D1188335

DATE DUE

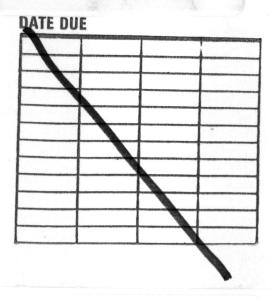

Crimes of Obedience

Crimes of Obedience
Toward A Social Psychology of Authority and Responsibility

Herbert C. Kelman and
V. Lee Hamilton

Yale University Press
New Haven and London

Published with assistance from the Louis Stern Memorial Fund.

Set in Electra type by Graphic Composition, Inc.
Printed in the United States of America by Vail-Ballou Press,
Binghamton, New York.

Library of Congress catalog
card number: 88–50549

International standard book number: 0–300–04184–5 (cloth)
0–300–04813–0 (pbk.)

The paper in this book meets the guidelines for permanence and durabil-
ity of the Committee on Production Guidelines for Book Longevity of
the Council on Library Resources.

10   9   8   7   6   5   4   3   2

To the Memory of
Martin Luther King, Jr.

. . . far more, and far more hideous,
crimes have been committed in the name
of obedience than have ever been
committed in the name of rebellion.
C. P. Snow (1961)

. . . an individual who breaks a law
that conscience tells him is unjust,
and willingly accepts the penalty by
staying in jail to arouse the
conscience of the community over its
injustice, is in reality expressing
the very highest respect for law.
Martin Luther King, Jr. (1963)

Contents

Preface

This book deals with the consequences that often ensue when authority gives orders exceeding the bounds of morality or law: with crimes of obedience. For both of us the book has roots in autobiography—in life experiences that shaped our scientific research interests.

Herbert Kelman grew up as a Jew in an anti-Semitic Vienna. He was eleven at the time of the Anschluss in 1938; he spent a year under Nazi rule and another year as a refugee in Antwerp. Along with his immediate family, he had the good fortune of escaping to the United States just a few weeks before the German invasion of Belgium. The experiences of the Nazi era, and especially the Holocaust, have deeply influenced his thinking and actions throughout his life. They have led him to focus attention on the question of how such atrocities become possible and how they can be prevented. As a social psychologist, he was drawn to research on the sources of unquestioning obedience versus principled resistance to unjust authority. As a citizen, he periodically felt the need to challenge policies that he considered immoral—for example, by actively participating in nonviolent direct action campaigns against racial segregation, by resisting the draft during the Korean War, and by refusing to pay war taxes during the Vietnam War.

Lee Hamilton was born in Dixie. Her concerns with authority, orders, and responsibility for the consequences were awakened while growing up in the American South in the 1950s and 1960s. Home was Richmond, Virginia, the former capital of the Confederacy. The moral dilemmas of these times were race and war. The civil rights movement was evident everywhere in Southern life; resistance to local laws and customs in the name of a higher law of justice was so common even a child could know about it. Late in the 1960s the antiwar movement came to the South. The reality of an unpopular conflict in Vietnam clashed with a tradition of military service and reverence for doing one's duty. Some of her friends resisted the draft; others served; some died. In that place and those times it was impossible not to ask questions about what right authority has to give orders and what right citizens have to resist them.

The research reported in this book began in 1971, as we observed the trial and conviction of Lt. William Calley for his part in the My Lai massacre. Other incidents such as the Watergate scandal and the Iran-contra affair—pieces of the autobiography of Americans in the 1970s and 1980s—continued to shape our thinking. This book presents a general picture of the social psychology of authority and responsibility in the hope that we may better prevent future excesses of obedience.

Many organizations and people made this book possible. The first of two surveys reported in this work was supported by U.S. Public Health Service Grant No. MH–17669 from the National Institute of Mental Health to H. C. Kelman, as well as by funds provided him by the Faculty of Arts and Sciences, Harvard University. The second was supported partly by a grant from the Gordon Allport Memorial Fund of Harvard University to Kelman and partly by National Science Foundation Grant No. 76–01113 and a Rackham grant from the University of Michigan to V. L. Hamilton. The sample of the first survey was selected and the interviews were conducted for us by the Roper Organization and its national staff; we are grateful to Carolyn Crusius and Burns Roper for their advice in the development of the interview schedule. The data for the second survey were gathered for us by the Survey Research Program of the University of Massachusetts–Boston under the direction of Floyd J. Fowler, whose help and advice were of great value to us throughout.

Kelman's work on this book in its earlier phases was greatly facilitated by a Guggenheim Fellowship and a year's residence as a fellow at the Woodrow Wilson International Center for Scholars in 1980–81. In 1985 he was able to continue work on the book as a resident scholar at the Rockefeller Foundation's Bellagio Study and Conference Center in Italy and at the Tantur Ecumenical Center for Theological Research in Jerusalem. He is deeply indebted to these organizations for providing material support as well as physical and intellectual environments conducive to scholarly pursuits.

A number of people contributed to the research itself. We would like to thank those members of the Vietnam Veterans Against the War who gave interviews to Hamilton during and after the Second Winter Soldier Investigations, held in Boston in 1971. Although we eventually decided not to report the interviews in this book, they helped to shape the image it portrays of the experience of following orders in Vietnam. We are grateful to Andre Modigliani, William Gamson, Neil Lutsky, and the late Paul Rosenkrantz, whose ideas helped us in planning the first survey and interpreting its results. Frederick D. Miller was a full collaborator in the development of the attitude scales described in chapter 12; we are greatly indebted to him for the time and effort he devoted to this project over several years and for the essential substantive contributions that he made to it. John D. Winkler also contributed to the scale development and testing. For several years Richard Hogan helped heroically in the data analysis.

Preparation of the book itself stretched across nearly a decade. Portions were written in four states, as well as Italy, Japan, Jerusalem, and the District of Columbia. We must offer a blanket thanks to all those secretaries and support staff without whom we could not have proceeded. We are particularly grateful to Becky Hunt and Ruth Grodinsky who processed the latest drafts of the manuscript with exceptional care, skill, and dedication.

We thank our editor at Yale University Press, Gladys Topkis, for being so kind to our text and so indulgent of its length. We are also grateful to her and to our copy editor, Cecile Watters, for polishing up the prose throughout the manuscript. Thoughtful editorial comments, many of which were heeded, were made by Maria Ascher, Charles Hamilton, Robert Wilcox, and Laura Wolff. Among our colleagues in social psychology, we thank William Gamson, Jeffrey Rubin, and Tom Tyler for their thoughtful and constructive reactions to the entire manuscript. For the end result and its remaining flaws, we take responsibility.

Speaking of responsibility, it may be of interest to readers to know which of us is more or less responsible for which parts of the work. Kelman handled the final drafts of all chapters and the continuity between chapters in the final editing. Hamilton handled the data analyses and structured the first draft of the entire manuscript. In first draft, each of us wrote portions of chapters 1 and 13; Kelman drafted all or most of chapters 2, 4, 5, 6, and 11; and Hamilton did all or most of chapters 3, 7, 8, 9, 10, and 12. The entire book, however, is a genuinely collaborative enterprise, based on a process of sharing ideas and learning from one another that extended over many years.

Special thanks go to Rose Kelman for assisting in the research itself by helping to develop coding categories for the open-ended questions in our first survey and personally coding all 989 interviews; for proofreading innumerable versions of the manuscript in all stages of its development; and for countless hours of helpful support to both of us during the research and writing. Kelman also thanks her for her unstinting encouragement, love, and friendship over the years. Hamilton thanks her husband, David Rauma, for putting up with her during the book's last several years of development.

H.C.K.
V.L.H.

April 1988

Crimes of Obedience

1 | The My Lai Massacre: A Military Crime of Obedience

March 16, 1968, was a busy day in U.S. history. Stateside, Robert F. Kennedy announced his presidential candidacy, challenging a sitting president from his own party—in part out of opposition to an undeclared and disastrous war. In Vietnam, the war continued. In many ways, March 16 may have been a typical day in that war. We will probably never know. But we do know that on that day a typical company went on a mission—which may or may not have been typical—to a village called Son (or Song) My. Most of what is remembered from that mission occurred in the subhamlet known to Americans as My Lai 4.

The My Lai massacre was investigated and charges were brought in 1969 and 1970. Trials and disciplinary actions lasted into 1971. Entire books have been written about the army's year-long cover-up of the massacre (for example, Hersh, 1972), and the cover-up was a major focus of the army's own investigation of the incident. Our central concern here is the massacre itself—a crime of obedience—and public reactions to such crimes, rather than the lengths to which many went to deny the event. Therefore this account concentrates on one day: March 16, 1968.[1]

Many verbal testimonials to the horrors that occurred at My Lai were available. More unusual was the fact that an army photographer, Ronald Haeberle, was assigned the task of documenting the anticipated military engagement at My Lai—and documented a massacre instead. Later, as the story of the massacre emerged, his photographs were widely distributed and seared the public conscience. What might have been dismissed as unreal or exaggerated was depicted in photographs of demonstrable authenticity. The

---

1. In reconstructing the events of that day, we consulted Hammer (1970), in addition to the sources cited in the text. Schell (1968) provided information on the region around My Lai. Concerning Vietnam and peasant rebellions, we consulted FitzGerald (1972), Paige (1975), Popkin (1979), and Wolf (1969).

1

dominant image appeared on the cover of *Life:* piles of bodies jumbled together in a ditch along a trail—the dead all apparently unarmed. All were Oriental, and all appeared to be children, women, or old men. Clearly there had been a mass execution, one whose image would not quickly fade.

So many bodies (over twenty in the cover photo alone) are hard to imagine as the handiwork of one killer. These were not. They were the product of what we call a crime of obedience. Crimes of obedience begin with orders. But orders are often vague and rarely survive with any clarity the transition from one authority down a chain of subordinates to the ultimate actors. The operation at Son My was no exception.

"Charlie" Company, Company C, under Lt. Col. Frank Barker's command, arrived in Vietnam in December of 1967. As the army's investigative unit, directed by Lt. Gen. William R. Peers, characterized the personnel, they "contained no significant deviation from the average" for the time. Seymour S. Hersh (1970) described the "average" more explicitly: "Most of the men in Charlie Company had volunteered for the draft; only a few had gone to college for even one year. Nearly half were black, with a few Mexican-Americans. Most were eighteen to twenty-two years old. The favorite reading matter of Charlie Company, like that of other line infantry units in Vietnam, was comic books" (p. 18). The action at My Lai, like that throughout Vietnam, was fought by a cross-section of those Americans who either believed in the war or lacked the social resources to avoid participating in it. Charlie Company was indeed average for that time, that place, and that war.

Two key figures in Charlie Company were more unusual. The company's commander, Capt. Ernest Medina, was an upwardly mobile Mexican-American who wanted to make the army his career, although he feared that he might never advance beyond captain because of his lack of formal education. His eagerness had earned him a nickname among his men: "Mad Dog Medina." One of his admirers was the platoon leader Second Lt. William L. Calley, Jr., an undistinguished, five-foot-three-inch junior-college dropout who had failed four of the seven courses in which he had enrolled his first year. Many viewed him as one of those "instant officers" made possible only by the army's then-desperate need for manpower. Whatever the cause, he was an insecure leader whose frequent claim was "I'm the boss." His nickname among some of the troops was "Surfside 5½," a reference to the swashbuckling heroes of a popular television show, "Surfside 6."

The Son My operation was planned by Lieutenant Colonel Barker and his staff as a search-and-destroy mission with the objective of rooting out the Forty-eighth Viet Cong Battalion from their base area of Son My village. Apparently no written orders were ever issued. Barker's superior, Col. Oran Henderson, arrived at the staging point the day before. Among the issues he reviewed with the assembled officers were some of the weaknesses of prior operations by their units, including their failure to be appropriately aggressive in pursuit of the enemy. Later briefings by Lieutenant Colonel Barker and his staff asserted that no one except Viet Cong was expected to be in the village after 7 A.M. on the following day. The "innocent" would all be at the market. Those present at the briefings gave conflicting accounts of Barker's exact orders, but he conveyed at least a strong suggestion that the Son My area was to be obliterated. As the army's inquiry reported: "While there is some conflict in the testimony as to whether LTC Barker ordered the destruction of houses, dwellings, livestock, and other foodstuffs in the Song My area, the preponderance of the evidence indicates that such destruction was implied, if not specifically directed, by his orders of 15 March" (Peers Report, in Goldstein et al., 1976, p. 94).

Evidence that Barker ordered the killing of civilians is even more murky. What does seem clear, however, is that—having asserted that civilians would be away at the market—he did not specify what was to be done with any who might nevertheless be found on the scene. The Peers Report therefore considered it "reasonable to conclude that LTC Barker's minimal or nonexistent instructions concerning the handling of noncombatants created the potential for grave misunderstandings as to his intentions and for interpretation of his orders as authority to fire, without restriction, on all persons found in target area" (Goldstein et al., 1976, p. 95). Since Barker was killed in action in June 1968, his own formal version of the truth was never available.

Charlie Company's Captain Medina was briefed for the operation by Barker and his staff. He then transmitted the already vague orders to his own men. Charlie Company was spoiling for a fight, having been totally frustrated during its months in Vietnam—first by waiting for battles that never came, then by incompetent forays led by inexperienced commanders, and finally by mines and booby traps. In fact, the emotion-laden funeral of a sergeant killed by a booby trap was held on March 15, the day before My Lai. Captain Medina gave the orders for the next day's action at the close of that funeral. Many were in a mood for revenge.

It is again unclear what was ordered. Although all participants were still alive by the time of the trials for the massacre, they were either on trial or probably felt under threat of trial. Memories are often flawed and self-serving at such times. It is apparent that Medina relayed to the men at least some of Barker's general message—to expect Viet Cong resistance, to burn, and to kill livestock. It is not clear that he ordered the slaughter of the inhabitants, but some of the men who heard him thought he had. One of those who claimed to have heard such orders was Lt. William Calley.

As March 16 dawned, much was expected of the operation by those who had set it into motion. Therefore a full complement of "brass" was present in helicopters overhead, including Barker, Colonel Henderson, and their superior, Major General Koster (who went on to become commandant of West Point before the story of My Lai broke). On the ground, the troops were to carry with them one reporter and one photographer to immortalize the anticipated battle.

The action for Company C began at 7:30 as their first wave of helicopters touched down near the subhamlet of My Lai 4. By 7:47 all of Company C was present and set to fight. But instead of the Viet Cong Forty-eighth Battalion, My Lai was filled with the old men, women, and children who were supposed to have gone to market. By this time, in their version of the war, and with whatever orders they thought they had heard, the men from Company C were nevertheless ready to find Viet Cong everywhere. By nightfall, the official tally was 128 VC killed and three weapons captured, although later unofficial body counts ran as high as 500. The operation at Son My was over. And by nightfall, as Hersh reported: "the Viet Cong were back in My Lai 4, helping the survivors bury the dead. It took five days. Most of the funeral speeches were made by the Communist guerrillas. Nguyen Bat was not a Communist at the time of the massacre, but the incident changed his mind. 'After the shooting,' he said, 'all the villagers became Communists'" (1970, p. 74). To this day, the memory of the massacre is kept alive by markers and plaques designating the spots where groups of villagers were killed, by a large statue, and by the My Lai Museum, established in 1975 (Williams, 1985).

But what could have happened to leave American troops reporting a victory over Viet Cong when in fact they had killed hundreds of noncombatants? It is not hard to explain the report of victory; that is the essence of a cover-up. It is harder to understand how the killings came to be committed in the first place, making a cover-up necessary.

Mass Executions and the Defense of Superior Orders

Some of the atrocities on March 16, 1968, were evidently unofficial, spontaneous acts: rapes, tortures, killings. For example, Hersh (1970) describes Charlie Company's Second Platoon as entering "My Lai 4 with guns blazing" (p. 50); more graphically, Lieutenant "Brooks and his men in the second platoon to the north had begun to systematically ransack the hamlet and slaughter the people, kill the livestock, and destroy the crops. Men poured rifle and machine-gun fire into huts without knowing—or seemingly caring—who was inside" (pp. 49–50).

Some atrocities toward the end of the action were part of an almost casual "mopping-up," much of which was the responsibility of Lieutenant LaCross's Third Platoon of Charlie Company. The Peers Report states: "The entire 3rd Platoon then began moving into the western edge of My Lai (4), for the mop-up operation. . . . The squad . . . began to burn the houses in the southwestern portion of the hamlet" (Goldstein et al., 1976, p. 133). They became mingled with other platoons during a series of rapes and killings of survivors for which it was impossible to fix responsibility. Certainly to a Vietnamese all GIs would by this point look alike: "Nineteen-year-old Nguyen Thi Ngoc Tuyet watched a baby trying to open her slain mother's blouse to nurse. A soldier shot the infant while it was struggling with the blouse, and then slashed it with his bayonet." Tuyet also said she saw another baby hacked to death by GIs wielding their bayonets. "Le Tong, a twenty-eight-year-old rice farmer, reported seeing one woman raped after GIs killed her children. Nguyen Khoa, a thirty-seven-year-old peasant, told of a thirteen-year-old girl who was raped before being killed. GIs then attacked Khoa's wife, tearing off her clothes. Before they could rape her, however, Khoa said, their six-year-old son, riddled with bullets, fell and saturated her with blood. The GIs left her alone" (Hersh, 1970, p. 72). All of Company C was implicated in a pattern of death and destruction throughout the hamlet, much of which seemingly lacked rhyme or reason.

But a substantial amount of the killing was *organized* and traceable to one authority: the First Platoon's Lt. William Calley. Calley was originally charged with 109 killings, almost all of them mass executions at the trail and other locations. He stood trial for 102 of these killings, was convicted of 22 in 1971, and at first received a life sentence. Though others—both superior and subordinate to Calley—were brought to trial, he was the only one convicted for the My Lai crimes. Thus, the only actions of My Lai for which *anyone* was ever convicted were mass executions, ordered and committed. We suspect that there are commonsense reasons why this one type of killing was singled out. In the midst of rapidly moving events with people running about, an execution of stationary targets is literally a still life that stands out and whose participants are clearly visible. It can be proven that specific people committed specific deeds. An execution, in contrast to the shooting of someone on the run, is also more likely to meet the legal definition of an act resulting from intent—with malice aforethought. Moreover, American military law specifically forbids the killing of unarmed civilians or military prisoners, as does the Geneva Convention between nations. Thus common sense, legal standards, and explicit doctrine all made such actions the likeliest target for prosecution.

When Lieutenant Calley was charged under military law it was for violation of the Uniform Code of Military Justice (UCMJ) Article 118 (murder). This article is similar to civilian codes in that it provides for conviction if an accused:

> without justification or excuse, unlawfully kills a human being, when he—
> 1. has a premeditated design to kill;
> 2. intends to kill or inflict great bodily harm;
> 3. is engaged in an act which is inherently dangerous to others and evinces a wanton disregard of human life; or
> 4. is engaged in the perpetration or attempted perpetration of burglary, sodomy, rape, robbery, or aggravated arson. (Goldstein et al., 1976, p. 507)

For a soldier, one legal justification for killing is warfare; but warfare is subject to many legal limits and restrictions, including, of course, the inadmissibility of killing unarmed noncombatants or prisoners whom one has disarmed. The pictures of the trail victims at My Lai certainly portrayed one or the other of these. Such an action would be illegal under military law; ordering another to commit such an action would be illegal; and following such an order would be illegal.

But following an order may provide a second and pivotal justification for an act that would be murder when committed by a civilian. As chapter 3 will discuss in more detail, American military law assumes that the subordinate is inclined to follow orders, as that is the normal obligation of the role. Hence, legally, obedient subordinates are protected from unreasonable expectations regarding their capacity to evaluate those orders:

An order requiring the performance of a military duty may be inferred to be legal. An act performed manifestly beyond the scope of authority, or pursuant to an order that a man of ordinary sense and understanding would know to be illegal, or in a wanton manner in the discharge of a lawful duty, is not excusable. (Par. 216, Subpar. *d*, Manual for Courts Martial, United States, 1969 Rev.)

Thus what *may* be excusable is the good-faith carrying out of an order, as long as that order appears to the ordinary soldier to be a legal one. In military law, invoking superior orders moves the question from one of the action's consequences— the body count—to one of evaluating the actor's motives and good sense.

In sum, if anyone is to be brought to justice for a massacre, common sense and legal codes decree that the most appropriate targets are those who make themselves executioners. This is the kind of target the government selected in prosecuting Lieutenant Calley with the greatest fervor. And in a military context, the most promising way in which one can redefine one's undeniable deeds into acceptability is to invoke superior orders. This is what Calley did in attempting to avoid conviction. Since the core legal issues involved points of mass execution—the ditches and trail where America's image of My Lai was formed—we review these events in greater detail.

The day's quiet beginning has already been noted. Troops landed and swept unopposed into the village. The three weapons eventually reported as the haul from the operation were picked up from three apparent Viet Cong who fled the village when the troops arrived and were pursued and killed by helicopter gunships. Obviously the Viet Cong did frequent the area. But it appears that by about 8:00 A.M. no one who met the troops was aggressive, and no one was armed. By the laws of war Charlie Company had no argument with such people.

As they moved into the village, the soldiers began to gather its inhabitants together. Shortly after 8:00 A.M. Lieutenant Calley told Pfc. Paul Meadlo that "you know what to do with" a group of villagers Meadlo was guarding. Estimates of the numbers in the group ranged as high as eighty women, children, and old men, and Meadlo's own estimate under oath was thirty to fifty people. As Meadlo later testified, Calley returned after ten or fifteen minutes: "He [Calley] said, 'How come they're not dead?' I said, 'I didn't know we were supposed to kill them.' He said, 'I want them dead.' He backed off twenty or thirty feet and started shooting into the people—the Viet Cong—shooting automatic. He was beside me. He burned four or five magazines. I burned off a few, about three. I helped shoot 'em" (Hammer, 1971, p. 155). Meadlo himself and others testified that Meadlo cried as he fired; others reported him later to be sobbing and "all broke up." It would appear that to Lieutenant Calley's subordinates something was unusual, and stressful, in these orders.

At the trial, the first specification in the murder charge against Calley was for this incident; he was accused of premeditated murder of "an unknown number, not less than 30, Oriental human beings, males and females of various ages, whose names are unknown, occupants of the village of My Lai 4, by means of shooting them with a rifle" (Goldstein et al., 1976, p. 497).

Among the helicopters flying reconnaissance above Son My was that of CWO Hugh Thompson. By 9:00 or soon after Thompson had noticed some horrifying events from his perch. As he spotted wounded civilians, he sent down smoke markers so that soldiers on the ground could treat them. They killed them instead. He reported to headquarters, trying to persuade someone to stop what was going on. Barker, hearing the message, called down to Captain Medina. Medina, in turn, later claimed to have told Calley that it was "enough for today." But it was not yet enough.

At Calley's orders, his men began gathering the remaining villagers—roughly seventy-five individuals, mostly women and children—and herding them toward a drainage ditch. Accompanied by three or four enlisted men, Lieutenant Calley executed several batches of civilians who had been gathered into ditches. Some of the details of the process were entered into testimony in such accounts as Pfc. Dennis Conti's: "A lot of them, the people, were trying to get up and mostly they was just screaming and pretty bad shot up. . . . I seen a woman tried to get up. I seen Lieutenant Calley fire. He hit the side of her head and blew it off" (Hammer, 1971, p. 125).

Testimony by other soldiers presented the shooting's aftermath. Specialist Four Charles Hall, asked by Prosecutor Aubrey Daniel how he knew the people in the ditch were dead, said: "There was blood coming from them. They were just scattered all over the ground in the ditch, some in piles and some scattered out 20, 25 meters perhaps up the ditch. . . . They were very old people, very young children, and mothers. . . . There was blood all over them" (Goldstein et al., 1976, pp. 501–02). And Pfc. Gregory Olsen corroborated the general picture of the victims: "They were—the majority were women and children, some babies. I distinctly remember one middle-aged Vietnamese male dressed in white right at my feet as I crossed. None of the bodies were mangled in any way. There was blood. Some appeared to be dead, others followed me with their eyes as I walked across the ditch" (Goldstein et al., 1976, p. 502).

The second specification in the murder charge stated that Calley did "with premeditation, murder an unknown number of Oriental human beings, not less than seventy, males and females of various ages, whose names are unknown, occupants of the village of My Lai 4, by means of shooting them with a rifle" (Goldstein et al., 1976, p. 497). Calley was also charged with and tried for shootings of individuals (an old man and a child); these charges were clearly supplemental to the main issue at trial—the mass killings and how they came about.

It is noteworthy that during these executions more than one enlisted man avoided carrying out Calley's orders, and more than one, by sworn oath, directly refused to obey them. For example, Pfc. James Joseph Dursi testified, when asked if he fired when Lieutenant Calley ordered him to: "No. I just stood there. Meadlo turned to me after a couple of minutes and said 'Shoot! Why don't you shoot! Why don't you fire!' He was crying and yelling. I said, 'I can't! I won't!' And the people were screaming and crying and yelling. They kept firing for a couple of minutes, mostly automatic and semi-automatic" (Hammer, 1971, p. 143).

Specialist Four Ronald Grzesik reported an even more direct confrontation with Calley, although under oath he hedged about its subject:

GRZESIK: Well, Lieutenant Calley—I walked past the ditch. I was called back by some-
    one, I don't recall who. I had a discussion with Lieutenant Calley. He said to take
    the fire team back into the village and help the second platoon search.
DANIEL: Did Lieutenant Calley say anything before he gave you that order?
GRZESIK: He said, "Finish them off." I refused.
DANIEL: What did you refuse to do?
GRZESIK: To finish them off.
DANIEL: What did he mean? Who did he mean to finish off?
GRZESIK: I don't know what he meant or who he meant by them. (Hammer, 1971,
    p. 150)

In preceding months, not under oath, Grzesik had indicated that he had a good idea what was meant but that he simply would not comply. It is likely that the jury at Calley's trial did not miss the point.

Disobedience of Lieutenant Calley's own orders to kill represented a serious legal and moral threat to a defense *based* on superior orders, such as Calley was attempting. This defense had to assert that the orders seemed reasonable enough to carry out, that they appeared to be legal orders. Even if the orders in question were not legal, the defense had to assert that an ordinary individual could not and should not be expected to see the distinction. In short, if what happened was "business as usual," even though it might be bad business, then the defendant stood a chance of acquittal. But under direct command from "Surfside 5½," some ordinary enlisted men managed to refuse, to avoid, or at least to stop doing what they were ordered to do. As "reasonable men" of "ordinary sense and understand-ing," they had apparently found something awry that morning; and it would have been hard for an officer to plead successfully that he was more ordinary than his men in his capacity to evaluate the reasonableness of orders.

Even those who obeyed Calley's orders showed great stress. For example, Meadlo eventually began to argue and cry directly in front of Calley. Pfc. Herbert Carter shot himself in the foot, possibly because he could no longer take what he was doing. We were not destined to hear a sworn version of the incident, since neither side at the Calley trial called him to testify.

The most unusual instance of resistance to authority came from the skies. CWO Hugh Thompson, who had protested the apparent carnage of civilians, was Calley's inferior in rank but was not in his line of command. He was also watching the ditch from his helicopter and noticed some people moving after the first round of slaughter—chiefly children who had been shielded by their mothers' bodies. Landing to rescue the wounded, he also found some villagers hiding in a nearby bunker. Protecting the Vietnamese with his own body, Thompson ordered his men to train their guns on the Americans and to open fire if the Americans fired on the Vietnamese. He then radioed for additional rescue helicopters and stood between the Vietnamese and the Americans under Calley's command until the

Vietnamese could be evacuated. He later returned to the ditch to unearth a child buried, unharmed, beneath layers of bodies. In October 1969, Thompson was awarded the Distinguished Flying Cross for heroism at My Lai, specifically (albeit inaccurately) for the rescue of children hiding in a bunker "between Viet Cong forces and advancing friendly forces" and for the rescue of a wounded child "caught in the intense crossfire" (Hersh, 1970, p. 119). Four months earlier, at the Pentagon, Thompson had identified Calley as having been at the ditch.

By about 10:00 A.M., the massacre was winding down. The remaining actions consisted largely of isolated rapes and killings, "clean-up" shootings of the wounded, and the destruction of the village by fire. We have already seen some examples of these more indiscriminate and possibly less premeditated acts. By the 11:00 A.M. lunch break, when the exhausted men of Company C were relaxing, two young girls wandered back from a hiding place only to be invited to share lunch. This surrealist touch illustrates the extent to which the soldiers' action had become dissociated from its meaning. An hour earlier, some of these men were making sure that not even a child would escape the executioner's bullet. But now the job was done and it was time for lunch—and in this new context it seemed only natural to ask the children who had managed to escape execution to join them. The massacre had ended. It remained only for the Viet Cong to reap the political rewards among the survivors in hiding.

The army command in the area knew that something had gone wrong. Direct commanders, including Lieutenant Colonel Barker, had firsthand reports, such as Thompson's complaints. Others had such odd bits of evidence as the claim of 128 Viet Cong dead with a booty of only three weapons. But the cover-up of My Lai began at once. The operation was reported as a victory over a stronghold of the Viet Cong Forty-eighth.

My Lai might have remained a "victory" but for another odd twist. A soldier who had not even been at the massacre, Ronald Ridenhour, talked to several friends and acquaintances who had been. As he later wrote: "It was late in April, 1968 that I first heard of 'Pinkville' [a nickname reflecting the villagers' reputed Communist sympathies] and what allegedly happened there. I received that first report with some skepticism, but in the following months I was to hear similar stories from such a wide variety of people that it became impossible for me to disbelieve that something rather dark and bloody did indeed occur sometime in March, 1968 in a village called 'Pinkville' in the Republic of Viet Nam" (Goldstein et al., 1976, p. 34). Ridenhour's growing conviction that a massacre—or something close to it—had occurred was reinforced by his own travel over the area by helicopter soon after the event. My Lai was desolate. He gradually concluded that someone was covering up the incident within the army and that an independent investigation was needed.

At the end of March 1969, he finally wrote a letter detailing what he knew about "Pinkville." The letter, beginning with the paragraph quote above, was sent to thirty individuals—the president, Pentagon officials, and some members of the Senate and House. Ridenhour's congressman, fellow Arizonian Morris Udall, gave it particular heed. The slow unraveling of the cover-up began. During the following months, the army in fact initiated an investigation but carried it out in strict secrecy. Ridenhour, convinced that the cover-up was continuing, sought journalistic help and finally, by coincidence, connected with Seymour Hersh. Hersh followed up and broke the story, which eventually brought him a Pulitzer Prize and other awards for his investigative reporting. The cover-up collapsed, leaving only the question of the army's resolve to seek justice in the case: Against whom would it proceed, with how much speed and vigor, and with what end in mind?

William Calley was not the only man tried for the events at My Lai. The actions of over thirty soldiers and civilians were scrutinized by investigators; over half of these had to face charges or disciplinary action of some sort. Targets of investigation included Captain Medina, who was tried, and various higher-ups, including General Koster. But Lieutenant Calley was the only person convicted, the only person to serve time.

The core of Lieutenant Calley's defense was superior orders. What this meant to him—in contrast to what it meant to the judge and jury—can be gleaned from his responses to a series of questions from his defense attorney, George Latimer, in which Calley sketched out his understanding of the laws of war and the actions that constitute doing one's duty within those laws:

> LATIMER: Did you receive any training . . . which had to do with the obedience to orders?
>
> CALLEY: Yes, sir.
>
> LATIMER: . . . what were you informed [were] the principles involved in that field?
>
> CALLEY: That all orders were to be assumed legal, that the soldier's job was to carry out any order given him to the best of his ability.
>
> LATIMER: . . . what might occur if you disobeyed an order by a senior officer?
>
> CALLEY: You could be court-martialed for refusing an order and refusing an order in the face of the enemy, you could be sent to death, sir.
>
> LATIMER: [I am asking] whether you were required in any way, shape or form to make a determination of the legality or illegality of an order?
>
> CALLEY: No, sir. I was never told that I had the choice, sir.
>
> LATIMER: If you had a doubt about the order, what were you supposed to do?
>
> CALLEY: . . . I was supposed to carry the order out and then come back and make my complaint. (Hammer, 1971, pp. 240–41)

Lieutenant Calley steadfastly maintained that his actions within My Lai had constituted, in his mind, carrying out orders from Captain Medina. Both his own actions and the orders he gave to others (such as the instruction to Meadlo to "waste 'em") were entirely in response to superior orders. He denied any intent to kill individuals and any but the most passing awareness of distinctions among the individuals: "I was ordered to go in there and destroy the enemy. That was my job on that day. That was the mission I was given. I did not sit down and think in terms of men, women, and children. They were all classified the same, and that was the classification that we dealt with, just as enemy soldiers." When Latimer asked if in his own opinion Calley had acted "rightly and according to your understanding of your directions and orders," Calley replied, "I felt then and I still do that I acted as I was directed, and I carried out the orders that I was given, and I do not feel wrong in doing so, sir" (Hammer, 1971, p. 257).

His court-martial did not accept Calley's defense of superior orders and clearly did not share his interpretation of his duty. The jury evidently reasoned that, even if there had been orders to destroy everything in sight and to "waste the Vietnamese," any reasonable person would have realized that such orders were illegal and should have refused to carry them out. The defense of superior orders under such conditions is inadmissible under international and military law. The U.S. Army's *Law of Land Warfare* (Dept. of the Army, 1956), for example, states that "the fact that the law of war has been violated pursuant to an order of a superior authority, whether military or civil, does not deprive the act in question of its character of a war crime, nor does it constitute a defense in the trial of an accused individual, unless he did not know and could not reasonably have been expected to know that the act was unlawful" and that "members of the armed forces are bound to obey only lawful orders" (in Falk et al., 1971, pp. 71–72).

The disagreement between Calley and the court-martial seems to have revolved around the definition of the responsibilities of a subordinate to obey, on the one hand, and to evaluate, on the other. This tension, described in more detail in chapter 3, runs through the analyses and empirical studies presented in this book. For now, it can best be captured via the charge to the jury in the Calley court-martial, made by the trial judge, Col. Reid Kennedy. The forty-one pages of the charge include the following:

> Both combatants captured by and noncombatants detained by the opposing force . . . have the right to be treated as prisoners. . . . Summary execution of detainees or prisoners is forbidden by law. . . . I therefore instruct you . . . that if unresisting human beings were killed at My Lai (4) while within the effective custody and control of our military forces, their deaths cannot be considered justified. . . . Thus if you find that Lieutenant Calley received an order directing him to kill unresisting Vietnamese within his control or within the control of his troops, *that order would be an illegal order.*
>
> A determination that an order is illegal does not, of itself, assign criminal responsibility to the person following the order for acts done in compliance with it. Soldiers are taught to follow orders, and special attention is given to obedience of orders on the battlefield. Military effectiveness depends on obedience to orders. On the other hand, the obedience of a soldier is not the obedience of an automaton. A soldier is a reasoning agent, obliged to respond, not as a machine, but as a person. The law takes these factors into account in assessing criminal responsibility for acts done in compliance with illegal orders.
>
> The acts of a subordinate done in compliance with an unlawful order given him by his superior are excused and impose no criminal liability upon him unless the superior's order is one which a man of *ordinary sense and understanding* would, under the circumstances, know to be unlawful, or if the order in question is actually known to the accused to be unlawful. (Goldstein et al., 1976, pp. 525–526; emphasis added)

By this definition, subordinates take part in a balancing act, one tipped toward obedience but tempered by "ordinary sense and understanding."

A jury of combat veterans proceeded to convict William Calley of the premeditated murder of no less than twenty-two human beings. (The army, realizing some unfortunate connotations in referring to the victims as "Oriental human beings," eventually referred to them as "human beings.") Regarding the first specification in the murder charge, the bodies on the trail, he was convicted of premeditated murder of not less than one person. (Medical testimony had been able to pinpoint only one person whose wounds as revealed in Haeberle's photos were sure to be immediately fatal.) Regarding the second specification, the bodies in the ditch, Calley was convicted of the premeditated murder of not less than twenty human beings. Regarding additional specifications that he had killed an old man and a child, Calley was convicted of premeditated murder in the first case and of assault with intent to commit murder in the second.

Lieutenant Calley was initially sentenced to life imprisonment. That sentence was reduced: first to twenty years, eventually to ten (the latter by Secretary of Defense Callaway in 1974).[2] Calley served three years before being released on bond. The time was spent under house arrest in his apartment, where he was able to receive visits from his girlfriend. He was granted parole on September 10, 1975.

Sanctioned Massacres

The slaughter at My Lai is an instance of a class of violent acts that can be described as sanctioned massacres (Kelman, 1973): acts of indiscriminate, ruthless, and often systematic mass violence, carried out by military or paramilitary personnel while engaged in officially sanctioned campaigns, the victims of which are defenseless and unresisting civilians, including old men, women, and children. Sanctioned massacres have occurred throughout history. Within American history, My Lai had its precursors in the Philippine war around the turn of the century (Schirmer, 1971) and in the massacres of American Indians. Elsewhere in the world, one recalls the Nazis' "final solution" for European Jews, the massacres and deportations of Armenians by Turks, the liquidation of the kulaks and the great purges in the Soviet Union, and more recently the massacres in Indonesia and Bangladesh, in Biafra and Burundi, in South Africa and Mozambique, in Cambodia and Afghanistan, in Syria and Lebanon. Sanctioned massacres may vary on a number of dimensions. For present purposes, however, we want to focus on features they share. Two of these are the *context* and the *target* of the violence.

2. The involvement of President Nixon in the case may have had something to do with these steadily lower sentences. Immediately after the Calley conviction, Nixon issued two presidential edicts. The president first announced that Calley was to stay under house arrest until appeals were settled, rather than in the stockade. The subsequent announcement was that President Nixon would personally review the case. These edicts received wide popular support. The latter announcement in particular brought sharp criticism from Prosecutor Daniel and others, on grounds that Nixon was interfering inappropriately with the process of justice in the case. Nevertheless, the president's interest and intention to review the case could have colored the subsequent appeals process or the actions of the secretary of defense. By the time of Secretary Callaway's action, of course, the president was himself fighting to avoid impeachment.

Sanctioned massacres tend to occur in the context of an overall policy that is explicitly or implicitly genocidal: designed to destroy all or part of a category of people defined in ethnic, national, racial, religious, or other terms. Such a policy may be deliberately aimed at the systematic extermination of a population group as an end in itself, as was the case with the Holocaust during World War II. In the Nazis' "final solution" for European Jewry, a policy aimed at exterminating millions of people was consciously articulated and executed (see Levinson, 1973), and the extermination was accomplished on a mass-production basis through the literal establishment of a well-organized, efficient death industry. Alternatively, such a policy may be aimed at an objective other than extermination—such as the pacification of the rural population of South Vietnam, as was the case in U.S. policy for Indochina—but may include the deliberate decimation of large segments of a population as an acceptable means to that end.

We agree with Bedau's (1974) conclusion from his carefully reasoned argument that the charge of U.S. genocide in Vietnam has not been definitively proven, since such a charge requires evidence of a specific genocidal *intent*. Although the evidence suggests that the United States committed war crimes and crimes against humanity in Indochina (see Sheehan, 1971; Browning and Forman, 1972), it does not show that extermination was the conscious purpose of U.S. policy. The evidence reviewed by Bedau, however, suggests that the United States did commit genocidal acts in Vietnam as a means to other ends. Central to U.S. strategy in South Vietnam were such actions as unrestricted air and artillery bombardments of peasant hamlets, search-and-destroy missions by ground troops, crop destruction programs, and mass deportation of rural populations. These actions (and similar ones in Laos and Cambodia) were clearly and deliberately aimed at civilians and resulted in the death, injury, and/or uprooting of large numbers of that population and in the destruction of their countryside, their source of livelihood, and their social structure. These consequences were anticipated by policymakers and indeed were intended as part of their pacification effort; the actions were designed to clear the countryside and deprive guerrillas of their base of operations, even if this meant destroying the civilian population. Massacres of the kind that occurred at My Lai were not deliberately planned, but they took place in an atmosphere in which the rural Vietnamese population was viewed as expendable and actions that resulted in the killing of large numbers of that population as strategic necessities.

A second feature of sanctioned massacres is that their targets have not themselves threatened or engaged in hostile actions toward the perpetrators of the violence. The victims of this class of violence are often defenseless civilians, including old men, women, and children. By all accounts, at least after the first moments at My Lai, the victims there fit this description, although in guerrilla warfare there always remains some ambiguity about the distinction between armed soldiers and unarmed civilians. As has often been noted, U.S. troops in Vietnam had to face the possibility that a woman or even a child might be concealing a hand grenade under clothing.

There are, of course, historical and situational reasons particular groups become victims of sanctioned massacres, but these do not include their own immediate harmfulness or violence toward the attackers. Rather, their selection as targets for massacre at a particular time can ultimately be traced to their relationship to the pursuit of larger policies. Their elimination may be seen as a useful tool or their continued existence as an irritating obstacle in the execution of policy.

The genocidal or near-genocidal context of this class of violence and the fact that it is directed at a target that—at least from an observer's perspective—did not provoke the violence through its own actions has some definite implications for the psychological environment within which sanctioned massacres occur. It is an environment almost totally devoid of the conditions that usually provide at least some degree of moral justification for violence. Neither the reason for the violence nor its purpose is of the kind that is normally considered justifiable. Although people may disagree about the precise point at which they would draw the line between justifiable and unjustifiable violence, most would agree that violence in self-defense or in response to oppression and other forms of strong provocation is at least within the realm of moral discourse. In contrast, the violence of sanctioned massacres falls outside that realm.

In searching for a psychological explanation for mass violence under these conditions, one's first inclination is to look for forces that might impel people toward such murderous acts. Can we identify, in massacre situations, psychological forces so powerful that they outweigh the moral restraints that would normally inhibit unjustifiable violence?

The most obvious approach—searching for psychological dispositions within those who perpetrate these acts—does not yield a satisfactory explanation of the phenomenon, although it may tell us something about the types of individuals most readily recruited for participation. For example, any explanation involving the attackers' strong sadistic impulses is inadequate. There is no evidence that the majority of those who participate in such killings are sadistically inclined. Indeed, speaking of the participants in the Nazi slaughters, Arendt (1964) points out that they "were not sadists or killers by nature; on the contrary, a systematic effort was made to weed out all those who derived physical pleasure from what they did" (p. 105). To be sure, some of the commanders and guards of concentration camps could clearly be described as sadists, but what has to be explained is the existence of concentration camps in which these individuals could give play to their sadistic fantasies. These opportunities were provided with the participation of large numbers of individuals to whom the label of sadist could not be applied.

A more sophisticated type of dispositional approach seeks to identify certain characterological themes that are dominant within a given culture. An early example of such an approach is Fromm's (1941) analysis of the appeals of Nazism in terms of the prevalence of sadomasochistic strivings, particularly among the German lower middle class. It would be important to explore whether similar kinds of characterological dispositions can be identified in the very wide range of cultural contexts in which sanctioned massacres have occurred. However general such dispositions turn out to be, it seems most likely that they represent states of readiness to participate in sanctioned massacres when the opportunity arises rather than major motivating forces in their own right. Similarly, high levels of frustration within a population are probably facilitators rather than instigators of sanctioned massacres, since there does not seem to be a clear relationship between the societal level of frustration and the occurrence of such violence. Such a view would be consistent with recent thinking about the relationship between frustration and aggression (see, for example, Bandura, 1973).

Could participation in sanctioned massacres be traced to an inordinately intense hatred toward those against whom the violence is directed? The evidence does not seem to support such an interpretation. Indications are that many of the active participants in the extermination of European Jews, such as Adolf Eichmann (Arendt, 1964), did not feel any passionate hatred of Jews. There is certainly no reason to believe that those who planned and executed American policy in Vietnam felt a profound hatred of the Vietnamese population, although deeply rooted racist attitudes may conceivably have played a role.

To be sure, hatred and rage *play a part* in sanctioned massacres. Typically, there is a long history of profound hatred against the groups targeted for violence—the Jews in Christian Europe, the Chinese in Southeast Asia, the Ibos in northern Nigeria—which helps establish them as suitable victims. Hostility also plays an important part at the point at which the killings are actually perpetrated, even if the official planning and the bureaucratic preparations that ultimately lead up to this point are carried out in a passionless and businesslike atmosphere. For example, Lifton's (1973) descriptions of My Lai, based on eyewitness reports, suggest that the killings were accompanied by generalized rage and by expressions of anger and revenge toward the victims. Hostility toward the target, however, does not seem to be the *instigator* of these violent actions. The expressions of anger in the situation itself can more properly be viewed as outcomes rather than causes of the violence. They serve to provide the perpetrators with an explanation and rationalization for their violent actions and appropriate labels for their emotional state. They also help reinforce, maintain, and intensify the violence, but the anger is not the primary source of the violence. Hostility toward the target, historically rooted or situationally induced, contributes heavily toward the violence, but it does so largely by dehumanizing the victims rather than by motivating violence against them in the first place.

In sum, the occurrence of sanctioned massacres cannot be adequately explained by the existence of psychological forces—whether these be characterological dispositions to engage in murderous violence or profound hostility against the target—so powerful that they must find expression in violent acts unhampered by moral restraints. Instead, the major instigators for this class of violence derive from the policy process. The question that really calls for psychological analysis is why so many people are willing to formulate, participate in, and condone policies that call for the mass killings of defenseless civilians. Thus it is more instructive to look not at the motives for violence but at the conditions under which the usual moral inhibitions against violence become weakened. Three social processes that tend to create such conditions can be identified: authorization, routinization, and dehumanization. Through authorization, the situation becomes so defined that the individual is absolved of the responsibility to make personal moral choices. Through routinization, the action becomes so organized that there is no opportunity for raising moral questions. Through dehumanization, the actors' attitudes toward the target and toward themselves become so structured that it is neither necessary nor possible for them to view the relationship in moral terms.

AUTHORIZATION

Sanctioned massacres by definition occur in the context of an authority situation, a situation in which, at least for many of the participants, the moral principles that generally govern human relationships do not apply. Thus, when acts of violence are explicitly ordered, implicitly encouraged, tacitly approved, or at least permitted by legitimate authorities, people's readiness to commit or condone them is enhanced. That such acts are authorized seems to carry automatic justification for them. Behaviorally, authorization obviates the necessity of making judgments or choices. Not only do normal moral principles become inoperative, but—particularly when the actions are explicitly ordered—a different kind of morality, linked to the duty to obey superior orders, tends to take over.

In an authority situation, individuals characteristically feel obligated to obey the orders of the authorities, whether or not these correspond with their personal preferences. They see themselves as having no choice as long as they accept the legitimacy of the orders and of the authorities who give them. Individuals differ considerably in the degree to which—and the conditions under which—they are prepared to challenge the legitimacy of an order on the grounds that the order itself is illegal, or that those giving it have overstepped their authority, or that it stems from a policy that violates fundamental societal values. Regardless of such individual differences, however, the basic structure of a situation of legitimate authority requires subordinates to respond in terms of their role obligations rather than their personal preferences; they can openly disobey only by challenging the legitimacy of the authority. Often people obey without question even though the behavior they engage in may entail great personal sacrifice or great harm to others.

An important corollary of the basic structure of the authority situation is that actors often do not see themselves as personally responsible for the consequences of their actions. Again, there are individual differences, depending on actors' capacity and readiness to evaluate the legitimacy of orders received. Insofar as they see themselves as having had no choice in their actions, however, they do not feel personally responsible for them. They were not personal agents, but merely extensions of the authority. Thus, when their actions cause harm to others, they can feel relatively free of guilt. A similar mechanism operates when a person engages in antisocial behavior that was not ordered by the authorities but was tacitly encouraged and approved by them—even if only by making it clear that such behavior will not be punished. In this situation, behavior that was formerly illegitimate is legitimized by the authorities' acquiescence.

In the My Lai massacre, it is likely that the structure of the authority situation contributed to the massive violence in both ways—that is, by conveying the message that acts of violence against Vietnamese villagers were *required*, as well as the message that such acts, even if not ordered, were *permitted* by the authorities in charge. The actions at My Lai represented, at least in some respects, responses to explicit or implicit orders. Lieutenant Calley indicated, by orders and by example, that he wanted large numbers of villagers killed. Whether Calley himself had been ordered by his superiors to "waste" the whole area, as he claimed, remains a matter of controversy. Even if we assume, however, that he was not explicitly ordered to wipe out the village, he had reason to believe that such actions were expected by his superior officers. Indeed, the very nature of the war conveyed this expectation. The principal measure of military success was the "body count"— the number of enemy soldiers killed—and any Vietnamese killed by the U.S. military was commonly defined as a "Viet Cong." Thus, it was not totally bizarre for Calley to believe that what he was doing at My Lai was to increase his body count, as any good officer was expected to do.

Even to the extent that the actions at My Lai occurred spontaneously, without reference to superior orders, those committing them had reason to assume that such actions might be tacitly approved of by the military authorities. Not only had they failed to punish such acts in most cases, but the very strategies and tactics that the authorities consistently devised were based on the proposition that the civilian population of South Vietnam—whether "hostile" or "friendly"—was expendable. Such policies as search-and-destroy missions, the establishment of free-shooting zones, the use of antipersonnel weapons, the bombing of entire villages if they were suspected of harboring guerrillas, the forced migration of masses of the rural population, and the defoliation of vast forest areas helped legitimize acts of massive violence of the kind occurring at My Lai.

Some of the actions at My Lai suggest an orientation to authority based on unquestioning obedience to superior orders, no matter how destructive the actions these orders call for. Such obedience is specifically fostered in the course of military training and reinforced by the structure of the military authority situation. It also reflects, however, an ideological orientation that may be more widespread in the general population, as some of the data presented in this volume will demonstrate.

ROUTINIZATION

Authorization processes create a situation in which people become involved in an action without considering its implications and without really making a decision. Once they have taken the initial step, they are in a new psychological and social situation in which the pressures to continue are powerful. As Lewin (1947) has pointed out, many forces that might originally have kept people out of a situation reverse direction once they have made a commitment (once they have gone through the "gate region") and now serve to keep them in the situation. For example, concern about the criminal nature of an action, which might originally have inhibited a person from becoming involved, may now lead to deeper involvement in efforts to justify the action and to avoid negative consequences.

Despite these forces, however, given the nature of the actions involved in sanctioned massacres, one might still expect moral scruples to intervene; but the likelihood of moral resistance is greatly reduced by transforming the action into routine, mechanical, highly programmed operations. Routinization fulfills two functions. First, it reduces the necessity of making decisions, thus minimizing the occasions in which moral questions may arise. Second, it makes it easier to avoid the implications of the action, since the actor focuses on the details of the job rather than on its meaning. The latter effect is more readily achieved among those who participate in sanctioned massacres from a distance—from their desks or even from the cockpits of their bombers.

Routinization operates both at the level of the individual actor and at the organizational level. Individual job performance is broken down into a series of discrete steps, most of them carried out in automatic, regularized fashion. It becomes easy to forget the nature of the product that emerges from this process. When Lieutenant Calley said of My Lai that it was "no great deal," he probably implied that it was all in a day's work. Organizationally, the task is divided among different offices, each of which has responsibility for a small portion of it. This arrangement diffuses responsibility and limits the amount and scope of decision making that is necessary. There is no expectation that the moral implications will be considered at any of these points, nor is there any opportunity to do so. The organizational processes also help further legitimize the actions of each participant. By proceeding in routine fashion—processing papers, exchanging memos, diligently carrying out their assigned tasks—the different units mutually reinforce each other in the view that what is going on must be perfectly normal, correct, and legitimate. The shared illusion that they are engaged in a legitimate enterprise helps the participants assimilate their activities to other purposes, such as the efficiency of their performance, the productivity of their unit, or the cohesiveness of their group (see Janis, 1972).

Normalization of atrocities is more difficult to the extent that there are constant reminders of the true meaning of the enterprise. Bureaucratic inventiveness in the use of language helps to cover up such meaning. For example, the SS had a set of *Sprachregelungen*, or "language rules," to govern descriptions of their extermination program. As Arendt (1964) points out, the term *language rule* in itself was "a code name; it meant what in ordinary language would be called a lie" (p. 85). The code names for killing and liquidation were "final solution," "evacuation," and "special treatment." The war in Indochina produced its own set of euphemisms, such as "protective reaction," "pacification," and "forced-draft urbanization and modernization." The use of euphemisms allows participants in sanctioned massacres to differentiate their actions from ordinary killing and destruction and thus to avoid confronting their true meaning.

DEHUMANIZATION

Authorization processes override standard moral considerations; routinization processes reduce the likelihood that such considerations will arise. Still, the inhibitions against murdering one's fellow human beings are generally so strong that the victims must also be stripped of their human status if they are to be subjected to systematic killing. Insofar as they are dehumanized, the usual principles of morality no longer apply to them.

Sanctioned massacres become possible to the extent that the victims are deprived in the perpetrators' eyes of the two qualities essential to being perceived as fully human and included in the moral compact that governs human relationships: *identity*—standing as independent, distinctive individuals, capable of making choices and entitled to live their own lives—and *community*—fellow membership in an interconnected network of individuals who care for each other and respect each other's individuality and rights (Kelman, 1973; see also Bakan, 1966, for a related distinction between "agency" and "communion"). Thus, when a group of people is defined entirely in terms of a category to which they belong, and when this category is excluded from the human family, moral restraints against killing them are more readily overcome.

Dehumanization of the enemy is a common phenomenon in any war situation. Sanctioned massacres, however, presuppose a more extreme degree of dehumanization, insofar as the killing is not in direct response to the target's threats or provocations. It is not what they have done that marks such victims for death but who they are—the category to which they happen to belong. They are the victims of policies that regard their systematic destruction as a desirable end or an acceptable means. Such extreme dehumanization becomes possible when the target group can readily be identified as a separate category of people who have historically been stigmatized and excluded by the victimizers; often the victims belong to a distinct racial, religious, ethnic, or political group regarded as inferior or sinister. The traditions, the habits, the images, and the vocabularies for dehumanizing such groups are already well established and can be drawn upon when the groups are selected for massacre. Labels help deprive the victims of identity and community, as in the epithet "gooks" that was commonly used to refer to Vietnamese and other Indochinese peoples.

The dynamics of the massacre process itself further increase the participants' tendency to dehumanize their victims. Those who participate as part of the bureaucratic apparatus increasingly come to see their victims as bodies to be counted and entered into their reports, as faceless figures that will determine their productivity rates and promotions. Those who participate in the massacre directly—in the field, as it were—are reinforced in their perception of the victims as less than human by observing their very victimization. The only way they can justify what

is being done to these people—both by others and by themselves—and the only way they can extract some degree of meaning out of the absurd events in which they find themselves participating (see Lifton, 1971, 1973) is by coming to believe that the victims are subhuman and deserve to be rooted out. And thus the process of dehumanization feeds on itself.

Conceptions of Authority and Responsibility: The Social-Psychological Sources of Crimes of Obedience

In the chapters that follow, our primary focus is on the role of authorization in creating the conditions for crimes of obedience. We shall refer to the processes of routinization and dehumanization as they become relevant to the analysis.

Authorization processes in crimes of obedience must be understood in the context of authority in general. Legitimate authority creates the *obligation* to follow rules, regardless of personal preferences or interests: Without this obligation it is difficult to maintain a dependable and equitable social order. Crimes of obedience are a consequence of authority run amok. They become possible when individuals abandon personal responsibility for actions taken under superior orders, continuing to obey when they ought to be disobeying. What are the conceptions of authority and responsibility that enable or impel people to participate in crimes of obedience? What alternative conceptions of authority and responsibility enable or impel people to resist participation in such crimes? These are the questions this book seeks to explore.

To begin our exploration, the next chapter expands the definition of crimes of obedience beyond sanctioned massacres by applying the concept to a number of recent cases, including the Watergate scandal and other civilian crimes. Chapter 3 outlines the historical and legal conflict between the duties to obey and to disobey. Chapters 4, 5, and 6 then present a social-psychological analysis of legitimate authority: Chapter 4 describes the structure of authority situations, treating authority as a special case of the broad category of social influence; chapter 5 discusses the determinants of perceived legitimacy, suggesting the conditions under which demands from authority can in principle be rejected as illegitimate; chapter 6 shows why, in practice, it is so difficult for people to avail themselves of the right to challenge authority in the face of the macro- and microlevel obstacles to doing so.

In chapter 7 we interrupt the theoretical argument in order to present some empirical findings bearing on people's reluctance to challenge authority and their tendency to obey without question. The data come from a survey of public reactions to the Calley trial in the U.S. population, which we conducted within a few weeks after the end of the trial. The survey was prompted partly by our desire to understand the massive outcry against Calley's conviction. Such survey data do not tell us how people actually behave in the face of destructive orders from authority, but they do tell us about people's attitudes toward obedience and their views of the social norms that apply to authority situations—about their conceptions of authority and responsibility.

Chapter 8 resumes the theoretical argument with an analysis of how people attribute responsibility for actions that occur in response to authoritative orders. In chapter 9 we apply this analysis to the data from the national survey, focusing on respondents' approaches to the attribution of responsibility. The issue of responsibility was central to the American public's response to the Calley trial. Individuals differing in their responsibility orientation displayed markedly different attitudes toward the My Lai massacre and the Calley trial; they also tended to differ in their demographic characteristics. On the one hand, a sizable group of Americans *denied* the responsibility of a soldier in a situation like My Lai and therefore disapproved of Lieutenant Calley's trial and conviction. On the other hand, those Americans who approved of the trial most often did so because they *asserted* the individual responsibility of subordinates for their own actions. We try to show how the dominant conception of responsibility in the U.S. population at the time, responsibility denial, can help explain the massive outcry against Calley's conviction.

In chapter 10 we turn to a second survey, conducted in the Boston area in 1976, in which we assessed reactions to My Lai as well as nonmilitary crimes of obedience (including Watergate) and tested some of our theoretical interpretations. This chapter explores the generality of our findings regarding approaches to responsibility by seeing how well they hold up in a different sample, at a later period, and in public reactions to crimes in different settings.

In chapters 11 and 12, we present the final strand of our theoretical argument, which concerns the role of individual differences in conceptions of authority and responsibility. Our primary focus is on three broad orientations to political authority, anchored in our earlier analysis of social influence and legitimacy: rule, role, and value orientation. We propose that rule and role orientations, for different reasons, foster a tendency to obey without question and to deny personal responsibility for actions taken under superior orders; value orientation, in contrast, fosters a questioning attitude toward authority and an assertion of personal responsibility for actions taken under superior orders. Chapter 12 presents data from the Boston survey that bear on these hypotheses.

Finally, the concluding chapter reexamines the issue of obedience to authority in the light of the results of our two surveys. It discusses the effect of situational factors as well as individual differences on the extent to which people are caught up in the structure of the authority situation or are able to break out of its confines and exercise independent judgment. One goal of this book, addressed in the conclusion, is to draw implications for patterns of socialization and political participation, and associated structural changes, that would increase individual responsibility in the face of orders from authorities and encourage citizens to challenge authority when its demands are illegal or immoral. We shall argue that what is required is a redefinition of the citizen role that stresses citizens' obligation to question authoritative orders in terms of the meaning of the actions they are asked to perform and the human consequences of the policies they are asked to support. Paradoxically, such a role presupposes not only sufficient closeness to authority to avoid excessive awe but also a capacity to distance oneself from authority so as to avoid entrapment in its mystique and its perspective.

2 | The Scope of Crimes of Obedience: Recent Cases, Persistent Issues

The quintessential examples of crimes of obedience are sanctioned massacres. But genocidal policy and military authority are not the only contexts in which such crimes occur. The Watergate scandal in recent American history provides illustrations of crimes of obedience in a political/bureaucratic context. Even in unofficial settings, it seems to be surprisingly easy to induce people to engage in actions that constitute crimes of obedience, broadly defined. This, at least, is a conclusion one can draw from a widely discussed series of social-psychological experiments, the studies of obedience carried out by Milgram (1963, 1974) to be discussed in detail in chapter 6. Under orders from an authority, it appears that many normal people respond with obedience, despite their own scruples and discomfort about actions that they and others would usually regard as illegal, immoral, and even unthinkable.

Just as sanctioned massacres are not the only kinds of crime that flow from authoritative orders, so lower-level personnel—such as Charlie Company's foot soldiers—are far from the only participants in these crimes. Even sanctioned massacres obviously require the collaboration of organizational levels across an entire chain of command. The degree of unquestioning obedience to orders shown by officers and functionaries at high levels of the organizational hierarchy is often striking. These people clearly do not belong to the more powerless segments of society. Yet they too seem to assume that superior orders override the moral considerations that might apply in other situations, freeing them of responsibility for their actions. The Watergate scandal can provide some insight into the dynamics of unquestioning obedience among those at middle or moderately high levels within an authority structure.[1] At the same

1. Sources consulted on the Watergate episode, in addition to those specifically cited in the text, include Bernstein and Woodward (1974), Dickinson (1973), Doyle

time, it extends the scope of our study of crimes inspired by authority from the realm of sanctioned massacres to an array of civilian crimes.

Civilian Crimes of Obedience

Authority in political bureaucracies differs from military authority in ways that crucially affect the meaning and course of crimes of obedience committed in that sphere. In political bureaucracies, unlike the military setting, obedience is not prescribed by law, and disobedience is therefore not subject to legal penalties. Political functionaries have available the two options for expressing dissent distinguished in Hirschman's classic book (1970): exit and voice. They can choose to resign rather than carry out an objectionable order—an option that is clearly not available to military personnel, at least not in the heat of battle. Alternatively, they can voice their dissent from within the organization in the hope of producing a change in policy and practice. If their criticisms become too vociferous and too public or if they verge on obstructionism or outright disobedience, they risk being fired. The loss of office, whether by resignation or dismissal, is a severe penalty, but it is qualitatively different from the legal penalties to which disobedient soldiers expose themselves. In short, obedience is less psychologically compelling in the political arena.

Political subordinates—like all subordinates—nevertheless face potentially competing duties or obligations. On the one hand, they are expected to obey authorities. On the other hand, we have seen that even in the military context subordinates are expected to evaluate orders and to *dis*obey unlawful commands. Chapter 3 traces the history and legal implications of these duties to obey and to disobey. For present purposes it is important to recognize that both the duty to obey and the duty to disobey in political bureaucracies have powerful normative supports in our society, each being linked to its own set of moral principles. The duty to obey—particularly among those working directly under the president—largely derives from the value of loyalty to the president and the president's policies. In the governing ideology of the Nixon White House, loyalty to the president as a person and to his mission was the highest value. This was reinforced by the shared belief that the president's political opponents were—wittingly or unwittingly—subverting national security (see Kelman, 1976). The duty to disobey largely derives from the value of personal integrity even at the cost of power and privilege.

In practice, political subordinates, both in the civil service and in appointed positions, are used to receiving and following orders in which they have no real investment or that they find disagreeable. Like other subordinates, they are less used to giving voice to objections or reservations, to finding and communicating rationales for possible disobedience to those orders. And like other subordinates,

(1977), Jaworski (1976), Knappman (1973), Kurland (1978), Mankiewicz (1975), Lang and Lang (1983), *New York Times* Staff (1973a, 1973b), Vidich (1977), and Woodward and Bernstein (1976).

even when driven by disagreement to choose exit—to resign—political functionaries are reluctant to make waves. As one study of political resignation put it, "Of
. . . 389 American top officials who resigned of their free will and in their prime
between 1900 and 1970, 355 (91.3 per cent) left government without any trace of
public protest. Only 34 (8.7 per cent) resigned with public protest" (Weisband and
Franck, 1975, p. 59).

The Watergate episode of the 1970s, a landmark in American political scan-
dals, exemplifies all these reactions. Among the White House subordinates, we
can observe many instances of unquestioning obedience, but also some cases of
exit and voice. Watergate encompassed multiple crimes of obedience and at least
one drama of principled disobedience.

ABUSE OF AUTHORITY IN THE OVAL OFFICE

A single event and a single day gave the name to Watergate: the June 17, 1972,
break-in and attempted bugging of Democratic National Headquarters in the Watergate apartment complex. To simplify the issues and actors in "Watergate," we
concentrate on two crimes of obedience: the burglary itself and the later erasure of
more than eighteen minutes of a taped presidential conversation. The first of these
was a crime pure and simple; the second was criminal if intentional, because it
destroyed evidence in an investigation of the initial crime. Much detail is known
about the burglary participants, but less about what and who induced them to
participate. Efforts were quickly made to obscure any connections to higher-ups.
The second crime, the erasure, can only be inferred, but its cast of characters
reaches to the heart of the White House.

Early in the morning of June 17, 1972, a Watergate security guard who spotted
a taped-over lock set off a search that located an odd group of burglars at Democratic headquarters. The credentials of those on the spot and those later implicated
in the bungled burglary suggest that someone should have been more competent.
The five burglars included Virgilio Gonzalez and Eugenio Martinez, both anti-
Castro Cuban exiles then living in Miami; Bernard Barker, also of Miami, a real-
tor and former Central Intelligence Agency (CIA) employee; and Frank Sturgis of
Miami, an associate of Barker's with CIA connections. The fifth and the only local
figure at the burglary scene was James McCord, Jr., a former FBI agent who was
on the CIA payroll—until the day after the burglary. Others later indicted for their
connection to the burglary were E. Howard Hunt, Jr., a former CIA employee,
and G. Gordon Liddy, a former FBI agent who was at the time serving as counsel
to the Finance Committee to Re-elect the President.

This was no ordinary burglary and no ordinary group of burglars. Their objective seemed to be political espionage geared toward the 1972 contest for the presidency. The revelation of the burglary attempt gradually set off a chain reaction of
other revelations about wiretaps, bugs, campaign dirty tricks, illegal campaign
contributions, tax fraud, and similarly illegal or questionable practices. Furthermore, many of these practices predated the 1972 election campaign. It turned out
that the apparatus responsible for many of the illegal operations had originally

been set up as an intelligence-gathering unit directed at the protest movement against the Vietnam War. For example, this unit—nicknamed the Plumbers—was charged with an earlier break-in at the office of Daniel Ellsberg's psychiatrist. (Ellsberg, who had copied and released the Pentagon Papers to the press, was a primary target for the Plumbers.)

Information was painfully dragged out of administration members and White House staff over a period of more than two years. Among the actors in this effort were a federal judge (John Sirica, whose law-and-order tendencies had earned him the nickname of "Maximum John"); the Senate Watergate Committee (Senate Select Committee on Presidential Campaign Activities), headed by Sen. Sam Ervin, Jr.; an independent special prosecutor, Archibald Cox, appointed by the president (since former Attorney General John Mitchell and other administration officials were implicated and eventually tried); a second special prosecutor, Leon Jaworski, appointed after the president fired the first; journalists, including eventual Pulitzer Prize winners Bob Woodward and Carl Bernstein of the *Washington Post*; and the House Judiciary Committee charged with an impeachment investigation.

The ultimate goal of these probes was reached only with the Nixon impeachment inquiry. The fundamental questions were how high in the chain of political command it was possible to trace (*a*) the issuance of orders to carry out the Watergate burglary, (*b*) knowledge of those orders, (*c*) orders to cover up involvement in the burglary, and (*d*) knowledge of the cover-up. Other related crimes of political espionage before and after the burglary were rapidly added to the list of questions, with a whole second layer of criminal cover-ups for each. All were potential ammunition for impeachment. Therefore, in each case the issue was what Nixon had ordered and what Nixon knew.

The Watergate burglars considered themselves to be acting under orders, to be acting in the national interest, and to be acting for the government in the fight against communism and especially against Cuban Premier Fidel Castro. It proved difficult to pin down the precise source of their orders and to discover who had known what about those orders. It appears that heroic efforts were made to insulate the entire White House, first, from the taint of the Watergate burglary, and then from the taint of other crimes and dirty tricks. As President Nixon prophetically put the issue in a news conference on August 29, 1972, "What really hurts in matters of this sort is not the fact that they occur, because overzealous people in campaigns do things that are wrong. What really hurts is if you try to cover it up."

President Nixon's downfall was probably sealed by cover-up operations that were already in full swing when he made that remark. The burglary had been carried out by political refugees and former intelligence agents—"foot soldiers" of political espionage. Cover-up actions similarly reached down the chain of command to the clerical staff and included the apparent destruction of taped evidence. But it also appeared that the president may well have been more deeply, personally, causally connected to some of these offenses than is often true of high command in a war crime.

Among the most startling revelations of the Senate Watergate hearings of 1973 was White House aide Alexander Butterfield's admission that President Nixon had a system for surreptitiously recording conversations in the Oval Office. Therefore, if he had participated in Watergate planning or covering up, there was an ample supply of testimony against him; if he was innocent of all involvement, he could almost surely establish it. But Nixon resisted release of these tapes in court battles all the way to the Supreme Court, claiming that their release would violate the doctrine of executive privilege. His efforts eventually failed. Piecemeal releases of transcripts revealed much, as did the discrepancies between White House versions of transcripts and versions others would later make. Perhaps more revealing were the missing tapes or tape segments for some meetings between Nixon and key aides—all of whom were later indicted, forced from office, or both.

The most symbolic hole in the evidence occurred in a tape from June 20, 1972, three days after the Watergate break-in. A period of over eighteen minutes was missing from a crucial meeting between Nixon and H. R. Haldeman, his chief of staff at the time and one of the most powerful men in the government. What caused this gap was as legally relevant to impeachment as what the missing segment might have contained. Destruction of evidence is criminal—and impeachable.

Nixon's longtime secretary, Rose Mary Woods, testified in Judge Sirica's court on November 8, 1973, that she had taken every possible precaution against erasing the tapes on which she worked. After the tape gap was revealed, she returned to court on November 26 for three days of testimony during which she indicated that she must have erased the tape by pressing "record" when she meant to press "stop" while taking a telephone call during transcription. Yet she also insisted that she was responsible for only about five minutes of the erasure, the duration of the phone call. Therefore, by Miss Woods's testimony, her usual care had slipped in this case, but not enough to account for the outcome. And the president had been the only one to know of the error. Court-appointed electronics experts concluded that the full gap was not accidental. This mystery may never be resolved. It remains a probable cover-up and a possible crime of obedience.

No one was willing to admit to virtually anything about taped evidence until after the event of principled disobedience that came to be known as the "Saturday Night Massacre." Pressure to bring the tapes into the legal fray began as soon as Butterfield's testimony made their existence known. Among those who wanted the tapes was Watergate Special Prosecutor Archibald Cox, appointed by the president to oversee prosecution of Watergate-related offenses. Cox sought to subpoena nine key tapes as evidence in Judge Sirica's court; Nixon steadfastly resisted their release on grounds of executive privilege. Judge Sirica's order to release them was confirmed by the U.S. Court of Appeals on October 12, 1973. Nixon then offered Cox a "compromise" alternative. By its terms, Nixon would have provided summaries of the tapes' contents and Sen. John Stennis would have listened to them to vouch for the accuracy of the summaries. Agreement to this arrangement would have eradicated the victory Cox had just won and left him with useless hearsay testimony by Nixon and Stennis instead of taped evidence (Ervin, 1980,

p. 230). Cox refused the offer on October 19 and held a televised press conference the next day to spell out his disagreements.

Nixon had Cox fired on October 20 for his refusal to obey orders about the tapes, but this did not happen without a certain amount of difficulty. First Nixon ordered then-Attorney General Elliot Richardson to fire Cox, but Richardson refused and resigned instead. Deputy Attorney General William Ruckelshaus (Richardson's successor at that point) was then asked (by Gen. Alexander Haig, on Nixon's order) to fire Cox. Ruckelshaus also refused and announced that he was resigning; Nixon announced that Ruckelshaus was fired. Finally, Solicitor General Robert Bork, third in command at the Justice Department, obeyed orders and fired Cox. Bork's act of obedience was to become an important issue some four-teen years later in his Senate confirmation hearings for a seat on the U.S. Su-preme Court. We shall return to that episode below.

All the disobedient participants made their justifications for disobedience pub-lic. In a news conference on October 23 Richardson affirmed his view of the attorney general as guarantor of "the independence of the special prosecutor" and his belief "in the public interest embodied in that role." Richardson further claimed, "I would have done what he [Cox] has done" (Drossman and Knapp-man, 1974, p. 98). On the same day Ruckelshaus claimed that his own refusal to obey orders to fire Cox was a "very easy" decision. "Ruckelshaus added that any-one in public life must always keep open 'the option to resign' when there is 'a fundamental disagreement' and that 'there has to be a line over which any public official refuses to step'" (Ervin, 1980, p. 14). On October 20, Archibald Cox, when fired, had issued the statement, "Whether ours shall continue to be a gov-ernment of laws and not of men is now for Congress and ultimately the American people [to decide]" (Drossman and Knappman, 1974, p. 97).

The American people decided quickly in a barrage of correspondence—in-cluding, it is claimed, the heaviest concentration of telegrams in Western Union records to that point (Drossman and Knappman, 1974). The correspondents were overwhelmingly opposed to the president's actions. By October 23, in a move that surprised virtually everyone, Nixon gave up and agreed to release the nine tapes. Missing tapes, tape gaps, and damning tapes followed, and the Nixon presidency entered its last days.

The principled disobedience of Richardson and Ruckelshaus, expressed through resignation accompanied by public protest, seemed to have had the direct effect of compelling the president to retreat. Weisband and Franck (1975) cite several factors to account for the success of this action. Inter alia, they point out:

> Since the central issue of the resignations was so directly within the resigners' area of responsibility and expertise, their views carried particular weight. Perhaps most signifi-cant, the circumstances under which Richardson and Ruckelshaus resigned made clear that they were not acting out of self-interest. They had not, themselves, been directly attacked but were sacrificing their careers to defend a colleague and, more important, a principle. Their evident integrity of purpose created an ideal backdrop for an appeal to the public conscience. (p. 16)

Richardson and Ruckelshaus were clearly responding to what the public perceived as a duty to disobey under the circumstances in which they found themselves. The ultimate impact of their action served to reinforce social norms in support of disobedience.

Instances of principled disobedience were, nevertheless, ·more the exception than the rule during the Watergate scandal. Civilian crimes inspired by authority show continuities with sanctioned massacres in the operation of processes of authorization, routinization, and dehumanization (Kelman, 1976). We will briefly review these in the context of the Watergate episode, with major emphasis on the insights this episode may provide into the participation of higher-ups in such enterprises.

Authorization. Many of the illegal acts during the 1972 campaign were orchestrated by the Committee to Re-elect the President (CREEP). As Jeb Magruder, White House staffer and former deputy director of CREEP, put it: "During this spring, when Liddy was presenting his break-in plan, I should have been aware that it was illegal, but somehow it seemed acceptable, perhaps because we were discussing it in the office of the Attorney General of the United States" (1974, p. 104). Clearly the potency of authorization to produce obedience is not restricted to powerless foot soldiers. Indeed, testimony before the Senate committee by Watergate participants often included reference to unquestioning obedience to superior orders.

There are many reasons, mundane as well as ideological, why higher-level functionaries in government or politics might go along with illegal or immoral policies. These can include holding on to a job, advancing a career, protecting one's turf, being a good team player. Granting the importance of such concerns, we still need to ask how the voice of conscience is subdued. We propose that, for bureaucratic actors, authorization may override normal moral considerations either by elevating loyalty to leader or organization to the highest obligation or by invoking a transcendent mission.

In certain authority structures, of which the Nixon White House was a prime example, the governing ideology or operating style places supreme value on functionaries' loyalty. For those who are committed to such an organization, authoritative orders call forth what they would consider a moral obligation that overrides any other scruples they might have. Once an order has been given, they see themselves as having no choice but to obey—not out of powerlessness, as might be the case for the foot soldier, but out of a personal commitment to the organization and its leadership. They are so close to the centers of power, like the attorney general's office in Magruder's reminiscences, that they identify with the authority structure and are caught up in its glory and mystique. They thus tend to exaggerate the authorities' moral claim on their loyalties. Such functionaries, like the powerless, do not expect to be held personally responsible, but not because they see themselves as helpless pawns. Rather, they see themselves as agents and extensions of the authorities and therefore assured of their protection.

Authorization may also override moral scruples by invoking a transcendent mission. The authorities are seen as agents of a larger set of corporate purposes that place them outside the realm of ordinary morality. This view derives from a theory of the state that asserts it is not subject to moral law in the protection or promotion of its interests. The central authorities, acting for the state, are similarly not subject to moral restraints that might operate in their personal lives. Kren and Rappoport (1980) describe Bismarck's version of this position as he confronted the contradiction between his official behavior and the moral principles governing his private behavior: "He reasoned that when acting as servant of the state, a man was not bound by the same morality binding him as an individual. His official duty was to exercise stewardship for the state, and since the state could not be limited by ordinary moral law in the pursuit of its interests, neither could be the individual who was acting as a part of that state" (p. 25). According to this view, decision makers could use the same justifications as those lower in the hierarchy, claiming that they had no choice—that they were responding to the demands of the state. Such claims have been discredited in international law as a defense against war crimes accusations: The Charter for the Nuremberg trials rejected the claim of "head of state" in Article 7, just as it rejected the claim of "superior orders" in Article 8 (Bosch, 1970). Still, political leaders continue to invoke transcendent missions, such as "national security" or "containment of Communist aggression," to justify illegal actions. National security was the justification for the White House operations that eventually led to the Watergate break-in, as well as for Richard Nixon's unsuccessful effort to prevent release of his tapes.

Functionaries close to the centers of power may come to share the view that the top national decision makers' actions—and their orders—relating to such transcendent missions cannot be judged according to the usual moral or legal criteria. In acting on these orders, the functionaries themselves become part of the transcendent enterprise. When authorized to play their particular roles in the larger enterprise, they may feel justified, and indeed obligated, to overcome ordinary moral and legal restraints.

Routinization and Dehumanization. As in any bureaucracy, the flow of paperwork and decision making in and around the Nixon White House was routinized. Dirty tricks were carried out alongside and in conjunction with normal bureaucratic functions, often by the same individuals (such as the attorney general). The momentum was too much for most participants to overcome. Characteristically, routinization obviated the need to make decisions and made it easier to avoid the implications of actions. As Magruder (1974) put it, "the cover-up . . . was immediate and automatic; no one even considered that there would *not* be a cover-up" (p. 104). Moreover, the use of language that assimilated the Watergate activities into such domains as law enforcement, intelligence gathering, and protection of national security made it easier to avoid confronting their criminal character and to see them, instead, as legitimate operations.

And as in any sanctioned massacre, the criminal activities of those in power and their employees were accompanied by derogation and dehumanization of the targets of the crimes. The Watergate break-in and related activities were a direct continuation of operations aimed at political dissidents, who were treated as subversive and dangerous, and even of clandestine operations aimed at foreign enemies. President Nixon's Democratic opponents in the 1972 campaign were placed in the same category; they were regarded not as advocates of different policies within a common democratic framework but as enemies representing a serious threat to the national interest. As one of the Watergate burglars, Bernard Barker, told the Senate Watergate Committee, Democratic party headquarters was the "enemy," and George McGovern was a front for inimical forces that had to be stopped. As far as he was concerned, his Watergate activities were a continuation of his covert CIA activities in the Bay of Pigs. In sum, the targets of Watergate actions were dehumanized, placed into a category of people defined as foreign, insidious, and dangerous—as threats to national security that had to be eliminated by whatever means were necessary.

The outcome of the Watergate episode was not a literal massacre—only a Saturday Night Massacre and a series of felonies and misdemeanors involving the theft and destruction of property and information. But as a civilian example of authority overstepping the bounds of legitimacy it is a striking case: a constitutional crisis in which two branches of government acted to rein in the third. For all practical purposes a president was impeached, spared only the final stages of what was a sure defeat.

Crimes of Obedience in the Recent News

We have dwelt at length on My Lai and Watergate because these two cases (My Lai in particular) were subjects of our own empirical research on public reactions to crimes of obedience, to be discussed in later chapters. These cases, however, are hardly isolated events and rare anomalies of merely historical interest. Crimes of obedience of different varieties and in different settings continue to make news virtually every day. To illustrate the pervasiveness of the phenomenon and the issues raised by it, let us review sketchily several cases that occupied—sometimes even preoccupied—the news media during the summer months of 1987. Some of the cases represent new (or newly discovered) crimes of obedience, others the reverberations of crimes committed in earlier years.

THE BARBIE TRIAL

The murderous actions of the Nazi regime and particularly its systematic program to annihilate the Jews of Europe provided history with the prototype of crimes of obedience. "I was only following orders" is a phrase many automatically associate with the bureaucrats, soldiers, and security forces of the Nazi era. The echoes of that period were heard repeatedly in 1987 in a series of trials held in different parts of the world. The most notorious of these was the trial of Klaus Barbie, "the butcher of Lyons," which has been described as perhaps the last of the great Nazi war crimes trials.

Barbie, as a young second lieutenant in the SS, became chief of the Gestapo for Lyons, France, and the surrounding region in 1942. In this capacity, he was in charge of police operations that involved the arrest, torture, and deportation of Jews and members of the French Resistance. He was selected for this assignment because of his ideological zeal (Morgan, 1987). Even within the SS, there were differences in behavior among officers; an SS major in the Kiev region, for example, refused to obey an order to massacre Jews and, as punishment, his battalion was sent to the front. Lyons, however, "with its Resistance activity and its large population of Jews, required someone who was not prey to moral qualms or self-doubt, who had an appetite for his work—a man like Klaus Barbie" (Morgan, 1987, p. 27). By all accounts, Barbie enjoyed his work; he was sadistic and personally participated in torturing his victims (Morgan, 1987; Painton, 1987).

After the war, Barbie fled to avoid prosecution. He was twice, in 1952 and 1954, tried in absentia in a Lyons military court and sentenced to death for the commission of specific war crimes. In 1972 he was found in Bolivia by Serge and Beate Klarsfeld, the well-known war-crimes researchers and activists. As a result of a campaign led by the Klarsfelds, he was finally, in 1983, extradited to France to stand trial. The eight-week trial in Lyons, ending on July 4, 1987, focused on specific crimes against humanity that were not known to the military court that convicted him in the 1950s. The new charges were necessary both because of the need to avoid double jeopardy and because the statute of limitations had run out on war crimes, the focus of the earlier charges. The crimes against humanity—atrocities committed against civilians because of their religion or race—with which Barbie was charged included the deportation of forty-four Jewish children from a children's home in the village of Izieu to the gas chambers of Auschwitz and the ordering of the last train from Lyons, filled with Jews and members of the Resistance, to Auschwitz and other camps—at a time when Germany's defeat was already assured (Bernstein, 1987; Morgan, 1987).

Early in the trial, Barbie depicted himself as a minor official acting under superior orders: "When I heard the accusations, I thought I was at the Nuremberg trial. I understood that I was described as acting in Lyons like a crazy man, that I was pursuing the Jews. But there were 120 of us. We were a unit. I wasn't in charge. You'd think I was the master of the region. I was under the authority of the regular army" (Koven, 1987, p. 12). On the third day of the trial, Barbie announced that he would henceforth stay away from the courtroom—as French law entitled him to do—because his extradition from Bolivia was illegal. He was brought back only twice during the trial, to be identified by witnesses, and at the end, to hear his verdict. On the basis of overwhelming evidence—much of it provided in testimony by French Jews and Resistance members—the court found him guilty on all 341 counts of crimes against humanity with which he was charged. He was given the maximum sentence: imprisonment for life.

THE WALDHEIM CONTROVERSY

Another, very different case harking back to World War II and Nazi atrocities continued to make news in the summer of 1987: the controversy that has surrounded the former secretary-general of the United Nations, Kurt Waldheim, since the spring of 1986. Waldheim ran for the Austrian presidency as the candidate of the People's party and was elected by about 54 percent of the vote on June 8, 1986. In the course of the campaign, new information was revealed about his service in the German army during World War II, which potentially implicated him in war crimes and crimes against humanity.

It is not clear, as of now, to what extent Waldheim participated directly in the crimes with which he has been connected. What is clear, however, is "that he had for years been concealing the truth about his military service during World War II and that, instead of spending the greater part of that conflict as a student in Vienna, as he claimed, he had been in the Balkans as a staff officer with German army units that committed atrocities" (Craig, 1986, p. 4). During most of 1942–44 he served in Nazi-occupied Yugoslavia and Greece with German army units involved in antipartisan operations, which included reprisal executions of hostages and led to the deaths of many unarmed civilians and the deportation of thousands of others to concentration camps. One of his tours of duty in Greece coincided with the transfer of forty thousand Salonika Jews to Auschwitz in *Wehrmacht* freight cars, although Waldheim denies any connection with or knowledge of this action (Craig, 1986, p. 4). It is likely, however, that he knew about some of the other actions in his capacity as a staff officer whose functions included the transmission of orders to combat units, interrogation of prisoners, analysis of intelligence, and briefing of his superiors.

Waldheim has described his role as routine, essentially involving secretarial chores. His defense has been that he was only doing his duty as a soldier—that what he did during the war was no different from what hundreds of thousands of other Austrians did. This defense no doubt appealed to large segments of the Austrian population, who have not so far come to terms with Austrian involvement in the Nazi enterprise and with their own—or their parents' or grandparents'—"dutiful" and even enthusiastic participation in the mass destruction of civilian populations (Botz, 1987). The attacks on Waldheim may very well have contributed to his electoral victory.

Waldheim has not, however, been able to enjoy the fruits of this victory. He has been isolated internationally and is unwelcome in many of the world's capitals. His efforts to rehabilitate himself received a serious blow on April 26, 1987, when the U.S. Department of Justice in effect barred him from traveling to the United States because of his presumed implication in Nazi war crimes (see Markham, 1987). According to the department's announcement, "a prima facie case of excludability exists with respect to Kurt Waldheim as an individual, and his name is being placed on the 'Watchlist.' This determination was based on United States law prohibiting entry to any foreign national who assisted or otherwise participated in activities amounting to persecution during World War II."

Two months later, the Waldheim case again made news when the Austrian president—head of a predominantly Roman Catholic state—paid an official visit to the Vatican, where Pope John Paul II welcomed him as a man of peace and made no mention of his wartime activities. For the pope, the visit and particularly his failure to put distance between himself and his visitor have been a source of considerable criticism. For Waldheim, the visit broke his diplomatic isolation, but it probably provided only temporary relief. There are increasing signs that even in Austria political and media figures are having second thoughts about Waldheim's presidency and are withdrawing their support from him (Markham, 1987).[2]

THE ARGENTINE "DUE OBEDIENCE" LAW

The military regime that ruled Argentina between 1976 and 1983 has been described by some Argentines as "an occupation army that spoke our language" (Elon, 1986, p. 74; see also Gonzalez, 1987). After ousting the government of Isabel Perón in March 1976, presumably in response to the chaos caused by the escalating violence of both left-wing guerrillas and right-wing death squads, the military rulers instituted a brutal reign of terror of their own. As part of what they called a *proceso de reorganizacion nacional* designed to "save" the country from subversive influences, they declared war against left-wing terrorists. According to their definition, however, a terrorist or *subversivo* was "not just someone with a gun or a bomb but also someone who spreads ideas that are contrary to Western and Christian civilization" (Elon, 1986, p. 75).

In fact, only a small proportion of the victims of Argentina's "dirty war" was guerrillas, most of whom were eliminated early in the process. Large numbers of the victims were people who were either involved in entirely nonviolent political activities or not involved in politics at all. Some were victimized because they were known to be liberal dissenters or because they had criticized the military dictatorship; others merely because they were students, psychoanalysts, sociologists, social workers, or members of other professions associated in the junta's mind with subversive ideas or actions; and still others because of mistaken identity, or because they inquired about or were related to earlier victims, or even because they owned property coveted by the kidnap squads which abducted the victims and were "authorized" to confiscate their possessions (Elon, 1986, p. 78). The largest single category of victims consisted of workers—mostly industrial labor-

---

2. In February 1988, a commission of historians appointed by the Austrian government reported that Kurt Waldheim "must have been aware of atrocities committed around him and did nothing about them, and that he tried to conceal his military past. But the panel said it had no evidence that Mr. Waldheim himself was guilty of war crimes" (Schmemann, 1988, p. A1). The report has intensified the internal debate within Austria and has led to increasing demands for Waldheim's resignation.

ers—since a major objective of the military was to promote discipline in the workplace.

The method applied systematically by the military government has contributed a new term to the vocabulary of human cruelty: the word "to disappear" used as a transitive verb. The victims of the dirty war are known as *desaparecidos*—the disappeared. Typically they were kidnapped from their homes or off the street by military or police squads, brought to concentration camps or interrogation centers, and brutally tortured or raped. They were not charged with crimes or brought to trial; in fact, their "arrests" were never officially acknowledged. Only a very few of the disappeared were ever heard from again. Most were killed, some in mass executions on the edge of a pit; their bodies were cremated, or buried in mass graves, or dumped into the sea from army helicopters. Some of the victims were still alive when they were pushed out of airplanes into the water. The Argentine National Commission on the Disappeared (1986) documented almost nine thousand cases of individuals who "were disappeared" by the military regime and identified 340 secret concentration camps and nine crematoria that operated during that period. Unofficial estimates raise the number of the disappeared to thirty thousand or even more, of whom the vast majority were between the ages of twenty and thirty-five; 40 percent were women (Disch, 1987). Perhaps 400,000 others went into exile. "The effects of government atrocities were felt in the entire population," not only because disappearances or exiles eventually touched almost every family, but because "the irrationality of the pattern of disappearance left no one safe" (Disch, 1987, p. 4).

The military dictatorship was finally brought down in 1983—largely because it lost the Malvinas/Falkland Islands war and because the economy was in a state of virtual collapse—and Raúl Alfonsín was democratically elected to the presidency. Within days of assuming office he established the National Commission on the Disappeared (which issued its report in 1984) and set in motion criminal procedures against the generals responsible for the dirty war and its abuses of human rights. The president's actions were specifically directed at the top military commanders, including the leaders of the successive military juntas, and not at the many hundreds of lower-ranking officers known to have been directly involved in abductions, torture, and killings. After many delays, nine former junta members were tried in civilian courts in 1985; five were convicted and sentenced to prison terms, including life terms for Gen. Jorge Rafael Videla and Adm. Emilio Massera. Since that time, other trials have been held and several additional top-ranking military and police officers have been found guilty. Argentine human rights activists have been critical of the small numbers (out of the thousands who participated in the crimes) who have been tried and convicted, of the slowness of the process, and of the lenient treatment accorded to those who have been found guilty. Still, these trials were unique in that, "unlike the trials in Nuremberg, where the victors had sat in judgment over the vanquished, here was a government being judged by its own people, according to its own laws—laws that had not been made retroactively. It was the first time that such a thing had happened in a Latin American country" (Elon, 1986, p. 78).

Efforts to go beyond the top commanders and bring to justice the hundreds or even thousands of members of the armed forces and police who actually carried out the criminal acts have confronted major obstacles. By the end of 1986, charges against some five hundred of these men had been filed, and many more such charges were in prospect. President Alfonsín expressed "concern that the trials were dragging on too long and creating tension in the armed forces" (Christian, 1987) and that the resulting military arrests might make the country ungovernable (Willey, 1987). Therefore, in December 1986, he asked and obtained a law from the Argentine Congress establishing a *punto final*—a legal deadline, to take effect February 22, 1987 (sixty days after passage of the law), for any indictments on charges arising from the abuses of the military regime. In effect, the law granted amnesty to the vast majority of those accused of the crimes committed during the years of the regime, and it provoked widespread public protest. But it also produced a spark of activity in human rights circles and in the courts, as a result of which 170 new cases were filed and accepted by the courts before the February 22 deadline (Disch, 1987). Alfonsín's attempt to mollify the military thus backfired. By the spring of 1987 there were still several hundred men, mostly former or current military officers, under active investigation by the courts. Anger and resentment within the military ranks increased. Some refused to cooperate with judicial proceedings and threatened a coup. Finally, in April 1987, a series of rebellions by mid-level officers erupted and were quieted only by Alfonsín's personal intervention (Christian, 1987). The officers demanded an end to the trials and amnesty for the accused.

Several weeks after these rebellions, Alfonsín came up with a new proposal for effective amnesty, more far-reaching than the punto final of December 1986. The proposal eventually took form in a "due obedience" law, passed by the Argentine Congress and approved by the Supreme Court in June 1987. The law grants immunity to military men below the rank of brigadier general accused of kidnapping, torture, and murder during the dirty war. "The law 'presumes, lacking evidence to the contrary,' that such men were 'under subordination to superior authority and carried out orders, lacking the possibility of inspection, opposition or resistance regarding need or legitimacy' of the orders" ("Wider Argentine Immunity Bill," 1987). The immunity does not extend to cases involving rape, kidnapping of children, or appropriation of property through extortion. As a consequence of the due obedience law, the trials of most officers involved in atrocities have been halted. Numerous cases have been struck from the records and the accused set free. Moreover, the Supreme Court overturned a number of earlier convictions and ordered the release of men who had been found guilty of torturing political prisoners ("Rights Advocates Bitter," 1987). Only some thirty or forty men—mostly senior retired officers who had primary responsibility for issuing orders or preparing plans for the dirty war—remained subject to prosecution.

It may well be that the due obedience law saved Argentine democracy from another military coup. In doing so, however, it established the presumption that all but the top military officers have no choice but to follow superior orders, even if these orders call for torture and murder. The law thus defines conditions under which a soldier may engage in torture and murder—although, ironically, not in looting—without fear of legal liability.

THE BORK NOMINATION

The summer of 1987 also brought echoes of the Watergate scandal. It will be recalled that Robert Bork, solicitor general and acting attorney general after the resignation of Elliot Richardson and the dismissal of William Ruckelshaus, obeyed President Nixon's order to fire Special Prosecutor Archibald Cox during the Saturday Night Massacre of October 20, 1973. In July of 1987, Robert Bork—who in the meantime had been appointed to the U.S. Court of Appeals for the District of Columbia by President Reagan—was nominated to fill the seat on the Supreme Court vacated by Justice Lewis Powell. In the course of the heated debate generated by this nomination and the confirmation hearings in the U.S. Senate, Judge Bork's role in the Saturday Night Massacre frequently came up as a consideration in assessing his judicial philosophy and his likely behavior on the Supreme Court.

By firing Cox, Bork clearly performed an *act* of obedience that associated him with the president's refusal to comply with a court order, which ultimately came to be seen as part of the Watergate cover-up. Bork's action as such did not, in our view, constitute a *crime* of obedience, although the issue is debatable. Judge Gerhard A. Gesell of the Federal District Court for the District of Columbia ruled, on November 14, 1973, that the firing of Cox was illegal because it violated the regulations establishing the Special Prosecutor's Office. According to these regulations, which in Judge Gesell's opinion had the force of law, the special prosecutor could be removed only for extraordinary impropriety, and there was no finding of such impropriety on Cox's part. The Justice Department did not appeal the ruling, but, since Cox did not want the job back, the issue was considered moot (Noble, 1987). In any event, violation of the regulations would not have made Bork subject to criminal penalties. Some of Bork's critics have viewed the firing of Cox not merely as an act of obedience that was technically illegal but as conscious participation in an obstruction of justice (Chang, 1987) or at least as a failure to ask himself whether the president's order was directed toward the unlawful purpose of obstructing justice (Gillers, 1987).

The discussion in the summer of 1987 of Bork's role in the Saturday Night Massacre, apart from raising questions about the legality of Cox's dismissal, focused on the more general philosophy that may have prompted Bork to act as he did. Some observers pointed out that Bork was concerned primarily with issues of legal procedure, involving the powers of the president and of the special prosecutor, rather than with the substance of Cox's investigation of the president (Noble, 1987). According to these observers, it was Bork's view that the special prosecutor, as a member of the executive branch subject to presidential authority, had no legal right to mount a court challenge against the president, and that the president therefore had the power to dismiss him for doing so. This view, in turn, was linked to "an important strain of Judge Bork's views for many years," namely, "his strong sense of deference to authority, in particular Presidential authority," which, according to one critic, has turned him into "an advocate of disproportionate powers for the executive branch of Government, almost exclusive supremacy" (Noble, 1987, p. 23). This view of presidential power, according to Anthony Lewis (1987), "made him insensitive to the moral and constitutional challenge that Watergate represented."

Bork's role in the Watergate affair was not as critical as several other factors to the Senate's decision to reject his nomination to the Supreme Court. It did contribute, however, to his image as a man whose deference to government authority and presidential prerogatives reduces his sensitivity to broader issues, such as the protection and expansion of individual and group rights.

THE IRAN-CONTRA HEARINGS

The major U.S. media event during the summer of 1987—the congressional hearings on the sales of U.S. arms to Iran and the diversion of profits from these sales to the Nicaraguan contras—focused on another set of political-bureaucratic crimes of obedience, with far greater implications for foreign and military affairs than the Watergate episode. The hearings and report of the joint Senate-House committee on the Iran-contra affair left little doubt that many of the actions associated with this affair were candidates for criminal charges and, within our framework, probably constituted crimes of obedience—actions involving secret arms sales to Iran contrary to declared U.S. policy, privatization of foreign policy, disruption of normal government processes, misappropriation of government funds, covert actions without congressional notification, establishment of secret funds and infrastructures to carry out future covert actions outside of government channels, soliciting funds for the contras and supplying weapons to them in disregard of the Boland Amendment, secret diversion of funds from the sale of U.S. arms to support of the contras, repeated and systematic lying to congressional oversight committees, and alteration and destruction of official documents in the midst of an investigation. The subsequent indictment against four key actors in the Iran-contra affair issued on March 16, 1988, by a federal grand jury at the recommendation of the independent counsel Lawrence E. Walsh, did indeed present criminal charges relating to these and other actions (Shenon, 1988; "Key Sections of Conspiracy Indictment," 1988).

The Iran-contra affair has been described as the work of a "secret government-within-the-government" consisting of President Reagan, the late CIA director, William Casey, the National Security adviser, Adm. John Poindexter, and his deputy, Lt. Col. Oliver North (Shannon, 1987, Aug. 5). Theodore Draper (1987, October 8) prefers the term *junta*. According to Draper,

> this junta was not a fully premeditated plot worked out by practiced conspirators. It arose by degrees because some officials were so possessed by determination to impose

their own beliefs and policies on the country that they were willing to violate its most fundamental principles of government and to form a band of true believers bonded together against all those who did not agree with them. We usually think of a junta as plotting to overthrow a president; this junta came into being to overthrow an established constitutional rule of law with the help of a president. (p. 47)

To think of the junta as a plot against the president designed to usurp his power is to miss the point of the whole affair. The president became, in effect, the head of a faction within a government in which top officials from the CIA and the National Security Council staff were arrayed against the secretary of state, the secretary of defense, and the Congress (Draper, 1987, Oct. 8, p. 58). There is no implication that the president necessarily knew the details of every operation. But even if he did not know, for example, about the diversion of funds (as Poindexter testified), it is clear that he shared the objectives of Poindexter, North, and Casey and that they were acting with at least his tacit approval (Shannon, 1987, Aug. 5). Backed with the authority of the president, they felt free to ignore the niceties of the law. "Reagan's men hardly seemed to have asked themselves where the statutory limits were. They believed in what they were doing, they believed in the authority of the President, and that was that—even though what the President knew or remembered of their doings was often unclear to them" (FitzGerald, 1987, pp. 37–38).

The president's role is also essential to our analysis of the actions of Poindexter, North, and their subordinates—such as North's secretary, Fawn Hall, and his assistant, Robert Owen, who described himself as "but a private foot soldier who believed in the cause of the Nicaraguan democratic resistance" ("Iran-Contra Hearings at a Glance," 1987)—as crimes of obedience. To illustrate the meaning of obedience in this political context, let us briefly explore the actions of three key witnesses in the congressional hearings, each representing a different position in the bureaucratic hierarchy: Fawn Hall, Oliver North, and John Poindexter.

Fawn Hall admitted to altering official documents at Colonel North's request, to shredding classified papers and interoffice memos, and to smuggling documents out of the White House inside her clothing. The language she used in explaining her actions to the congressional committees provided almost classical illustrations of the response of participants in a bureaucratic crime of obedience at lower levels of the hierarchy. She apparently acted out of intense loyalty to her boss and in the conviction that he would not have asked her to do anything improper. "I believed in Colonel North," she said, "and there was a very solid and very valid reason that he must have been doing this. And sometimes you have to go above the written law, I believe" ("Iran-Contra Hearings at a Glance," 1987). She saw herself as "part of the team," engaged in a vital mission that transcended legal constraints. She shredded and smuggled documents in order "to protect the initiative." The word *protect* was her euphemism for what would otherwise appear to be illegal actions. Asked if she was participating in a cover-up, she replied: "I don't use the word cover-up. I was in a protective mode" (Magnuson, 1987, p. 21). She also provided illustrations of the way in which illegal actions can become routinized and integrated into one's daily work. "It was a policy of mine not to ask questions," she said

at one point during the hearings. When asked whether she realized the significance of altering official documents, she replied: "That was my job, and I wasn't
reading or trying to find out what his motives were or what he was trying to hide"
(Magnuson, 1987, p. 21). And her response to another question, probing her
awareness of the nature of the documents she was shredding, was: "I really didn't
notice, sir. I was just purely doing my job" (p. 22).

Colonel North himself, of course, was doing more than his job. There is some
ambiguity about how to characterize his actions, many of which seemed to show
a marked indifference to legal and ethical constraints. Was he engaged in "ordinary" crimes, using his position for personal gain? Or was he engaged in crimes of
obedience, carrying out the orders of his superiors with unusual vigor? Was he
acting out of ideological zeal, taking advantage of his powerful connections to
pursue his favorite causes? Or can it even be said that he was committing acts of
civil disobedience, conscientiously breaking laws that he considered to be in violation of higher principles? In our view, his actions can best be described as a
combination of the second and third of the four options: Many of his actions
constituted probable crimes of obedience, motivated and justified by a transcendent mission to which he had an intense ideological commitment. The evidence
brought out at the congressional hearings did not seem to support the first possibility. Whatever personal profit North may have derived from the Iran-contra
affair was apparently of minor proportions and probably due to the lack of accountability that pervaded the whole operation rather than to venal motives. This
assessment still seems warranted despite his grand jury indictment on charges of
conspiracy to defraud the Internal Revenue Service and of receiving an illegal
gratuity (Shenon, 1988). As for the fourth possibility, North's refusal at the hearings to accept any personal responsibility for violations of the law hardly fit the
image of a person who reluctantly breaks a law for reasons of conscience and is
prepared to bear the consequences of this principled act.

Two seemingly contradictory images of North emerged from the congressional
hearings. On the one hand, he seemed to present himself as a self-propelled actor.
He fully identified himself with the objectives of the covert projects of selling arms
to Iran and supporting the Nicaraguan contras. He embraced the doctrine behind
these covert actions, which called for rolling back the spread of communism by
"actively assisting, and perhaps even trying to create, resistance movements struggling against Soviet-allied Marxist governments in the Third World" (Church,
1987, p. 25). He was particularly committed to keeping the contra program alive,
whatever the cost might be. He justified irregular approaches to this and related
ends by announcing that "it's a dangerous world" ("Iran-Contra Affair," 1987),
picturing himself as the protector of America's future in the face of an indifferent
and intransigent Congress. Self-righteously and alliteratively he declared that he
had to choose "between lives and lies." The lives he was referring to were, presumably, those of the U.S. hostages in Lebanon and of the Nicaraguan contras; the
lives of the innocent victims of the weapons supplied to Iran and to the contras
apparently did not enter into his moral calculations.

Colonel North also emerged as a man with considerable influence. He was at the center of a wide range of operations carried out by the National Security Council staff; his position enabled him to interpret policy directives and thus to determine the form in which they would be carried out; he seemed to take many initiatives, often using extragovernmental channels and unconventional means; and he had extensive human, financial, and material resources at his disposal. From his testimony it seemed clear that North enjoyed his power and took pride both in what he was able to achieve for his cause and in how he was able to circumvent a reluctant Congress and officialdom. In fact, he had a tendency to embellish his exploits and to exaggerate his importance, although there is no doubt that he played a central role in initiating and guiding a wide range of covert operations (Church, 1987).

On the other hand, the same Colonel North who presented himself as a man who took initiatives and wielded influence in pursuit of his ideological agenda also seemed to take recourse in the familiar defense of superior orders. Although he did not imply that he was "merely" following orders in the face of personal objections or reservations, he emphasized repeatedly that everything he did was authorized by his superiors, including the National Security advisers, CIA Director Casey, and supposedly the president himself: "Throughout the conduct of my entire tenure at the National Security Council, I assumed that the President was aware of what I was doing and had, through my superiors, approved it. I sought approval of my superiors for every one of my actions. . . . I never carried out a single act, not one, in which I did not have authority from my superiors. . . . I haven't in the 23 years that I have been in the uniformed services of the United States of America ever violated an order, not one" ("Iran-Contra Hearings at a Glance," 1987; "Iran-Contra Affair," 1987). Moreover, he maintained that his superiors—and certainly the president—were entitled to his unquestioning obedience: "If the commander-in-chief tells this lieutenant colonel to go stand in the corner and sit on his head, I will do so." When asked why he had never inquired into Poindexter's failure to forward to the president his (North's) memoranda about the diversion of funds, he replied: "I'm not in the habit of questioning my superiors. If he deemed it not to be necessary to ask the President, I saluted smartly and charged up the hill" (Shannon, 1987, July 15).

North's defense of superior orders prompted Sen. Daniel K. Inouye, chairman of the Senate committee, to point out that the military code to which North is beholden requires him to obey only the lawful orders of a superior officer. In fact, Inouye went on to say, "members of the military have an obligation to disobey unlawful orders. This principle was considered so important that we, we the Government of the United States, proposed that it be internationally applied in the Nuremberg trials" ("Panel's Case," 1987). Inouye's reference to the Nuremberg trials was interrupted by an angry outburst from Brendan Sullivan, North's attorney. Inouye did not pursue the issue, but the point had been made: Superior orders is not a sufficient defense even in a military context, and much less so in a civilian context. "Officials are expected to ask questions of their superiors, and to be morally and legally responsible for their own actions. . . . They realize that they owe a president something more precious than obedience; they owe him their independent judgment" (Shannon, 1987, July 15).

The two images conveyed by Colonel North, far from being contradictory, can actually be described as two manifestations of the same attitude: He seemed to see himself as the bearer of presidential authority. His activist, enterprising, and unrestrained pursuit of his ideological agenda derived its impetus from that presidential authority. He was not just a zealous ideologue and an indomitable doer who would pursue his agenda come what may; he was a zealous ideologue and indomitable doer who felt fully authorized by the president. He believed in what he was doing and enjoyed exercising power in behalf of these beliefs, but the power was derivative. He assumed—with good reason—that the president shared his agenda and that his actions either were specifically approved by the president or reflected the president's wishes.

Moreover, he seemed to believe that the president was above the law, at least in the conduct of foreign policy and certainly in the pursuit of the transcendent mission of rolling back the spread of communism in Nicaragua and elsewhere. As the president's agent, he saw himself as also above the law and operated from the premise that everything he did was legal (Healy, 1987; Wicker, 1987).[3] His behavior suggests that he was carried away by the power he believed to have at his disposal as the president's agent and by his supposed freedom from legal restraints. One consequence of his view was that he believed his operations to be fully protected against legal action. Thus, the appointment of a special prosecutor in December 1986 came as a great shock to him: "I never in my wildest dreams or nightmares envisioned that we would end up with criminal charges" ("Iran-Contra Affair," 1987). He had been prepared, he said, to be the "fall guy" if some of the operations he was involved in became public, but he changed his mind when he realized that he might face indictment and decided to point the finger at the superiors who authorized the operations and others who knew about them.

One superior who accepted responsibility for authorizing North's operations, including the most questionable one—the diversion of the profits from the arms sales—was Admiral Poindexter. In fact, Poindexter acknowledged several times over the course of the hearings that he had unilaterally made certain controversial decisions. But the image he conveyed was hardly of an independent actor usurping presidential power, but rather of a dutiful staff officer. If some of his actions were criminal, they were not crimes of rebellion against presidential authority but crimes of obedience of the kind one finds toward the top of a bureaucratic hierarchy. Poindexter, like North, no doubt believed in the doctrine that prompted the covert arms sales to Iran and aid to the contras. But whereas North appeared

---

3. North was obviously aware that there were at least serious questions about the legality of his operations, which is probably why he rushed to destroy the evidence when these operations began to unravel. What he believed was that the laws were not—or should not have been—binding on him because he was acting on behalf of the president and in pursuit of the vital interests of the country. He was not, however, prepared to challenge the laws and defend his actions on grounds of principle.

to be driven primarily by commitment to a transcendent mission, Poindexter's readiness to do his part without question seemed to derive primarily from an overriding obligation: a sense of loyalty to the president that superseded loyalty to the law or any other consideration.

Poindexter's view of his obligation to the president was revealed in his account of the presidential finding of December 1985, which retroactively authorized a November 1985 arms shipment to Iran. A year later, after the investigation into the arms sale had begun, Poindexter decided to tear up that finding. He felt that the finding gave the impression "that the whole Iranian project was just an arms-for-hostages deal." Under the circumstances, the finding "was a significant embarrassment to the President and I wanted to protect him from possible disclosure of this." He went on to explain: "I think it's always the responsibility of a staff to protect their leader, and certainly in this case where the leader is the Commander-in-Chief" (Draper, 1987, Oct. 8, p. 55). In Poindexter's eyes, then, protection of the leader was a central obligation of the National Security adviser.

Poindexter's role in the diversion of funds provides the clearest illustration of how his sense of obligation to his commander in chief led him to make controversial decisions in apparently unilateral fashion—or at least to take public responsibility for such decisions. In his congressional testimony, Poindexter accepted full responsibility for authorizing the diversion after North first proposed the idea to him in February 1986: "After thinking about what authority I had, what the President would do if he were asked, the controversy that would exist if this became public, I considered all of these factors and at the end of the conversation, I told Colonel North to go ahead, because I thought it was a good idea. In my view, it was legal. It was very similar to the third country and private support for the contras. And in my view it was an added benefit of the Iranian project" (Draper, 1987, Oct. 22, p. 48). In further testimony, Poindexter elaborated on his reasons for failing to seek the president's approval of the diversion plan or even informing him of it:

> The President's policy with regard to support for the contras had not changed since 1981. The various versions of the Boland Amendment came and went, but the President was steadfast in his support for the contras. . . . So I was absolutely convinced as to what the President's policy was with regard to support for the contras. I was aware that the President was aware of third-country support, that the President was aware of private support. And the way Col. North described this to me at the time, it was obvious to me that this fell in exactly the same category, that these funds could either be characterized as private funds . . . or they could be characterized as third-country funds. . . . Now, I was not so naive as to believe that this was not a politically volatile issue. . . . So, although I was convinced that we could properly do it, and that the President would approve, if asked, I made a very deliberate decision not to ask the President so that I could insulate him from the decision and provide some future deniability for the President if it ever leaked out. . . . This clearly was an important decision, but it was also an implementation of very clear policy. If the President had asked me, I very likely would have told him about it. But, he didn't and . . . the important point here is that on this whole issue, you know the buck stops here with me. I made

the decision; I felt that I had the authority to do it; I thought it was a good idea; I was convinced that the President would, in the end, think it was a good idea. But I did not want him to be associated with the decision. ("Iran-Contra Hearings/Excerpts," 1987; Draper, 1987, Oct. 22, p. 49)

Thus, in explaining his action, Poindexter argued that it was neither necessary nor desirable to seek the president's approval. It was unnecessary because the use of the Iranian funds was compatible with earlier policies that the president had already approved; the diversion was not a new policy but implementation of a policy that had the president's full support. Moreover, Poindexter felt certain that the president would approve the decision if asked—a conviction based on his close familiarity with the president's passionate support for the contra cause. In short, Poindexter seemed to believe—for good reason—that he was carrying out the president's policies and acting under his authority. Since he felt certain about the president's wishes anyway, he considered it best not to inform him of the diversion and thus to provide him future deniability. By deflecting responsibility from the president to himself, he was, in his view, performing the loyal staff officer's duty to protect the president from potential political embarrassment.

The White House quickly challenged Poindexter's testimony on one point: The president denied that he would have approved of the diversion if he had been asked about it. When confronted with this denial later in the hearings, Poindexter replied: "I understand that he said that, and I would have expected him to say that. That's the whole idea of deniability" (Draper, 1987, Oct. 22, p. 49). And, indeed, the point of deniability is to enable the president to issue precisely the kind of denial that he issued in this instance. In his reply, Poindexter remained entirely consistent with the basis of his defense—that his motive had been the duty to protect the president—without compromising the president's position that he had no knowledge of the diversion.

Many observers have found it hard to believe Poindexter's claim that he decided on the diversion of the funds without the president's knowledge and direct authorization. Whether or not Poindexter's account is true, however, his behavior is not inconsistent with his model of the dutiful officer. It is conceivable that his account was in fact true and that he did not inform the president of the diversion. He may well have acted under what he saw as a blanket presidential authorization. Thus, he may have seen no need to inform the president because he was convinced that he knew the president's wishes and was carrying out his policies. More important, in keeping with an explicit or implicit understanding with the president, he may have deliberately withheld the information in order to provide the president *absolute* deniability. It is equally conceivable that Poindexter's account was *untrue* and that the president did in fact know about the diversion. After all, Poindexter admitted to misrepresenting the facts on other occasions in order to protect presidential policies and covert operations. He may well have done the same during the congressional hearings in order to fulfill his obligation of providing the president continuing deniability. In either event, Poindexter's actions seem consistent not with those of a usurper of presidential power pursuing his own foreign-policy agenda but with those of a dutiful officer who saw himself as acting under presidential authority and whose loyalty to the president superseded all other moral and legal obligations. His idea of loyalty was such that he seemed prepared to take upon himself the burden of making controversial decisions—or claiming to have made such decisions—in order to protect his commander in chief.

THE CHRYSLER ODOMETER CASE

To show that crimes of obedience are not necessarily restricted to official settings—whether military or political—we conclude this sample of recent cases with a brief discussion of a corporate crime that made the news during the summer of 1987. Earlier examples of cases in this category, to which we shall return in the concluding chapter, are the Ford Motor Company's Pinto case, involving a defective gas tank, and the case of the space shuttle booster rocket's defective O-rings, which apparently contributed to the *Challenger* tragedy.

In June 1987, the Chrysler Corporation was indicted by a federal grand jury for selling sixty thousand cars and trucks as new even though they had been driven by company executives. Two executives were indicted on criminal charges in the matter. According to the indictment, "executives at Chrysler assembly plants routinely took new cars off the assembly line and drove them for as much as 400 miles with the odometers disconnected." The odometers were then reconnected and the cars were sold without informing the buyers of the accumulated mileage. "In addition, the indictment charged, some cars were damaged in the testing and were only superficially repaired before being shipped to dealers to be sold" (Holusha, 1987, p. D9). Again, buyers were not informed of the damage and repair. The indictment covered only the sixty thousand vehicles that were built and allegedly tampered with during an eighteen-month period in 1985 and 1986. It charged, however, that the company had engaged in the practice of regularly disconnecting odometers on cars produced in its plants since 1949 (Eisenstein, 1987) and that millions of cars had been sold over the decades with inaccurate mileage readings.

Lee Iacocca, chairman of the Chrysler Corporation, apologized for the practice and offered to supply new cars to replace the forty that had been damaged during the testing and to extend and expand the warranties of the other cars that were involved in the test program. He called the company's actions "dumb" and "unforgivable," although he continued to insist that the practice was not illegal (Holusha, 1987). The issue of legality will, of course, be determined by the courts. There seems little doubt, however, that the practice of systematically and routinely deceiving car buyers is not just "dumb" (at least after it has been discovered) but unethical. What makes the case interesting from our point of view is that it suggests a corporate crime of obedience, involving a large number of participants over many years. We do not know at present where in the company's hierarchy the decision was made to institute this practice, how the "orders" were communicated, and how they were enforced. It seems likely, however, that the practice represented company policy and that company executives at different levels carried out this policy—obeyed orders—with few questions. It also seems reasonable to suppose that many participants knew that the practice was unethical and suspected that it was illegal—or at least that they should have.

Issues in the Definition of Crimes of Obedience

A crime of obedience is an act performed in response to orders from authority that is considered illegal or immoral by the larger community. Both "crime" and "larger community" need to be thought of loosely in order to encompass the varieties of evil our definition is meant to cover. For example, in Nazi Germany, the protoypical arena of crimes of obedience, many thousands of employees and soldiers carried out instructions and orders that resulted in an unprecedented destruction of innocent life. Yet the orders given to those subordinates came from duly constituted authorities. They were in fact legal under German law at the time, and thus, technically, they were not crimes within the confines of Germany itself. In this case, the rest of the world serves as the larger community, and its judgment creates the crime. In an attempt to capture the peculiar legal status of the German activities, Hannah Arendt (1964) dubbed them "legal crimes." We attempt both to broaden the scope of the discussion and to retain its paradoxical flavor by referring to such acts as crimes of obedience.

The paradoxical nature of crimes of obedience creates ambiguities in the definition of both terms of this concept. Judges as well as analysts of crimes of obedience have to grapple with two definitional issues: When does an act of obedience become a *crime* of obedience? And when does an ordinary crime become a crime of *obedience?* For judges, the answers to these questions help determine the degree of guilt and the appropriate level of punishment in any given case. For analysts, they help clarify the meaning of this class of crimes and the range of conditions that may give rise to them.

DEFINING CRIME

The most obvious criterion for defining an act of obedience as a *crime* of obedience is evidence that the actors knew their orders were illegal or inconsistent with general moral principles. One line of defense against this charge, to which those accused of crimes of obedience often resort, is that their actions were in fact completely within the law. Thus, North and Poindexter have argued that their activities in support of the contras were legal because the Boland Amendment did not apply to the National Security Council; the Chrysler Corporation has insisted that selling cars that had been test-driven as new cars was "dumb" but not illegal. A variant of this defense is that the actions were necessary parts of a larger enterprise, such as protecting the country against internal subversion or external threats, that the government was legally entitled—even obligated—to pursue. This line of defense is compromised by the central role that secrecy or cover-up has played in all the cases we reviewed. The participation of those charged with crimes of obedience in elaborate schemes to keep their activities secret, or in efforts to destroy the evidence once these activities have been exposed, suggests awareness that what they had been doing was at least of doubtful legality.

Nevertheless, it is conceivable that some participants in crimes of obedience, particularly at lower levels of the hierarchy, are unaware of the illegal character of their orders. Indeed, the potential for such ignorance arises from the inherent ambiguity that marks crimes of obedience. When subordinates receive orders from duly constituted authorities operating within an apparently legal framework, they may well assume that the orders themselves are legal. More often than not, the question of legality does not even enter their minds, especially when they are working in official settings—military or civilian—surrounded by the trappings of legitimacy. Our earlier quotations from Jeb Magruder and Fawn Hall illustrate how common it is for functionaries at different levels in a hierarchy simply not to ask questions. Those who are close to the top of the hierarchy, such as members of the White House staff, may implicitly assume that legal constraints do not apply to their actions as long as they are authorized by the president. Thus, for a variety of reasons, those charged with crimes of obedience may in fact be right in claiming that they did not know their orders were illegal.

But here a second criterion for defining an act of obedience as a crime of obedience comes into play: the judgment that the actor *should* have known that the order was illegal. In military law, as we noted in the discussion of the Calley case, the judgment of what a soldier should have known is based on what people of "ordinary sense and understanding" can reasonably be expected to know. Thus, Colonel Kennedy, in his charge to the jury in Calley's trial, pointed out that a defendant is criminally liable for actions taken under superior orders if "the superior's order is one which a man of ordinary sense and understanding would, under the circumstances, know to be unlawful, or if the order in question is actually known to the accused to be unlawful" (Goldstein et al., 1976, p. 526). In general, the higher the status of officers, the greater the expectation that they be able to discriminate between lawful and unlawful orders. The conviction of a low-level officer like Lieutenant Calley for a crime of obedience was actually exceptional and, as we suggested above, was probably due to his role in both ordering and committing mass executions. Calley's defense was not helped by the evidence that some of the enlisted men under his command sensed that the orders of the day were illegal; it was hard to sustain the argument that he, as an officer, was unable to do so.

In sum, in civilian as well as in military settings, an act of obedience becomes a crime of obedience if the actor knows that the order is illegal, or if any reasonable person—particularly someone in the actor's position—"should know" that the order is illegal.

DEFINING OBEDIENCE

The classical line of defense by those accused of crimes of obedience is that they were "only following orders."[4] The presence of superior orders in itself, of course, is not an acceptable defense, according to the Nuremberg Principles and most military codes. As Colonel Kennedy pointed out to the jury in the Calley trial and as Senator Inouye remarked to North at the end of his congressional testimony, soldiers are not obligated to follow orders that are unlawful; in fact, they are obligated to disobey them. Nevertheless, in view of the inherent ambiguity of crimes of obedience, the defense of superior orders does carry considerable weight. It is generally recognized that it is difficult for subordinates to evaluate whether an order is legal or illegal and to choose between obedience and disobedience on that basis, particularly in military settings with their strong presumption that subordinates will follow orders. Thus there is often a tendency to accept the defense of superior orders, as long as the defendants have a reasonable basis for claiming that they did not know the orders were illegal. In Argentina, as we have seen, the defense of superior orders has actually been legally established in the due obedience law, which applies to all but the highest military officers.

Furthermore, even if superior orders are not accepted as full exoneration, they may at least serve as mitigating factors. Thus, those accused of crimes have potentially much to gain from the claim that they were only following orders, since it may help them escape punishment or reduce its severity. The self-serving potential of this claim always makes it suspect. Therefore, the definition of obedience—the question of when a war crime, or a crime against humanity, or an obstruction of justice, or a misappropriation of funds, or a conspiracy to break the law becomes a crime of *obedience*—is a matter of some moment to those who are called upon to judge such actions. Needless to say, it is also important to the analyst who is seeking to identify the distinctive features of this class of crimes.

The simplest cases, from the point of view of defining crimes of obedience, are those in which the actors show reluctance to carry out the actions ordered but nevertheless do so because they feel obligated to follow orders. These are clear cases of obedience, in which the actors experience a conflict between obligation and preference but act in accordance with their perceived obligation. Some of the men acting under Calley's orders at My Lai fit this pattern.

In many cases that we would describe as crimes of obedience, however—including most of the cases reviewed here—the picture that emerges is much more complicated. One major category of cases we have in mind consists of those in which the evidence clearly suggests that the actors had *motives* for their criminal

---

4. The defense of superior orders may be used simultaneously with the defense that the action was entirely legal. Colonel North, for example, pursued both lines of defense. He argued, in effect, that his actions were legal (because, for example, the Boland Amendment did not apply to the National Security Council), but that even if they turned out to have been illegal, he was duly authorized to take them.

acts beyond the duty to obey.[5] They may act out of ideological zeal, as North apparently did in his support of the contras or Barbie in the performance of his Gestapo functions. They may derive personal gratification from their activities, such as North's evident enjoyment of the wide-ranging power he exercised, or the sadistic pleasure that Barbie and some of the Argentine officers found in torturing and raping their victims, or the release of accumulated anger and frustration among participants in massacres. They may reap material gains from their activities, as Nazi storm troopers and Argentine kidnap squads did at times by confiscating their victims' property and as some Chrysler executives may have done by driving the company's new cars. Or, finally, they may have seen their activities— or indeed their dutiful acts of obedience themselves—as ways of advancing their careers, as Adolf Eichmann and perhaps Kurt Waldheim did in the context of Nazi Germany, and as William Calley may have done in the context of the Vietnam War.

Many of the cases we have reviewed deviate from the simple case of reluctant obedience in another respect: The *nature* of the action suggests a level of involvement that goes well beyond the call of duty. Thus, actors may take considerable initiative in the implementation of the orders they receive, as both Calley and North did in their very different ways. In some cases, an actor's initiative may come close to crossing the line between implementation and formulation of policy. High officials, such as Poindexter, may at times act without specific orders, making important decisions on the basis of a broad authorization to pursue a general policy line. In effect, they are acting according to their interpretation of their superior's wishes. Apart from the taking of initiative, actions may also suggest a level of involvement beyond the call of duty if they are carried out with a great deal of enthusiasm and diligence.

In all these instances, the motives and nature of the actions make it difficult to conceive of the defendants as reluctant participants in crime who were merely following orders because they saw themselves as having no other choice. One can reasonably ask in these cases whether one is really dealing with crimes of obedience or with cynical use of the defense of superior orders to avoid or reduce criminal responsibility. From a legal point of view, evidence that the criminal actions satisfied one or another personal motive or represented a high level of personal involvement clearly undermines the credibility of a defense of superior orders and greatly reduces whatever exonerating or mitigating role it may have played. Moreover, the psychic or material gains that accrued to the actors and their active identification with the actions increase their personal culpability, even if the actions took place in the context of superior orders. We therefore agree with the legal view that, if obedience to superior orders ever has an exculpatory effect,

5. It is possible to see mixed motives nearly everywhere in obedient actions. For example, the reluctantly obedient subordinate may be responding out of fear in addition to, or even instead of, obligation. The discussion here focuses on those motives that might lead a subordinate to participate willingly or autonomously in the actions in question.

that effect is removed or considerably diminished if the actors took initiative or derived personal benefits from their criminal actions. Thus, it strikes us as reasonable that the most likely to be tried and convicted for crimes of obedience should be individuals who clearly went beyond the call of duty in following unlawful orders.[6]

From an analytic point of view, however, we want to stress that the fact that a criminal action serves various personal motives or is carried out with a high degree of initiative and personal involvement does not necessarily remove it from the category of crimes of obedience. To be sure, those charged with a crime may be using superior orders as an ex post facto justification for actions they took for other reasons and on their own initiative, or they may be exaggerating the role that superior orders played in their decision. It is equally possible, however, that obedience to authority is in fact a central element in such cases. As we tried to show in our discussion of North's and Poindexter's roles in the Iran-contra affair, an individual may be acting with a great deal of initiative and single-minded zeal, pursuing sundry personal and ideological agenda in the process, and yet be operating fully under the umbrella of superior orders. Even elaborate and innovative initiatives, and even initiatives that are not specifically known to the superior, may be viewed by the subordinates—sincerely and often realistically—as implicitly authorized: as following broad guidelines for implementation of the superior's policy and reflecting what the superior wanted (or would have wanted) them to do.

As for personal motives and ideological agenda, these may mix and interact with the actor's sense of duty in a variety of ways. Perhaps the most plausible possibility is that superior orders or authorization create an opportunity and a sense of entitlement to pursue activities that are personally satisfying to the individual. In some cases, individuals may come to see their own agenda—such as the vigorous promotion of their ideological preferences in disregard of legal constraints—as an integral part of the mission covered by their orders. In other cases, they may see their personally motivated actions—such as the rape or sadistic torture of "enemies of the state"—as not exactly ordered, but encouraged or at least condoned by their superiors. In yet other cases, they may simply take advantage of the power they derive from acting on behalf of high authorities to pursue personal gains, such as enriching themselves. In all these cases, it may be entirely true that they would not have committed their respective criminal acts in the

---

6. By this logic, there should be a greater tendency to try and to convict individuals higher in the hierarchy, since they are more likely to be in a position to take initiative (even if they are following orders from their own superiors) and to derive personal benefits from their actions. Moreover, they can be presumed to be better able to discriminate between legal and illegal orders and to challenge orders that they find questionable. This tendency clearly prevailed in the Nuremberg trials as well as in the recent Argentine trials, but it may at times be overshadowed by other considerations. The trials generated by My Lai, for example, focused on the massacre itself rather than the policies that may have led to it. As a result, Calley became the prime target because he was the only officer who both ordered the killings and personally participated in them.

absence of orders or authorization from their superiors. There is no particular reason to believe, for example, that Colonel North would have engaged in a host of illegal activities in pursuit of his ideological cause or out of his sense of drama had he not perceived himself as acting under the president's authority, which placed him above the law. It is possible even that some of the murderers and torturers in Nazi Germany or in the juntas' Argentina might have lived out their lives as law-abiding citizens had they not been operating in systems that gave them a license to act out their sadistic fantasies.

In sum, we speak of a crime of *obedience* if criminal actions are linked to the explicit or implicit orders of authorities in one of two ways (or some combination of both). First and most obviously, superior orders may *cause* the action entirely, in the sense that the subordinates take it reluctantly and strictly out of a sense of obligation. Alternatively, superior orders may serve to *justify* (not just ex post facto, but ab initio) actions that correspond to the subordinates' own preferences and with which they readily identify themselves. Both cases constitute crimes of obedience on the presumption that the subordinates would not have taken the action without authorization: in the first case because they would not have wanted to take it, and in the second because they would not have felt free to do so.

In including some actions that satisfy personal motives and that involve a high level of initiative under the rubric of crimes of obedience, we are not suggesting that the actors' culpability is thereby reduced. Having gone beyond the call of duty, they have made the actions their own and must be judged accordingly. We define such acts as crimes of obedience because we believe that they cannot be adequately explained without taking the role of authorization into account.

PUBLIC REACTIONS

One further consequence of the ambiguity inherent in crimes of obedience must be noted at this point. There is often a sharp divergence in public reactions to individuals accused of such crimes. They are castigated, reviled, and treated as minor or major villains by large segments of the public. At the same time, there are those who defend them, support them, applaud them, and even elevate them—at least temporarily—to the status of heroes. The most recent example is Oliver North, who became a hero in the eyes of a sizable, vociferous minority of the U.S. population after he began his congressional testimony. His popularity gradually declined, but at its height he was a favorite subject of ballads and object of fads among his admirers (and among those ready to cash in on his hero status). In his day, William Calley too was a hero in certain quarters and became the subject of a popular ballad. But even among those who did not regard him as a hero, there was a widespread feeling that he had been treated unjustly, as we shall see in later chapters that present our own research on public reactions to the Calley trial. To take another example, the charges against Kurt Waldheim seem to have increased his popularity in Austria and, as noted above, probably contributed to his electoral victory. Again, there are some indications that his popularity is now on the decline.

The divergent reactions to those charged with crimes of obedience reflect the paradoxical character of such crimes. It is hardly surprising that perpetrators of these crimes would be widely perceived as villains in view of our description of crimes of obedience as acts performed in response to orders from authority that are considered illegal or immoral by the "larger community." Within that community, they are bound to be faulted both for the acts themselves and for their failure to stand up against authorities who ordered such acts. But there is also the "smaller community" (which could be as large as a nation-state), in which those acts are considered to be proper and necessary, or were at least at one time considered to be so. That community is the obvious source of the defense, support, and applause that the perpetrators of crimes of obedience enjoy. Within that community, some may support them and even elevate them to hero status because they approve of the substance of their actions. Others may applaud their obedience to authority and admire their devotion to duty, even if it required them to take controversial actions. Some may defend them out of their own identification with their dilemma. (For example, many Austrians seem to feel that Waldheim did only what they themselves or their parents did and had to do during the Nazi era; many Americans believe, as our data show, that Calley did what they themselves would have done and would have been obligated to do under similar circumstances.) Finally, many may sympathize with them out of a feeling that they are being treated unfairly and crucified for having done their duty.

3 | The Duty to Obey and the Duty to Disobey

The unique feature of crimes of obedience is that they arise from a conflict between two competing duties: the duty to obey and the duty to disobey. The duty to obey is inherent in the very concept of authority. It is supported by widely shared social norms, rooted—in our society—in Western religious and moral teachings. In the military context, norms that spell out the duty to obey are explicitly codified in military law. The norms of obedience are so strong that they create a presumption of obedience to authority—notably in military situations—even when the actions ordered would otherwise be perceived as immoral or illegal. To counteract this presumption would require another set of social norms that clearly support the right and even the duty to disobey under specified circumstances. The very fact that acts of obedience can come to be regarded as crimes implies that such an alternative set of norms does exist. Such norms have, in fact, been spelled out in Western religious and moral writings over the centuries and, again, explicitly codified in military law.

In this chapter we explore the continual dialectic between the duty to obey and the duty to disobey in several contexts. We begin with a brief examination of the concept of authority, in which the duty to obey is a direct corollary of the right to command. Since authority sets conditions and limits on the use of power, the concept provides an opening for the right, if not the duty, to disobey. We then turn to Western religious and moral teachings, which develop norms in support of the duty to obey, but which also contain the primary normative basis for the duty to disobey. Finally we turn to military law, in which the duty to obey is most explicitly formulated, but which also offers the most explicit statement of the conditions under which a duty to disobey prevails.

Historical and Contemporary Conceptions of Authority

Social scientists and political theorists typically agree that authority involves two components: the right to command others and the power to do so. Legitimacy, the right to command, is based in social organization. Weber's (1947) famous discussion of legitimacy is a useful starting point for uncovering some of these bases. Weber argued that there are three fundamental types of legitimate authority: traditional, charismatic, and legal or rational-bureaucratic authority. These types correspond to three bases of legitimacy itself. Legitimacy can rest on the traditional or historical origins of the authority, as in hereditary kingship or tribal succession. It can rest on the individual charisma (literally, the "gift of grace") of a new leader, as is typical of a new, initially rebellious organization in either the political or religious sphere. Finally, and commonly in modern civil societies, legitimacy can rest on rational-bureaucratic procedures for change of government, for promulgation of law, and for delegation of authority.

Weber also argued that in the bureaucracies of modern civil societies and organizations, hierarchical position and expertise or knowledge tend to go together. Parsons (1947), in his translation of Weber, and Blau (1968), among others, have pointed out that position and knowledge are not necessarily linked and may represent different types of authority-subordinate relationships. Blau explicitly contrasted bureaucratic authority, as exemplified by the military command hierarchy, with professional authority, as exemplified by the doctor-patient relationship. In a bureaucratic authority relationship, which rests on the authority holder's superior position in a hierarchy, obedience may be encouraged by coercive means. In a professional relationship, which rests on the authority's greater expertise, compliance is largely voluntary.[1] These distinctions (discussed more fully in chapter 5) should not be overdrawn, however. Bureaucratic authorities are generally assumed or required to possess superior knowledge or competence, and professional authorities can often call on coercive supports for their commands or instructions or can at least behave as if they had such supports.

In modern secular conceptions, authority is usually considered a property of a role rather than, for example, residing in the person of a king, a god, or a god-king (Peabody, 1968).[2] Moreover, authority is fundamentally a relational concept: A person holds authority only over, or with respect to, another person. Thus, authority refers to a role relationship between two sets of actors within a social unit: the authority holders (or "authorities") on the one hand and the subordinates or ordinary members on the other. The social unit involved may be a small group

---

1. Coleman (1980) has suggested a related distinction between *disjoint* and *conjoint* authority systems. In the first of these, "the interests that the subordinate expects will be pursued in the exercise of authority are not the same as those of the subordinate, while in the second those interests are the same" (p. 147). In Coleman's terms, bureaucratic authority is typically disjoint, and professional authority is typically conjoint.

2. In the terms of another distinction made by Coleman (1980), we refer here essentially to *complex* rather than *simple* authority systems. In the latter, the authority is exercised directly by the actor in whom it is vested; in the former it is exercised by a "lieutenant" or an "agent." It is "in the complex authority relation that the concept of position apart from the person—and the notion of a person 'occupying a position' in the organization—arises" (p. 150).

or an organization or it may be as large as the society or the political state. In the political arena, we might describe the two sets of actors as officials and citizens, keeping in mind that officials are also citizens and that officialdom is itself hierarchically organized, so that those in higher positions serve as authorities to those below them.

Since authority is a relationship, the role of each of the two parties is defined with reference to the role of the other: The role of authorities entitles them to make certain demands on citizens, and the role of citizens obligates them to accede to those demands. Similarly, the role of superior in an explicit hierarchy entitles its incumbent to give certain orders to subordinates, and the role of subordinate requires obedience to these orders. Both parties share the assumption that authorities have the right to issue commands and that citizens have the duty to obey them. Authority differs from sheer power by virtue of this right to command and expect obedience. The distinction is reflected in the language with which authority is discussed. Words like *orders, obedience, obligation,* and *duty* imply a relationship that is based not merely on superior power.

As in all reciprocal relationships, however, rights are not all on one side and obligations on the other. Along with the right to give orders, authorities also carry responsibility for the consequences of the actions they have ordered. Subordinates, on their part, have a duty to obey, but a corresponding right to expect that the authorities will take responsibility for any untoward outcomes of actions performed under superior orders. But neither the subordinates' right to be absolved of responsibility nor the authorities' right to make demands or give commands is unlimited. Subordinates are not totally free of the responsibility to exercise judgment, as Lieutenant Calley's court-martial argued. And authorities' right to demand and command generally applies to a restricted domain and is subject to a specified set of procedural rules. Indeed, the constrained (in contrast to arbitrary) exercise of power is an essential part of the definition of *legitimate* authority.

The term *legitimate authority* is, in a literal sense, redundant since authority itself implies the right to make demands and give orders. Yet this redundancy adds to the analytic usefulness of *authority* as a concept. Authority, at least in the modern Western context, generally derives from position within a social structure. As we have already stated, those who occupy positions of authority usually possess not just the right to give commands but also the power to do so. They have at their disposal the means necessary for enforcing their orders and sanctioning disobedience. Furthermore, if they are perceived as legitimate, they are also accorded the *right* to use coercive means, within specified limits, to deal with disobedience.[3] But occupants of authority positions may not be perceived by citizens

---

3. The monopoly or near-monopoly of coercive power is so striking that some theorists (such as Stinchcombe, 1968) treat it as the defining characteristic of legitimacy. In our view, the possession by authorities of coercive means for enforcing their orders may be an indicator of their legitimacy, but it is not a source of that legitimacy. The essence of legitimacy is that it contributes to *voluntary* acceptance of the demands of authority holders, which enables them to govern far more effectively than they would if they had to rely entirely on coercive means.

as using their power rightfully. Their legitimacy may be undermined in several ways, as we shall elaborate below. For now, some examples from the political sphere can serve to illustrate why authorities may lack legitimacy in the eyes of the population: The government itself may be oppressive and unrepresentative and hence considered illegitimate; or the incumbent leaders may have gained power through fraudulent or violent means; or their specific commands or the policies within which these are embedded may fall outside their domain of authority or violate the procedural rules that govern the exercise of authority.

Thus, individuals who have many of the objective features that characterize authority—who occupy authority positions, who possess all the trappings of authority, who have the power to enforce their demands, who claim the right to give orders, and whose claim may even be recognized by external actors (for example, by other governments in the international system)—may nonetheless lack legitimacy. Lack of legitimacy can be an objective phenomenon within the terms of a particular framework for legitimization. For example, if legitimacy rests on an electoral process, a power holder who came into office through a military coup may be objectively defined as illegitimate. From our point of view, however, the lack of legitimacy as *perceived* by group members is of primary importance, since we treat legitimacy as a social-psychological concept referring to members' acceptance of the authority's right to make demands upon them. In either event, the situation we have postulated—power holders possessing many of the objective features of authority yet lacking legitimacy—can most parsimoniously be described as one of *illegitimate authority*. Once such a category is recognized, the phrase *legitimate authority* loses its redundancy. To put it succinctly: We can speak of authority when officeholders *claim the right* to give orders by virtue of their positions; this authority is legitimate insofar as members *accept that claim*.

Legitimacy can be assessed at several levels. A specific order, a general rule or law, a particular officeholder, or an entire institution or government may be deemed legitimate or not. (Note, in this connection, Easton's distinction between legitimacy of the authorities and that of the regime [1965, chap. 18].) Furthermore, one can distinguish procedural and substantive standards for assessing legitimacy at any of these levels. The procedure by which an order is issued or a law is enacted may be legitimate while the substance of the order or law is illegitimate. Similarly, an officeholder who attained power through legitimate means may use this power for illegitimate purposes. Substantive standards are more vague and difficult to apply than procedural standards; it is easier to establish whether the appropriate steps were taken and the appropriate channels used in passing a law than to determine the constitutionality of that law.

Whatever standard they employ, citizens must judge authority to be illegitimate at some level before resorting to open, principled disobedience. Resistance to a specific order, civil disobedience of a rule or law, rebellion against an incumbent administration, and revolt against a system of government share the prerequisite that authority must be perceived as illegitimate in whole or in part. But people find it extremely difficult to arrive at such a judgment, for reasons to be elaborated in chapter 6. There is a general tendency to accord authorities the presumption of legitimacy. One is reminded here of Homans's (1976) observation, echoing an earlier Augustan thinker, that stable power relations tend eventually to be accepted as legitimate, such that "whatever is, is right." It typically requires the introduction of a new ideological framework (often presented as the revival of an old framework) to enable citizens to challenge the legitimacy of the established order.

Such ideological frameworks are of necessity a collective product, which is one of the reasons that challenges to the legitimacy of authority and hence principled disobedience are usually collective phenomena (Gamson et al., 1982). Walzer (1970) argues forcefully that "disobedience, when it is not criminally, but morally, religiously, or politically motivated, is almost always a collective act, and it is justified by the values of the collectivity and the mutual engagements of its members" (p. 4).

Although the perception of illegitimacy may be a necessary condition for disobedience, it is not a sufficient condition. Disobedience also requires overcoming the powerful habit of obeying authorities that seems to manifest itself wherever human groups are found. The phenomenon of obedience to authority is so ubiquitous that Milgram (1974) evoked an evolutionary argument for its prevalence. The habit of obedience is further bolstered by strong social norms in its support. To overcome this habit and its supporting norms, people need recourse to a countervailing set of norms that permit disobedience and even require it under certain circumstances. Such norms are crucial for two reasons. First, they provide citizens with the knowledge that disobedience is actually possible. Given the long history of obedience in the face of apparently intolerable orders, this is not a trivial contribution. Second, they provide people with a language and a socially acceptable justification for saying no—and they provide observers (and judges) with a basis for endorsing that action. Disobedience thus becomes an act that may at times be right and worthy of approval. In short, social norms in support of the right and duty to disobey serve to legitimize the act of disobedience.

Justifying Disobedience to Authority: Religious Roots

Western culture is surprisingly rich in normative support for disobedience, but it does not make the decision to disobey an easy one.[4] Obedience, rather than disobedience or vacillation, is presumed to be the normal course of action in the laws, rules, and edicts to which we have access. These documents, however, also

4. In addition to the sources cited in the text, we consulted a number of works in the preparation of the broad historical overview presented in this and the following sections. Sources for the discussion of ancient Judaism and early Christianity include Claburn (1968), Davies (1965), Drane (1982), Gager (1975), M. Grant (1968), R. M. Grant (1977), Herrman (1973), Markus (1974), Moore (1984), Noth (1958), and Smith (1971). Works covering the Middle Ages, the Reformation, and the development of the state include Brooke (1971), Buck and Zophy (1972), Carlyle and Carlyle (1936), Franklin (1967), Gierke (1958), Kantorowicz (1957), Laski (1919), E. Lewis (1954), McIlwain (1947), Moeller (1972), Strayer (1970), Tawney (1962), Walzer (1976), Wilks (1963), and Yinger (1961).

prescribe limits on the exercise of authority, and, in so doing, they inevitably suggest conditions for disobeying authority and set out justifications for such disobedience.

What is the source of the limits of authority and who sets those limits? The answer to this question can be traced across millennia of Western history in a recurring theme of conflict between religious and secular authorities. Disobedience of the latter is frequently justified in the name of the former—or in the name of a yet "higher authority" that both supposedly acknowledge. The higher authority sets limits on the actions not only of the secular authorities but also of the religious authorities themselves. For example, Berman's (1983) sweeping work on the Western legal tradition spells out the limits on papal action: "Within the church itself, . . . there were theoretical as well as practical limitations upon arbitrariness. . . . Even Pope Innocent IV (1243–1254), one of the most authoritarian of papal monarchs, admitted the possibility of disobeying a pope if he should command an unjust thing by which the status ecclesiae [state of the church] could be disturbed" (p. 214). When there is a religious authority willing and able to set limits for itself and for secular authority, there is rich potential for justified disobedience. Normative support for disobedience in the modern West is thus rooted in Judeo-Christian tradition.

The Bible can be conceived as a book of norms: a historical window into the "oughts" and "ought nots" of long-ago cultures in what was then the crossroads of the world. From it we can glean images of an evolving concept of authority, which helped shape modern norms about obedience. Two caveats must be kept in mind in evaluating the biblical record. It is important not to read into an older era the relatively strict modern separation between the religious and political domains. Even today, religions are always political forces. But in traditional cultures, religion and politics were much closer to a unity; political leaders were often also religious leaders, and what we would interpret as political revolts were often cloaked in the mantle of religion. It is equally important to be aware of what may have been left out of the record. For example, almost all the New Testament's records were compiled not only substantially after the death of Jesus but also after the fall of Jerusalem to Roman forces. This conjunction suggests why early Christianity's politically rebellious character may have been downplayed. Thus the Bible is a book of norms for a world in which politics and religion were much of a piece, and whose messages were composed or preserved by political winners and political survivors.

JEWISH BIBLICAL FOUNDATIONS

Around 1250 B.C. several tribes found their way out of bondage in Egypt and migrated into Canaan. Some of these migrants traced their lineage back to a patriarch named Abraham. During their nomadic wanderings they established a loose political federation, using a form of agreement that was fairly typical for the region: a covenant. Mendenhall (1955) has convincingly argued that, although the covenant was a common arrangement, these tribes hit upon an unusual variant. In the typical covenant of that time, a people agreed to be ruled by a king and accepted certain obligations toward him in return for his good works and protection. In contrast, the covenant adopted by the Israelites under the guidance of Moses was an agreement between an emerging people and its special God (who at the same time was the only and hence universal God), in which the people promised to follow God's commandments and He in turn promised to nurture and protect them.

The biblical story of Abraham and Isaac (Genesis 22) presents a personalized version of this covenant. As the familiar tale goes, God put Abraham to the test by asking him to sacrifice his only son, Isaac, a son whose very birth had been a miracle accomplished with God's aid. As Abraham prepared to do God's bidding, an angel stayed his hand and told him that God would not require such a sacrifice. In return for Abraham's demonstrated obedience, God reaffirmed His covenant with him, promising to make his offspring into a great nation. On the face of it, Abraham's action seems to be an almost paradigmatic case of unquestioning obedience, to the point of readiness to engage in criminal behavior. This is surprising in view of earlier accounts of Abraham's give-and-take relationship with God, particularly the story in which he questions the justice of God's decision to destroy Sodom and bargains with Him over the fate of the city (Genesis 18). The sacrifice story seems to give unequivocal normative support to the duty to obey. On closer examination, however, the message turns out to be more complex and more ambiguous.

First, it must be noted that God does not in fact permit Abraham to carry out the sacrifice. Some have proposed that the rejection of human sacrifice is actually the main message of the story. Such a message would be consistent with the frequent biblical admonition to the Israelites against adopting the religious practices of the surrounding nations: "Thou shalt not do so unto the Lord thy God; for every abomination to the Lord, which he hateth, have they done unto their gods; for even their sons and their daughters do they burn in the fire to their gods" (Deuteronomy 12:31). According to this view, it can even be argued that Abraham *failed* the test to which God had put him by his willingness to obey an order that God could not possibly have meant for him to carry out. Such an interpretation, however, does not conform to the text, in which the angel clearly tells Abraham that God is rewarding him "because thou hast done this thing, and hast not withheld thy son, thine only son" (Genesis 22:16).

A more likely interpretation is that the story was meant to convey a dual message: Abraham did indeed pass the test by demonstrating his inner readiness to make a supreme sacrifice at God's bidding, but God did not really want the death of Isaac and in fact abhors human sacrifice (see "From Mt. Moriah," 1975). Perhaps Abraham knew this and, although proceeding with the preparations for the sacrifice, had faith that God would in the end intervene and (as he told Isaac) "provide Himself the lamb for a burnt-offering" (Genesis 22:8). Perhaps Abraham did not know this, in which case the episode was designed to teach him that lesson. In either event, the message regarding the duty to obey is more nuanced than it might at first appear: Yes, God must be obeyed, but He observes certain limits beyond which He will not ask His subjects to go. By implication, an authority that does not accept limits is not entitled to unquestioning obedience.

There is a second ambiguity in the message about obedience that the story of Abraham and Isaac conveys. The story endorses the duty to obey the highest authority. But what does it imply about obedience to earthly authorities, such as kings and priests? On the one hand, insofar as kings and priests derive their legitimacy from their relationship to God, the right to expect obedience from God's subjects devolves on them. On the other hand, the duty to obey the highest authority without question, regardless of the sacrifice this may entail, provides a justification for disobedience with regard to lesser authorities. Clearly, when there is a conflict between the commands of a king and those of God, the duty to obey the highest authority takes precedence, no matter what the consequences. Disobedience under these circumstances is further justified by the fact that royal decrees in violation of God's commandments are ipso facto illegitimate.

Throughout the books of the Jewish Bible—particularly the prophets—we encounter the message that the king's power is limited, since the king himself is accountable to a higher law on which his legitimacy rests. This message is explicitly formulated in a passage in Deuteronomy that, according to Greenberg (1978), contains "the only ordinance concerning kings in the Torah" (p. 211). The passage states that a king over Israel must be chosen by God, that he must himself be a member of the community, and that he must abide by certain constraints. It goes on to decree

> that he shall write him a copy of this law in a book, out of that which is before the priests the Levites. And it shall be with him, and he shall read therein all the days of his life; that he may learn to fear the Lord his God, to keep all the words of this law and these statutes, to do them; that his heart not be lifted up above his brethren, and that he turn not aside from the commandment, to the right hand, or to the left; to the end that he may prolong his days in his kingdom, he and his children, in the midst of Israel. (Deuteronomy 17:18–20)

Many other biblical passages communicate implicitly, yet firmly and often eloquently, the limits of the king's power and his duty to adhere to the same divine commandments by which his subjects are bound.

The statement of such limits clearly suggests the conditions under which disobedience of royal orders would be justified and indeed obligatory. Yet the Bible itself does not explicitly address this issue (Greenberg, 1978). It is implicit, however, in several discussions of relevant biblical incidents found in the talmudic literature. Greenberg argues that these discussions reflect a coherent underlying doctrine, which he sums up in the following three propositions regarding a person's duty if "he finds himself with an order he knows to be illegal":

1. He must refuse to carry out the order even if it means a fall in rank and status;
2. He must actively oppose the order and prevent its execution; otherwise he will be guilty before God.

3. If he voluntarily obeys the order, he is not only guilty before God, but legally culpable as well. He cannot exempt himself on the ground of being merely the king's agent, for there is no agency for wrongdoing. (p. 218)

This doctrine was eventually formalized in the Code of Maimonides, which states explicitly that "if a king ordered violation of God's commandments, he is not to be obeyed" (Laws of Kings 3:9; cited in Greenberg, 1978).

Similar conclusions are reached by Kirschenbaum (1974) in an interesting analysis of the defense of obedience to superior orders in Jewish law. According to his analysis, Jewish law, when applied to the military situation, "recognizes the duty of a soldier to obey the orders of his superiors and regards the crimes of insubordination, disobedience and rebellion with the utmost severity" (p. 193), but this duty of obedience is not absolute. Orders to commit a crime need not—in fact must not—be obeyed. Following orders is not an acceptable defense if those orders were illegal. Thus, if a soldier follows orders to commit a criminal act—and was aware of the criminal nature of that act—he bears personal responsibility for it.

The Role of the Prophets. The Jewish Bible makes it clear that the power of kings and priests is limited in that they are subject to the same ethical rules, based in religious law, that apply to the general population. Their actions and policies can therefore be criticized—and, in principle, their orders can be disobeyed—if they violate God's commandments. But who is to judge whether such violations have occurred? It is difficult for the ordinary member of the community to make such judgments and risky to act upon them. There is a need, therefore, for authoritative interpreters of the requirements of God's higher law.

The function of interpreting God's commandments to kings, elites, and masses was institutionalized, during the biblical period following the establishment of the monarchy, in the role of the prophet. The biblical prophets, known to us as central figures in the historical books that deal with the period from the conquest of Canaan to the Babylonian exile (such as Samuel, Nathan, Elijah, Elisha) and as authors of the literary books of prophecy (such as Amos, Isaiah, Jeremiah, Ezekiel), took it upon themselves to protest specific actions or general policies of the rulers and to criticize the practices and way of life of the broader society. They presented themselves as speaking at the behest and in the name of God and described the actions they attacked as violations of God's commandments and sinful in His eyes. Whenever the king's actions had the backing of priests and other religious authorities (including other prophets) beholden to him, the prophets were in a position of offering *alternative* interpretations of God's commandments and insisting that theirs was the authentic interpretation.

The prophets' authority derived from their recognition as a special class of preachers and reformers (Albright, 1949, p. 34) who had direct access to God and served as the vehicles for divinely inspired visions. Their role might be described as that of an institutionalized deviant. Although the role as such was accepted and legitimate, individual incumbents had to prove their authenticity. The earlier prophets often did so through recourse to devices used by more primitive diviners or soothsayers from whom they nevertheless generally tried to dissociate themselves. Thus, a prophet might perform miracles, issue oracles following a trance or an ecstatic spell, "produce a sign as evidence of the truth of his message, or dramatize his theme by strange behavior" (Gordis, 1949, p. 471).

Later prophets relied on the power and content of their messages to establish their authority. They demonstrated the authenticity of their message by speaking in the name and in the language of a religious tradition to which their listeners felt committed, even if they did not always live up to it in practice. All the prophets' criticisms and exhortations were anchored in the tradition of Mosaic monotheism. They denounced any cultic practices that deviated from strict adherence to that tradition, and they bitterly attacked the luxurious life-style of the elites, their corruption, hypocrisy, immorality, injustice, and oppression of the poor as violations of their religious heritage. "The prophets called upon the people to 'return' to their God and his law" (Gordis, 1949, p. 467). Gordis points out that the Mosaic tradition itself reflected values growing out of the Israelites' historic experience as slaves in Egypt and nomads in the desert (1949, pp. 475–80). The prophets sought to revive these earlier values while transforming them in the light of new socioeconomic and political conditions. In sum, the prophets' evocation of traditional values provided the main proof of their legitimacy as interpreters of God's will and of the authenticity of their antiestablishment messages.

However excellent their credentials, the critical, nonconformist prophets could never count on automatic acceptance. They had to compete with other prophets, some of whom were actually attached to the royal court, who were inclined to support the policies and defend the actions of the reigning monarch (Gordis, 1949, pp. 471–73). There are many references in the Bible to the "false prophets" with whom the biblical prophets had to contend. Since the Bible is written from the standpoint of the rebellious prophets—the social critics passionately dedicated to strict monotheism and the pursuit of justice—it is easy to distinguish between the "true prophets" and the "false prophets." At the time, however, there was probably considerable controversy about whose prophecy was the more authentic.

In the early days of the monarchy, critical prophets—such as Samuel, Nathan, and Elijah—often influenced the behavior of the king and had a significant impact on national policy. Later, particularly in the period between the middle of the eighth century B.C. and the Babylonian exile of the early sixth century, the prophets generally became marginal figures. Most of them were rejected, despised, and ridiculed; some were declared to be traitors; and some were even killed. Amos, for example, was exiled; Micah was tried for treason; Jeremiah was imprisoned (Gordis, 1949, p. 474). In the Babylonian exile, the influence of the prophets began to rise again. Many of the exiles were strict monotheists, and they accepted the exile and the destruction of Jerusalem as fulfillments of the earlier prophecies. The prophets of the exile, particularly Ezekiel and the prophet the scholars named Deutero-Isaiah, were widely respected. One legacy of the exile, which carried over into the subsequent period of restoration, was the strengthened role of the prophets. Ultimately, of course, the critical prophets prevailed. Their adherents wrote the history of the biblical period, and their viewpoint dominated the interpretation of the religious commandments that gave shape to normative Judaism.

There is little if any indication in the Bible of the extent to which the prophets actually induced or encouraged disobedience among the general population. What we know is that they personally criticized the policies and practices of the political authorities, dissented from them, and rebelled against them. They did so in witness to a higher authority, whose commandments—in their view—were being violated by the kings and their cohorts. For later generations, they provided a language and justification for challenging authority and a normative basis for the duty to disobey.

EMERGENCE AND ADAPTATION OF CHRISTIANITY

The period of the Jewish exile in Babylon, during which the role of prophet as politico-religious dissenter was crystallized, stands out as critical in the building of Judeo-Christian ideology about obedience and justified disobedience. A second watershed is the period in which Christianity emerged. Its religious versus political character was initially unclear, as was its distinctiveness from Judaism. Rome's crushing of Jewish nationalism, however, led Christianity to develop a separate path of "peaceful coexistence" with Rome.

In the decades before the birth of Jesus, the Romans gained a military and political hold on Palestine. They did not do so unopposed. Herod the Great came to power as a Roman puppet in 39 B.C. after crushing a bandit revolt. Such revolts by outlying peasants against the Romans and their allies in the Jerusalem upper class were common. In this traditional culture's fusion of religion and politics, revolts were occasionally accompanied by claims of messiahship for the leaders. Unrest was particularly strong in 4 B.C., following the death of Herod, and in A.D. 6, when the Romans attempted a census as part of their incorporation of Palestine into the empire. Galilee was a hotbed of revolt throughout this era. Judas of Galilee was a key leader, advocating resistance to participation in the Roman census and to payment of Roman tax.

Thus Jesus emerged from a politically unstable region in an equally unstable time. Since the record of his activities was produced by chroniclers who had good reason to emphasize their peaceful character, it may never be clear to what extent he was perceived as a potential military messiah. But it is plausible that he was seen as such by the Roman forces and their wealthy Jerusalemite allies.

In this context, a key teaching by Jesus on the boundaries of secular authority is open to diametrically opposed interpretations. When questioned regarding the crucial issue of payment of tribute to Rome, Jesus reportedly replied, "Render unto Caesar that which is Caesar's and unto God that which is God's." This statement was later commonly considered to legitimate the coexistence of Christianity and secular authorities. It has also been argued that the chronicler, Mark, included the quote in part to dissociate the budding church from Jews rebelling against Rome (Brandon, 1968). But it may have had a more pointed meaning:

> This [statement] could only mean one thing to the Galileans who had participated in Judas of Galilee's tax revolt—namely, "Don't pay." For Judas of Galilee had said that everything in Palestine belonged to God. But the authors of the Gospels and their readers probably knew nothing about Judas of Galilee, so they preserved Jesus' highly provocative response on the mistaken assumption that it showed a genuinely conciliatory attitude toward the Roman government. (Harris, 1974, pp. 190–91)

We will never know. It is evident, however, that religious statements were also political statements in that time and place, and that religious leaders were political leaders. What they said about obeying or defying the might of Rome mattered.

The emerging Christian tradition regarding obedience was directly affected by the eventual failure of Jewish armed rebellion against Rome. Jewish political revolts bubbled over into full-scale military revolt in A.D. 66. But Jerusalem finally fell four years later, and the back of the resistance was broken. This failure shaped the role of the Christian church in the Roman Empire. The Gospels, all apparently written after the fall of Jerusalem, downplayed the political character of the movement and emphasized its independence from Judaism, as was probably prudent in the face of Roman might.

The history of Christianity in its first three hundred years was a complex adaptation to circumstances. Once the immediate Roman wrath against Jewry had faded, the new church faced troubles. Jews had previously won legal and social support for their religion among the Romans, who were generally willing to absorb or acknowledge the religions of clients and conquered foes. The new religion had no such official status. It was also suspect for its rejection of traditional Roman views of citizenship, which treated emperors as divine, and for its adherents' refusal to enter military service, which required an oath to the emperor. For whatever reasons, several emperors carried out campaigns to weaken or wipe out the new religion.

The struggling church developed a number of survival tactics. One was to come to terms with Rome in ways more peaceful and palatable to Roman authority than had been true of its parent religion. The second century of Christianity is characterized by the writings of apologists who argued that Christianity was good for Rome and that its adherents were good Romans and faithful taxpayers. The key event leading to the acceptance of Christianity in the Roman world was the conversion of Emperor Constantine prior to an important battle, which he won. Constantine's conversion was actually somewhat indecisive, but he removed paganism as the official Roman state religion. Christianity could then flourish as the de facto state religion with the emperor's support; it could, and did, at last force others to adapt as Christians had been forced to adapt in the past.

Early Christianity evolved along with its Roman host empire. This evolution included a gradually developing split between Eastern and Western branches that corresponded to the growing gulf between Rome and Byzantium. The centuries of gradual cleavage and collapse of Roman administrative control witnessed a growing, then flourishing—and thoroughly civilized—Christian religion. Its organization gave it an increasingly important administrative role in the remnants of empire.

In the millennium we know as the Middle Ages, the Catholicism that evolved in the Western empire played a role unique in world history. Historical sources are in general agreement that the Catholic church in some fashion served as the inheritor and transmitter of Roman administration and civilization. It had a relatively well-oiled administrative apparatus, was relatively multinational and urban, and retained ties to the more developed East until the eleventh century. The church was not itself a state, at least not in the modern sense of the term; instead it stood in a constantly shifting relationship to secular powers. It has been described by modern writers in such terms as "quasi-state" (Southern, 1970) and "paradoxical" state (Berman, 1983). In this duality of authority we might find one key to the West's evolution of an ideology of justified disobedience.

THE DEVELOPMENT OF DIVIDED AUTHORITY IN THE WEST

Conflict between authorities was not new in the Judeo-Christian tradition. Religion and "state" had often been in conflict in ancient Judaism because of foreign domination. Judaism further incorporated an internal tension between prophetic and priestly elements: between institutionalized deviants and the institution itself. What was new, however, was a stable duality of authority. Historians disagree about when the Catholic church developed its legal and moral autonomy from secular rule (see, for example, Berman, 1983), but they do not dispute that some separation occurred—that authority in the West, by about 1200, was divided.

Principled disobedience, as act and as ideology, requires divided authority. One social unit must be as capable of commanding obedience as another, and the two must stand in occasional opposition. It is our suspicion that these social units must also share some common allegiance to a higher authority; else they would simply fight out their disagreements. In this case, religious and secular authorities claim a common allegiance to God, with secular authorities holding a predominance of physical force and religious authorities possessing stronger claims as interpreters of divinity. As Berman (1983) puts it, "Perhaps the most distinctive characteristic of the Western legal tradition is the coexistence and competition within the same community of diverse jurisdictions and diverse legal systems. . . . Legal pluralism originated in the differentiation of the ecclesiastical polity from secular polities. The church declared its freedom from secular control, its exclusive jurisdiction in some matters, and its concurrent jurisdiction in other matters" (p. 10).

In other cases, two branches of government might both claim their particular interpretations of the Constitution to be the "higher authority" for opposing actions. For example, in the Watergate scandal the Nixon White House claimed that the doctrine of executive privilege made Nixon's tapes immune from examination by a Congress or court pursuing its constitutional prerogative to search for evidence of lawbreaking. A multiplicity of jurisdictions builds in rationales for disobedience as long as the actor can defy one authority in the name of the other.

The ideological tensions that accompanied split authority throughout the Middle Ages are reflected in the writings of church thinkers. Given the era, these thinkers represented an upper class writing to and for an upper class. But until recently, justified disobedience has been a heady wine usually reserved for such groups. The record of thought from Augustine through Aquinas through Luther to today traces the democratization of disobedience.

St. Augustine, writing in the first part of the fifth century, was the most influential of early church thinkers who grappled with the question of the tension between secular and sacred authority. His monumental work, *The City of God* (see Oates, 1948), was written between 413 and 426 partially in response to the sacking of Rome. The model of Roman justice and a fear of post-Roman chaos drove Augustine to conclude that the order provided by political control is itself worthy of support and obedience. Augustine's writings on church-state conflict are colored both by fear of anarchy and by tension within the church itself. The result is a cautious doctrine, but one that retains a fundamental dichotomy between the secular world's imperfections and the religious ideal. Justice, or some approximation to it, is seen as a key goal and virtue of secular rulers; for, in Augustine's famous query, without justice what is any kingdom but a great robber band? Despite the regrettable likelihood that medieval kingdoms might be closer to robbery than to justice, Augustine's analysis considered only specific violations of scriptural commands by secular authorities as grounds for disobeying them.

Throughout the early Middle Ages, church and state were in fact relatively intermingled. Some writers place more emphasis on the dominance of church forces; others emphasize the role of kings; but accounts, like Berman's (1983), that stress the differences between medieval and modern concepts of church and state, may be closest to the truth. In this view, the medieval world was characterized by an un-modern overlap between sacred and secular categories or roles. Politics and religion were not quite all of a piece, but their degree of fusion exceeded and stretched modern definitions.

Berman (1983) identifies the period of the Gregorian Reform, roughly 1075–1122, as pivotal for the building of divided authority and the creation of separate legal jurisdictions. By its end, if not before, the church had firmly asserted the separateness of spiritual and secular rule; as Pope Gregory VII put it, "Kings and princes of the earth, seduced by empty glory, prefer their own interests to the things of the spirit, whereas pious pontiffs, despising vainglory, set the things of God above the things of the flesh" (Berman, 1983, p. 110). Although authority was divided, and the church supreme, this did not limit the authority of secular power except when the two clashed:

> Gregory VII and his supporters never doubted that secular government, though subordinate to the church in spiritual matters and even—though only indirectly—in secular

matters, represented divine authority, that the power of the secular ruler was established by God, and that secular law flowed ultimately from reason and conscience and must be obeyed. . . . Gregory was full of hope for the future of secular society—under papal tutelage. In this, he and his followers were poles apart from St. Augustine. (p. 111)

Writing in the relative security and with the relative optimism of the late Middle Ages, St. Thomas Aquinas (see Bigongiari, 1953) provided a more spirited thirteenth-century justification of disobedience. Historically, Aquinas stood at the pinnacle of church supremacy—both legal and theological—over Western secular rulers. Between about 1100 and 1300, popes presided over the consolidation of Catholic legal and theological doctrine; arbitrated secular disputes, including key issues of warfare and marriage, between major secular powers; and instigated the great wave of Crusades that both bled Europe and opened it to trade with the East. Yet historical hindsight enables us to see in Aquinas's day, with the church's separation from and assertion of dominance over secular authority, the seeds of its loss of power to the state. Secular states were developing their own administrative control, their own regular taxation, and their own use of arms. Secular rulers were becoming much worthier opponents when they wished to be.

In addition, what the church lacked as a "quasi-state" was intermediate-range sanctions (Southern, 1970). To the extent that Catholicism could use its own tools to compel obedience, it presented secular rulers with a formidable organizational opponent. For example, we have the powerful historical image from January 1077 of a Holy Roman emperor (Henry IV)—barefoot in the snow—contritely petitioning the pope (Gregory VII) to lift his excommunication and reinstate him as rightful emperor. But popes could do very little in the way of small steps and small sanctions, especially at any distance. Papal use of direct military force was feasible only over a restricted geographic range. Papal use of the ultimate ideological weapons of excommunication and interdict had to be carefully selective to work at all. Hence, in the day-to-day conflicts that always characterize divided power, bargaining and conciliation had to be the rule.

As the real authority of secular rulers began to grow, Catholic ideology more sharply asserted the supremacy of sacred authority (and the church's own role as interpreter of it). Aquinas's justification of disobedience deserves noting at length:

There are two reasons for which a subject may not be bound to obey his superior in all things. First on account of the command of a higher power. For as a gloss says on Romans xiii. 2, "They that resist the power, resist the ordinance of God. If a commissioner issue an order, are you to comply if it is contrary to the bidding of the proconsul? Again if the proconsul command one thing and the emperor another, will you hesitate to disregard the former and serve the latter? Therefore if the emperor commands one thing and God another, you must disregard the former and obey God." Secondly, a subject is not bound to obey his superior if the latter command him to do something wherein he is not subject to him. For Seneca says: "It is wrong to suppose that slavery falls upon the whole man; for the better part of him is excepted. His body is subjected and assigned to his master, but his soul is his own." Consequently in matters touching the internal movement of the will man is not bound to obey his fellow man, but God alone.

Nevertheless man is bound to obey his fellow man in things that have to be done externally by means of the body. . . . in matters concerning the disposal of actions and human affairs a subject is bound to obey his superior within the sphere of his authority; for instance, a soldier must obey his general in matters relating to war, a servant his master in matters touching the execution of the duties of his service, a son his father in matters relating to the conduct of his life and the care of the household, and so forth. . . .

Accordingly we may distinguish a threefold obedience: one, sufficient for salvation and consisting in obeying when one is bound to obey; secondly, perfect obedience, which obeys in all things lawful; thirdly, indiscreet obedience, which obeys even in matters unlawful. (*Summa Theologica*, in Bigongiari, 1953, pp. 169–71)

Of course, even in the heydey of church authority, "indiscreet obedience" (support of secular objectives in opposition to church will) was probably on the increase— if only because the distinction between secular and spiritual authorities and objectives was becoming easier to draw.

A further important difference between Augustine and Aquinas, between the growing church and the dominant church, was the increased subjectivity of the judgments about obedience demanded in the later era. When conflict is envisioned or engaged in only over specific writ, it can be clearly delineated and controlled. When conflict expands to cover the entire political arena, the resulting vagueness leaves the way open for interpretation. One actor's interpretation is another's heresy. Thus sweeping claims carry within themselves the potential loss of the power so confidently being asserted.

INDIVIDUALIZATION OF DIVIDED AUTHORITY

The Protestant Reformation added further to the divisions between powers. Although it took place in a religious context, the Reformation accomplished substantial changes in the secular order of Western life. In confronting Catholicism, the reformers were challenging an adversary that dominated Western law; that often intervened directly in political or military affairs; that controlled substantial agricultural and other economic resources, which it protected from secular claims; and that held a monopoly on ideological justification of the whole enterprise. It now appears that Protestantism played a substantial role in legitimating trade, freeing the cities from domination by agricultural interests, and sealing the rise of mercantilists and bourgeoisie as political powers in Western urban life.

The Reformation produced secular changes more sweeping than many of its founders either foresaw or desired. The deeply conservative German monk Martin Luther, for example, allegedly was driven to nail the famous Ninety-five Theses to the door at Wittenberg in 1517 by carefully considered religious objections. The church practice that moved him was the immensely popular selling of salvation by means of indulgences. Luther appears to have been as opposed to money-lending and other eventual concomitants of trade in the Protestant world as was the stern John Calvin. Luther's "revolt" sharply separated itself from mass dissatisfactions of the time and was supported by German princes who wanted to loosen papal control. Luther and these princes decisively opposed peasant revolts under Protestant banners.

Despite its conservative roots, Protestantism heralded a democratization of disobedience by shifting the relation of the individual to established authority. This shift is perhaps most sharply visible in the availability of theological independence to broader population groups. The advent of printing presses made it possible to distribute perhaps a third of a million copies of Luther's tracts, in Latin and in translation, between 1517 and 1520. Luther himself was surprised by this, having failed to appreciate the power that could be wielded at great distance through print. In the cities, the educated elites were growing. These cities were fertile ground for Reformation thought and action. Protestantism's goal of individual citizens reading the Bible and serving as their own priests could be rapidly realized via Bibles published throughout the West in the vernacular. The Ninety-five Theses in Latin tacked onto a door could never have such impact. The translated Bible, available to the middle classes, could and did.

Such democratization of independent religious thought and action through print was essentially closed off to the Catholic world by the Council of Trent's reaction to the Reformation in 1546. As E. L. Eisenstein (1974) has argued, the Council's failure to agree on any strategy for encouraging the laity to read and for promoting the production of vernacular Bibles had substantial long-term implications for the citizenry of the Protestant versus Catholic West. For example, literacy was encouraged in the Protestant but not in the Catholic world as the means to personalized enlightenment.

In Protestantism, potential opposition between religious and secular authority was carried to its logical extreme: the independent opinion of the individual. And those to whom options became available spread beyond the upper class to include educated urbanites. The democratization of justified disobedience was carried to lengths that it was not to exceed for over four centuries.

By the twentieth century in America, two developments had laid society open to further democratization. Education had extended beyond the middle classes, and the notion of citizenship had extended beyond propertied males. The new citizens made considerable use of their culture's ideology of justified disobedience, reaching a height of political effectiveness in the civil rights conflicts of the 1950s and 1960s. One stirring voice of the ideology, that of Martin Luther's modern namesake, evoked a cultural tradition that stretched back to Augustine and beyond:

My Dear Fellow Clergymen:

While confined here in the Birmingham city jail, I came across your recent statement calling my present activities "unwise and untimely." . . . You express a great deal of anxiety over our willingness to break laws. This is certainly a legitimate concern. Since we so diligently urge people to obey the Supreme Court's decision of 1954 outlawing segregation in the public schools, at first glance it may seem rather paradoxical for us consciously to break laws. One may well ask "How can you advocate breaking some laws and obeying others?" The answer lies in the fact that there are two types of laws: just and unjust. I would be the first to advocate obeying just laws. One has not only a legal but a moral responsibility to obey just laws. Conversely, one has a moral responsibility to disobey unjust laws. I would agree with St. Augustine that "an unjust law is no law at all."

Now, what is the difference between the two? How does one determine whether a law is just or unjust? A just law is a man-made code that squares with the moral law or the law of God. An unjust law is a code that is out of harmony with the moral law. To put it in the terms of St. Thomas Aquinas: An unjust law is a human law that is not rooted in eternal law and natural law. Any law that uplifts human personality is just. Any law that degrades human personality is unjust. All segregation statutes are unjust because segregation distorts the soul and damages the personality. (King, 1969, pp. 72, 77)

King's philosophical rationale for secular disobedience was not new. The ideal future he later described in his "I have a dream" speech was his Augustinian City of God. By the twentieth century, the individual could draw on a long-standing and coherent ideology of disobedience, and more individuals had the knowledge and resources to do so.

To sum up: Authorities rarely invite their own destruction. They rarely provide the individual facing them with the tools to disobey effectively. But historically, Western culture at least provides potentially powerful counterweights to an authority's stance that obedience is both compulsory and obligatory. The individual can judge that the authority's demand is illegitimate, having assessed authority's commands against alternative religious or moral standards. Normative buttressing for disobedience is clearly not psychologically available to everyone. Yet Western history has seen its availability spread, first into the middle classes and eventually to include dissident groups that suffer injustice at authority's hands. The existence of such normative buttressing may require the kind of divided political and social power that has characterized the West for millennia. In any case, the search for the social origins of the right to say no must continue.

At least two questions remain. Who takes advantage of the normative supports for disobedience that the culture provides? And what can facilitate taking an independent stance vis-à-vis authority? The following chapters will develop these themes. First, however, we continue to lay the groundwork for understanding justified disobedience in modern times. Because law codifies the norms and expectations of a social group, legal rules provide some indication of what a society considers permissible and what it considers wrong. Legal debates also provide hints about social-structural supports for norms and social-structural conflicts about them. We therefore turn to the most carefully codified dilemmas of obedience in the Western world, those of military law.

Authority and Obedience in Military Law

It is hardly surprising that the greatest legal attention to orders and obedience to them can be found in military law.[5] Military organizations have long demanded

5. A number of works were consulted in the preparation of this section, in addition to those cited in the text. General sources on obedience, law, and warfare include Dinstein (1965), Falk (1968),

and usually received unquestioning obedience from subordinates to superiors. Therefore, we examine military sources as exemplifying both the oldest and the most extreme normative push toward obedience.

We further concentrate on legal codifications by modern Western states. The debates of earlier eras, such as the medieval church-state conflicts over justified war, usually considered whether the conflict was legitimate in religious eyes and therefore whether any killing was justified. Adversaries were at the top of their respective secular and religious authority structures, rather than authority and subordinate within a single structure. Centuries of such debate over the justice or injustice of war probably touched the average soldier negligibly, if at all. Even in the modern era, legal protection of disobedience and legal demands for independent thought are hardly addressed to the foot soldier. It is only in the twentieth century that we even begin to find the common soldier as the target of the debate; by his claim Lt. William Calley was such a soldier.

Illegal actions by military subordinates under orders from superior officers are among the most clear-cut and well-documented examples of crimes of obedience. This clarity results from several factors: (a) a well-defined hierarchy, such that it is obvious who can give orders to whom and who must obey; (b) the regular commission of acts that would be crimes in other settings, such that their definition must be a cause of constant concern; and (c) the resulting development of codes to specify prescribed versus proscribed actions in and around the battlefield.

Modern military law concerning orders from superiors represents a balance between two extremes. On the one hand, it could be (and has been) argued that subordinates are *never* responsible for actions committed under orders. At the opposite extreme, it could be argued that they *always* are. Many military systems have at some time operated on the principle that the subordinate is never responsible. The opposite view has represented a point of philosophical debate rather than actual practice in any system of military law. It is a major irony of the post–World War II world, or a major lesson of that war, that the two modern military legal systems that most closely approximate a requirement of individual responsibility are those of Israel and West Germany.

The doctrine that a subordinate is never responsible for actions under orders rests on the assumption that the superior always is. This doctrine is known as *respondeat superior:* "let the superior answer." The superior's responsibility also traditionally goes beyond specific orders issued and includes the obligation to oversee the actions of subordinates. The supposedly reciprocal responsibilities of authority (to supervise) and subordinate (to obey) were the foci of two key military trials following World War II: the Nuremberg tribunal and the trial of the Japanese

---

Greenspan (1959), and Taylor (1970). Original legal sources include *The Law of Land Warfare* (Dept. of the Army, 1956), *The Manual for Courts Martial, United States* (1969), *The Trial of the Major War Criminals* (1947–49), and *Trials of War Criminals before the Nuernberg Military Tribunals* (1949–53). The issue of superior orders was originally reviewed in Hamilton (1975). Relevant political, legal, and moral-philosophical discussions can be found in Arendt (1964), Cohen et al. (1974), Falk et al. (1971), P. French (1972), Pennock and Chapman (1970), Sanford and Comstock (1971), and Walzer (1970, 1977). Relevant works on the nature of battle include Gray (1959) and Keegan (1976).

general Yamashita. Below and in chapter 8 we shall examine the assumption that these two responsibilities are reciprocal. First, however, we consider how the nations that conducted the trials arrived at their own positions on the issues.

The Allied victors emerged from World War II adhering to a somewhat uneven compromise between the notion that subordinates are never responsible and the contrary notion that they always are. The compromise doctrine, presented in chapter 1, asserts that superior orders ordinarily must and ought to be obeyed, but that illegal orders should be resisted. Under ordinary circumstances, a soldier is expected to obey all orders and can be punished for disobedience. Even if an order is illegal, a soldier may still be excused for obeying it. The soldier is held criminally responsible only if an order was "manifestly" illegal or if a "reasonable man" would have known it to be illegal. Even when a soldier is found guilty, obedience to orders may be a mitigating circumstance. Modern military doctrine therefore is closer to the ancient respondeat superior than to the concept of individual liability for actions performed.

This uneven compromise is the product of several twists in military law. On the eve of World War I, there was no international consensus on the validity of the doctrine of absolute obedience. British law, in a 1749 code, provided that obedience to superiors was legal only when the orders issued were also legal. But this provision was rescinded in a 1914 code, which reasserted superior orders as an absolute defense. Prior to 1914, American military law, in specific legal decisions, had rejected the absolute defense of superior orders. In 1914, however, the American military adopted a code clearly modeled after the British one. It asserted that violations of the law of war would not be prosecuted if the actions were committed under superior orders.

The German military code had never allowed superior orders as an absolute defense for subordinates. The first German military code of 1872 indicated that subordinates who obey an order that they know to be unlawful are accomplices to the crime. The version under which the Germans fought in World War II stated:

> If the execution of a military order in the course of duty violates the criminal law, then the superior officer giving the order will bear the sole responsibility therefor. However, the obeying subordinate will share the punishment of the participant: (1) if he has exceeded the order given to him, or (2) if it was within his knowledge that the order of his superior concerned an act by which it was intended to commit a civil or military crime or transgression. (*Reichsgesetzblatt*, 1926, No. 37, p. 278, Art. 47; quoted in Goldstein et al., 1976, p. 412. Drawn from the opening speech of the chief prosecutor, Nuremberg trials, Nov. 11, 1945)

German military courts upheld these limitations on the superior orders defense after World War I, most notably in a case involving the German sinking of a Canadian hospital ship, the *Llandovery Castle*. The code could not be applied, however, to German actions in World War II, which were later condemned as among history's most extensive war crimes, because those actions were *legal* under German law. As such, they presented the prosecuting countries with particularly complex legal problems in the war's aftermath.

During World War II the Americans and British changed their war crimes codes. According to cynical interpretations, they did so to be able to prosecute Germans more effectively for crimes committed under superior orders. Both codes were altered to reduce the scope of the superior orders defense into the modern compromise defense described above. Both changes were made in 1944: the British in April and the American in November. Abandonment of superior orders as an absolute defense came late and, one might guess, reluctantly.

A post–World War II international tribunal established certain principles under which Nazi war criminals were tried at Nuremberg. Two new international crimes were recognized, "crimes against peace" and "crimes against humanity." Aggressive war was declared a crime against peace. Genocidal policies against populations under one's own rule, such as Nazi actions against German Jews or nationals of subjugated countries, were declared crimes against humanity. For the first time internal sovereignty was declared not to be absolute, and national laws were declared subordinate to international law when the two were in conflict. It was also asserted that superior orders was not an absolute defense if the charge was a crime of war, crime against peace, or crime against humanity.

The Nuremberg tribunal convicted many leading Nazis of war crimes and crimes against humanity. Yet the judges clearly did not intend their decision to place an "intolerable burden" of responsibility on the individual soldier. Despite the supposed Nuremberg principle of individual responsibility, no rank-and-file Germans were held to such standards; only relatively high officials were denied the defense of superior orders. Indeed, the American prosecutors explicitly emphasized that the Nuremberg defendants, although obedient to still higher officials, were not ordinary actors:

> The [London] Charter recognizes that one who has committed criminal acts may not take refuge in superior orders nor in the doctrine that his crimes were acts of state. These twin principles working together have heretofore resulted in immunity for practically everyone concerned in the really great crimes against peace and mankind. Those in lower ranks were protected against liability by the orders of their superiors. The superiors were protected because their orders were called acts of state. Under the Charter, no defense based on either of these doctrines can be entertained. Modern civilization puts unlimited weapons of destruction in the hands of men. It cannot tolerate so vast an area of legal irresponsibility. . . . Of course, we do not argue that the circumstances under which one commits an act should be disregarded in judging its legal effect. A conscripted private on a firing squad cannot expect to hold an inquest on the validity of the execution. The Charter implies common sense limits to liability just as it places common sense limits upon immunity. *But none of these men before you acted in minor parts. Each of them was entrusted with broad discretion and exercised great power. Their responsibility is correspondingly great.* (Chief prosecutor's opening speech, Nuremberg trials, Nov. 11, 1945; quoted in Goldstein et al., 1976, p. 412; emphasis added)

Thus the principle of individual responsibility in international law was broadened. National laws were denied as the sole guideline for "legality," and superior orders was rejected as an absolute defense. The expanded net was neither intended nor used to catch small fish, however.

Gen. Tomoyuki Yamashita was no small fish. His trial embodied the modern extension of the principle of respondeat superior. Instead of being convicted of war crimes committed *as* a subordinate, he was convicted for war crimes committed *by* his subordinates. While Yamashita commanded the Japanese forces in the Philippines, the American offensive was gradually breaking down Japanese resistance. It apparently broke down Japanese lines of communication, Japanese morale, and Japanese scruples in the process. Numerous instances of war crimes were recorded during the last days of Japanese control in the Philippines. Yamashita clearly did not order the actions that occurred. The American prosecutors did not even assert that he necessarily knew about them. Instead, they argued that he was responsible for the actions of his men because he was their commander. Such arguments draw upon long-standing codes of warfare. The U.S. Supreme Court agreed, refusing to strike down the tribunal's conviction of General Yamashita. All noted that international understandings in the 1907 Hague Convention stated that the laws of war apply only to military troops "commanded by a person responsible for his subordinates." Yamashita was a commander, and therefore the person responsible in the eyes of the military tribunal and the Supreme Court.

The decision to convict Yamashita effectively broadened the notion of respondeat superior to include situations when the commander was such in name only. As Mr. Justice Murphy noted in dissenting from the Supreme Court's decision, "The only conclusion I can draw is that the charge made against the petitioner is clearly without precedent in international law or in the annals of recorded military history" (Goldstein et al., 1976, p. 435). Murphy attacked the notion that a commander can be so broadly responsible for actions of subordinates. He also cited several sources in international law to the effect that the concept of responsibility as stated in the Hague Convention is vague and ill defined. Murphy's arguments were to no avail. Yamashita was hanged.

The aftermath of World War II witnessed the creation of the modern legal compromises governing responsibilities of authority and subordinate in time of war. Compromise came accompanied by the tortuous logic and dubious motives that constitute the stuff of history. The Nuremberg Principles of individual responsibility on the part of subordinates were largely reaffirmations of ideas from previous military codes, including the German code itself. This reaffirmation did not occur in a way that directly touched on the guilt or innocence of ordinary foot soldiers, although it has since been popularly interpreted as doing so. The Yamashita case, for all its peculiarities and potential inequities, reaffirmed and broadened an even older notion: that of superiors' responsibility for the actions of those under their authority.

It was becoming clearer that the responsibilities of superior and subordinate in modern warfare were not likely to be simply reciprocal or zero-sum. The responsibility of subordinates had technically broadened to include the obligation to consider the legality of orders in almost Aquinian fashion. The responsibility of authority had broadened to include the obligation to oversee actions by subordinates despite difficult circumstances. Taken together, such trends might mean that the world would be safe from war crimes generated from above or below. Such is not apparently the nature of war or the crimes it spawns, however. America had the chance to use its newly affirmed principles on itself relatively soon in historical terms.

Chapter 1 has already spelled out the stories of the massacre at My Lai and the Calley trial. Lieutenant Calley was apparently convinced that his actions were justifiable because they constituted following orders. His court-martial disagreed, finding his actions not those of a reasonable man following the American military code. Large segments of the American public, including President Nixon, in turn disagreed with the court-martial. Subsequent chapters will attempt to unravel public opinion to understand why segments of the public felt as they did. For now, we simply conclude that military law does spell out conditions under which soldiers have a duty to disobey, although it is not surprising that soldiers—particularly of lower ranks—are expected to avail themselves of the option of disobedience only under rare circumstances and that authorities are reluctant to punish them for failure to do so.[6]

Conclusions

Human beings harm others for many reasons, including in response to orders from authority. In Western philosophy and practice the issue of obedience to orders has always been complex. Obedience to authority is legally and morally encouraged. Subordinates may be faced both with sanctions to compel obedience and with an ideology that glorifies it. Yet a long Western tradition of authority split between religious and secular organizations has helped create an escape route for the subordinate faced with a repugnant order. The subordinate can claim that the order defies moral or religious restrictions imposed by conscience or "natural law."

We have briefly described various kinds of authority against which such a claim could be made, noting that all authorities share the twin features of possessing greater power than subordinates and having the right to command or instruct them. These twin features are particularly potent in the cases of military and political authorities, whose potential for harm may also be the greatest.

The claim of conscience would appear to be a weak weapon; yet it is probably the most effective weapon short of revolt. It offers a justification for disobedience,

---

6. Two recent articles derive the military officer's duty to disobey superior orders on occasion from the requirements of the military organization itself. Both articles deal specifically with the case of Col. Eli Geva, an armored-brigade commander in the Israeli army, who asked to be relieved of his command position during the war in Lebanon in the summer of 1982 because of his moral objections to the campaign to take West Beirut. They argue that an officer's disobedience or dissent under such circumstances is an affirmation of the kind of commitment that is "the backbone of the military profession" (Gal, 1985, p. 553) and a "functional necessity" for an effective military organization (Hacohen, 1987, p. 134).

not merely an excuse. It renders disobedience acceptable, even laudable, in the eyes of *at least some countervailing authority*. Without the actual or implied presence of such an authority we assume that obedience is almost always the simplest and most prudent course of action. Even given countervailing authority, however, disobedience can entail an actual or perceived risk.

Military law is a formal codification of some of the most important Western rules regarding obedience. Such rules have incorporated two concerns: the accountability of superiors who give orders and that of subordinates who obey them. The traditional military doctrine establishing the responsibility of superiors for their subordinates' actions would appear to, and has sometimes been used to, imply subordinates' reciprocal *lack* of responsibility. Yet the post–World War II trials at Nuremberg and Tokyo suggest that it is possible legally to enlarge the responsibility of both authority and subordinate without contradiction.

Despite the historical availability of normative supports for disobedience, it is by no means clear that disobedience is psychologically available to those most in need of it: actors in crimes of obedience and those who stand in judgment over them. The theoretical availability of the right to say no may be meaningless if the right is not perceived or appropriately translated into judgment under pressure. In the following chapters we discuss the social psychology of obedience, first by presenting the concept of authority in more detail and later by examining the attribution of responsibility. By combining the study of authority and the study of responsibility we will indicate how the framework within which one views a crime of obedience can make it seem a crime, on the one hand, or obedience, on the other. Our goal is to clarify how responsibility may be "lost" where it is most essential to retain it: in the military and bureaucratic hierarchies of the modern world.

4 | The Structure of Authority

A central feature of authority, as we have seen, is its right and ability to activate a duty to obey among those over whom it holds sway. But we have also seen that this duty is by no means absolute. Even religious and military doctrines, which elevate the principle of obedience to authority to the highest priority, specify conditions under which individuals have a right—indeed a duty—to disobey. In this chapter we begin to develop a social-psychological framework for analyzing obedience and disobedience in authority relationships. Drawing on sociological and political theory, we view authority as a property of social structures. A social-psychological analysis enriches this structural view by examining the nature of the relationship between authorities and their subordinates, the conditions for perceived legitimacy of the authority, and the situational and personal factors that determine the behavioral outcomes of obedience or disobedience.

We have described authority as a role relationship between two sets of actors within a social unit. The role of authorities in that unit entitles them to make certain demands and the role of ordinary members obligates them to accede to those demands. Authority differs from sheer power in that the authority holders are perceived as having the right to command—as being legitimate. In modern secular conceptions, at least, legitimacy also implies that power will be used within certain constraints rather than in arbitrary fashion.

From a social-psychological perspective, the use of authority is one form of social influence. Insofar as the use of authority is perceived to be legitimate, it can be defined as *legitimate influence*. In other words, when we speak of the use of authority, we refer to influence exercised by authority holders over group members that is accepted as rightful by virtue of the respective positions of the two parties. The greater the perceived legitimacy of the authority, the higher the probability that group members will obey. In this chapter, we focus on the structural determinants of member obedience—on the elements of an authority situation that contribute to the perceived legitimacy of the authority that is invoked. Essentially, we will be proposing that obedience depends on the perceived legitimacy of the *where*, the *who*, and the *what* of authority—the social context in which authority is used, the character of the authority holders, and the nature of the specific demands they make. Obedience here refers not merely to people's *act* of following orders but to their doing so out of a sense of duty.

Since we treat authority as a special subcategory of the broader concept of social influence, we begin with a brief definition of social influence and discussion of the structure of social influence situations in general.[1] We then apply these formulations to the special case of legitimate influence and the structure of authority situations.

Social Influence

Social influence can be said to have occurred whenever a person changes his or her behavior[2] as a result of induction by some other person or group—the influencing agent. The term *induction* refers to any action whereby the influencing agent offers or makes available to the person a specific new behavior, attitude, or belief—or perhaps a new pattern of responding or a different way of interpreting events that challenges habitual reactions and existing beliefs. In doing so, the influencing agent also communicates something about the effect that adopting the induced behavior might have on the person. Thus, in inducing change, the agent points a way for the person; she provides a direction that can guide him in the selection of appropriate actions or attitudes.[3]

The induction may be deliberate and intentional, as in persuasion, orders, threats, and suggestions. Induction can also be unintentional to varying degrees, as when an influencing agent sets an example or serves as a model for a person—sometimes without even knowing of that person's existence. Induction often represents a mixture of intentional and unintentional elements, as when teachers, therapists, or scientific experimenters subtly and unwittingly communicate their expectations to students, patients, or experimental subjects and find those expectations confirmed (Brophy and Good, 1974; Murray, 1956; Rosenthal, 1966). Induction may take place through direct or symbolic contact with the influencing agent: at one extreme, in the course of face-to-face interaction, and at the opposite extreme, in the course of the person's exposure to mass communications or to public ceremonies rife with institutional symbols.

By *change* in our definition of social influence we mean that the person's behavior following induction is different from what it would have been without the

1. A more detailed discussion of these issues can be found in Kelman (1974b). See also Kelman (1961).

2. The term *behavior* is used throughout to refer not only to overt actions but also to attitudes, beliefs, and values. When we speak of "behavior, attitudes, or beliefs," we are being redundant in order to remind the reader that our analysis is not restricted to overt behavior.

3. In the interest of smoothness of exposition, we refer to the person being influenced as "he" and to the influencing agent as "she" through the remainder of this chapter and throughout chapter 5 (except, of course, in examples that specifically refer to a male influencing agent or a female recipient of influence).

influence attempt. Thus, the definition implies at least some degree of resistance to change that has to be overcome. Even when the person is eagerly seeking the other's guidance and direction, his original behavioral tendencies—diverted by the induction—constitute sources of resistance, however negligible their competitive strength might be. Change can be described as positive when influence results in acceptance of the induced behavior (that is, in conformity, if one uses that term in a strictly descriptive sense) or as negative when influence results in change in a direction opposite to that induced. Negative influence is different from resistance to change in that the person's behavior is very definitely affected by the other's induction; it reflects anticonformity rather than independence (Willis, 1965).

Our definition of social influence is broad, but it is not intended to cover all changes that can result from social interaction. It implies some meaningful connection—recognized in the wider society—between the induced behavior and the influencing agent. The agent is not just transmitting stimuli or reinforcers, as in a conditioning paradigm, but is offering behavior that is in some way linked to her—her preferences, her values, her social position. The induction points to something the influencing agent wants from the person, or expects of him, or represents (models) in his eyes. Social influence, therefore, is an aspect of the relationship of the influencer to the influencee; this relationship can be as rich and as structured as that of mother to child or as tenuous as our relationship to Brooke Shields when we wear the jeans she once advertised on television. The nature of the influencing agent's role and of the person's relationship to her in the collectivity to which they both belong has a direct bearing on the meaning of the induced behavior.

THE STRUCTURE OF A SOCIAL INFLUENCE SITUATION

In its most general form, an influence situation is one in which an influencing agent offers some new behavior or attitude to a person and somehow communicates that the person's chances of achieving his goals depend on whether or not he adopts that behavior. We assume that the person will be positively influenced to the extent he is persuaded that adopting the induced behavior will facilitate achievement of his goals.[4] What can we say about the characteristics of an influence situation that is conducive to such an outcome?

Let us answer this question by reference to a hypothetical illustration: a recruitment campaign by the U.S. Department of Defense designed to persuade young

4. Conversely, we assume that people will be *negatively* influenced if they anticipate that adopting a *contrary* behavior is most likely to facilitate goal achievement. The discussion that follows examines the structure of an influence situation that is likely to culminate in positive influence; conditions that are conducive to negative influence can be readily deduced from the logic of our scheme. Two further caveats are in order here. First, for the sake of convenience we may at times refer to what the influencing agent would have to do if she wanted to achieve positive influence. The model, however, applies to unintentional as well as to intentional induction. Second, in the effort to describe the psychological processes underlying social influence, we may picture the recipient of influence as a conscious, rational decision maker, deliberately weighing alternative courses of action. We assume, however, that in fact these processes often operate on an unconscious or unverbalized level.

men to sign up for service in the army. The illustration assumes the present conditions in the United States, in which there is no military draft. Thus, our hypothetical influence situation provides a nice contrast with recruitment through a draft—an influence situation governed by legitimate authority, to which we shall turn later in this chapter. There is, of course, another important way in which our illustrative campaign contrasts with the draft: The draft is aided in its recruitment efforts not only by the legitimate authority of the state but also by its coercive power. This conjunction between legitimacy and coercion, in fact, appears in many authority situations and will be discussed below. For present purposes, the important feature of our illustrative case is that the army's recruitment effort cannot rely on activating young men's duty to obey but—like standard influence attempts—must persuade them that signing up will facilitate achievement of their personal goals.

We postulate three conditions that must prevail if any given individual is to respond positively to the recruitment campaign. First, the campaign must capture the attention and arouse the interest of potential recruits. They will be inclined to listen if they come to see the situation as relevant to one or more of their important goals or concerns. The various appeals typically used in a recruitment campaign are designed to activate such goals. Thus, army service may be linked to certain material incentives; for example, the campaign may suggest that it offers decent pay and benefits along with job security, a chance to see the world, and an opportunity for specialized training and career advancement. Such an appeal may be particularly attractive to young people who otherwise face the prospect of unemployment or dead-end jobs. Another type of appeal seeks to enhance the self-image of the potential recruit by depicting military service as a glamorous occupation, symbolized by sharp uniforms and masculine pursuits. Yet another approach may appeal to patriotic values, offering young people an opportunity to serve their country, protect its security, and advance its interests.

If the recruitment campaign succeeds in bringing these goals into salience, and if one or more of them is important to a given individual, then he is likely to be responsive to the campaign and open himself up to it. How seriously he takes the invitation to join the army, however, depends on a second condition: He must be persuaded that the influencing agent is in fact relevant to the achievement of the goals that have been activated. In part, the potential recruit will base his conclusion on assessment of the individuals who do the recruiting and who provide the testimonials. How credible are they? Can their claims be believed and their experiences be generalized? And do they themselves manifest the personal achievement, the glamorous image, and the patriotic commitment they offer as the rewards of military service? In part, the conclusions of the potential recruit will depend on his assessment of the army itself. Does it have the capacity to deliver the rewards it promises? Does it have a record suggesting that its promises can be trusted? Does it have the prestige that is generally associated with favorable outcomes? If the answers to these questions are positive, the individual will be positively oriented to the influencing agent's recommendations.

Even though the individual may be responsive to the influence attempt and positively oriented to the influencing agent, a third condition must be met if he is actually to go out and enlist in the army. That specific behavior must come to stand out relative to the many other alternatives that may be available to him in the situation. One dominant alternative, whenever individuals are induced to undertake radical changes in their lives, is to drift along and delay a decision until the pressure or the temptation has passed. To overcome this tendency, the army recruiters may attempt to channel the individual into the path they want him to follow. They may do so by facilitating the induced behavior—making the steps required for enlisting in the army very clear and easy to undertake, perhaps by starting with a small, relatively noncommittal step that raises the likelihood the person will take further steps involving gradually increasing commitment (cf. Frank, 1944, on the "step-by-step approach"; Freedman and Fraser, 1966, and DeJong, 1979, on the "foot-in-the-door technique"). Alternatively, they may do so by applying pressure—for example, inducing the individual to make an immediate public commitment in a situation in which some of his peers have already stepped up to be enlisted. Even if the individual has been persuaded to enter military service, he can still choose among a number of alternatives to enlisting in the army. He may opt for the navy if he wants to see the world, or for the air force if he wants to acquire transferable skills, or for the marines if he wants to enhance his macho image. If the army's recruitment program is to succeed, the specific behavior of enlisting in the army has to become a sufficiently "distinguished path" so that the individual will select it in preference to other available alternatives.

The three conditions for positive influence described in our example correspond to three kinds of information that must be conveyed in an influence situation and that enter into the decision to accept influence. (See the first three boxes in figure 4.1, which depicts the structure of a social influence situation as seen from the perspective of the person subjected to influence.)

Definition of the Situation. Deliberate efforts by the influencing agent or other features of the setting inform the person being influenced about the nature of the situation in which he finds himself and, more particularly, about what is at stake for him in this situation. In a deliberate influence attempt, the influencing agent may present a challenge to the person's existing beliefs, attitudes, or actions by trying to show that these are not (or are no longer) most conducive to achieving his goals. If the challenge is successful—if the person is convinced that the situation is relevant to goals that are important to him—he is motivated to reconsider his current behavior or attitudes and to expose himself to the induction as a possible source of new directions to explore. The *exposure* may range from an active effort to seek out new information to passive, unreflective attention representing little more than a decision not to turn off the television set. If the challenge is unsuccessful—if the person remains unconvinced that important goals are at stake in the situation—he is inclined to leave the field by tuning out and directing his attention elsewhere. In that case, the influence attempt goes awry at the very

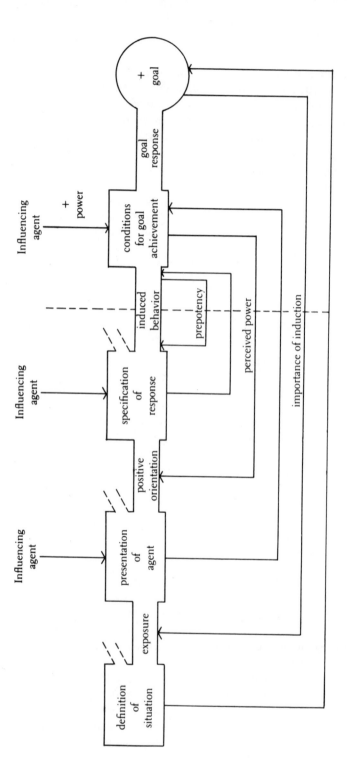

Figure 4.1 Diagram of the Structure of a Social Influence Situation. Reprinted from Kelman, 1974b, p. 133, by permission of the publisher.

Note: To the left of the vertical broken line, the diagram depicts what happens in a situation that produces positive influence; to the right it depicts the person's perception of the situation and anticipation of consequences. Arrows from left to right represent the effects of the information conveyed in the influence situation on the person's perception of (a) the goals at stake, (b) the instrumentality of the influencing agent to achievement of these goals, and (c) the precise behavior required to meet the conditions for goal achievement. Arrows from right to left represent the effects of these perceptions, in turn, on the person's response to the information conveyed. The broken-lined channels leading out of each box refer to situations in which the information is not sufficiently persuasive to lead to acceptance of influence.

outset by failing to define the situation in a way that motivates the person to expose himself to the induction.

The definition of the situation, then, bears on the first condition for positive influence described in our example. This first condition can be restated as a dimension or variable: the perceived *importance of the induction* (represented in figure 4.1 by the lowest of the three arrows moving from right to left). The importance of the induction refers to the extent to which the person views the influence situation as having motivational significance for him—the extent to which the situation has activated goals important to him relative to the other goals that he is currently pursuing (and that he may have to sacrifice or at least postpone if he changes his behavior). The importance of the induction depends both on the strength of the motives that have been aroused and on the perceived relevance of the situation to these motives. The more important the induction—for example, in the army recruitment campaign, the stronger the motives activated and the more relevant army service appears to the satisfaction of these motives—the greater the person's *responsiveness* to the communication. The probability of *acceptance* of the particular induction depends on the person's perception of the influencing agent.

Presentation of the Agent. A second type of information conveyed to the person, deliberately or otherwise, refers to the influencing agent's characteristics: for example, her prestige, status, special knowledge or expertise, representativeness, group membership, control of certain resources, or ability to apply sanctions. In deliberate influence attempts this information is designed to demonstrate that what the influencing agent says or does may have considerable relevance to the person's goal achievement. If this communication is successful—if the person is convinced that the influencing agent is in a position to facilitate or impede his goals—then he is inclined to be receptive to the options the agent offers: In other words, he is *positively oriented* to her induction. If the communication is unsuccessful—if the person remains unconvinced that the influencing agent is relevant to the achievement of his goals—he will turn elsewhere for direction and remain uninfluenced by her induction. If he is convinced that she is in fact detrimental to the achievement of his goals (because she represents a negative reference group or a hated ideology, for example, or because she is publicly identified with illegal or socially disapproved activities), he may be influenced negatively—in the direction opposite to her induction. In either event the person will be "lost" to the influence attempt at this point because he could not be persuaded to orient himself positively to the influencing agent.

Presentation of the agent bears on the second condition for positive influence described in our example, which—when restated as a dimension or variable—becomes the perceived *power of the influencing agent* (represented in figure 4.1 by the middle arrow from right to left). The agent's power with respect to a particular person refers to the extent to which that person perceives her as instrumental to the achievement of his goals. Thus, an influencing agent possesses power over someone insofar as she is in a position to facilitate or impede his goal achievement. The power of the influencing agent over that person depends on two factors. The first is her capacity to affect some of the conditions for his goal achievement, which might take the form, for example, of controlling resources he desires, or having the ability to apply certain sanctions, or possessing expert knowledge he would find useful in solving his problems. The second factor is the perceived likelihood that she will in fact use the capacities at her disposal in ways that would affect the person's goal achievement. This perception involves an assessment of the agent's motives and intentions—an assessment that is not necessarily based on a careful sifting and weighing of evidence, but is often automatic and visceral. Characteristics of the influencing agent that enter into the judgment of how she is likely to use the means at her disposal include manipulativeness, ruthlessness, and trustworthiness. The greater the influencing agent's power—the greater her perceived capacity and intention to affect the person's goal achievement—relative to the perceived power of competing influencing agents (including the person himself), the greater the likelihood that he will accept her induction.[5] The probability that he will adopt the specific behavior she recommends depends on a third type of information conveyed in the influence situation.

Specification of the Response. The influence situation conveys to the person the precise nature of the response being induced and facilitates its performance. The induced behavior thus becomes readily available to the person, both perceptually and behaviorally. In a deliberate influence attempt, the influencing agent may try to demonstrate the unique relevance of that behavior (in contrast to various possible alternatives) to the person's goal achievement. She may try to reduce ambiguities about the form and content of the induced response and to overcome the person's resistance to performing it. She may look for ways of easing the person into performance of the response (for example, a recruiter of hospital volunteers may make her appeal at a club meeting, where she can count on social facilitation to increase the rate of volunteering, and she may try to draw her prospects in gradually by asking them at first to come only to a tour of the hospital or to give only a very limited number of hours). If these various efforts are successful—if the person perceives the *induced behavior* as distinctive, readily performable, and uniquely relevant to goal achievement—then he will be both willing and able to adopt that behavior. If the efforts are unsuccessful—if the form and content of the behavior remain ambiguous or resistances to its performance have not been over-

5. It should be noted that we define power independently of influence. Power, in the present scheme, is a basic *determinant* of influence, but it is defined and assessed not in terms of ability to influence but in terms of the relationship between influencer and influencee. Although our propositions about the effects of power refer to the influencer's power as perceived by the influencee, it is possible to link her power over him systematically to her objective characteristics and her position within the social structure relative to his.

come—he is likely to opt for one of the alternative courses available to him.[6] Thus, even though he may be motivated to expose himself to the induction and positively oriented to the influencing agent, the influence situation will not culminate in positive influence unless the induced behavior has been transformed into a distinguished path.

Specification of the response corresponds to the third condition for positive influence described in the example of an army recruitment campaign. Again, this condition can be restated as a dimension or variable: the *prepotency or relative strength of the induced behavior* (represented in figure 4.1 by the highest of the three arrows from right to left). Prepotency of the induced behavior refers to the extent to which that behavior emerges as most clearly relevant in the context of the motivations that have been activated in the situation. The assumption is that, even though a person may be motivated to accept the induced behavior, he may select one of a number of alternative courses of action that are generally available to him. He may do so because he is uncertain about the exact nature of the induced behavior, or because he considers some of the alternatives equally effective, or because he finds the induced behavior excessively difficult or unpleasant. In short, resistances to the induced behavior may enter both at the point of perception and at the point of action.[7] The likelihood that a specific induced behavior will be accepted depends on the degree to which that behavior has become prepotent—that is, relatively stronger than the available alternatives.

The induced behavior becomes prepotent to the extent that it is strengthened within the influence situation—for example, by making the response itself more distinctive, by linking it clearly to the conditions for goal achievement, by minimizing discomforts that inhibit its performance, by structuring the situation so that the person is gradually eased into performing it, by socially facilitating performance of the response, or by introducing situational demands and pressures that can best be met by performing the induced response. Induced behavior also becomes prepotent to the extent that competing responses are weakened or eliminated in the situation—for example, by increasing the overall ambiguity of the situation, by demonstrating the ineffectiveness or counterproductiveness of these responses for the achievement of the person's goals, by blocking performance of such responses or making it uncomfortable, or by making it difficult for the person

6. Logically, the person is always choosing between different options. Psychologically, of course, situations differ in the number of options available to actors. As we shall discuss below, one of the ways of "encouraging" adoption of the induced response is by closing off alternative response possibilities. The question of whether the person sees himself as having options at all will become of central importance when we consider the structure of authority situations.

7. Many of these resistances serve as reminders of the nonrational factors that determine people's decisions in an influence situation, no matter what the cost-benefit calculations might yield. The influence techniques designed to increase the prepotency of the induced behavior are often ways of overcoming such nonrational resistances to change or of creating nonrational facilitators of change—that is, of easing the person into mindless performance of the induced behavior. This category of determinants of influence thus helps counteract what may appear to be—but is not intended to be—a rational bias in our model.

to engage in evasive maneuvers or to leave the field. Typically, prepotency is achieved through some combination of strengthening the induced behavior and weakening alternatives—for example, by making apparent the special advantages of that behavior relative to various other options.[8]

The Determinants of Influence in Concert. We do not assume that the different steps culminating in positive influence must occur in the order presented here. The three steps represent a logical sequence for analytical purposes, but in a given influence situation they could occur in different orders and combinations. The same feature of the influence situation, the same action or communication by the influencing agent, or—in the laboratory—the same manipulation by the experimenter may simultaneously generate two or more of the necessary inputs. For example, when a superior officer issues a command in a combat situation, subordinates are instantly aware—quite apart from any considerations of legitimacy—that they must pay attention to the orders if they wish to avoid a court-martial, that the officer has the power to enforce these orders, and that the only way they can forestall punishment is by doing precisely what they have been ordered to do. In a very different setting, Brooke Shields's appearance on television in her favorite jeans is intended to create an image that simultaneously arouses the viewers' desire to be glamorous and popular, focuses on someone with the proven ability to achieve this goal, and associates her glamour with the jeans she is wearing. (From the advertiser's standpoint, of course, the exercise would be a failure if it merely persuaded viewers that wearing jeans would make them glamorous; it has to persuade them that this particular *brand* of jeans is the distinctive path to that goal.)

What we are proposing is simply that, in some order and in some fashion, the information conveyed in an influence situation must satisfy three conditions if positive influence is to occur. If no important goal is activated, the recipient of the influence attempt has no motivation at all to seek change and is unlikely, therefore, to expose himself to the induction. If an important goal is activated, but the person perceives the influencing agent as irrelevant to its achievement, he lacks the motivation to accept her induction and is likely to turn elsewhere in his search

8. The importance of the induction, the power of the influencing agent, and the relative strength of the induced behavior can best be described as *classes* of variables because there are numerous forms that each of these determinants may take. From a social-psychological point of view, what matters is the particular form these variables take in a given influence situation. For example, the assertion that the probability of influence is a function of the power of the influencing agent is merely a way of identifying a class of variables that affect influence, based on a logical analysis of the generic structure of an influence situation. The statement becomes interesting only when we specify a particular type of power and explore the conditions under which it affects the probability and magnitude of influence and the kind of influence it produces. Thus, if we find that coercive power, or power based on the ability to punish—one of the bases of power distinguished by French and Raven (1959; for later formulations, see Raven, 1965, 1983)—increases public conformity with the influencing agent's instructions, but actually decreases private acceptance of her evaluation (Raven and French, 1958), we have learned something of substantive significance about the uses and limits of a particular variety of influence attempt.

for new behavior. If both the first and second conditions are met, there is sufficient motivation to accept the induction, but this motivation will not translate into specific action unless the induced behavior or viewpoint stands out relative to other options.

We have restated these three conditions as variables or dimensions that can be viewed as the three basic determinants of the probability of influence. In doing so, we have identified three structural elements in the generic influence situation that determine the probability of influence. These are the *where*, the *who*, and the *what* of influence—the social context in which the influence is exerted, the character of the influencing agent, and the nature of the specific behavior induced in the situation. Each of these elements has to be persuasive if positive influence is to ensue. The person has to be persuaded that the situation is relevant to important goals, that the influencing agent has the power to facilitate or impede achievement of these goals, and that the specific induced behavior is optimally suited to goal achievement. It should be noted that persuasiveness at each of these levels depends on the person's preferences. That is, the situation, the influencing agent, and the specific recommendation are each persuasive insofar as the person perceives them as conducive to his preferred outcomes. This feature of the generic case of social influence becomes a relevant point of contrast as we apply the scheme to the special case of legitimate influence in authority situations.

THE SOCIAL CONTEXT OF SOCIAL INFLUENCE

Before we turn to the discussion of legitimate influence and the structure of the authority situation, we should comment on our conception of social influence in general as a process (or set of processes) linking individuals to social structures. Social influence always occurs within a larger social context. Even interactions between strangers on a train or between friends and lovers are defined and at least minimally structured by the larger society. Participants enact prescribed roles and their interaction is governed in part by the expectations associated with those roles. Many social influence situations are more thoroughly embedded in the organizational or societal context than these informal relationships. They represent episodes in the functioning of social units—part of the process whereby the society or organization (through its designated authorities) socializes and controls its members and carries out its daily business, and whereby the members advocate policies, protest against existing practices, or seek to advance their personal or subgroup interests.

Our model of social influence is designed to address the larger social context in which particular episodes (or sequences of episodes) of social influence are embedded. We assume throughout that influence—even in clearly defined authority relationships—is a two-way process in which members influence authorities and thus contribute to social change, just as authorities influence members, thus contributing to individual change. For the moment, however, we focus primarily on one side of that relationship: influence from the social unit (and specific authorities within it) directed at the individual member. We are concerned here with the way in which societal or organizational demands and expectations are communicated to members and accepted by them, and in chapter 5 with the way in which such acceptance in turn affects members' integration in the society or organization. This analysis has implications for the reverse side of the relationship, to which we shall return at a later point: The particular way in which a person accepts influence from his society or organization and is integrated in it helps shape the way in which he in turn exerts influence upon that social unit.

The social unit with which we are primarily concerned in this book is the government or nation-state, since this is the arena in which crimes of obedience are most likely and most damaging. Much of the discussion, therefore, dwells on the relationship between government and citizen or between superior and subordinate in a military or political-bureaucratic hierarchy. Our analysis is applicable, however, to a variety of social units of differing size and complexity, ranging from an entire society, through a community, organization, and institution, to a smaller and less structured group. To encompass the entire range of social and political units, we use the term *social system,* by which we mean a patterned set of human activities that have some definition, regularity, and continuity beyond the particular individuals engaged in them at a given time and that are governed by certain shared norms and expectations. The term is used here merely for descriptive purposes, and we make no assumption about equilibrium in the system.

In our discussion of the structure of the generic social influence situation (and our depiction of it in figure 4.1), we have conceptualized it at the level of social interaction. Description focuses on what happens in the influence situation proper and the basic variables are designed to capture the microlevel interactions between the participants in that situation. Yet each of the independent variables in the model—each of the factors contributing to positive influence—though stated at the level of social interaction, refers at least implicitly to conditions in the larger social system. The importance of the induction ultimately depends on the definition of the influence situation within a societal or organizational context; the power of influencer over influencee in the particular situation is often a function of their positions in the larger society; and the prepotency of the induced behavior is affected by the alternatives the society makes available in this type of situation.

The implicit links between determinants of social influence and the larger system become explicit and obvious when an influence attempt is carried out *on behalf of* a government or organization. When, for example, military or bureaucratic authorities issue orders to their subordinates, the message is clear that the induction is important because it is backed by the norms and sanctions available to the government, that the authorities possess power in the immediate situation by virtue of their official positions in the larger structure, and that the induced behavior is prepotent because official codes preclude alternative options. We are now ready to turn to this special case of social influence.

Legitimacy

THE OBLIGATORY CHARACTER OF LEGITIMATE INFLUENCE

Social influence is legitimate insofar as the person to whom it is directed accepts the influencing agent's *right* to make certain demands or to present certain requests. For example, if the person has promised to contribute funds to an organization, a demand for payment constitutes a legitimate influence attempt. The influencing agent has a right to make the demand and the person has an obligation to accede to it. Similarly, if the relationship between the two parties is characterized by reciprocity, the influencing agent has a right to ask the person for services commensurate with those she previously performed for him. These examples point to the general character of legitimacy in an influence situation as the perceived rightfulness of a demand; but the most clearly structured cases of legitimate influence, and those of greatest interest to us, occur in the context of an authority relationship. In modern bureaucratic settings, such a relationship means that the authority holder is entitled to make demands (within specified limits) and the subordinate is obligated to accede to them by virtue of their respective positions in the political or organizational hierarchy.

The distinctive feature of legitimate influence is the obligatory character of the induced behavior. Once a demand is categorized as legitimate, the person to whom it is addressed enters a situation where his personal preferences become more or less irrelevant as determinants of behavior. In this respect, the structure of an authority situation contrasts sharply with the structure of the standard influence situations discussed above. In those situations, the person is presumed to choose his behavior on the basis of his personal preferences. The influencing agent has to communicate to the person in some fashion that accepting the induced behavior would be desirable to him from the point of view of achieving his own goals. The agent may do so through persuasion, negotiation, setting an example, offering rewards, or even through coercion. In all these cases, the person has to become convinced that adopting the induced behavior is preferable for him. Even coercion may be conceptualized in terms of choice. Although an individual may feel that he is being forced to comply, he in fact has the choice of complying or suffering the consequences. When an influencing agent uses coercive power, she is structuring the situation so that the person will be inclined to accept the induced behavior in preference to the limited and noxious alternatives available to him. Still, the choice is up to him. This conceptualization of coercion as offering a choice underlies the refusal of the law to accept duress as an across-the-board excuse.

In the pure case of legitimate authority, in contrast, the influencing agent does not need to convince the person that adopting the induced behavior is preferable for him, given the available alternatives, but merely that it is required of him (although in practice, as we shall elaborate below, authorities typically buttress their demands with the capacity to coerce and the attempt to persuade). Authorities activate commitments or obligations that are inherent in the definition of the citizen's role (Gamson, 1968, pp. 127–35), spelling out the requirements of that role under the existing circumstances. The person's focus is not on what he wants to do, given available alternatives, but on what he sees as required of him. In this sense, one might say that his reactions are governed not so much by motivational processes as by perceptual ones. Legitimate demands have the quality of required-ness that is often associated with external reality, which determines the dimensions of the situation to which people must relate themselves and the parameters of their response. Put most broadly, the legitimacy of a social group or social order is tantamount to its right to define reality for its members. Legitimate authorities are the carriers of reality.

Psychologically, once a demand is seen as legitimate, the person acts as if he were in a nonchoice situation. In Coleman's (1980) terms, he has transferred control over his own actions to the authority holder. He does have choices if he is willing and able to *redefine* the issues, the relationship to the authority holder, or the broader social context. But, as recent theories of social action have empha-sized, people rarely reflect on the social definition and the wider context of the situation in which they find themselves. They tend to react "mindlessly" (Chan-owitz and Langer, 1980; Langer et al., 1978; Langer and Piper, 1987) and to enact routine scripts (Schank and Abelson, 1977) once they have entered into an action sequence. Moreover, Abelson (1982) has pointed out that attitudes and personal preferences are often irrelevant to a person's entry into a script—to the action rule that sets a scripted routine into motion.

Thus, when a person is presented with a demand in a situation that has all the earmarks of legitimacy, he does not usually ask himself what he would like to do. The central question he confronts is what he must do or should do—his obliga-tions rather than his preferences. And indeed, when legitimate authorities—such as the administration of a legitimate political system—make certain demands, people accept them whether or not they like them. Individual citizens may or may not be convinced of the value of the actions their government asks them to take or policies it asks them to support; they may or may not be enthusiastic about carry-ing them out; they may even find them objectionable on various grounds. Under ideal-typical conditions, however, if the demands are within the limits of legiti-macy, citizens willingly meet them without feeling coerced, and consider it their duty to do so.

We have overdrawn the contrast between authority situations and ordinary in-fluence situations in order to highlight the nonchoice character of the authority situation as perceived by individuals who find themselves in it. In actuality, people do make choices in situations of legitimate authority, and personal preferences do play a role in these choices. To balance this unidimensional description of the authority situation, we therefore turn to a discussion of where and how elements of choice and preference enter into people's reactions to authority in real life.

The essence of a situation of legitimate authority, as we have argued, is the participants' perception of its obligatory character. As long as the situation continues to be defined as one of legitimate authority, people focus on what is required of them and they tend to meet these requirements regardless of their personal preferences. This psychological orientation is central to our understanding of obedience to authority, as well as of the conditions under which disobedience becomes possible. Yet, within these constraints, people do make choices that are at least partly governed by their preferences. To some extent, such choices flow from the concept of legitimacy itself; to some extent they reflect the reality that in most social interactions more than one definition of the situation may prevail. The various ways in which preferential choice qualifies the definition of authority situations will be particularly germane to our analysis of individual differences in reaction to authoritative demands (chapter 11).

Activation of Commitments. We noted above that people's reactions in an authority situation are governed not so much by motivational processes—what they want—as by perceptual ones—what they see as required of them. This may be so, once a person's commitments have been activated. But the very concept of the activation of commitments (Gamson, 1968) has built-in motivational assumptions. The person is committed to his role as group member or citizen—and therefore is ready to meet his role obligations once that commitment has been activated—because the role is personally meaningful to him. His commitment to the member role reflects his desire to maintain his relationship to the group and his self-definition as a good group member. Furthermore, development of role commitment itself must be understood in a motivational context. Commitment and loyalty to the group—and the concomitant acceptance of its legitimacy—ultimately depend on the perception that the group meets the psychological and material needs of its members.

Although it is correct, then, to say that in an authority situation people respond on the basis of their role requirements rather than their personal preferences, they do so in part because (and to the extent that) they cherish their roles as group members. Role commitment, in turn, can be traced to the satisfactions such membership provides. The seeming paradox in the statement that people perceive a situation of legitimate authority as a *nonchoice* situation in which they *willingly* perform the behavior required of them can be readily understood in these terms. In effect, people willingly suspend their right to make choices. Legitimacy implies, however, that this right has been only suspended, not surrendered. Over the long run, at least, members maintain the right to judge whether the trust they have placed in the authorities is justified by the quality and the consequences of the authorities' performance. In effect, subordinates voluntarily *vest* authority in a superordinate and they may "*divest* the superordinate of the vested authority, that is, withdraw authority previously vested" (Coleman, 1980, p. 151).

Judgments of Legitimacy. Adherence to an authoritative demand is obligatory *if* the person accepts the legitimacy of that demand. We mentioned in chapter 3 and will elaborate in chapter 5 that legitimacy can be assessed at different levels and by different criteria at each of these levels. Thus, at least implicitly, the person is making judgments and hence choices in the authority situation: He determines whether the demand is legitimate and on that basis decides whether he is required to obey.

In actuality, authority situations often elicit an automatic response on the part of many people. As we suggested in chapter 3, authorities benefit from the presumption of legitimacy, which carries over to the demands they issue. The definition of most authority situations, communicated by the authorities and accepted by the subordinates, takes it for granted that the demand will be obeyed. Resistance becomes possible only through an active process of redefining the situation. In some cases, the definition of the situation is so compelling that almost everyone accepts its obligatory character without question. In other cases, one finds marked individual differences in the tendency to question the obligatory character of the situation or to accept it automatically. In principle, however, it can be said that in all cases there is some choice involved in people's perception of the situation as one in which obedience is required or optional.

Within the framework of legitimate authority, of course, the nature of the choices that people are entitled to make is strictly limited. They cannot choose to disobey simply on the basis of their preferences. To be sure, people often do, but such actions constitute violations of the norm and, in most cases, violations of the law as well. In principle, people are entitled to disobey an authority's order only if they judge the order to be illegitimate by reference to a countervailing authority which supports a countervailing interpretation. But such judgments are often affected by preferences, even when people are operating within the framework and norms of authority. Typically, people are more inclined to raise questions about the legitimacy of an order if they find the behavior demanded of them to be incongruent with their interests or values. They are also more likely to conclude that the order is indeed illegitimate under these circumstances. The incongruities themselves may be insufficient grounds for disobedience, but insofar as they enter into judgments of legitimacy, they may make the choice of a disobedient response more likely.

Coercion and Legitimacy. Even a clearly defined situation of legitimate authority brings into play additional forces that might induce individuals to accept influence—or, by the same token, to resist influence—strictly on the basis of their own preferences. For example, a young man drafted for military service may be happy to obey, quite apart from his citizen obligation to do so, for reasons discussed earlier: He finds the pay or training opportunities rewarding, or soldiering enhances his masculine self-image, or he believes in a strong national defense and wants to contribute to it. Authorities often introduce such incentives or value considerations as a way of bolstering their legitimate demands, even though, in principle, activation of role commitments is all that would be needed. They may do so in order to encourage citizens to go beyond the minimum requirements and obey with greater enthusiasm, or to discourage them from searching for ways of evading their obligations. With or without deliberate efforts by the authorities, behavioral outcomes are often determined by some combination of what the individual perceives as his role requirements and what he prefers to do in the light of other goals that have become salient in the situation.

The most obvious instance of such a combination of influences is the interaction between legitimacy and coercive power in many authority situations. Legitimate authorities often possess some degree of coercive power with which they can back up their demands, particularly in political and military settings where the authority of officials and officers rests on a legal framework. Within this framework, authorities have not only the right to give orders but also both the right and the capacity to enforce those orders by imposing penalties for disobedience. Although we reject the view that the authorities' enforcement power is the essence of their legitimacy (which would make the concept of legitimacy superfluous and meaningless), we do see an integral relationship between legitimate power and coercive power. At the very least it can be said that the right to give orders gains support from the *right* to enforce those orders even if not from the *capacity* to enforce them.

There are both advantages and disadvantages, however, to the coercive power that political and military authorities have at their disposal. It clearly enhances their capacity to elicit compliance from those subordinates who do not accept the legitimacy of the political or military system, or from those—found in any group—who break some of the rules despite their acceptance of the system's legitimacy. In their relationship to subordinates who accept the system's legitimacy and generally abide by its rules, however, the authorities' possession of coercive power may well decrease their ability to elicit obedience as much as it may enhance it.

On the one hand, if the authorities place too much stress on the penalties incurred by disobedience, they may encourage citizens simply to comply—to adhere to the rules in order to avoid punishment—instead of drawing on their sense of obligation to meet the requirements of the citizen role. Continued role adherence would then depend on surveillance by the authorities, in contrast to the self-monitoring that controls the fulfillment of role obligations. Thus, to capitalize on their legitimacy, it would be to the authorities' advantage to activate citizens' commitments to the system and to downplay the penalties for disobedience.[9]

On the other hand, awareness of penalties for disobedience may bolster obedience. The existence of legal sanctions for disobedience enhances the perceived

---

9. Blau (1964) discusses the costs in overall influence that managers entail by excessive use of their sanctioning power. He argues (p. 206) that managers can enhance their legitimate authority by *refraining* from exercising the sanctioning power at their disposal. For an interesting discussion of the limits of coercive power in influencing behavior, see Sykes (1958).

legitimacy of a demand by clearly distinguishing behavior that is obligatory from that which is optional. In other words, the threat of legal punishment is not just an incentive for complying but a cue indicating that obedience is required rather than a matter of preferential choice. When authorities fail to attach sanctions for disobedience to a law or an order, or when they habitually fail to enforce it, they are signaling that citizens can at least discreetly choose to ignore it.

Furthermore, the existence of penalties for disobedience may weight the scales toward obedience among those who have doubts about the legitimacy of a particular demand. A soldier, for example, who believes that an order may be illegal must consider the consequences of acting on that judgment. If he disobeys and it then turns out that his judgment was wrong—that he rejected or ignored an order whose legality is subsequently confirmed by higher authorities or by a court-martial—he is subject to punishment. The risk of punishment discourages him from challenging the legitimacy of the order and makes him more likely to obey it. He may also risk punishment, of course, if he obeys an order that is later determined to have been illegal, but the fear of punishment for disobedience is more likely to influence behavior because it reinforces the already strong push toward obedience built into the structure of the authority situation.

It should be noted that, in this example, we are not proposing that the person merely *complies* because of fear of punishment. Rather, we assume that he *obeys* because he considers the order legitimate; the fear of punishment contributes to his obedience by inclining him to accept the legitimacy of the order in view of the potential cost of challenging it. The risk of punishment is integrally related to the legitimacy of the order: If a person is to be punished for disobedience, it is precisely because the order was (or is later judged to have been) legitimate and he was required, therefore, to carry it out.

In authority situations that do not rest on a legal framework and in which the authorities are not entitled to impose penalties, the fear of embarrassment may perform a function similar to that of punishment in legally structured situations. People are often inhibited from challenging the legitimacy of a demand because of concern over the possible consequences of such a challenge. If their judgment turns out to have been wrong—if they rejected a demand that later proves to have been appropriate and within the domain of authority of the one who made it—they may find themselves deeply embarrassed. Thus, doubts about the legitimacy of a demand—issued, for example, by airline, hospital, or museum personnel, or others who appear to be in charge—are often resolved in favor of obedience.

Other Bolstering Factors. Obedience to legitimate demands may be bolstered not only by the threat of punishment or embarrassment for failure to obey but also by a variety of positive inducements. Thus, people may be presented with medals, citations, or other awards for outstanding performance of their roles. Such rewards, of course, are usually given for performance "above and beyond the call of duty," but their existence may encourage citizens and soldiers at least to perform their duty. Furthermore, performance of the obligations of one role may be bolstered by commitment to another role. For example, soldiers in a combat situation are often induced to take the heavy risks demanded of them—to meet their obligations as soldiers—out of loyalty to their comrades in the immediate fighting unit (Shils and Janowitz, 1948; Lang, 1968).

Obedience to legitimate demands may also be bolstered by people's perception that the required behavior—and the policy supported by it—contribute to the maximization of some of their values. The values brought into play may be organically linked to the legitimacy of the demand. For example, when imposing new taxes, the authorities may invoke the principle of fairness in distributing the burdens of citizenship, or the importance of maintaining the long-run health of the economy. In doing so, they are calling attention to values on which their legitimacy partly rests in the eyes of many citizens. That is, citizens perceive the authorities as ruling rightfully insofar as they believe that they are enhancing precisely values such as these; and they give the authorities the freedom of action implied by legitimacy in order to enable them to develop long-term policies consistent with such values. In this case, then, invocation of the principles of fairness and a healthy economy enhances the perceived legitimacy of the demand—and hence obedience to it—by justifying that legitimacy in terms of underlying societal values.

The bolstering effect of personal values was demonstrated in a study by Tyler (1987), which found that obedience to laws is greater when people view the law as consistent with personal morality. It can be presumed that the link between legally prescribed behavior and moral values enhances the perceived legitimacy of the law itself. Obedience may also be bolstered, however, when the required behavior supports values that are independent of the sources of legitimacy. For example, school attendance is likely to be more reliable and regular among those lucky adolescents for whom the requirement to attend school coincides with an intrinsic valuing and love of learning.

Although the invocation of supporting values can be presumed to bolster obedience, it may on occasion undermine it, just as excessive reliance on penalties for disobedience may have a boomerang effect, as we pointed out above. A legitimate demand that is promoted on the basis of its relevance to the person's own values may create some ambiguity in the definition of the situation; the person may respond as if he were operating in the realm of preferences rather than in the realm of obligations. As a result, if he finds the specific demand objectionable, he may choose to disobey it, whereas he might have obeyed if the situation had been defined strictly in terms of legitimate authority. For example, a teacher may be more successful in inducing students to carry out an onerous assignment by simply presenting it as a requirement than by trying to justify it as an unusually valuable learning experience (Brophy et al., 1983).[10]

10. It may well be that disobedience under the latter circumstances may occur more readily among those students who actually value the learning process and who are therefore responsive to the teacher's invocation of value considerations than among those who are indifferent to these considerations and

Fluidity of the Definition of the Situation. In principle, if a situation is defined as one of legitimate authority, role obligations override personal preferences. This quality of authority situations serves as the basis for the dramatic outcomes of influence that we associate with legitimate authority. On the one hand, authority is able to induce individuals to take actions that clearly go against their personal desires and short-term interests, often calling for considerable sacrifices. At its best, this feature of authority allows political systems to function on the basis of consent, with relatively little need to resort to coercion and to confront challenges at every step of the way. On the other hand, authority is able to induce individuals to take actions that they would otherwise consider antisocial and immoral because they have relinquished control and responsibility to authorities whose orders they obey without question.

In actuality, authority situations are more fluid then these instances of unquestioning obedience would suggest. Although the demands of legitimate authority must be taken into account, personal preferences and values do not become entirely irrelevant. Such preferences may, as we have noted, coincide with role obligations and hence reinforce them; but they may also contradict these obligations and conflict with them. The conflict between requirements and preferences cannot be understood in quantitative terms—as one whose outcome depends simply on which of the two elements is the stronger. Rather, it generally takes the form of a conflict between two competing definitions of the situation—a conflict over which decision rule is to prevail.

Thus, if a person finds an order to be objectionable, he will look for ways of escaping the nonchoice definition of the situation. He will first try to do so without challenging the legitimacy of the authority by ascertaining whether the behavior is indeed required. In this connection, he may seek to establish whether the authority's induction constitutes a *demand* or merely a *request*. According to the useful distinction offered by Hofeller (1966), a legitimate request—in contrast to a legitimate demand—refers to the case in which authorities are entitled to exert influence, but citizens are entitled to refuse without thereby incurring legal penalties. The right to make certain requests—and to back them up with a degree of social pressure and moral suasion—is not a trivial perquisite of authority, since there are many things people ordinarily do not have a right to ask of others. It does not, however, imply the reciprocal duty to obey as does the right to make demands.

---

therefore react to the assignment strictly as a demand from a legitimate authority. This reasoning is based on Margaret Hofeller's (1966) analysis, which distinguishes different processes of legitimacy. She derives the paradoxical prediction that a legitimate demand to perform an otherwise undesirable behavior is more likely to be carried out by people who do *not* particularly value the purposes behind that behavior than by those who do. The assumption is that the former are more likely to be bound into the definition of the situation as one strictly governed by legitimate demands, leaving them no choice but to obey. In an experiment designed to test this proposition, Hofeller obtained indirect support for it. In chapter 11, we develop the related proposition that individuals whose commitment to the group is based on shared values feel freer to disobey an occasional order because they tend to assess the legitimacy of specific demands in terms of these values and to reject those demands they find wanting.

If people can interpret an objectionable order as a request rather than a demand—if they can define it as not actually required, as not applying to themselves or to their particular circumstances—then they are likely to take advantage of that option. Furthermore, orders are often vague, as our description of the My Lai incident amply illustrates. There is thus room for individuals to construe the order in ways that are congruent with their preferences. Most people would rather evade or reinterpret objectionable orders in these ways than enter into direct confrontation with authority. On the other hand, if they determine that the objectionable behavior is indeed required and that the orders cannot be reinterpreted to their liking, they may have to resort to more confrontational means of redefining the situation. They may in that case opt out of obedience by challenging the legitimacy of the order, as we proposed in our discussion of judgments of legitimacy. Alternatively, they may resolve their conflict by claiming allegiance to a higher authority that requires disobedience.

If a person is unable to redefine the situation in one of these ways, he is likely to obey despite his misgivings. Even under these compelling circumstances, however, obedience is not ubiquitous and personal preferences may at times win out. Soldiers in combat situations often do not shoot even though they fully accept the legitimacy of the order to do so. People ordered to participate in massacre or torture may refuse to do so without challenging the legitimacy of the order itself, simply on the ground that they cannot bring themselves to carry out such actions. It may be that, for some people, the urge to survive or the revulsion against hurting others may be more compelling than the demands of legitimate authority. There remains, thus, an irreducible element of personal preference that operates in the most tightly structured authority situation.

Nevertheless, the distinguishing characteristic of situations of legitimate authority is their ability to focus individuals on their role obligations at the expense of their personal preferences. We shall explore why it is so difficult to break out of the constraints of this definition of the situation, and why some people can do so more readily than others, after first examining in greater detail the structure of authority situations and the determinants of obedience.

THE STRUCTURE OF SITUATIONS GOVERNED BY LEGITIMATE AUTHORITY

Keeping in mind the various ways in which choice and preference enter into real-life reactions to authority, let us describe the structure of situations governed by legitimate authority in ideal-typical terms. In doing so, we focus on the obligatory character of legitimate demands in order to bring out how and under what conditions the citizen or subordinate comes to perceive an authority situation as one in which he has no choice but to obey.

In the generic influence situation, described at the beginning of the chapter, the influencing agent offers some new behavior to the person and communicates the implications adoption of this behavior will have for his goals; the person, in turn, adopts the behavior if he is persuaded that doing so will facilitate achievement of his goals. In the authority situation, in contrast, the agent presents the person with a demand or order to carry out some behavior and communicates that performance of the behavior is required, regardless of how or whether it dovetails with his personal goals; the person, in turn, performs the behavior without regard to his own preferences if he concludes that it is indeed required.

In specifying the characteristics of an authority situation that is conducive to such an outcome, we shall use as our example an order from the Selective Service System requiring young men to register for the draft when they reach their eighteenth birthday. Paralleling our discussion of positive influence, we assume that three conditions must be present if obedience is to occur—obedience in the sense of the individual's willing performance of the behavior demanded by the authorities because he sees it as a requirement of his role as a citizen.

First, the order must activate a positive commitment to the political system and a sense of obligation to meet the requirements of the citizen role. If this commitment is lacking, or if the order from the Selective Service System fails to bring it into salience, the individual is unlikely to be responsive to the information conveyed.

Second, assuming the communication succeeds in activating the young citizen's role commitments, he must also perceive the draft agency as having the right to determine how these commitments are to be fulfilled. Only if he accepts the agency's authority will he turn to it in his search for information about the precise behavior required of him.

Third, the specific behavior required has to be sufficiently distinctive so that the individual will perceive it as the only acceptable way of meeting his obligation. Obedience is more likely if the steps to be taken are explicitly spelled out and facilitated, if there is no ambiguity about when and where registration has to take place, and if there is a clear distinction between permissible and impermissible options.

A person may adopt the induced behavior even in the absence of one or more of these conditions, but he will not have done so out of the sense of duty to obey legitimate authority. For example, he may comply in the face of the authorities' coercive power, performing the induced behavior unwillingly in order to avoid punishment. This is possible because authorities such as the Selective Service System typically possess the means to enforce their demands, thus superimposing the elements of a standard influence situation on those of an authority situation.

The three conditions for obedience correspond to three kinds of information that must be conveyed in an authority situation and that enter into the decision to obey. (See the first three boxes in figure 4.2, which depicts the structure of a situation of legitimate authority from the perspective of the subordinate.)

Definition of the Situation. Deliberate efforts by the authorities or other features of the setting help establish a definition of the situation as an "authority situation"—a situation governed by the authority relationship between the two parties, which entitles one to make demands and obligates the other to accede to these demands. Often the definition of the situation is built into the physical

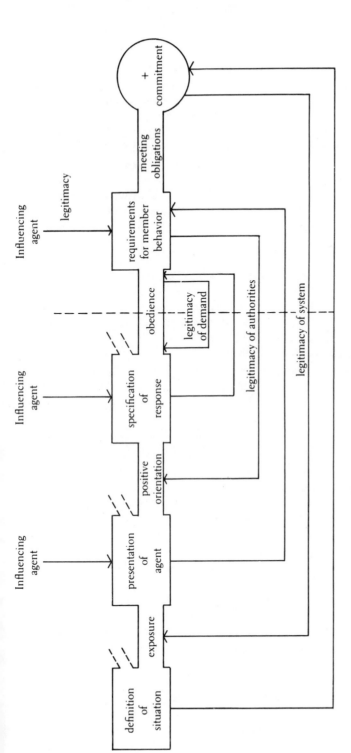

Figure 4.2 Diagram of the Structure of a Situation Governed by Legitimate Authority.

Note: To the left of the vertical broken line, the diagram depicts what happens in an authority situation that produces obedience; to the right it depicts the person's perception of the situation. Arrows from left to right represent the effects of the information conveyed in the situation on the person's perception of (*a*) commitments that have been activated, (*b*) the right of the authority to activate such commitments, and (*c*) the precise behavior required to live up to these commitments. Arrows from right to left represent the effects of these perceptions, in turn, on the person's response to the information conveyed. The broken-lined channels leading out of each box refer to situations that are not perceived as sufficiently legitimate to lead to obedience.

structure of the setting in which the two parties interact: Inductions that take place in a courtroom, at a police station, in a government office, or on the battlefield are readily perceived in an authority framework. The definition of the situation is designed to activate the person's commitment to the role of citizen or group member (or to his subordinate role within the particular hierarchy) and to fulfilling the obligations of that role. If he feels a sense of commitment to his role—which depends to a large extent on the legitimacy the system itself possesses in his eyes— and if that commitment is effectively mobilized in the situation, then he will seek out and readily attend to information indicating what is required of him. If he feels no commitment, or if the situation has not been made relevant to whatever commitment he does feel, then he is unlikely to be responsive to messages alluding to his role obligations.

Commitment to the role need not be deep in order to create the conditions for obedience, as long as there are no alternative authorities claiming legitimacy. Often people accept the legitimacy of a social order—including a pattern of social stratification that places their subgroup at a disadvantage—because they have never known things to be different or conceived of alternative arrangements. Thus, the system is legitimate in their eyes almost by default, and they are responsive to its demands, albeit without enthusiasm and out of "mindless" habit—to use Langer's term (see, for example, Langer et al., 1978). Disobedience is likely to occur only when there are competing definitions of the situation anchored in alternative claims to legitimacy (see chapter 3; also Gamson et al., 1982). From the point of view of eliciting obedience, the commitment activated in the authority situation needs to outweigh only such alternative *commitments*,. but not preferences for alternative behaviors in the pursuit of *personal goals*.

Presentation of the Agent. The authority situation conveys to the person— deliberately or otherwise—information about the influencing agent's credentials as an authority who has the right to speak for the system and make demands on its behalf. In modern bureaucratic contexts, this right generally derives from the influencing agent's position in the hierarchy relative to the person's own position. If the influencing agent's authority is convincingly conveyed, the person will look upon her as a source of valid ("authoritative") information about the behavior required of him in the situation. He will therefore be positively oriented to any demands coming from her. He may be positively oriented toward the influencing agent for various reasons other than her hierarchical position, including her coercive or reward power, her attractiveness, or her credibility—the characteristics that usually endow an influencing agent with the capacity to induce behavior (French and Raven, 1959; Kelman, 1961; Raven, 1965). These other sources of power may contribute to the person's acquiescence on preferential grounds, but the only dimension relevant to his *obedience* is the agent's perceived legitimacy as an authority holder, which entitles her to spell out the person's obligations. If she fails to meet that test, the person will look elsewhere for authoritative information about what is and is not required of him.

Specification of the Response. The authority situation conveys to the person the precise nature of the response demanded of him and facilitates the performance of that response. Some of the means applied to that end are similar to the induction techniques used in ordinary influence situations to enhance the relative strength of the induced behavior. Thus, the authorities may try to reduce ambiguities about the form and content of the required behavior, to overcome the person's resistance to performing the behavior, and to find ways of easing him into performing it. The essential information that must be communicated, however, in order to ensure obedience is that the particular response demanded is the only way for the person to meet his obligations in the present situation. The authorities must see to it that there is no ambiguity about the obligatory character of the behavior demanded, thus giving the subordinate minimal leeway to reinterpret the behavior as merely suggested and optional rather than demanded and required. In the absence of such specification of the desired response, people may select alternative means of meeting their obligations even though their role commitments have been activated in the situation and even though they accept the authorities' legitimacy.

One of the major factors conducive to obedience, as distinct from a self-selected alternative response, is the perceived legitimacy of the demand itself. If the demand clearly falls within the legally or otherwise prescribed domain of the agent's authority and follows the prescribed procedures for exercising authority, the person is likely to obey without considering alternatives. The existence of legal sanctions for disobedience enhances the perceived legitimacy of a demand. This is in one sense obvious but in another sense paradoxical: If a demand is legitimate, people feel obligated to obey it, which should make punishment unnecessary or even counterproductive. But, as we noted in our discussion of the relationship between coercion and legitimacy, the specification of sanctions for failure to perform a particular behavior helps distinguish behaviors that are obligatory from those that are optional. The role of punishment here is not to motivate obedience (in the sense of acceding to the demand out of a sense of duty) but to provide distinctive cues for the obligatory nature of the induced response. Negative sanctions may, of course, also serve as motivators for compliant behavior insofar as group members are not sufficiently committed to their roles to follow orders out of a sense of duty.

Levels of Legitimacy: The Determinants of Obedience. In the earlier discussion of the generic influence situation, we restated the three conditions for influence in terms of three dimensions, which we identified as the basic determinants of influence (represented in figure 4.1 by the three arrows moving from the right to the left side of the diagram). In comparable fashion, we can identify the three basic determinants of obedience in an authority situation (represented by the arrows moving from right to left in figure 4.2). We propose that the three determinants of influence—importance of the induction, power of the influencing agent, and prepotency of the induced behavior—correspond, in an authority situation, to the three levels of legitimacy to which we have already alluded in chapter 3: the legitimacy of the system, the legitimacy of the authorities or power holders within the system, and the legitimacy of their specific demands.[11] Although these three classes of variables may not encompass all the determinants of obedience, they point to those factors that are uniquely related to the special character of the authority situation as one in which influence takes the form of activating role obligations.

To the extent that people perceive the *system* as legitimate—relative to other systems that may be making competing demands at the same time—an authoritative demand will activate their commitment to their membership roles and thus enhance their responsiveness to that demand. To the extent that they perceive the particular *authorities* as legitimate—relative to other authorities within the same social unit who may be demanding or permitting different behavior—they will accept these authorities' right to define member obligations and to make demands upon them. To the extent that they perceive the specific *demand* as legitimate— relative to alternative ways of fulfilling their role obligations that they might otherwise find more attractive—they will be inclined to obey without question. Perceived legitimacy at these three levels, taken together, determines the probability of obedience in an authority situation.

11. "Legitimacy of the system" in our scheme refers essentially to what Easton (1965) calls "legitimacy of the regime." However, our use of the term *system* here is meant to include not only the *regime* but also the *political community* as defined by Easton. "Legitimacy of the authorities" in our scheme is similar to Easton's use of the same term.

5 | The Dynamics of Authority

In chapter 4 we identified the structural elements of an authority situation, distinguishing three levels at which legitimacy has to be established in the eyes of group members or subordinates if they are to obey out of a sense of duty. The interesting task for social-psychological analysis is to explain *how* legitimacy is established at each of these levels—how social expectations and individual motivations are articulated with one another to produce perceived legitimacy. In this chapter, therefore, we move from the discussion of the where, who, and what of authority to a consideration of the how of authority.

In examining the dynamics of authority—that is, the sources of legitimacy of the system, the authorities, and the demand—we shall draw on earlier analyses of the dynamics of social influence (Kelman, 1958, 1961, 1963, 1974b). For present purposes, these analyses point to societal or organizational differences in the way in which authority's expectations are communicated and to individual differences in the way in which authority is assessed and experienced. We begin this chapter with a review of the earlier work. We will then draw on this work to focus on the way in which legitimacy is established at the levels of the system, the authorities, and the specific demand.

Three Processes of Social Influence

The structural model of social influence, described in chapter 4 and summarized in figure 4.1, yielded three basic determinants of social influence—the importance of the induction, the power of the influencing agent, and prepotency, or the relative strength of the induced behavior—each of which can take qualitatively different forms. It is these qualitative differences that give the model its dynamic character. Following this logic, earlier publications (especially Kelman, 1961, 1974) used the structural model of the influence situation as a starting point for a distinction among three processes of social influence: compliance, identification, and internalization. Each of these processes is defined by a distinctive combination of the three determinants of social influence. The following description of the three processes should give some indication of the conditions under which each is likely to arise and the nature of the changes it is likely to generate. The three processes will be characterized as ideal types in order to clarify their qualitative differences, although we do not see these processes as mutually exclusive.

COMPLIANCE

Compliance can be said to occur when an individual accepts influence from another person or a group in the hope of achieving a favorable reaction, or avoiding an unfavorable reaction, from the other. The person may be interested in attaining certain specific rewards or in avoiding certain specific punishments that the other controls. For example, an employee may be careful to express only the opinions favored by his boss[1] in order to gain promotion or avoid dismissal. Or the person may be concerned with gaining approval or avoiding disapproval from the other in a more general way. For example, people who are new in a community, or perhaps generally insecure, may be anxious to say what is expected in all situations and to please everyone with whom they come in contact, out of a disproportionate need for direct and immediate reassurance that others accept them.

When people comply, they do what the influencing agent wants them to do, or what they think she wants them to do, in order to achieve a positive response from her. They adopt the induced behavior, such as a particular opinion response, not because they agree with its content but because its expression is instrumental in producing a desired social effect. They learn, essentially, to say or do the expected thing in particular situations, regardless of what their private beliefs may be. Opinions adopted through compliance are likely to be expressed only when the behavior is observable by the influencing agent.

IDENTIFICATION

Identification can be said to occur when an individual adopts behavior associated with a satisfying self-defining relationship to another person or a group. A "self-defining relationship" refers to a role relationship that forms a part of the person's self-image. Accepting influence from another through identification, then, is a way of establishing or maintaining the desired relationship to that other and the self-definition that is anchored in this relationship. Identification essentially involves taking over a role or adopting some aspect of behavior that goes with a particular role. The process need not be conscious. The little girl who cradles her doll and the medical student who patronizes patients may not be aware that they are imitating role models and preparing for future role relationships.

The relationship an individual tries to establish or maintain through identifi-

1. As in chapter 4, we refer to the person to whom the influence attempt or authoritative demand is directed as "he" and to the influencing agent or authority holder as "she."

cation may take different forms. In the most common and classical usage of the term by psychologists, identification takes the form of a relationship in which the individual takes over all or part of the role of the influencing agent. To the extent that such a relationship exists, the person defines his own role in terms of the other's role. He attempts to be like or actually to be the other person. An influencing agent likely to be an attractive object for such a relationship is one who occupies a role desired by the person or who possesses characteristics the person lacks, such as control in a situation in which he is helpless, direction in a situation in which he is disoriented, or belongingness in a situation in which he is isolated.

The case of Patricia Hearst, which gained a great deal of public attention during the 1970s, provides a dramatic example of classical identification. After being kidnapped by the Symbionese Liberation Army, a radical fringe group, Patty Hearst joined their ranks, participated in a bank robbery with them, and maintained an underground existence with several members of the group until she was eventually captured. She was tried and convicted for her crimes as Tanya—the SLA nom de guerre she had adopted. The rationale behind the conviction was that she had stayed with the SLA and participated in their crimes by choice, even though her association with the group began through an act of coercion. From all indications, Patty did indeed become converted. She adopted an SLA identity and a set of beliefs associated with it. But these beliefs were isolated from and superimposed upon her earlier values and were entirely dependent on her continuing relationship to the SLA. After her capture, she went through a period of confusion, in which she fluctuated between the two identities of Patty and Tanya—quite understandably, since she was being put on trial in her role as Tanya. Soon, however, she reverted to her earlier identity and the beliefs and behavior patterns associated with it. Thus, the beliefs she adopted under SLA pressure did not survive her departure from that social environment and return to her former surroundings. A similar pattern was found among Westerners returning home after being subjected to "thought reform" in China (Lifton, 1956). The quality of the belief change produced by brainwashing and similar influence processes is nicely captured by the term *coercive persuasion,* coined by Schein and his associates (1961). It represents more than public conformity designed to placate the interrogator, but less than private acceptance of new beliefs in the sense of stable integration into the person's own value structure.

The brainwashed prisoners and Patricia Hearst attempted to regain their identity, which had been subjected to severe assaults, by adopting the attitudes and beliefs of their keepers—including these keepers' evaluation of them. But classical identification is not restricted to such crisis situations. It can be observed in childhood socialization, as in our example of the little girl cradling her doll. There the taking over of parental attitudes and actions is a normal and probably crucial part of personality development. A similar process is at work in the more or less conscious efforts an individual makes in learning to play an occupational role by imitating an appropriate role model, as in our example of the medical student. In the work setting people can of course be much more selective in the attitudes and actions they take over from others. What is at stake is not their basic sense of self or their sex-role identity but a more limited professional identity.

The self-defining relationship an individual tries to establish or maintain through identification may also take the form of a reciprocal-role relationship— that is, a relationship in which the roles of the two parties are defined with reference to each other. A person may be involved in a reciprocal relationship with another specific individual, as in a friendship, or he may enact a social role that is defined with reference to another (reciprocal) role, as in the relationship between patient and doctor or student and mentor. A reciprocal-role relationship can be maintained only if the participants have mutually shared expectations of each other's behavior. Thus, if a person finds a particular relationship satisfying, he will tend to behave in a way that meets the other's expectations. Behavior in line with the requirements of a reciprocal relationship should manifest itself whether or not the influencing agent is watching. Quite apart from the other's reaction, it is important to the person's self-concept to meet the expectations of his friendship role or occupational role.

Identification may also serve to maintain an individual's relationship with a group or collectivity in which his self-definition is anchored. Such a relationship may include elements of classical identification as well as of reciprocal roles. To maintain a self-definition as a group member, one typically has to model one's behavior along particular lines, as well as to meet the expectations of fellow members. People may identify with their nation—for example, gaining a sense of vicarious power, achievement, and identity through their self-definition as part of a group that has shaped history, commands respect, and is destined to live to eternity. In combat situations, soldiers' identification and solidarity with their immediate group of comrades have been found to be major determinants of attitudes and of behavior under stress (Shils and Janowitz, 1948; Lang, 1968). Group identification processes at lower degrees of intensity probably account for many of the conventions that people acquire in the course of socialization.

Identification is similar to compliance in that the person does not adopt the induced behavior because its content is intrinsically satisfying, at least initially, but identification differs from compliance in that he believes in the actions and opinions he adopts. The behavior is accepted both publicly and privately and is likely to manifest itself whether or not the influencing agent is able to observe it. Manifestation of the behavior does depend, however, on the role the person takes at any given moment. Only when the appropriate role is activated—only when he is acting within the relationship upon which the identification is based—will he express the induced behavior. In other settings, dominated by different role relationships, the behavior may not come to the surface. In identification, in contrast to compliance, the person is not primarily concerned with pleasing the other, with giving her what she wants, but he is concerned with meeting the other's expectations for his own role performance. Thus, behaviors adopted through identification, though accepted privately, remain tied to the external source and dependent on social support. They are not integrated into a personal value system, though they may be quite stable as long as the person operates in a social environment that is relatively unchanging.

INTERNALIZATION

Internalization can be said to occur when a person accepts influence because the induced behavior is congruent with his value system. Milton Rokeach, who has written more extensively on the subject of values than any other social psychologist, defines *value* and *value system* as follows: "A *value* is an enduring belief that a specific mode of conduct or end-state of existence is personally or socially preferable to an opposite or converse mode of conduct or end-state of existence. A *value system* is an enduring organization of beliefs concerning preferable modes of conduct or end-states of existence along a continuum of relative importance" (1973, p. 5). These definitions are closely linked to Rokeach's measuring instrument, which has proved to be a powerful tool in his empirical research. Although our use of the terms is consistent with Rokeach's definitions,[2] we have found Kluckhohn's (1952) broader definition more suitable for our purposes. According to Kluckhohn, "a value is a conception, explicit or implicit, distinctive of an individual or characteristic of a group, of the desirable which influences the selection from available modes, means, and ends of action" (p. 395). In defining values as conceptions of the *desirable,* Kluckhohn goes on to stress that "a value is not just a preference but is a preference which is felt and/or considered to be justified—'morally' or by reasoning or by aesthetic judgments, usually by two or all three of these. Even if a value remains implicit, behavior with reference to this *conception* indicates an undertone of the desirable—not just the desired" (p. 396).

Values are socially derived and shared. They are themselves products of social influence, acquired from the various socializing agents to whom the person is exposed and the various groups with which he is affiliated. The combination and organization of any person's values, however, are idiosyncratic to that person. Each person is exposed to a different set of influencing agents and groups and thus experiences a unique mix of value inputs. Moreover, people respond selectively to these influences, picking and choosing among different sources, as well as among the different values offered by any one source. Selectivity in response to external stimuli can be traced to individual differences in temperament and behavioral style that have been observed in numerous studies of neonates (for example, Escalona, 1968; Thomas and Chess, 1977). The temperamental dispositions that each infant possesses at birth or develops shortly thereafter (such as its activity level and its sensitivity to stimulation) constitute a set of special demands that it makes of the environment from the very beginning. Thus, even infants have personal criteria by which they find some environmental inputs congenial

2. Rokeach's more recent description of values as "shared prescriptive or proscriptive beliefs about ideal modes of behavior and end-states of existence that are activated by, yet transcend object and situation" (1980, p. 162) is even closer to our use of the term *value.*

and others uncongenial. For example, some infants may seek out stimulation from adult caretakers while others may tend to withdraw from it. One might describe an infant's particular combination of temperamental characteristics as a rudimentary personal structure that allows it to react to some environmental inputs as "right for me" and others as "wrong for me." Such a structure may provide the initial basis for selecting among the different values to which the growing individual is exposed. This rudimentary structure is gradually built up into a personal value system, which then provides the basis for further selection among the values offered by different influence sources. Such externally derived values are modified and adapted, arranged, and related to one another, as they are integrated into the ever-evolving value system that is unique for each person.

One of the functions of a value system is to generate a set of personal standards by which the person accepts or rejects induced behavior. When we speak of internalization, then, we refer to the acceptance of influence because the induced behavior meets such personal standards. In the case of internalization, in contrast to compliance and identification, the content of the induced behavior is intrinsically rewarding. The person adopts it because it appears useful for solving a problem, or is congenial to his worldview, or is demanded by his moral convictions—in short, because he perceives it as inherently conducive to the maximization of his values. The characteristics of the influencing agent do play an important role in internalization, but the crucial dimension is her credibility. That is, the agent's ability to exert influence via internalization rests on her relation to the content conveyed rather than on her control over rewards and punishments or her attractiveness as an object for identification.

The most obvious examples of internalization involve evaluation and acceptance of induced behavior on rational grounds. For example, a hospital administrator may call in an organizational consultant to help deal with a situation of low staff morale and high absenteeism. He may adopt a more participatory style of management, as recommended by the consultant, because he finds her recommendations relevant to his problems and congruent with his values. Insofar as his change is based on internalization (recommendations of experts may, of course, also be adopted for reasons of compliance or identification) he will probably not accept these recommendations in toto but will modify them to fit his unique style and situation.

Internalization, however, does not necessarily represent a rational process, despite the rationalist overtones in our description of it. If people adopt beliefs because of their congruence with a value system that many regard as irrational—for example, racist attitudes that fit their paranoid view of the world—we would still describe the process as internalization, since it is the content of the induced behavior that is intrinsically appealing to them. Furthermore, congruence with a person's value system does not necessarily imply logical consistency. It may simply mean affective appropriateness. For example, a young man who hears about the option of conscientious objection to a military draft may immediately decide that it "feels right" for him without requiring further analysis. He may see this new option as behavior that naturally fits with his value system and is demanded by it and that provides him an opportunity to actualize his self-concept.

Behavior adopted through internalization is in some way—rational or otherwise—integrated with the person's existing values. It becomes part of a personal structure, as distinguished from a set of social-role expectations. Such behavior gradually becomes independent of the external source. Its manifestation depends neither on observability by the influencing agent nor on the salience of the relevant role relationship but on the extent to which the underlying values have been made relevant by the issues under consideration. This does not mean that people invariably express internalized attitudes or carry out internalized action tendencies regardless of the social situation. In any specific situation, they have to choose among competing values in the face of a variety of situational requirements. It does mean, however, that these behaviors and attitudes will at least be psychologically available whenever their content becomes relevant and thus enter into competition with alternative considerations.

Each type of influence—compliance, identification, and internalization—should be viewed as the outcome of a reciprocal process involving a certain degree of mutual influence rather than a totally one-sided process in which a person passively incorporates behavior imposed by an influencing agent. But the concept of internalization is especially designed to capture the person's own contribution to the influence relationship. It reminds us that influence may result from an active engagement between outside forces and the person's own values. Internalization, in essence, refers to a process of integrating socially induced behavior into a personal value system. Whereas the concept of identification points to the possibility that influence may be privately accepted and yet remain dependent on the external source, the concept of internalization points to the possibility that influence may become independent of the external source from which it was originally derived.

RELATIONSHIPS AMONG THE THREE PROCESSES

Compliance, identification, and internalization are not mutually exclusive. Although we have defined them as ideal types, they do not generally appear in pure form in real-life situations. They do not, as such, constitute personality dispositions. The same individual may be susceptible to influence via each of the processes at different times and in different contexts, although individuals may differ in their susceptibility to one or another process in a given type of situation. For example, although everyone complies under some circumstances, individuals may differ in their readiness to comply when subjected to peer pressure. The same person may respond to influence via all three processes, not only in different situations, but sometimes even in the very same situation. Thus, all three of the processes may be involved simultaneously in the same relationship, such as that between student and mentor in the course of professional socialization. The precise mix of influence strategies and responses may shift over the course of the relationship. For example, one may well find a gradual shift in emphasis from compliance to internalization, in line with Blau's (1964) argument that social relations tend to move from extrinsic to intrinsic exchanges. Yet elements of compliance or identification may persist or reappear.

All three of the processes may also be engaged simultaneously around the same issue. For example, many of the Americans who were induced to buy war bonds during World War II may have been responding, at one and the same time, to social pressure and the threat of disapproval, to the desire to live up to the expectations of the citizenship role and their self-images as good citizens, and to the conviction that the action was necessary for the welfare of the country and the promotion of the patriotic values to which they were personally committed. We suspect that influence processes coexist more often than not: that individuals rarely act for just one reason and that social groups and organizations rarely rely on just one means of persuasion.

Compliance, identification, and internalization therefore mix and overlap in a given person, a given situation, a given relationship, and even a given influence attempt. Yet the distinction among these processes is analytically useful, particularly since at different times, in different contexts, and for different individuals, one or another of them predominates. Furthermore, organizations and societies differ in the degree to which they use the various processes to socialize and control their members. And within an organization or society, different processes tend to be emphasized in the socialization and treatment of different subgroups: Some are expected merely to comply with the rules, others to identify with the organization, and still others to internalize its values. We will address such subgroup differences more fully in chapter 8, when we discuss different patterns of accountability for wrongdoing. For now we wish merely to raise the possibility that strategies of influence may be differentially employed and that such differentiation is likely to have a social meaning.

ANTECEDENTS AND CONSEQUENTS OF THE THREE PROCESSES

Each of the three processes is characterized by a distinct set of antecedent and consequent conditions, summarized in table 5.1. The antecedents of each process flow directly from our structural model of social influence. In each case, the three variables identified by that model—the importance of the induction, the power of the influencing agent, and the relative strength of the induced response—determine the probability that influence will occur, whether in the form of compliance, identification, or internalization. The three processes differ, however, in the *qualitative* form these basic determinants take. As table 5.1 specifies, they differ with respect to the *basis* for the importance of the induction, the *source* of the influencing agent's power, and the *manner* of achieving prepotency of the induced response. (See Kelman, 1961, for an explanation of the distinct antecedent conditions postulated for each process.)

We postulate further that each of the three processes of influence corresponds

Table 5.1 Summary of the Distinctions between the Three Processes

	Compliance	*Identification*	*Internalization*
ANTECEDENTS			
1. Basis for the *importance of the induction*	Concern with social effect of behavior	Concern with social anchorage of behavior	Concern with value congruence of behavior
2. Source of *power of the influencing agent*	Means control	Attractiveness	Credibility
3. Manner of achieving *prepotency of the induced response*	Limitation of choice behavior	Delineation of role requirements	Reorganization of means-ends framework
CONSEQUENTS			
1. Conditions of performance of induced response	Surveillance by influencing agent	Salience of relationship to agent	Relevance of values to issue
2. Conditions of change and extinction of induced response	Changed perception of conditions for social rewards	Changed perception of conditions for satisfying self-defining relationships	Changed perception of conditions for value maximization
3. Type of behavior system in which induced response is embedded	External demands of a specific setting	Expectations defining a specific role	Person's value system

Source: Reprinted from Kelman, 1961, p. 67, by permission of the publisher.

to a characteristic pattern of thoughts and feelings in the person, generated by the antecedent conditions peculiar to that process. These different reactions in turn account for differences in the nature of the changes produced by each of these processes. We do not assume that the processes differ systematically in their capacity to produce change or in the amount and strength of the changes they produce. Rather, we propose differences in the quality and the subsequent fate of the behavior adopted via each process. These differences are summarized in the lower half of table 5.1. As the table indicates, the changes produced by the three processes differ with respect to the conditions under which the new behavior is manifested, the conditions under which it is likely to be changed or abandoned, and the behavioral system in which it is embedded. (For an explanation of the distinct consequent conditions postulated for each process, see Kelman, 1961.)

The underlying logic of the distinction among compliance, identification, and internalization can be summarized briefly. The basic determinants of social influence, specified in our description of the generic influence situation, take a qualitatively different form for each of the three processes. Thus, each process is characterized by a different package of antecedent conditions. These in turn make for differences in the induced behavior and in the nature of the resulting changes. Given a particular set of conditions—associated with each of the three types of influence situations identified by the model—we can, therefore, predict the outcome of the influence attempt.

Social Influence as Linkage between the Individual and the Social System

In order to apply the distinction among the three processes of influence to an analysis of the dynamics of authority, we must first spell out the implications of our microanalysis of social influence for the relationship between the individual and influencing agents at a more macro, systemic level. We have already indicated in chapter 4 that we conceive of social influence as a process (or set of processes) linking individuals to larger social structures. We pointed out in that connection how each of the basic determinants of influence—importance of the induction, power of the influencing agent, and prepotency of the induced behavior—refers at least implicitly to conditions in the larger social system.

The relationship of these three determinants of social influence to the social system becomes particularly evident when we examine the distinct forms they take in compliance, identification, and internalization (as summarized in table 5.1). Thus, the different bases for the importance of the induction postulated by the three-process model can be analyzed in terms of the nature of the person's relationship to the society or organization and the kind of integration he hopes to achieve or maintain.[3] The different sources of power of the influencing agent can be analyzed in terms of the relationship between the person and the agent within the society or organization that provides the context for their current interaction.[4] The different ways of achieving prepotency of the induced behavior—the specific

---

3. A person's focus on the social effect of his behavior represents a concern with how adequately he conforms to the societal rules; his focus of social anchorage represents a concern with how securely he is embedded in his roles within the society; and his focus on value congruence represents a concern with how fully he lives up to societal values that he shares.

4. Means control (the influencing agent's ability to supply or withhold material or psychological resources on which a person's goal achievement depends) may refer to those agents whom the person perceives to be in a position to allocate societal resources and administer sanctions; attractiveness (the agent's possession of those qualities that make a continued relationship to her particularly desirable) may refer to those in a position to define the requirements of being a good group member; and credibility (the agent's expertness and trustworthiness) may refer to those in a position to assess the society's needs in terms of its underlying ideology and long-term goals.

induction techniques used in the influence situation—may be related to different functions of the society or organization.[5]

The three processes of social influence can thus be restated with reference to the social unit within which they are generated and to which a person's acceptance of influence is directed. When viewed within the context of a particular social unit, each process represents a different way in which the person meets the demands of that unit and maintains his personal integration in it. Compliance reflects an orientation to a society's *rules* (including its laws and customs)—the behavioral requirements it sets for its members. In accepting influence through this process, the person is acknowledging the rules and adhering to them, thus presumably assuring himself of continued access to rewards or approval (or avoidance of penalties or disapproval) contingent on following these rules. Identification reflects an orientation to the *role* of citizen or to some particular role within the society, not just as a set of behavioral requirements, but as an important part of the person's self-definition. In accepting influence through this process, he is meeting the expectations of that role, thus maintaining the desired relationship to the society and his self-concept as someone fully in possession of the role. Internalization reflects an orientation to societal *values* that the individual personally shares. In accepting influence by this process, he is living up to the implications of these shared values, thus maintaining the integrity of his personal value system.

In our restatement of the processes of compliance, identification, and internalization, we have distinguished three components of a social system that are interrelated but analytically separable: its rules, its roles, and its values (see also chapter 11). Each of these components can be described as a set of *standards* for the behavior of individual members: criteria against which to evaluate the quality of their performance. When using rule-based standards, we evaluate the person's overt behavior by its correspondence to the requirements set out in the rules. When using role-based standards, we evaluate the way in which the person carries out the behavior in terms of the commitment it shows to the role and to the social unit in which that role is embedded. When using value-based standards, we evaluate the behavior by its intended contribution to the achievement of group goals. Compliance, identification, and internalization are designed to meet these three types of standards, respectively.

The three components of a social system also provide some of the *contents of socialization*. In being socialized into a society or into a particular organization or group, the individual learns and adopts rules, role expectations, and values that govern member behavior. The relationship of these three types of socialization content to the three processes of influence is somewhat complex. A person may develop an internalized commitment to certain societal roles and readiness to adhere to certain societal rules because he sees these as necessary to the fulfillment of collective values that he shares. Similarly, the person may be committed to

5. Limitation of choice behavior may occur most readily in the context of allocating resources and applying sanctions; delineation of role requirements, in the context of mobilizing group support as in a time of crisis; and reorganization of means-ends conceptions, in the context of setting and evaluating societal goals, perhaps in periods of major social change.

societal rules out of identification, accepting the need to adhere to them faithfully as one of the requirements of a role that has become central to his self-definition. In any given instance, he may adhere to a rule or law out of compliance (he may obey the speed limit, for example, in order to avoid a traffic ticket), but he may have a general attitude of respect for a body of rules (such as the legal system) based on internalization, or a general self-image as a law-abiding citizen, based on identification.

Despite these complexities one can postulate a hierarchy in the socialization of rules, roles, and values that can probably be stated most clearly in the negative. Insofar as a person's socialization has not proceeded beyond the acceptance of rules, we can describe him as integrated into society by way of compliance. Insofar as his socialization has not proceeded beyond the acceptance of a role, without linking it to the promotion of larger values, we can describe his means of integration as identification. And insofar as his socialization has led to the acceptance and incorporation of societal values into a personal value system, we can speak of integration by way of internalization. Compliance, identification, and internalization can thus be seen as three ways of achieving, promoting, and protecting people's personal integration in a society or organization.

Conceptualizing social influence in terms of properties of the social system helps to bridge analyses of social influence, which are usually made at the microlevel, with those of social control, which usually proceed at the macrolevel. Both focus on the link between the individual and societal or organizational forces. But a social-influence analysis does so from the perspective of the individual subjected to influence, whereas a social-control analysis does so from the perspective of the larger society. More generally, by attempting to bridge a microanalysis of social behavior with a macroanalysis, our approach to social influence can help conceptualize the effect of the individual on larger social units; it can clarify how individual patterns of relating to society affect the way in which society functions and how individual change affects social change. Conversely, this approach may be helpful in conceptualizing how the structural features and institutional patterns of a society affect the integration and functioning of its individual members.

The operation of rules, roles, and values in socialization and social control is illustrated in an analysis of people's emotional reactions when they find themselves deviating from societal standards in the domains of responsibility or propriety (Kelman, 1974a, 1980). Actions that depart from societal standards of responsibility (or morality) typically involve causing harm to others or to society in general; actions that depart from societal standards of propriety typically involve performing in ways that are deemed inappropriate for a person in the actor's position or, in many cases, for any adult in the society. Deviations from standards in either of these domains may take the form of violations of rules, role expectations, or values. Which violation a person focuses on depends on the level at which a given standard is represented in his cognitive structure, which in turn is in part a function of his socialization. If the standard has been adopted at the level of compliance, he will focus primarily on rule violations; if it has been adopted at the level of identification, he will focus on deviations from role expectations; and if it has been internalized, he will focus on violations of values.

The person's primary focus will determine his reaction when he finds himself deviating from a particular standard. At each level, violation of standards should arouse different concerns and emotional responses in the person. Moreover, he can be expected to go about handling the concerns and resolving the tensions aroused in different ways—to use different strategies for avoiding or minimizing the consequences of deviation and for rectifying the situation and coming to grips with it psychologically.

Thus, if a person has violated compliance-based standards—if he has broken rules—he will be concerned primarily with the way others will react to his violations. His dominant emotional reaction can be characterized as *fear* of the social consequences of the deviant action if he has violated standards of responsibility, or *embarrassment* if he has violated standards of propriety. If he has violated identification-based standards or role expectations, his primary concern will be to reestablish his desired relationship to society and his self-definition as a worthy, securely anchored member of society. The dominant emotional reaction in this case can be described as *guilt*[6] if he has acted irresponsibly, or *shame* if he has acted improperly. Finally, if he has violated internalized standards, which are integral parts of a personal value system, he is primarily concerned with the object of his failure—the person he has harmed by his irresponsible action or the task on which he has fallen short of proper performance—as well as with the implication of this failure for his ability to live up to his own standards of morality and competence. The dominant emotional reaction here can be described as *regret* or *remorse* in the domain of responsibility, or *self-disappointment*[7] in the domain of propriety.

The various reactions to violations of societal standards suggest how the three processes of social influence might affect the exercise of social control. Individuals operating at the level of compliance are "insufficiently" socialized. Their adherence to social norms depends on surveillance, which makes them less reliable and more difficult to control. Individuals operating at the level of internalization are, in a sense, "excessively" socialized from the point of view of agencies charged with social control. Since societal standards are integrated with their personal value systems, they tend to make their own judgments about the validity of authoritative demands. Their conformity to such demands is, thus, more conditional. Individ-

---

6. Guilt is used here in the sense of a person's concern that the deviant action has thrown his relationship to society into question and undermined his self-definition within it. Through his irresponsible behavior he has incurred a debt to society that he must repay in order to reinstate himself. The core meaning of this reaction is well conveyed by the German word *Schuld*, which means both guilt and debt.

7. Rokeach (for example, 1980, pp. 296–98) has shown experimentally that self-dissatisfaction—which he induces through a method of self-confrontation—is a significant source of value change. His term *self-dissatisfaction* encompasses violations of internalized standards in the domains of both propriety and responsibility (or competence and morality in Rokeach's terms).

uals operating at the level of identification are likely to conform to authoritative demands with less surveillance than those at the level of compliance and with less questioning than those at the level of internalization. Identification, with its associated emotions of guilt and shame, can thus be seen as the influence process most conducive to social control.

The distinctions among compliance, identification, and internalization—and among the corresponding societal components of rules, roles, and values—help us specify what society expects of different members and what they expect of themselves. In so doing, it can contribute to our understanding of the dynamics of authority. We will draw on it in the remainder of this chapter as we proceed to examine how legitimacy is established at each of the three levels specified by our structural analysis of authority—the levels of the system, the authorities, and the specific demands. In chapter 11 we will take this argument further by proposing that rule orientation, role orientation, and value orientation represent different ways in which people relate themselves to the political system, which have direct implications for their conceptions of authority and responsibility in the face of authoritative orders.

Legitimacy of the System

In our discussion of the first level of legitimacy, we focus on the political system—specifically, the modern nation-state. It is the nation-state, and crimes committed in its name, that are the primary concern of this book. The basic analysis, however, should be equally applicable to other social units.

From a psychological viewpoint, the government of a nation-state is legitimate insofar as the population perceives it as (a) reflecting its ethnic and cultural identity and (b) meeting its needs and interests.[8] A well-functioning nation-state derives legitimacy from both of these sources. It is possible, however, to distinguish among different states, or different historical periods for the same state, in terms of the relative weights of these two ultimate bases of legitimacy.

In the long run, a political system cannot maintain its legitimacy unless at least a significant portion of the population perceives it as meeting their needs and interests (although it can, of course, retain power by relying on coercive means, even if only a small elite are well integrated into the society). In shorter runs, however, a state can maintain its legitimacy even if it is not working effectively, or is facing serious economic difficulties, or is torn by internal conflicts, so that it can provide adequately for the needs and interests of only some segments of the population at the expense of others. It can do so as long as it is strong in the

8. Using Easton's (1965) distinction between the political community and the regime as separate components of the political system and objects of diffuse support, we can rephrase this proposition as follows: A population will feel committed to the political community and extend diffuse support to it insofar as it perceives it as reflecting its ethnic and cultural identity and meeting its needs and interests. Commitment to the political community, in turn, enhances the population's belief in the legitimacy of the regime.

second base of legitimacy—that is, as long as it is seen by wide segments of the population as representing their national (their ethnic-cultural) identity. By appealing to the common national ties of the people, the leadership may be able to elicit their loyalty despite internal divisions and inequities. Thus, the perception of the state as representing national identity can compensate—temporarily and sometimes for extended periods—for its failures in meeting public interests and needs, and gives it a continuity it might otherwise lack. This is a particularly valuable resource in the initial stages of political development, when elites typically have to mobilize mass support without being able to offer many concrete benefits to the majority of the population.

One of the basic assumptions of nationalism, the ideology of the modern nation-state or of movements directed toward the establishment of a new nation-state (Kelman, 1969), is that the nation-state—as its name implies—represents the population by virtue of the fact that its political boundaries also constitute national boundaries. That is, the political entity corresponds to an ethnic, cultural, and historical entity with which at least large portions of the population identify. In practice, of course, this correspondence often does not exist; most states comprise a variety of distinct ethnic and cultural groups, sometimes with a long history of intergroup conflict. Insofar as the state does correspond to a nation, however, people tend to see it—almost by definition—as most capable of protecting their interests, even if it is not serving them well in the short run. Thus, common identity can substitute for economic shortcomings. Conversely, a sense of economic well-being can substitute for ethnic divisions. If people perceive the state as adequately meeting their needs and interests, it can maintain its legitimacy even though it does not fully reflect the population's ethnic-cultural identity or does so only for a small proportion of the population.

Aside from substituting for one another, the two sources of legitimacy can reinforce each other and each can potentially facilitate the development of the other. Thus, if citizens perceive the state as being genuinely representative and reflective of their group identity, they are inclined to feel confident that it will meet their needs most faithfully and provide the best protection of their interests. Supported by this initial confidence of the citizens and by their willingness to give it the benefit of the doubt, the government is in a stronger position to push for economic development and to organize the society in a way that will in fact meet the needs and interests of the population. The government, in this case, enhances its legitimacy by drawing on a type of nationalism in which the primary push is from nation to state: An existing national consciousness is used in the process of state building. The creation of the modern state of Israel exemplifies this process. The Palestinian national movement illustrates the process of mobilizing national consciousness in an effort to establish a political state.

The mutual reinforcement of the two sources of legitimacy also works in the reverse direction. A well-functioning society that provides meaningful roles for its citizens, establishes networks of transaction and communication between them, creates interdependence among them, and adequately meets their needs and interests will develop a set of common values and traditions and a sense of unity that are tantamount to a national identity, even if the population was originally diverse in its ethnic and cultural identifications. This national identity need not displace the original ethnic-cultural identities of the component groups but can exist alongside of them. Legitimacy in this case is enhanced by the development of a type of nationalism in which the primary push is from state to nation: An existing sociopolitical structure is used in the process of nation building. Switzerland exemplifies one of the most successful outcomes of such a process.

In sum, we have proposed that the legitimacy of a political system will be accepted to the extent that there is a widely held perception of its representativeness and instrumentality within the population. These perceptions, however, are not equally strong or well articulated among all segments of the population. At the level of the individual, we can speak in this connection of differences in the strength and nature of sentimental and instrumental attachment to the nation state. Attachment refers to how much people care for the state and how much loyalty they feel toward it—the psychological counterpart of perceived legitimacy. Sentimental and instrumental attachment can thus be seen as two different (though not mutually exclusive) types or aspects of nationalism. They correspond, at the system level, to the respective perceptions that the state reflects the ethnic-cultural identity of the population and that it meets the population's needs and interests.

Individuals are sentimentally attached to the national political system when they see it as representing them and feel that their own identity is closely linked to it. For the sentimentally attached, the system is legitimate and deserving of their loyalty because it is the embodiment of a group in which their personal identity is anchored. They have a particular investment in maintaining the integrity of national symbols.

Individuals are instrumentally attached to the national political system when they see it as dedicated to and capable of meeting the needs and interests of the population. For the instrumentally attached, the system is legitimate and deserving of their loyalty because it provides the organization for a smoothly running society beneficial to its members. They have a particular investment in the effective functioning of the mechanisms for handling the society's affairs.

Whether a person's attachment to the nation-state is largely sentimental or largely instrumental or some fairly balanced combination of the two depends on various personal and social characteristics—such as the person's place in society, education, residence, religious and ethnic identifications, personal history, and personality dispositions. One can also examine societal conditions that make one or the other of these two types of attachments more probable in a given environment and at a given time. Thus, for example, the source of loyalty that predominates in a society may depend on its stage of development.[9] It may also be affected

---

9. In this connection, the sentimental-instrumental dichotomy is reminiscent of Durkheim's (1947) distinction between the mechanical solidarity of more traditional societies and the organic solidarity of more industrialized societies.

by the kinds of appeals that the national leadership makes at a given time; these in turn depend on the major societal functions that the leaders attempt to perform and on the dispositions available within the population on which they can draw for popular support.

Each of the two types of attachment may be expressed in different ways, depending on whether it is channeled through societal rules, roles, or values. The cross-cutting of attachment and orientation yields a typology of six patterns of personal involvement in the nation-state. This typology, adapted from an earlier formulation (Kelman, 1969) and summarized in table 5.2, is based on the assumption that different individuals and groups within the population may relate themselves in different ways to the nation-state. The six patterns distinguished here are not meant to be mutually exclusive; although one or the other of these patterns may be the predominant one for a given individual or subgroup within the population (or indeed for a given state), various combinations of them are possible and likely. We should also reiterate that this typology, although it explicitly focuses on personal involvement in the nation-state, is applicable to any larger institution or unit that may command obedience and loyalty.

The rows of table 5.2 refer to the two sources of attachment or loyalty to the state that we have distinguished—sentimental and instrumental. The columns distinguish three types of political orientation, defined in terms of the three components of a political system through which members may be bound to it—its rules, its roles, and its values—which we described above and linked to the processes of compliance, identification, and internalization, respectively. When defined in relation to legitimacy of the state, the two sources of attachment refer to the bases of perceived legitimacy; the three types of orientation refer to the processes and criteria by which perceived legitimacy is generated, assessed, and maintained. The three orientations are central to people's relationship to authority and to their conception of responsibility in authority situations; as such, they will be emphasized in our empirical work on crimes of obedience.

Table 5.2 Patterns of Personal Involvement in the National Political System

Sources of Attachment to the Political System	Types of Orientation to Political Processes		
	Rule orientation (Compliance with societal rules)	Role orientation (Identification with societal roles)	Value orientation (Internalization of societal values)
Sentimental	Acceptance of rules that secure person's inclusion in society	Involvement in role of national citizen which enhances person's sense of status	Commitment to basic cultural values for which the society stands
Instrumental	Acceptance of rules that protect person's interests	Involvement in societal roles that contribute to person's status	Commitment to values underlying institutional arrangements

RULE, ROLE, AND VALUE ORIENTATIONS TO POLITICAL PROCESSES

In order to describe how rule, role, and value orientations affect the nature of people's attachment to the political system, we shall treat the three as ideal types. We stress again, however, that these orientations are not mutually exclusive.

For rule-oriented individuals, sentimental attachment takes the rudimentary form of feeling included within the society's boundaries. They accept the state's legitimacy because it gives them the assurance of being reliably covered by the definition of citizen. The sense of inclusion and security is at the core of their relationship to the state; they do not develop a more active identification with the citizen role. They may see the state as a sacred but distant object and focus their attention on the rules by which citizenship is defined.

For rule-oriented individuals instrumental attachment takes the rudimentary form of feeling protected by the state's operative rules. They accept the state's legitimacy because it gives them a sense of assurance that they have access to their fair share of resources and to fair treatment by the authorities, so that their basic needs will be met. Their involvement in various societal roles is limited and tenuous. They tend to perceive law and order as an end in itself and focus their attention on adherence to legal rules.

Thus, insofar as rule-oriented individuals are sentimentally attached, they see the nation-state as conferring identity upon them by virtue of their sense of inclusion according to the rules defining societal membership; they feel personally protected by the stability of the state and concerned with upholding the symbols of its authority. Insofar as they are instrumentally attached, they see the nation-state as meeting their needs and interests by providing and maintaining a body of rules that guarantees at least minimal regard for their welfare; they feel protected by the mechanisms for allocating resources and administering law and order on a fair basis. Rule-oriented individuals consider it their primary obligation as citizens to live up to societal rules, and they expect the authorities, in turn, to maintain the integrity of these rules.

For role-oriented individuals, sentimental attachment takes the form of a more active emotional involvement with the role of national citizen. Individuals derive a sense of personal-status enhancement from their identification with the nation-state as an actor in the international system. They accept the state's legitimacy on an affective level, without developing an articulated cognitive framework in support of this attitude. They react with pride and fervor to the symbols of the state's power and status, such as the flag, the national anthem, the head of state, and often religious symbols that are linked to the nation.

Governments attempt to develop such national symbols and to promote emotional commitments to them so that they can appeal to them in mobilizing popular support. They are aided in this process by their direct and indirect control over the way in which children are socialized. In the course of this socialization at home, at school, and in places of worship, emotional conditioning to respond to national symbols typically goes on. Insofar as the state has control over the schools and is linked to such primary, affect-laden socializing agencies as the family and the church, it has ready avenues for fostering emotional responses to national symbols. These can then be brought into play to heighten emotional arousal whenever it becomes necessary—as in periods of crisis—to mobilize the population.

For role-oriented individuals instrumental attachment takes the form of active participation in a variety of social roles that are mediated by the national political system. They accept the state's legitimacy because it provides them with status satisfactions and opportunities to advance economically, professionally, and socially. Governments are often in a position to promote instrumental attachment through involvement in such roles because of their extensive control over the economic and social institutions of the society. In the complex, bureaucratically structured modern nation-state, individual citizens are highly dependent on the central authorities in carrying out their occupational, local-community, and other social roles. As a result, many citizens become thoroughly entangled in the national political system. Defending the system becomes tantamount to defending their total way of life. This entanglement of citizens enables political authorities to co-opt the leaders of various groups and institutions within the society in the service of the state, particularly in times of crisis.

Thus, insofar as role-oriented individuals are sentimentally attached, they see the nation-state as extending their identity by virtue of their sense of identification with the role of national citizen; they feel personally involved with and enhanced by the nation as an actor in the international system and concerned with upholding the symbols of national status. Insofar as they are instrumentally attached, they see the nation-state as meeting their needs and interests by enabling them to participate in various social roles mediated by the state; they feel involved in various subunits through which the society carries out its functions and satisfied that these units assure them the status to which they consider themselves entitled. Role-oriented individuals see their primary obligation to be the faithful performance of the citizen role and of their other social roles and they expect the authorities, in turn, to maintain the integrity of these roles.

Finally, for value-oriented individuals, sentimental attachment takes the form of ideological commitment to the nation-state, based on the perception that it reflects the ethnic-cultural identity of the population. Here, individuals perceive the state as legitimate because they share many of the cultural values around which it is defined.

Instrumental attachment for these individuals goes beyond personal integration and takes the form of an ideological commitment to the political system. The commitment is based on the perception that the state is an effective and equitable instrument for meeting the needs and interests of the general population. Value-oriented citizens accept the legitimacy of the state because they believe that its institutional arrangements are founded on values they share.

Thus, insofar as value-oriented individuals are sentimentally attached, they see the nation-state as reflecting their identity by virtue of their personal commitment to basic cultural values for which—in their view—the nation stands. Insofar as they are instrumentally attached, they see the state as dedicated to meeting people's needs and interests through institutional arrangements grounded in values they share. They consider it their primary obligation as citizens to advance the fundamental values that shape the national culture and underlie the society's institutional arrangements, and they expect the authorities, in turn, to maintain the integrity of these values.

In speaking of the fundamental values of a nation-state, we do not assume that there is a single, objectively identifiable, and universally shared set of values that characterizes any society. Although some values may be widely shared within the society, there are a variety of other values to which different segments of the population may have differing degrees of commitment. Even values that virtually everyone in a society such as ours considers basic—such as freedom, equality, and justice—may be subject to sharply differing interpretations. The societal values (or interpretations of them) to which different individuals or groups subscribe may at times be not only different but mutually contradictory—and yet have equal claim to traditional status and authenticity. Individuals and groups select from the range of values made available in any society the ones they consider fundamental and authentic; they emphasize some and deemphasize others; they interpret the tradition in ways most congenial to them.[10]

There is often conflict between different subgroups in a society over which set of values is the most authentic, or which interpretation of values they all profess is most consistent with the national tradition. The existence of such conflicts does not make the definition of the "fundamental" values of a society entirely arbitrary and self-serving. In any society there are bound to be divergent traditions, each of which has a justified claim to historical authenticity—although the values linked to any given tradition may not be the *only* set of societal values that justify such a claim. Conflict over which definition of societal values is to prevail is an integral part of the dynamics of any complex society and a legitimate feature of pluralistic democracies.[11]

MAINTAINING LEGITIMACY

Sentimental and instrumental attachments constitute the ultimate sources of legitimacy of the nation-state. They are most significant, at least at the conscious level, when a new state is being established or when an existing state is experiencing crisis. They can be seen then, primarily, as conditions critical to the *creation* and *revitalization* of legitimacy. The *maintenance* of legitimacy, once a state has

10. Our conception of "the" basic values of a society as being subject to selection and interpretation helps highlight the relationship between value orientation and internalization. Internalization implies that values are adopted from an external source selectively and with modifications, so that they can become integrated in a personal value system. Value orientation, which represents a commitment by individuals to shared societal values, implies that they have selected from the range of available values and interpretations those that are most congruent with their personal values—those suitable for internalization.

11. This view of societal values is consistent with a conflict model of society. It assumes, however, that conflict over values—particularly cultural values—may have an independent basis rather than being merely a rationalization of competing class interests.

been established and is running its normal course, depends primarily on the perception that certain mechanisms for legitimate rule exist, that they are intact, and that they are being used as necessary. Mechanisms of legitimate rule, in essence, refer to procedures and criteria for preventing the arbitrary use of power. Four broad conditions for maintenance of perceived legitimacy can be suggested.

1. The political system prescribes and faithfully follows certain *procedures and criteria for accession to power.* These may take a variety of forms: For rational-bureaucratic authorities, legitimate accession to power is evidenced by possession of the task qualifications appropriate for their positions; in democratic political systems, the election process confers legitimacy on officeholders; in traditional political systems, the legitimacy of rulers is usually determined on a hereditary basis. Whatever their specific nature, rules of accession and qualifications for holding power seem to be present in all authority structures. Power holders with questionable legitimacy often go to great lengths to demonstrate that they meet the criteria for accession—for example, by manipulating election results or fabricating family trees. Disputes about the legitimacy of accession to power may produce violent conflicts or secessionist movements, as illustrated by the origins of the Shi'a branch of Islam.

2. Authorities are subject to certain *external norms or standards, which derive from a normative framework shared by the authorities and the citizens*—such as a constitution, a body of religious doctrine, or a widely accepted oral tradition. In biblical Judaism, for example, as noted in chapter 3, rulers along with their subjects were held accountable to the Mosaic law, which formed part of the covenant between God and Israel. In all authority structures, the authorities' rights and the citizens' obligations are both anchored in such a shared normative framework.

3. The norms governing the actions of legitimate authorities generally include certain *rules that define limits to the use of their power.* Such rules often include specification of the domain within which they may make demands, the circumstances under which they are entitled to do so, and the procedures they are expected to follow. Lon Fuller's eight standards for assessing the "inner morality" of laws can be viewed as a set of limits on the use of the lawmaking power. He discusses the requirement that laws take the form of general rules, that they be made known to the citizenry, that they not be retroactive, that they be clearly expressed, that they avoid self-contradiction, that they not demand the impossible, that they not be changed too frequently, and that they be administered as announced (Fuller, 1969, chap. 2). Departures from any of these standards violate, in our terms, some of the procedures and criteria for legitimate rule. Consistent with Fuller's standards, an important program of research by Tyler and his colleagues (for example, Tyler, 1984; Tyler, Rasinski, and McGraw, 1985; Tyler, Rasinski, and Griffin, 1986) demonstrates that citizens' satisfaction with various governmental and legal authorities depends on their perception that procedures have been followed justly, independent of the outcome of personal gain or loss.

This third condition for legitimate rule may not apply universally. For example, an absolute monarchy may be perceived as legitimate by its subjects even though it imposes no constraints on the exercise of authority. We propose that rules limiting the exercise of power are a necessary condition for legitimacy at least in modern bureaucratic authority and that they enhance the perceived legitimacy of all authorities.

4. The political system provides *mechanisms of recourse for citizens* who feel that their rights or expectations have been violated by authorities, *and of accountability for officials* who have overstepped the limits of their authority. Mechanisms of recourse may include the office of ombudsman or the availability of courts to test the constitutionality of laws. Mechanisms of accountability include procedures and criteria for delegitimizing authorities whose failures to abide by the limits of their power have been extensive and excessive. One might argue that, to maintain its legitimacy, any social unit must have functioning mechanisms for the delegitimization of its authorities—such as the impeachment of political officials, the demotion of military officers, the defrocking of priests, the disbarment of attorneys. Even charismatic authorities can be delegitimized—they can fall from grace—although it is more difficult to institutionalize criteria and procedures to govern that process. In short, a claim that the use of power is legitimate becomes meaningless if there is no way of determining when power is used illegitimately and of acting on that determination. In the absence of mechanisms of delegitimization, the use of power may be legitimate in principle but arbitrary in practice. Such mechanisms must not only be available, but be occasionally used—in response, of course, to clear abuses of power—in order to give empirical substance to a political system's claim to legitimate authority.

Occasional abuses of power, if properly dealt with, do not necessarily reduce the perceived legitimacy of the state itself. But repeated failures of the authorities to adhere to the criteria and procedures for the legitimate exercise of power, particularly if these failures remain uncorrected, will gradually erode the legitimacy of the state. Such continuing systematic failures may also direct the attention of the citizenry to the ultimate sources of the state's legitimacy, which tend to remain in the background in an established, smoothly running regime. That is, when abuses of power become the norm rather than the exception in a government's daily operation, people may begin to question its adequacy in representing their group identity and in meeting their needs and interests.

THE PRESUMPTION OF LEGITIMACY

It is now time to return to the specific situation in which political authorities are presenting citizens with a particular demand. In such a situation, how does legitimacy of the system—the first basic determinant of obedience that we have identified—contribute to the probability of obedience? In an established state, in which the mechanisms of legitimate rule appear to be intact, the invocation of this determinant of obedience tends to be almost automatic. That is, once the situation is defined as one governed by political authority, people's commitment to the state as a legitimate entity and their sense of obligation to meet the requirements of the citizen role are readily activated. Thus, they are at least responsive to the demand from the authorities. Whether or not they will actually obey still depends, in the terms of our scheme, on establishing the legitimacy of the authorities and of the demand itself, but they have been induced to take the first step toward obedience. In short, the state can be said to benefit from the presumption of legitimacy.

In the context of this book, with its focus on obedience to destructive orders, the presumption of legitimacy of the system is a disturbing phenomenon. Insofar as acceptance of the state's legitimacy is an automatic response to the invocation of authority, it steers the individual in the direction of unquestioning obedience. Without wishing to minimize this dangerous implication, we think it important to place it in perspective by pointing out that the presumption of legitimacy also performs some very positive functions for political and other social systems. Without this presumption of legitimacy, it would be virtually impossible to run a society or organization effectively and equitably. Under such circumstances, Easton (1965) argues, "no authorities could ever commit themselves or the members of the system except through a process of continuing referenda or force. But with a belief in their legitimacy, the authorities can rest assured that if their activities fall within a definable range, they can obtain at least the acquiescence of other members and at best, their enthusiastic cooperation." The belief in the authorities' legitimacy "implies a predisposition to accept [their] outputs regularly as authoritative or binding" (p. 280). Easton proceeds to show that it is possible for political systems to persist without legitimacy by depending either on force or on expediency to gain acceptance of their outputs as binding. Such arrangements, however, entail high costs and "under most conditions . . . there is a pressure to stabilize political relationships through diffusion of sentiments of legitimacy" (p. 286).

Legitimacy serves as a basis for trust in the system's leadership. Indeed, trust is implied in the very concept of legitimacy (see Gamson, 1968). Because of this trust, citizens are prepared to give legitimate authorities the benefit of the doubt— to proceed on the assumption that the authorities have the citizens' interests at heart, that they know what they are doing, that they take full responsibility for their policies and actions. These very assumptions, it must be conceded, support the tendency to unquestioning obedience in political and military authority situations with its frequently disastrous consequences. At the same time, these assumptions provide the foundation for fair and effective government. They enable political leaders to operate on the basis of consensus rather than coercion, since citizens willingly accept certain sacrifices that the leadership considers necessary for the general welfare. They make it possible for leaders to respond to crises and to pursue long-term policies, even though these actions entail short-term costs for the population, because citizens are prepared to give them the benefit of the doubt—in effect, to extend them credit, so that they can undertake actions whose value will not be proven (or disproven) until some time in the future. They increase citizens' readiness to accept conditions that are not entirely satisfactory from the point of view of their subgroup interests (at least in the short run) because they regard these conditions as consistent with the requirements of equity and conducive to long-term benefits for the entire society.

Rasinski, Tyler, and Fridkin (1985) found, in line with this analysis, that perceived legitimacy of political leaders serves to buffer the political system from the drop in support that would otherwise be expected after poor performance (measured by decreased personal outcomes). The public's readiness to maintain trust in political authorities despite perceived shortcomings in their performance facilitates continuity of policy and strengthens the hands of the authorities in the adjudication of domestic conflicts, in the allocation of scarce resources, and in the conduct of external relations. Finally, the presumption of legitimacy of the system and the associated trust in the leadership provide a set of decision rules that permit an orderly process of change in a sharply divided society.

Legitimacy of the Authorities

Once the legitimacy of the system has been established, obedience further depends on the perceived legitimacy of the specific authorities who are issuing the order in the name of that system. Perceived legitimacy of these authorities depends on people's assessment of (a) their qualifications for the positions they are occupying, and (b) the way in which they comport themselves within these positions.

QUALIFICATIONS FOR OFFICE

Authorities are deemed to possess the qualifications for their positions—and hence to be legitimate—if their accession to power conformed to the procedures and criteria prescribed by the particular social unit. The precise nature of the qualifications depends on the type of authority structure involved. Weber's (1947) classic typology, briefly discussed in chapter 3, identifies three pure types of authority distinguished by "the kind of claim to legitimacy typically made by each": traditional, charismatic, and legal authority (p. 325).

Traditional authority rests in the sanctity of an order that has been handed down from the past and is presumed "to have always existed." Thus "the person or persons exercising authority are designated according to traditionally transmitted rules" (p. 341). Highest authority in a patriarchy—the archetype of traditional authority—is exercised by a "chief," who is designated by a definite rule of inheritance or election. When a traditional chief exercises authority with the aid of an administrative staff, the staff is typically recruited from persons bound to the chief by traditional ties (such as relatives, slaves, or dependents who are officers of the household) or by personal loyalty (such as favorites, vassals, or tributary princes). Patriarchal rule may give way to estate systems, in which individuals with some independent social status acquire rights to an office because the patriarchal chief has either bestowed it upon them by privilege or else sold or leased it to them by contract. The legitimacy of both patriarchal and estate authorities rests on their traditional status. Their claim to legitimacy is considered valid if they attained their positions of authority in accordance with traditional rules, which generally means through inheritance or through appointment by or contract with the hereditary chief.

In contrast, charismatic authority, Weber's second fundamental type, is typically found in new political or religious movements formed in opposition to the established order and often with the aim of replacing it. "Charismatic authority repudiates the past, and is in this sense a revolutionary force" (p. 362). Legitimacy does not rest on bureaucratic position or traditional status, but on the leader's personal charisma (gift of grace), expressed through what are seen as superhuman—or at least highly extraordinary—powers or qualities, such as heroic strength, prophetic insight, or therapeutic or legal wisdom. Possession of charisma must be "proven" to the satisfaction of the followers by the performance of miracles, by defeat of their enemy in battle, or by contributions to their welfare. Failure to provide such evidence on a continuing basis may be interpreted as a fall from grace. If a leader "is for long unsuccessful, above all if his leadership fails to benefit his followers, it is likely that his charismatic authority will disappear" (p. 360). Charisma might be related to the two ultimate sources of legitimacy of a system—the extent to which it is perceived as representing the population's group identity and as meeting their needs and interests—which, as we proposed above, play an especially significant role in the establishment of a new order. Leaders may acquire charisma by demonstrating their power to unite the people and to improve their living conditions; they may lose it in the wake of continuing deterioration of economic conditions as a result of their policies and erosion of their personal status as unifying symbols. Both the rise and fall of such quintessential charismatic leaders of the post–World War II period as Kwame Nkrumah and Sukarno—the founding fathers of Ghana and Indonesia, respectively—can be understood in these terms.[12]

Since charismatic authority is based on personal qualities of the leader rather

12. Charisma is an inherently circular concept. Authorities are recognized as legitimate because they have charisma. But an important proof of their charisma, and hence an important determinant of their perceived legitimacy, is the recognition they enjoy among the masses. Weber (1947) points out that "it is recognition on the part of those subject to authority which is decisive for the validity of charisma" (p. 359). He explains that this recognition is not the *basis* of the authorities' claim to legitimacy, as it would be in the case of leadership by consent of the led, but it provides evidence in support of their claim. When charismatic leaders are deprived of this recognition—when followers lose faith in their special leadership qualities—their charismatic authority declines. Thus, one can say that, at least in part, leaders have charisma because they are recognized—but they are recognized because they have charisma. The circularity of charisma means that both the achievement and the loss of charisma-based legitimacy are self-feeding processes. As leaders become recognized, they build up charisma, which in turn enhances and spreads their perceived legitimacy. By the same token, once charismatic leaders begin to lose support, their charisma declines, which in turn accelerates their loss of legitimacy. Removal from office is generally taken as a strong indicator that leaders have lost the gift of grace and leads to a dramatic decline in their legitimacy. Thus, when Nkrumah and Sukarno were each deposed while out of the country, their legitimacy seemed to vanish instantly, despite the immense popular following they had earlier amassed through their personal leadership qualities. Apparently nothing erodes one's charisma more effectively than the loss of power.

than on legal or traditional rules, it faces problems in providing for delegation of authority and particularly for succession to the leadership. Charisma "cannot itself become the basis of a stabilized order without undergoing profound structural changes" (Parsons, 1947, p. 66). These problems create a tendency toward what Weber calls "the routinization of charisma"—at least after the charismatic leader has left the stage—whereby authority becomes traditionalized or legalized. Initially, the leader selects the administrative staff on the basis of their own charismatic qualities, their enthusiasm for the cause, and their devotion to the leader. These qualifications enhance their legitimacy, which ultimately derives from their appointment by the leader and their identification as her disciples and agents. With routinization, norms for the recruitment of staff may develop, often involving training or tests of eligibility. Succession can be handled in several ways that help to preserve the original leader's charisma and to transfer her legitimacy to successors. Charismatic leaders may designate their own successors or someone may be designated by their charismatic followers. Alternatively, hereditary charisma may develop, based on the assumption that charismatic qualities are transmitted through inheritance; in a modified version of this principle, the leaders's heirs may have to demonstrate the possession of charismatic qualities before being entitled to the succession.

Legal or rational-bureaucratic authority, Weber's third type, is the one with which this book is centrally concerned. Legal authority, as exemplified by modern political states and economic enterprises, rests in an impersonal order, shaped by a rational system of abstract normative rules. The purest type of legal authority, as described by Weber, employs a bureaucratic administrative staff. Authorities occupy "offices," which are organized according to a principle of hierarchy, and authority is exercised along hierarchical lines. Within such a structure, authorities' claim to legitimacy is considered valid if they attained their offices in accordance with the legal rules. For those at the top of the hierarchy, the legitimating procedure may take the form of election or it may embody various other principles of succession. For the bureaucracy itself, however, Weber—in keeping with his emphasis on the rational character and efficiency of bureaucracy—specifies technical qualifications as the primary criterion of appointment. Ideally, these would be "tested by examination or guaranteed by diplomas certifying technical training, or both" (Weber, 1947, p. 333).

Later writers (Parsons, 1947; Blau, 1968) have criticized Weber's failure to distinguish between professional and bureaucratic authority and have argued that these two bases of legitimacy need not go together. The legitimacy of authorities within a bureaucratic structure derives strictly from their positions in the hierarchy. The legitimacy of professionals (such as medical or legal "authorities") rests in their possession of technical knowledge and skills. A bureaucracy is a disjoint complex authority system (Coleman, 1980), whereas professional-client relationships can generally be characterized as conjoint simple authority systems. Professional authorities, in contrast to bureaucratic authorities, are not entitled to give orders that their clients are obligated to obey. In our terms, the relationship between a professional and a client is governed by considerations of preference rather than obligation: Clients follow a professional's recommendations because—and insofar as—they consider it in their interest to do so.

Linguistic usage seems to contribute to the tendency to equate these two types of modern authority. A professional is an authority in the sense of having command over a body of knowledge, as in the statement "Dr. X is an authority on tropical diseases." This is different from being an authority in the sense of having the right to command a subordinate to "take out" a machine-gun nest. The distinction is further blurred when we speak of a physician as "prescribing" treatments and of a patient as "following doctor's orders." Perhaps the gap between these two uses of the term *authority* can be partly closed by reference to Hofeller's (1966) distinction, discussed in chapter 4, between legitimate demands and legitimate requests. Bureaucratic authorities have the right to make demands and expect obedience; professional authorities, by virtue of their technical qualifications and their legal status, have the right to make requests of their clients, but they cannot demand obedience.

Despite the differences between bureaucratic and professional authority, there are important continuities between them. Bureaucratic authority in task-oriented organizations often presumes certain professional skills. Although a superordinate's right to give orders to subordinates may derive from her hierarchical position, her legitimacy in the eyes of these subordinates is enhanced if she possesses the skills normally associated with her position. Conversely, professional authority often carries with it high bureaucratic status. For example, by virtue of their professional credentials, physicians represent the highest authority in medical institutions and are entitled to give orders to the nonmedical staff. Thus, whereas professional credentials may not be defining (or even necessary) criteria for legitimacy in legal or rational-bureaucratic authority structures, they contribute to the perceived legitimacy of authority holders.

The continuity between the different bases of legitimacy of rational-bureaucratic authorities is consistent with our view of legitimacy as cutting across the three influence processes of compliance, identification, and internalization.[13] Legitimate influence, of course, contrasts with all three processes, as originally formulated, in that it rests on obligation rather than preference. But there may be different motivational underpinnings for the activation of obligations, corresponding to the three processes. In its purest form, acceptance of legitimacy represents identification with the role of citizen or group member. At that level, the authorities' legitimacy is based on their attractiveness to the person in the sense that he

13. We differ, in this respect, from French and Raven (1959), who view legitimacy as a separate base of power, commensurate with the other four bases that they distinguish—coercive power and reward power (similar to means control in our formulation of compliance), referent power (similar to attractiveness in our formulation of identification), and expert power (similar to credibility in our formulation of internalization). Raven (1965, 1983) has extended the original scheme to include a sixth base of power, information, but he continues to treat legitimate power as commensurate with the other five bases.

wishes to maintain a reciprocal-role relationship with them. Their position enables them to define the requirements of being a good group member, and it is important to the person's self-definition to meet their expectations. Acceptance of legitimacy may, however, be mediated by an underlying concern with socially controlled rewards and punishments or with maximization of shared values—that is, by concerns linked to compliance or internalization, respectively. Insofar as this is true, the authorities' legitimacy may be based in part on their means control or credibility. Weber's failure to make a clear distinction between bureaucratic and professional authority reflects the fact that legitimacy based on hierarchical position is often bolstered by other bases of legitimacy. Bureaucratic authority typically implies means control since higher positions in a hierarchy are usually accompanied by control over rewards and punishments; and where the authority holder also possesses professional credentials, her legitimacy is enhanced by the element of credibility.

BEHAVIOR IN OFFICE

Continuing legitimacy of authorities depends on people's assessment of how they comport themselves in office. The criteria by which the legitimacy of their behavior in office is assessed are directly linked to the conditions that help maintain legitimacy of the system, as discussed earlier. These conditions include (in addition to the existence of procedures and criteria for accession to power, with which we have already dealt): the existence of a shared normative framework, of limits to the use of power, and of mechanisms of recourse and accountability. Thus, the perceived legitimacy of authorities is affected by the assessment of their behavior in office with respect to the following questions:

1. Do they acknowledge and show commitment to the normative framework they share with other members of the society? This framework may take the form of a constitution, a body of law, a set of traditionally transmitted rules, a religious doctrine, a nationalist manifesto, or a political ideology. Authorities are deemed legitimate to the extent they demonstrate by their behavior that they are faithful to this framework and abide by its norms, that they consider themselves fellow members of the community beholden to this framework rather than standing above or apart from the community, and that they recognize that their right to command derives from that framework no less than the ordinary members' duty to obey.

2. Do they abide by the limits on the use of their power set by the rules under which they exercise authority? Such limits are clearly defined in the legal rules governing rational-bureaucratic authority, which spell out the sphere of competence for the various positions in the organizational hierarchy and the procedures to be followed in the exercise of authority. Traditional rules also define the limits of authority, setting out what commands can be given to whom under what circumstances, but tradition usually leaves a certain sphere open for the personal decision of the ruler. For charismatic movements, "there is no such thing as a definite sphere of authority and of competence. . . . There may, however, be

territorial or functional limits to charismatic power and to the individual's 'mission'" (Weber, 1947, p. 360). With the routinization of charisma, further limits are introduced. Whatever the limits set out by a particular framework, authorities who overstep them, by exercising power outside of their designated domain or under improper circumstances, or by using unacceptable procedures, lose legitimacy in the eyes of the population.

3. Do they hold themselves accountable for their actions? Do they recognize the rights of citizens and subordinates to make use of available mechanisms of recourse if they feel that the authorities have abused their power? Do they cooperate with efforts, undertaken within the rules of the system, to call them to account for their policies and actions, and do they respect the decisions and carry out the recommendations generated by such efforts? Authorities lose legitimacy if they sidestep, ignore, or show contempt for the mechanisms of recourse and accountability provided by the society.

Repeated failures by authorities to respect, in their official behavior, the criteria and procedures for the legitimate use of their authority will gradually erode their legitimacy in the eyes of the population. Continuing, uncorrected failures by authorities to meet these criteria and adhere to these procedures will affect the perceived legitimacy of the political system itself.

Legitimacy of the Demand

Perceived legitimacy of the system and the authorities does not ensure obedience unless citizens also perceive the specific demand itself to be legitimate. Two questions arise in determining the legitimacy of a demand. First, is the message conveyed by the authorities in fact a legitimate *demand*, which obligates citizens to obey, in contrast to a request or some other influence attempt, whose acceptance is optional and subject to personal preference? And second, if it is a demand, is it a *legitimate* demand: a proper order that the authorities are entitled to give?

ASSESSING THE OBLIGATORY CHARACTER OF THE DEMAND

To answer the first question, people use different cues to assess the obligatory character of the induced behavior. Three kinds of indicators can be distinguished, corresponding to the three processes of influence (table 5.1) and to the three types of political orientation (table 5.2).

One indicator of the obligatory character of the induced behavior is the existence of sanctions for disobedience. We have already mentioned that sanctions often serve as distinctive cues that enable people to differentiate what is obligatory from what is optional: An influence attempt by authorities is likely to be categorized as a legitimate demand if the rules provide penalties for failure to accept the influence. In the absence of penalties, the influence may still be regarded as legitimate but categorized as a legitimate request (such as "doctor's orders"), which citizens are free to accept or reject. The criterion for determining the obligatory character of the induced behavior in this case, then, is based on the anticipated consequences of disobedience.

A second indicator of the obligatory character of the induced behavior is the invocation of national symbols—or comparable group symbols in the case of social units other than the nation-state—that automatically bring the role of citizen (or group member) and its associated requirements to the fore. The display of the national flag and of the pictures of national leaders, heroes, or martyrs, the playing of the national anthem, the recitation of slogans proclaiming national goals, the recollection of crucial events in the national history, and the parading of troops and military equipment—all have the effect of arousing national loyalty and a sense of duty to support the national cause. Influence attempts surrounded by such symbols are likely to be categorized as legitimate demands to which the individual citizen is obligated to accede. The criterion for determining the obligatory character of the induced behavior in this second case is based on the power of the group symbols to which it is linked.

The third indicator of the obligatory character of the induced behavior is the invocation of central societal values in justification of the demand. The values invoked are legitimating values, in the sense that they are among the values on which the perceived legitimacy of the authorities and of the political system itself ultimately rests. That is, many citizens regard the authorities and the system as legitimate precisely because they see them as promoting and protecting these very values. In chapter 4 we cited the example of authorities who invoke the principle of fair distribution of the burdens of citizenship, or the need to maintain the long-run health of the economy, as justification for the imposition of new taxes. Another example might be the invocation of the need to maintain national security and to protect freedom around the world as justification for a new draft law. In both examples, the demand (to pay taxes or serve in the armed forces) is presented as part of a policy necessary to the achievement and protection of central legitimating values. The point of invoking the legitimating values in this context is not to persuade the public that the policy serves the common interest and should therefore be voluntarily supported but to signal that the demand is indeed legitimate and must be obeyed. Influence attempts that are successfully justified by reference to central values that the authorities are expected to uphold are likely to be categorized as legitimate demands. In this case, then, the criterion for determining the obligatory character of the induced behavior is based on the anticipated consequences of the policy that prompted it.

These different ways of assessing the legitimacy of demands clearly suggest the three processes of influence. In standard influence situations, the introduction of sanctions motivates compliance, the invocation of group symbols motivates identification, and the presentation of value-linked justifications motivates internalization. In the context of legitimate authority, sanctions, group symbols, and societal values perform more of a cuing function than a motivating function. Still, these two functions cannot be entirely separated from each other. Different people, at different times, may be especially responsive to one or the other of these cues, and this responsiveness may reflect their particular motivational orientation to the authorities' demand. Responsiveness to sanctions may indicate an underlying concern with state-controlled rewards and punishments, which makes the person sensitive to the existence of penalties for disobedience as the primary cue for obligatory behavior. Responsiveness to group symbols may indicate an underlying concern with self-definition as a good group member, which makes the person sensitive to the invocation of such symbols as the primary cue for obligatory behavior. Responsiveness to value-linked justifications may indicate an underlying concern with maximizing shared values, which makes the person sensitive to the presentation of such justifications as the primary cue for obligatory behavior.

In our view, then, as we have already mentioned, legitimate authority cuts across the three processes of influence. One can distinguish a compliance-like reaction to a legitimate demand, in which the activation of role requirements and hence the readiness to obey are enhanced by the existence of sanctions, spelling out the consequences of disobedience; an identification-like reaction, in which role requirements are activated and hence obedience is induced by the invocation of group symbols, which bring the role of group member into salience; and an internalization-like reaction, in which the activation of role requirements and the readiness to obey are enhanced by justifications for the demand, alluding to the consequences of the policy behind it for the achievement of group values.[14] Thus, all three types of reactions take place within a framework of legitimacy, but the perception of requiredness takes a qualitatively different form in each case.

We may postulate different motivational bases for these three patterns of reaction to demands from legitimate authorities. In keeping with the distinct antecedents for the three processes of influence (table 5.1), these motivational bases can be briefly described as, respectively, a concern with the social effect, the social anchorage, and the value congruence of one's behavior in response to the authoritative demand. Similarly, we may postulate differences among the three reaction patterns in the nature of the obedient response. In the compliance-type reaction, it tends to be a calculative response, narrowly focused on that which is specifically required; in the identification-type reaction, it tends to be a more enthusiastic response, conforming to a broader image of how a good citizen ought to act; and in the internalization-type reaction, it tends to be a somewhat conditional response, partly shaped by the person's own view of how the behavior demanded of him fits into the larger policy process and relates to the values this process seeks to maximize.

The three indicators of the obligatory character of the induced behavior—sanctions for disobedience, group symbols, and value-linked justifications—are not mutually exclusive and may even be used simultaneously. They may be thought of as a checklist of criteria to which individuals implicitly refer in deter-

14. The second type of reaction represents legitimacy in its purest form, since it focuses directly on the requirements of the citizen role without further inducements. However, sanctions for disobedience and justifications by reference to societal values are both integrally related to the legitimacy of the demand—the first because the authorities' right to issue demands is characteristically accompanied by the right to impose penalties for disobedience, and the second because the legitimacy of demands is ultimately rooted in their presumed contribution to the achievement of societal values.

mining whether a given induction constitutes a legitimate demand. But responsiveness to these different cues and the tendency to react to demands from legitimate authorities in the qualitatively different ways associated with each—in a compliance, identification, or internalization mode—may reflect broader orientations to the political system on the part of different individuals and subgroups. We have already referred to these in table 5.2 as rule, role, and value orientations.[15] These three, in turn, represent different ways in which an individual is integrated into the political system. That is, rule-oriented individuals are primarily integrated through adherence to societal rules, role-oriented individuals through involvement in societal roles, and value-oriented individuals through commitment to societal values. Thus, there is an intimate relationship between the criteria a person uses in assessing the legitimacy of a demand and the way in which the political system acquires legitimacy for him. Rules, roles, or values may be, for any given individual, both the primary source of standards for judging authoritative demands and the primary vehicle for integration in the political system.

ASSESSING THE LEGITIMACY OF THE DEMAND

So far, we have been dealing with the first question a person must answer in determining the legitimacy of a demand—whether the authorities did in fact issue a *demand* that he is obligated to obey. If the person recognizes the induced behavior as a demand, the question still remains whether it is a *legitimate* demand, one that the influencing agent is entitled to issue by virtue of her position. In most authority situations, the legitimacy of specific demands is accepted automatically, as long as the system and the authorities speaking on behalf of it are perceived as legitimate, and as soon as it is clear that the authorities have indeed issued a demand that they mean to be obeyed. Such automatic acceptance of the legitimacy of specific demands—even when issued by otherwise legitimate authorities—is not universal, however. There are a number of criteria by which citizens can judge whether a particular demand is legitimate, closely related to the proce-

---

15. It should be noted that all three of these orientations refer to the *role* of the group member and its requirements. In role orientation, however, the emphasis is on the role as an end in itself; the person is primarily concerned with his self-concept as a good group member, who lives up to the obligations of his role. In rule orientation, the emphasis is on adherence to the rules—on conforming to the specific behavioral requirements of the member role. In value orientation, the emphasis is on maximization of the societal values that underlie the member role. In the normal course of events, value orientation implies a commitment to the member role and readiness to follow the rules. Similarly, role orientation implies a readiness to follow the rules. In a sense, then, the three orientations are hierarchically related to one another. They are qualitatively distinct, however, and the "higher" orientations do not simply subsume the "lower" ones. Thus, for example, as we shall elaborate in chapter 11, value-oriented citizens—though they normally follow the rules, since they regard them as essential to maintaining the integrity of the state to which they are committed—are prepared on occasion to break certain rules, when they see these as inconsistent with what they regard as fundamental societal values.

dural criteria discussed above for judging the continuing legitimacy of a system and of the authority holders within it:

1. Is the demand within the "sphere of competence" of the authorities—within the domain in which they are entitled to issue demands?
2. Does the demand conform to the procedures for exercising authority prescribed by the rules (legal or traditional) to which the authorities are subject?
3. Is the demand being applied equitably to the different individuals and subgroups that make up the population?
4. Is the demand consistent with the larger normative framework the authorities share with other citizens? For example, apart from being executed according to the legally prescribed procedures, is the demand itself constitutional?
5. Is the policy in which this demand is embedded congruent with the stated values of the political system—values on which its perceived legitimacy ultimately rests?

A negative answer to one or more of these questions constitutes grounds, within a democratic framework of legitimacy, for challenging the legitimacy of the demand and for refusing to obey it. Indeed, having criteria for challenging the legitimacy of demands is implicit in the concept of legitimacy itself. Nevertheless, empirical evidence shows that it is extremely difficult to mount such challenges— and more so for some individuals than for others. In the next chapter, we turn to a discussion of the sources of these difficulties. Subsequent chapters will discuss individual differences in the ability to surmount them.

6 | Challenging Authority

In exploring the difficulties faced by individuals who contemplate challenging authority, we focus primarily on political authority: on the relationship of the citizen to the state and to the various institutions that are backed by the laws and power of the state or its subdivisions. These include, for example, the institutions charged with administering criminal justice, collecting taxes, selecting men for military service, ensuring public safety, regulating business activities, and distributing benefits. Military authority—a central concern of this book—is a special case within this larger category. Members of the military—whether they volunteered or were drafted—are part of a strict hierarchy with a strong tradition of obedience, whose rules and regulations are backed by the political state. The backing of the state and its legal structure lend a unique quality to the relationships between citizens and officialdom or among the different ranks within the military hierarchy, but many of the issues to be discussed apply to authority relationships in other settings as well. What we learn about political or military authority may thus contribute to our understanding of other authority situations, and vice versa, as long as we remain sensitive to the special features of each type of situation. (See also chapter 13.)

Difficulties in challenging political authority arise at both the macrolevel and the microlevel. At the macrolevel, we refer to the confrontation between the prerogatives of the state and the rights of the individual. In a similar vein, one can speak of the rules and regulations that govern the relationships between superiors and subordinates in any bureaucratic authority structure. At the microlevel, we refer to face-to-face encounters between citizens and the officials who represent political authority for any given purpose. Here, the detailed studies of interactions with authority in nonpolitical settings (for example, Milgram, 1974; Gamson et al., 1982) can be a source of useful insights into what happens in political or military contexts.

A macrolevel analysis, as we have seen in the preceding chapter, suggests that there are many bases for challenging the legitimacy of a demand from political (or other) authorities. At the most fundamental level, a demand is automatically illegitimate if those who issue it—the state itself or the incumbent authorities—lack legitimacy in the eyes of the population or a particular segment of the population. It does not follow, however, that citizens will necessarily challenge authority and disobey under these circumstances. For one thing, they often obey simply out of compliance—that is, in order to avoid the punishment that disobedience would bring upon them. Moreover, a regime that falls short in providing the usual sources of legitimacy for a population group—in that it does not adequately represent their group identity or meet their needs and interests—is often accepted as legitimate because these conditions have prevailed over a long period of time and people have never conceived of alternative arrangements. In the absence of an alternative ideological framework that defines the existing order as unjust, people tend to ascribe legitimacy to the established pattern of social stratification even though it operates to their own disadvantage and does not fully include them in the national identity and the society's benefits. When people disobey because they have come to see the regime as unjust and illegitimate, they have essentially reached the point of rebellion or revolution.

We do not propose to address the conditions for rebellion or revolution directly here. We intend, instead, to take a narrower focus: to examine the possibilities for challenging the legitimacy of specific demands among individuals who on the whole accept the legitimacy of the state and of the incumbent authorities. The challenge to authority under these circumstances may take legal or extralegal forms, sometimes both in combination. The ultimate legal form in the United States is a challenge to the constitutionality of a law, brought before the Supreme Court. The ultimate extralegal form is civil disobedience.

At the end of chapter 5, we listed five criteria by which citizens can assess and potentially challenge the legitimacy of a specific demand. The right to challenge demands on these or comparable bases is built into the very definition of legitimacy. To be perceived as legitimate, a demand must conform to certain criteria and citizens must be in a position to evaluate it accordingly. Yet the striking phenomenon of hierarchies of authority—brought to its most dramatic and devastating expression in the twentieth-century state—is the readiness of citizens to accept orders unquestioningly. More often than not citizens obey, even when obedience entails enormous personal sacrifices or the commitment of actions that, under other circumstances, they would consider morally reprehensible.

The explanation for this paradox is not hard to find. Central to the logic underlying the concept of legitimacy is the existence of a high threshold for disobedience. Legitimate rule tends to instill among citizens a sense of trust in the authorities and to incline citizens to give the authorities the benefit of the doubt, even when particular policies are incongruent with their personal preferences or group interests. In pluralistic democracies, differences in interests and values among subgroups are contested through the electoral process and the policy debate. However, once a law is passed, once a policy is put into effect, once an order is issued, the individual citizen is expected to obey. This expectation is written into the structure and the social definition of authority situations. Although authority situations differ in how tightly they are structured, the built-in expectation of obedience is a characteristic they all share—one that follows from our earlier discussion of authority as an influence situation in which individuals focus on role obligations in contrast to personal preferences.

At the microlevel, the expectation of obedience is conveyed in the typical authority situation through various cues: visible indications that this is an "official" situation (such as the government seal or the president's picture prominently displayed), trappings attesting to the legitimacy of the resident authorities (such as the name plates on their doors, the diplomas on their walls, the uniforms they wear), and concrete ways of distinguishing between those who give the orders and those who are expected to follow them (such as differences in the insignia on their uniforms or in their way of dressing, or perhaps in their gender or skin color). Moreover, the expectation of obedience is heavily supported by social norms and sanctions, which may take the form of legal penalties when an individual disobeys military or other official orders. The net effect of these built-in expectations is that individuals are channeled into a pattern of behavior marked by automatic, unquestioning obedience. In the normal course of events, the option of disobedience does not even enter into consideration. Both parties play their respective parts in the prescribed script by which the situation is defined. Everything proceeds on the assumption that the individual must and will obey.

To avail themselves of the right to challenge authority's demands on the basis of one or another of the criteria we have described, citizens have to break out of the pattern of behavior into which they have been channeled and violate the assumption on which their relationship to the authorities has been proceeding—in short, they have to redefine the situation. They cannot simply ignore the authoritative demands or choose to overrule them on the basis of personal preferences or group interests. They can base their challenge only on the claim that the demands are illegitimate—that, contrary to the way in which the situation has hitherto been defined, the authorities are not entitled to make these demands and the citizens, therefore, are not obligated to obey them. But in this case the burden of proof lies almost entirely with the citizens who seek to mount the challenge. The authorities' demands are presumed to be legitimate until proven illegitimate.

The ability to redefine the authority situation and hence to challenge authoritative demands—at the macro- and the microlevels—presupposes two psychological conditions that are not readily available. In the cognitive sphere, individuals must be aware of—or able to conceive of—alternative definitions of the situation and interpretations of its requirements. In the motivational sphere, they must be prepared to disrupt the established social order and the smoothness of social interaction and to suffer the consequences of such disruption. These two psychological conditions are closely linked to access to material resources, without which individuals are often unable to learn about available options or to afford the risk of disruption. As long as people are unaware of alternatives and unwilling to risk disruption, they are likely to accept the conventional definition of the situation as self-evident and inevitable and to shy away from any effort to challenge it.

The cognitive and motivational obstacles to redefining an authority situation manifest themselves both at the macrolevel and at the microlevel, and we now turn to a discussion of each.

Macrolevel Obstacles to Challenging Authority

At the macrolevel, the definition of an authority situation as self-evidently legitimate and hence requiring obedience is anchored in established social structures and institutions. Thus, an invoice presented by the Internal Revenue Service, an induction notice from the Selective Service System, a command issued by a military officer to a subordinate, or a demand conveyed by a police officer, a welfare official, a school principal, a public health doctor, or an airline pilot within their respective domains is ultimately backed by the authority of the state. Each of these orders occurs within a clearly demarked institutional context; it is supported by an established ideology; it is executed through formal offices and official agents; it is prescribed by a set of legal and administrative rules; and compliance to it is enforced by codified sanctions. To challenge such a demand, the individual must step outside this definition of the situation and redefine the demand as illegitimate.

Such a challenge almost invariably requires recourse to an alternative authority that is at least equal in status to the one issuing the demand. Preferably, this can be described as a "higher authority," making countervailing demands. The higher authority may be within the system, taking the form of a person who outranks the one who gave the initial order in a hierarchical authority structure or the form of a set of legal regulations or a constitution. Alternatively, the higher authority may be outside the system, taking the form of the will of God or one's personal conscience. If the appeal to higher authority is to have any standing, both parties— superior and subordinate—must accept its legitimacy. Even when they do, the demands of the higher authority are often a matter of interpretation. The issue is usually straightforward if we can challenge a lieutenant's order by reference to a captain's contrary order. But as we move from this relatively simple case to challenges based on the authority of legal rules, the Constitution, the will of God, or personal conscience, we face the progressively more difficult problem of differences in the *interpretation* of demands from higher authority. Thus, if individual citizens are to claim the right to challenge an authority's demands and to have any hope of prevailing in such a claim, they must have a credible basis for an alternative interpretation of the demands of higher authority.

Authority systems—and the political state, in particular—function in a way that tends to inhibit members' recourse to alternative sources of authority within and outside the system. Authorities typically operate in a framework that supports their claim to having the final say and takes citizens' obedience for granted. Citizens are not encouraged to question, to negotiate, or to seek second opinions. Rarely are they made aware of the existence of higher authorities with potentially competing demands or of the possibility of alternative interpretations of what higher authority requires. To acknowledge the existence of such alternatives would weaken the authorities' position and reduce the automatic obedience on which the smooth functioning of their offices depends. Even when citizens are aware of the existence of higher authorities, they are often discouraged from appealing to them. Access may be available only at considerable cost and only to those who are prepared to disrupt the established order. Moreover, higher authorities may at times be inclined to support the lower authorities rather than the citizens who challenge their demands. Thus, individuals seeking the support of higher authorities in their challenge to authority must, at best, enter into an uneven competition with those they are challenging. What are the possibilities and limits of the recourse to higher authority available to them, both outside and within the political system?

RECOURSE TO HIGHER AUTHORITY OUTSIDE THE SYSTEM

Acceptance of a higher authority outside the system clearly represents a threat to the modern nation-state's sovereignty—to its claim to be the social unit in which paramount authority is vested. Thus, citizens are granted the right to challenge demands of the state by recourse to a higher outside authority only rarely and in a very circumscribed form. Perhaps the best example, within Western democracies, of the state's willingness to grant such a right is conscientious objection to military service. Citizens of the United States, for example, are entitled to claim the status of conscientious objector on the basis of the higher authority of a religious framework—and, only recently and cautiously, on that of a personal moral framework.

The special status accorded to religion as an acceptable higher authority under narrowly prescribed circumstances is probably due to the historic relationship between religion and the state. Historically, the legitimacy of the state in the West ultimately rested in the will of God. In principle, therefore, individuals were entitled to disobey the king's law if it violated God's law. In practice, of course, any potential challenge to the king had to confront the question of who determines the will of God. The official religious hierarchy often supported the king's version of God's will. An effective challenge based on higher authority was possible, therefore, only when the religious hierarchy used its authority to support such a challenge, or when credible religious authorities outside of the official hierarchy— such as the Hebrew prophets or the Christian saints—were available to offer an alternative interpretation of God's will.

The modern nation-state, in keeping with its historic link to religion, does admit of some higher law against which its dictates can be tested. Consistency with the will of God remains an implicit source of the state's legitimacy—a source to which symbolic and ritualistic references are often made—as well as a criterion for assessing its legitimacy. It is not surprising that in Catholic countries as diverse as Poland, Nicaragua, and the Philippines the church has been an effective vehicle for challenging the legitimacy of the state. This continuing role of the church in political legitimation helps explain the acceptability of religiously based conscientious objection. In a sense, when citizens ground their objection to military service in the higher authority of religion, they are appealing to the ultimate authority recognized by the state itself, though they disagree with the state in their interpretation of that authority's demands. The state can "afford" to be magnanimous to those claiming a different interpretation, as long as the scope of the disobedience is limited and the number of citizens involved remains small.

The history of the legal and judicial treatment of conscientious objection in the United States demonstrates that the state is most comfortable with claims for C.O. status based on obedience to specific religious authorities and on minimal individual judgment. Thus, claims for conscientious objection based on membership in one of the historic peace churches for whom pacifism is a matter of church doctrine—such as the Quakers, Mennonites, and Brethren—were most readily granted. Next, the Selective Service law accepted claims based on membership in an organized church for which pacifism is not doctrinally required, but which recognizes it as an option. Gradually, the right to conscientious objection was broadened to include those who base their position on religious training and belief in a Supreme Being, even if it is outside an organized church. Finally, the Supreme Court accepted claims based on a coherent set of deeply held moral or ethical beliefs, equivalent to beliefs based on a relationship to a Supreme Being.

It is significant that the law recognizes conscientious objection only on the basis of belief—whether religious or moral—"against participation in war in any form." The law as of now does not recognize selective conscientious objection, that is, objection based on opposition to a specific war. Apparently, the state can tolerate exempting a small minority of citizens from obedience to one of its demands because a higher authority leaves them no other choice—because the religious or moral law to which they are beholden bars them from participation in any war. These exceptions reinforce the general rule that the individual citizen is obligated to obey the demands of authorities; the exception is permitted only because the individual claims an overriding obligation to a higher authority—one, moreover, to which the state itself gives obeisance. What is far more difficult for the state to tolerate is disobedience based on a citizen's personal judgment about the morality of a particular war. Such judgments may be dictated by ideological commitments or group loyalties—alternative sources of authority that the state does not accept. Even if they are anchored in religious beliefs, they come dangerously close (from the state's point of view) to making obedience a matter of preference rather than obligation.

Selective conscientious objectors typically also have recourse to a higher authority: their individual conscience. In a religious framework, conscience reflects their personal interpretation of God's will. In a secular framework, it reflects their personal determination of what is required for the common good. In either event, an open-ended right of citizens to condition their obedience on personal judgment of what their conscience requires, on a case-to-case basis, has historically been seen as an unacceptable threat to the authority of the state. In fact, of course, as Walzer (1970) points out, when people announce that they are bound to God or higher law "in conscience," they are usually not acting as isolated individuals. He argues that "the individual's understanding of God or the higher law is always acquired within a group" and the individual's "obligation to either is at the same time an obligation to the group and to its members" (p. 5). But such groups themselves are no more acceptable to the state than individual conscience as alternative sources of authority.

In general, conscientious objection to military service still represents an option that is not readily available to most young men. For example, the Selective Service System in the United States, while duly informing draft registrants of the right to claim C.O. status, does not go out of its way to explain the criteria by which qualification is determined, to specify the evidence that claimants are expected to provide, or to inform them of the appeals to which they are entitled. Potential C.O.s thus need outside help in order to become fully aware of the options they have and the steps they must take in order to take advantage of them. If they seriously consider taking a C.O. position, they need access to historical and philosophical information about conscientious objection, to legal counseling about their rights under the draft regulations, and to legal defense if their stand brings them into conflict with the law. It is not surprising, therefore, that this alternative is rarely considered or even conceived of by men outside of the white, middle-class, college-bound or college-educated population (Perry, 1985).

In processing claims of conscientious objection, the Selective Service System has tended to place the burden of proof on the claimant. The regulations define a C.O. as someone "who has been found, by reason of religious, ethical, or moral beliefs to be conscientiously opposed to participation in war in any form." The instructions to registrants, however, go beyond the requirement to demonstrate belief when they state: "To qualify, you must establish to the satisfaction of the board that your conscience, spurred by deeply held moral, ethical, or religious beliefs, would give you no rest or peace if you participate in . . . military service and training in any war. You must also show that you are sincere in your claimed beliefs" (see Yolton, 1986). The manual for Selective Service personnel and board members goes even further in stating that "the registrant must *prove* to the satisfaction of the board that his claim is truly held in order to be found eligible for the classification" (emphasis added). The manual also specifies that "moral, ethical, or religious beliefs do not include essentially political, sociological, or philosophical views."

The relatively narrow definition and the even narrower interpretation of the criteria for C.O. status tend to place potential C.O.s in an adversarial relationship vis-à-vis the authorities. They may find themselves in a position of noncooperation with the system, particularly if they want to base their stand on individual conscience without institutionalized authority support, or if their objection is directed to a particular war rather than to all wars, or if they are reluctant to deal with the draft system at all. Thus, despite official recognition of the right to conscientious objection to military service, those who choose to exercise that right must take the risk of being viewed (and treated) as deviants or toublemakers, or even as cowards or traitors.

Apart from conscientious objection to military service, there is little precedent for the state's willingness to grant citizens the right to challenge an order by recourse to a higher authority outside of the system. There have been many cases throughout history, however, in which individuals—often joining forces in a social movement—have challenged authority at their own risk, justifying their action in the name of a higher authority. A recent example in the United States is the sanctuary movement. Churches and synagogues in different parts of the country have been sheltering Central American refugees, declared to be illegal aliens by the Immigration and Naturalization Service, and preventing their deportation to their countries of origin (for most of them Guatemala or El Salvador). In doing so, they are knowingly violating a law whose enforcement they consider to be inconsistent with their obligations to God's higher law.

The religious foundation of the sanctuary movement is a major source of its strength. For the participants in the movement, their religious commitment and membership in a religious community provide the ideological and social supports necessary to sustain their willingness not only to take risks and make sacrifices, but also to stand outside of the law. While this function could also be fulfilled by a secular movement, the sanctuary movement's religious foundation provides another and more unique advantage: Religion, as we have noted, enjoys a special status as a higher authority which the state respects and to which it extends limited recognition. By basing its challenge to the state on the higher authority of religion, therefore, the movement has been effective in arousing public sympathy and is causing embarrassment to the political authorities. Nevertheless, the authorities have not been deterred from bringing eight religious activists from the movement to trial in New Mexico, declaring their motives irrelevant, and convicting them of the crime of assisting illegal aliens. Clearly, the right to challenge the authority of the state by recourse to the higher authority of God is severely circumscribed and citizens are not encouraged to avail themselves of that right.[1]

RECOURSE TO HIGHER AUTHORITY WITHIN THE SYSTEM

Challenges to authoritative demands by recourse to higher authority *within* the system are less threatening to the authority structure than challenges attributed to

1. There is another condition under which disobedience may be justified by reference to an outside authority, which is not necessarily higher than that of the state but is entitled to make alternative claims of its own. Western democracies recognize certain domains of life to which the authority of the state does not extend. Once again, religion provides a good example: Citizens may be excused from certain obligations if these come into conflict with religious requirements. Other examples come from those domains that are considered private, such as family relations, professional relations (those between doctor and patient or attorney and client, for example), and the relationship between journalists and their sources. The state is expected to maintain the integrity of these relationships and to interfere in them only with great reluctance. Thus, citizens may refuse official requests for information derived from these relationships by claiming the right to privileged communication. Even though these private domains are accorded a certain independent status, the state can at times overrule claims based on them if it declares such actions to be required by the public interest and if it follows the procedures prescribed for such occasions. Citizens who insist on giving priority to the obligations of an alternative domain—as journalists periodically do when they defy court orders to reveal their confidential sources—run the risk of fines and incarceration.

the demands of outside authorities. Even so, they are problematic for the authority holders because they undermine the social expectation that obedience to authoritative demands is the normal, ubiquitous response of citizens. Thus, average citizens generally are not informed of the availability of higher authorities who might offer alternative interpretations of what is required of them, and access to such alternative authorities tends to be costly and difficult.

Recourse to higher authority within the system may take several forms. The simplest, least ambiguous way of challenging the demand of an authority is to appeal to that authority's own superior or to any higher authority within the same bureaucratic hierarchy. For example, an enlisted man could neutralize a demand from his lieutenant by confronting it with a countervailing demand from the captain or with the captain's contrary interpretation of what is required. Mounting such challenges, however, often has its own complications. It is not always clear what a citizen's or subordinate's rights of appeal are and to which office a particular appeal is to be directed. Those who succeed in getting a hearing find that higher authorities within a bureaucracy tend to give the benefit of the doubt to the lower authorities; they are reluctant to overrule them out of concern with maintaining the efficiency and morale of the entire authority structure. Moreover, those who challenge an order by turning upward in the hierarchy risk being identified as troublemakers and suffering the consequences. If they lose their appeal, they can anticipate retaliation from the authorities whom they challenged. And even if they win their appeal, they are by no means protected against retaliation. Thus, the cognitive and motivational obstacles to challenging authoritative demands arise even in this relatively simple case.[2]

A second and more difficult form of challenge within the system is by recourse to the higher authority of the law or of the regulations governing the particular bureaucracy. Here challengers maintain, on procedural or substantive grounds, that the order violates the law or regulations. Procedurally, they may argue that the order exceeds the authority of the one who gave it—which is to say, that it is outside of her or his domain of authority; or that it deviates from the prescribed rules by which power is to be exercised within the bureaucracy. Substantively, they may argue that the order is invalid because it requires actions that are themselves illegal or prohibited by the governing regulations (see Kadish and Kadish, 1973, pp. 100–120). Such challenges are difficult because they imply a level of detailed knowledge about the law and the mechanisms for invoking it that is not available to average citizens. To obtain such information and to pursue the challenge through the appropriate channels, citizens generally require technical and financial resources that are beyond their means, unless they find public organizations—dedicated to legal aid, civil rights, civil liberties, or a particular substantive issue—to take on their case. A further difficulty in mounting a legal challenge

---

2. The fate of whistle-blowers in industry or government provides an excellent illustration of the personal cost of challenging authority—whether or not the challenge succeeds (see, for example, Glazer and Glazer, 1986; Perrucci, Anderson, Schendel, and Trachtman, 1980; Peters and Branch, 1972).

arises from the fact that it is often necessary to refuse an order before contesting its legality. Thus, if the challenge fails, challengers run the risk of being penalized for having refused a legal order (see Kadish and Kadish, 1973, pp. 153–70). Even if the challenge ultimately succeeds, challengers place themselves in the position of lawbreakers, deviants, and troublemakers, subject to all of the social opprobrium attendant upon such acts. Challenges of this sort, therefore, are unlikely to occur in the absence of a strong social network providing both material and emotional support.

Similar difficulties, but of even greater magnitude, are likely to confront a third type of challenge to an order—a challenge based on recourse to the higher authority of the constitution (or its functional equivalent in polities that have no written constitution). The claim here is that the order is illegitimate, even though it conforms to existing law, because the law itself violates the constitution (or the basic law) of the state. Operationally, such a challenge in the United States takes the form of an appeal to the Supreme Court. Thus, during the 1950s, various laws that mandated racial segregation were challenged in the courts and were eventually overturned when the Supreme Court declared them unconstitutional. These court tests often started with deliberate violations of the laws to be challenged—for example, refusal by black citizens of an order to leave facilities that were, by state law, restricted to whites. Challenging the constitutionality of a law is even more difficult than challenging the legality of an order because judgments of what the constitution requires are very much subject to differences in interpretation. To make such a challenge is, therefore, extremely risky, since one cannot readily predict its outcome. Of course, bringing a case before the Supreme Court also requires enormous technical and financial resources.

A constitutional challenge clearly implies a claim that existing law violates the underlying values of the society, which are embodied in the constitution. It is also possible, however, to base a challenge directly on the claim that an order—or the policy from which it emerged—violates societal values, without taking legal action or even without claiming that the order is illegal. The distinction between a constitutional challenge and this fourth type of challenge is similar to that drawn by Kadish and Kadish (1973, p. 182) between legitimated disobedience and civil disobedience. Challenges of this kind are the most difficult of all, since the claims they are based on are clearly in the realm of judgment and interpretation. In particular, if the challenge is directed at policies formulated and executed by legal and traditional procedures, it rests entirely on the claim that the policy is immoral. The uncertain legal standing of such a claim probably led the proponents of civil disobedience in opposition to the Vietnam War to couple their attack on the morality of the war with an attack on its legality: The argument that the war was illegal provided a more concrete, objective justification for their own illegal challenge.

The challenge to authoritative orders on the grounds that they are inconsistent with fundamental societal values represents an appeal to higher authority within the system in the sense that the promotion of certain values—relating to the common good—is the ultimate source of the system's legitimacy. Those who mount such a challenge are in effect claiming that their interpretation of the common good, and hence of the requirements for legitimate rule, is more authentic than that of the authorities. Such a claim is reminiscent of the statements of the ancient prophets, except that they benefited from the presumption of direct access to the highest authority, which greatly enhanced the credibility of their alternative interpretations.

In a secular context, dissent and disobedience in the name of fundamental societal values often have no greater credibility than challenges based on individual conscience alone, but they do have one advantage: The disobedience is justified, not by obligations to external forces, but by the requirements of the society itself. Americans who engaged in acts of civil disobedience directed at racial segregation or U.S. involvement in Vietnam generally spoke as true patriots, trying to uphold the integrity of the country and in fact enhance the legitimacy of the government by insisting on policies congruent with the system's legitimating values. Such claims can be effective—not unlike the claims of the ancient prophets—insofar as they are linked to authentic traditional values widely shared within the society, even if these values have been latent for some time.[3] The credibility and effectiveness of the challengers is enhanced to the extent that their commitment to the system is beyond question and has been demonstrated by prior occupancy of high positions within the social structure and contributions to the general welfare. Such a history lends authenticity to the claim that their disobedience is responsive to a higher authority within the system.[4]

The difficulty in challenging the legitimacy of authoritative demands on the grounds that they are inconsistent with underlying societal values—and, even more so, on the grounds of individual conscience—is inherent in the nature of legitimate authority. There is an inevitable tension between the requirement to maintain the legitimacy of the state, thus enabling the authorities to govern effectively and justly, and the citizens' right and obligation to make independent judgments and follow the dictates of conscience. Although we believe that a just society cannot do without (civil) disobedience any more than it can do without (legitimate) authority, we also consider it impossible to extend an *automatic* right to disobey legitimately generated demands to any citizens who claim that these demands contradict their interpretation of the common good or violate their individual conscience. As we shall explicate in the concluding chapter, our image of a good society is one that fosters among its members a capacity and willingness

3. An important contributing factor to the success of the civil rights movement, including its campaigns of civil disobedience and nonviolent resistance, was the fact that it spoke to values widely shared within the U.S. population—even if these values were also widely ignored and violated in practice. Gunnar Myrdal's classic work, *An American Dilemma* (1944), foresaw the significance of these values in focusing its analysis on the conflict between "The American Creed," with its requirement of equal treatment on the basis of universalistic criteria, and the particularistic requirements of loyalty to one's own race and color.

4. See, in this connection, E. P. Hollander's (1958) concept of "idiosyncrasy credits."

to challenge the authorities' interpretation of what is consistent with societal values and required for the common good, but we also assume that such challenges—particularly when they take the form of outright disobedience—cannot be undertaken without some cost to the individual.

Even less basic challenges—such as appeals up the hierarchy or refusal to obey an order that is deemed illegal—are confronted with macrolevel obstacles inherent in the nature of legitimate authority. The obligation to obey is supported by powerful social norms. To counteract this sense of obligation requires a redefinition of the situation which, as we have proposed, depends on cognitive and motivational conditions that are not readily available. Challenging the legitimacy of an order presupposes a degree of awareness of and certainty about alternative definitions that the average citizen does not possess. In contrast to their own perceived lack of knowledge, most citizens tend to ascribe special knowledge and expertise to the authorities (that is, to blend professional authority into their image of bureaucratic authority) that the average citizen could not possibly match. Moreover, challenging the legitimacy of an authoritative demand presupposes a readiness to disrupt the social order despite all of the repercussions that this might entail: stigmatization as a troublemaker or traitor—which, with current technology, could easily become part of a person's computerized record for life; legal sanctions if the challenge is denied by the higher authority to whom the individual appealed; and various forms of harassment and retaliation even if the challenge is sustained. In sum, the very nature of legitimate authority, while providing built-in rights to challenge authoritative demands, also militates against the use of these rights. Institutional changes can make it easier for citizens to avail themselves of their right to challenge. But, even under the best of circumstances—given the structure of authority systems—individuals contemplating disobedience will have to take some initiative in informing themselves of alternative definitions of the situation and will have to be prepared to pay the price for disrupting the social order. Such a stance by individual citizens presupposes, in turn, the availability of effective social supports for challenging authority.

Microlevel Obstacles to Challenging Authority

The individual's relationship to authority structures at the macrolevel is typically acted out at the microlevel. It is in the course of face-to-face interactions in concrete authority situations that individuals encounter authority and make the decision whether to obey or disobey. To challenge an order, citizens must redefine not only the larger social context in which the authority is embedded, but also the immediate interaction situation in which they are encountering the authority. The structural obstacles to challenging authority discussed in the preceding section are reflected and further reinforced at the microlevel. Cognitively, in addition to being only dimly aware of alternative authorities or interpretations of authority, citizens are generally unfamiliar with the dimensions of the situation in which they find themselves and the options available to them within it. Motivationally, in addition to being concerned about possible sanctions and other negative consequences of disobedience, citizens worry about the embarrassment to which they would expose themselves by disrupting the smooth flow of interaction.

These obstacles manifest themselves in the microlevel situations in which citizens encounter the representatives of political authority. We shall specify and clarify their operation, however, by examining experimental studies of obedience and, in particular, the well-known experiments by Stanley Milgram (1974). The stylized character of the experiment makes it easier to see the structure of the authority situation and the dynamics of the individual's encounter with authority. Moreover, Milgram's research has the advantage of exploring a series of variations of the standard experimental situation, which help us identify some of the conditions that strengthen or weaken the obstacles to challenging authority—the binding and opposing forces that push the level of obedience up or down.

THE STRUCTURE OF THE EXPERIMENTAL SITUATION

In describing the main features of Milgram's experiments, we will focus on the standard experimental situation, from which the most dramatic and most widely cited findings are derived. The research program included seventeen additional experiments in which one or another feature of the standard situation was varied, making it possible to assess the effects of each variation on the observed level of obedience.

The participants in the experiment were male volunteers from New Haven, Connecticut, who responded to a newspaper advertisement or mail solicitation.[5] They were between twenty and fifty years of age and covered a wide range in educational background and occupational status. The experiment took place at Yale University.

On arriving at the laboratory, each participant received four dollars (plus fifty cents for carfare)—the payment promised for his participation in a one-hour experiment. At the laboratory, each participant joined another man who was introduced as a fellow participant but who actually had been trained to perform the role of the victim in this experimental drama. The two men were told that they would be taking part in a study of memory and learning, in which one would act as "teacher" and the other as "learrner." They were asked to draw slips of paper as "the fairest way" of designating who was to perform which function. The drawing was rigged, however, so that the naive participant was always chosen to be the teacher.

The experimenter explains that the study is concerned with the effects of punishment on learning. The learner is conducted into a room, seated in a chair, his arms strapped

---

5. In one of the experiments, the naive participants (the teachers, not the learners) were women (see Milgram, 1974, pp. 62–63, 77–85). The level of obedience among female participants was virtually identical to that for males, although Milgram reports that the women generally demonstrated a higher level of conflict.

to prevent excessive movement, and an electrode attached to his wrist. He is told that he is to learn a list of word pairs; whenever he makes an error, he will receive electric shocks of increasing intensity.

The real focus of the experiment is the teacher. After watching the learner being strapped into place, he is taken into the main experimental room and seated before an impressive shock generator. Its main feature is a horizontal line of thirty switches, varying from 15 volts to 450 volts, in 15-volt increments. There are also verbal designations which range from SLIGHT SHOCK to DANGER-SEVERE SHOCK.[6] The teacher is told that he is to administer the learning test to the man in the other room. When the learner responds correctly, the teacher moves on to the next item; when the other man gives an incorrect answer, the teacher is to give him an electric shock. He is to start at the lowest level (15 volts) and to increase the level each time the man makes an error, going through 30 volts, 45 volts, and so on. (Milgram, 1974, p. 3)

As the experimental task proceeded, the teacher, according to his instructions, administered shocks of increasing intensity after each error made by the learner. Starting at the 75-volt level, the learner began to indicate discomfort with increasing degrees of intensity. Although, in the baseline condition, the learner was in another room, his reactions could be clearly heard by the teacher. The learner, in fact, was not connected to the generator and received no shocks at all. His reactions—which sounded very convincing and whose authenticity was not questioned by the naive participants—were prerecorded so that each learner was exposed to a standardized set of protests from the victim. Starting with short grunts, the learner's protests gradually escalated—as the shock level increased—to verbal complaints, painful groans, vehement demands to be released from the experiment, and finally an agonized scream. In one version of the baseline experiment, the learner, having alluded to a mild heart condition during the initial briefing, shouted repeatedly that his heart was bothering him.[7]

Finally, the learner announced that he would no longer provide answers to the memory test. After the next shock he merely screamed, and after that, he fell completely silent. The experimenter instructed the learner to treat the absence of a response as a wrong answer and to continue administering shocks of increasing intensity each time the learner failed to respond.

Throughout the experiment, whenever the teacher turned to the experimenter for advice on whether to continue in the face of the learner's protests, he was simply asked to continue. If the teacher asked whether the shocks might cause injury to the learner, the experimenter responded: "Although the shocks may be painful, there is no permanent tissue damage, so please go on." If the teacher persisted in his questioning or expressed unwillingness to continue, the experimenter responded with a series of three successively more forceful prods: "the experiment requires that you continue"; "it is absolutely essential that you con-

---

6. This designation in fact appeared under the switch for 375 volts. The last two switches (435 and 450 volts) were simply marked XXX.

7. This variation, incidentally, had no effect on the average level of obedience displayed by the participants.

tinue"; "you have no other choice, you *must* go on." If the teacher refused to continue after this final prod, the experiment was terminated. The main measure of obedience was the maximum shock a participant administered before refusing to go further. In the baseline experiments just described, almost two thirds of the participants went all the way, administering shocks up to the highest level of 450 volts without breaking off.[8] Among those who refused to go on, there was considerable variation in the point at which they actually broke off.

We can gain some understanding of the high level of obedience manifested in this experiment by imagining how the naive participant may have experienced the situation. Such an exercise should put into relief the obstacles to challenging authority that arise in the microprocesses in which authority relationships are acted out. The laboratory situation is a genuine authority situation in its own right. One of the outstanding features of Milgram's research is that he utilized the structure and the social definition of the experimental situation itself as a vehicle for studying the phenomenon of obedience. Unlike most social-psychological experiments, the obedience studies were not mere simulations of the phenomenon to be studied. They observed the phenomenon of obedience to authority in situ— in one of the variety of real-life situations, namely, the scientific laboratory, in which it manifests itself. How much one can generalize from this situation to other situations remains an open question, of course, as it does in all empirical research. Clearly, there are vast differences between Milgram's laboratory and Nazi Germany or My Lai. Yet, we believe, these experiments shared many of the structural features of other authority situations.[9]

As in other authority situations, when Milgram's research participants agreed to come to his laboratory, they placed themselves under the control of the person in charge of that setting. They implicitly agreed to perform whatever actions the experimenter wished them to perform without questioning the purposes of those

8. The proportion of completely obedient participants was 62.5 percent in the version in which the learner did not refer to a heart condition and 65 percent in the version in which he mentioned a heart condition. The small difference is not statistically significant.

9. Various writers have criticized the obedience experiments on methodological grounds, arguing that they lack ecological validity or generalizability. These critiques and Milgram's response to some of them are thoroughly reviewed by Arthur Miller (1986, chap. 6). Some of the critics (for example, Orne and Holland, 1968) argue that Milgram's subjects concluded, from the calm reaction of the experimenter, that they were not really harming the learner. In effect, they *trusted* the experimenter not to allow harm to come to a participant in a scientific study. Trust in the authority, however, is one of the ubiquitous features of authority situations. To be sure, Calley and those who followed his orders had no doubt that they were harming their victims, but they too justified their actions by trust in the authorities—trust that the authorities would not have ordered these actions unless they were necessary, legal, and appropriate. Thus, even if Milgram's subjects trusted the experimenter not to cause harm to their fellow participants, they still manifested obedience to authority. The evidence suggests that most of them believed—or at least had good reason to believe—that the learner was experiencing pain and wanted to terminate the experiment. The question still remains, therefore, why two-thirds of the subjects continued to trust the experimenter (if the critics are right) rather than challenge him. Both the trust and the obedience that it justifies can be traced to the structure of the authority situation.

actions. In short, they accepted the experimenter's authority. A number of features of the relationship support this basic structure of the situation as one in which the participants adhere to the demands of the experimenter.

To begin with, the nature of the experimental contract, though usually implicit, clearly called for the research participants to do the experimenter's bidding. After all, they had agreed to come to the laboratory in order to serve as subjects. The payment of a fee for participating in the experiment helped to firm up the contract, to give it concrete expression. It is not surprising that the participants in the obedience experiments who had decided to quit—to break the contract—offered to return the $4.50 they received at the beginning of the session. In doing so, they both acknowledged that they were breaking the contract and expressed their hope that the experimenter—by taking back the payment—would free them of their obligation. The experimenter replied that the money was not the issue—and, indeed, he was right. The payment merely symbolized the understanding that the participants had come to serve in a scientific experiment, and return of the money would not change the fact that they were now violating that understanding.

Various features of the situation contributed to its aura of legitimacy—to the perception of the experimenter in his domain as a legitimate actor involved in a legitimate enterprise that could be fully trusted. One contributing factor was the prestige of the institution in which the work was being carried out. In order to assess the extent to which the prestige of Yale University, the institutional setting for Milgram's experiments, contributed to participants' readiness to obey, he repeated the experiment in a rundown office building in downtown Bridgeport, Connecticut, under the auspices of an organization he called "Research Associates of Bridgeport." In this unknown, less prestigious setting, the level of obedience did decline—47.5 percent of the participants went all the way compared to 65 percent in the comparable condition at Yale—but the difference falls short of statistical significance. Another factor contributing to the aura of legitimacy, in the Bridgeport office building as well as at Yale University, was the prestige of science itself—its social recognition as a worthy enterprise promoting human welfare. Furthermore, the setting was replete with the diverse trappings of legitimacy, ranging from the laboratory coat worn by the experimenter to the complicated, expensive scientific apparatus filling the room. The expensive appearance of the apparatus suggested that the research was amply funded—concrete evidence that it must be legitimate. Finally, the aura of legitimacy was enhanced by the implication that the experimenter had special knowledge and expertise that qualified him to take charge of this scientific laboratory. As is so often the case, the experimenter's presumed professional authority enhanced his bureaucratic authority.

In contrast, the participants saw themselves as lacking the knowledge and expertise to challenge the experimenter's judgments. There was a pronounced asymmetry between the two actors in this drama. It was clearly understood that the experimenter owned this setting, that he alone knew its dimensions, that he called the tune. Under the circumstances, participants typically conceded control of the situation to the experimenter and, by the same token, relinquished to him the responsibility for anything that might happen. They expected to do what they were told. They did not perceive themselves as having either the right or the capacity to contradict the experimenter. Nor were they concerned about this state of affairs; they trusted that no harm would come to any of the participants in this enterprise. They were reassured on this score during the initial briefing when—in response to a question by the learner—the experimenter confirmed that the shocks might be extremely painful but would not be dangerous.

The assumption that the experimenter has control and responsibility was built into the very definition of the situation, and the interaction between research participant and experimenter proceeded on that basis. In these respects, the laboratory situation closely resembles other authority situations, in all of which control and responsibility are turned over to the authorities in charge of the setting—whether they be government officials, military officers, hospital physicians, or airline pilots. There are many important differences between these situations, but in all of them we find an almost automatic readiness to relinquish control to the authorities in charge, who benefit from the presumption of legitimacy, trustworthiness, and expertise.

THE PARTICIPANTS' CONFLICT

As the interaction between participant and experimenter proceeded, predictably and smoothly, in keeping with the situational structure that we have just outlined, the participants suddenly found themselves confronted with the learner's pained cries of protest. The evidence reported by Milgram indicates that most participants were quite clearly disturbed by this development. In a film about the obedience experiments, produced by Milgram,[10] the participants display visible signs of distress. It is reasonable to conclude from this evidence that most of the experimental teachers would have preferred to stop administering the shocks, at least at the point at which the learner began to verbalize his complaints. They did not wish to harm or endanger the learner. They did not feel that he should be forced to continue in the experiment against his will—particularly in view of their assumption that, but for the luck of the draw, the positions might have been reversed and they themselves might have been strapped into the learner's chair. Despite their respect for science, they were probably not convinced of the need to complete this run of the experiment in the face of the learner's pain. In contrast to a military or medical context, in which inflicting pain on the enemy or the patient may be integrally related to the goals of the ongoing activity, the learner's excruciating pain in the present context appeared to be only an unnecessary and unfortunate by-product of an activity designed to fulfill the more abstract goals of scientific inquiry. For all of these reasons, it can be presumed that the typical participant would have preferred to stop the experiment at some point after the learner began to protest.

10. Milgram's film, *Obedience*, is distributed by the New York University Film Library.

Nevertheless, although they might have preferred to withdraw from the experiment, the participants did not stop outright. To do so would have been incongruent with the structure of the situation to which they had committed themselves. They tried instead to resolve the dilemma within the structure of the situation. They turned to the experimenter, to whom they had relinquished control and responsibility. They called his attention to the learner's complaints and asked him how to proceed—often suggesting that perhaps he ought to stop the experiment. Thus, they acknowledged the experimenter's authority; they hoped and expected that he would authorize a new course of action. The experimenter, however, refused to bail them out. He reiterated the structure of the situation and insisted on holding them to their contract.

The participants were thus placed in a conflict between their personal preferences and their role requirements. They were confronted with a difficult choice, given the role they had adopted on entering the situation and within which they had been operating up to this point. To refuse to go on meant to challenge the experimenter's authority—to question the legitimacy of his demands and, by implication, the legitimacy of the experimenter himself. Some participants—about a third in Milgram's baseline condition—were able to take that leap, although usually not without some delay and considerable conflict. The majority, under this particular set of conditions, found it impossible to redefine the situation and challenge the experimenter.

This finding is at odds with what most observers would have predicted—at least before the results of Milgram's research became widely known. Milgram (1974, chap. 3) described the experiment to various groups of respondents, including psychiatrists, college students, and middle-class adults. All the respondents predicted that they themselves would disobey, breaking off at least at the 300-volt shock level, and that only a minuscule proportion of other subjects would go all the way to 450. These predictions were probably based on the assumption that participants would be acting in terms of their personal preferences; they ignored the role constraints built into the very structure and definition of the situation within which the research participants were operating. No doubt, if people were asked to administer painful shocks to another person in a situation that was not marked by legitimate authority, the vast majority would refuse. Conversely, if people were ordered to inflict pain on another person in an authority situation in which such an order was more clearly within the superior's domain of authority—such as a military or medical context—most people would obey with less conflict than that shown by the participants in the obedience experiments. The conflict experienced in the obedience experiments was particularly intense, among both those who obeyed to the end and those who chose to disobey at some point in the process.

One side of the conflict can be understood quite readily. Most people would find it difficult to continue shocking a person who cries out in pain, asks to be released, and appears to be at risk of permanent damage. But why was the alternative so difficult, raising the conflict to such high intensity? What accounts for the participants' reluctance simply to refuse to go on? To understand their reluctance, we must consider what such a refusal means within the microcosm of the experimental situation. A refusal to continue transforms the entire situation and totally disrupts the relationship between experimenter and subject, violating the assumptions on which the interaction has been proceeding so far. Participants find it exceedingly difficult to take such a step, which implies a challenge to the legitimacy of the proceedings, distrust in the ongoing enterprise, doubts about the experimenter's credentials and judgment, and an assertion that he is exceeding his authority and making illegitimate demands. In taking this step, participants would be claiming the right and capacity to make judgments about matters that are outside of their range of knowledge and competence.

And what if their judgment turns out to be wrong—if they refuse to continue only to discover that the experimenter's demands were perfectly legitimate? In some authority situations, such as in a military context or in the context of a business organization, subordinates are understandably afraid that a wrong judgment—disobeying an order whose legitimacy is subsequently confirmed—may expose them to legal penalties or damage their careers. In the obedience experiments, participants had no reason to fear punishment (apart from the possible loss of $4.50), but they were afraid of possible embarrassment. They ran the risk of appearing ignorant, silly, and immature if they made an issue over actions by the experimenter that proved to be harmless and appropriate—entirely within the range of what is normally done and widely approved. It becomes clear that the participants' concerns about embarrassment were not completely unfounded when we imagine what would happen if we called the police because, while walking down a hospital corridor, we heard someone crying out in pain and asking to be released and discovered a man in a white coat trying to push a large pointed instrument into another, partially undressed, person who was vociferously protesting. The participants in the obedience experiments were never sure whether they were confronted with an abuse of authority or with a situation resembling our hospital scenario.

Apart from the potentially embarrassing consequences of disobedience, the act of disobedience itself was acutely embarrassing in this situation. It is improper and discourteous to deny an experimenter the authority that he claims for himself and that he appears to be entitled to claim. It was particularly difficult in this case for participants to stop cooperating once they had accepted the definition of the situation and proceeded accordingly for some period of time. To do so would have meant breaking the flow of the interaction and destroying the basis of the relationship that had been established. (See Gamson et al., 1982, p. 111.)

The concern about propriety and courtesy is well illustrated by one of the participants in the version of Milgram's baseline experiment in which the learner repeatedly referred to his heart condition. The participant had become increasingly concerned about the learner's failure to respond. When the experimenter instructed him, nonetheless, to continue administering shocks, he replied: "What if he's dead in there? I mean, he told me he can't stand the shock, sir. I don't mean to be rude, but I think you should look in on him. All you have to do is look in on him. All you have to do is look in the door. I don't get no answer, no noise. Something might have happened to the gentleman in there, sir" (Milgram, 1974, p. 76).

This participant is featured in Milgram's film on the obedience experiments. It is evident from his filmed reactions that he is concerned throughout about the welfare of the learner, and he is quite agitated when he makes these remarks. What is so startling about them is that, at a point at which he is entertaining the possibility that the learner may be dead or seriously hurt, he worries about being rude to the experimenter. The experimenter, of course, remains impervious to the participant's pleas that he look in on the learner. As always, he instructs the teacher to continue administering the shocks. And the teacher continues.

This particular participant provides a good illustration of someone who seems completely boxed into the definition of the situation and incapable of breaking out of it. Although he is clearly concerned about the learner and distressed about causing him pain and possible harm, he is unable to translate these feelings into a decision to say no. He makes his feelings known and even presses them on the experimenter (to the point of worrying about appearing rude). His reaction cannot really be described as *unquestioning* obedience. Yet, once he has raised his questions and articulated his concerns—without persuading the experimenter to change his orders—he continues to obey. He seems to feel that he has no other choice because he does not perceive himself as an independent agent in this situation. It is interesting that, in the postexperimental debriefing, he seems unable to understand a question about whether there are any conditions under which he might have stopped administering shocks to the learner. As far as he is concerned, he *did* stop—and he seems dismayed to learn that some participants did not stop. *He* stopped; it was the *experimenter* who continued. His hand may have been on the switch, but the decision and the responsibility were clearly the experimenter's.

To break out of the definition of the authority situation requires, as we have argued, cognitive and motivational conditions that would allow people to challenge the authority and adopt an alternative framework. The microstructure of authority situations, exemplified by the obedience experiments, poses major obstacles to any attempt to mount such a challenge. People often feel that they lack the knowledge and information on which to base an alternative definition of the situation, countering the one imposed by the authorities in charge; and they are reluctant to disrupt the smooth flow of their interaction with the authorities and risk the consequences of such disruption. Challenging the authority's definition of the situation is easier in some situations than in others, and some people seem better able to break out of the authoritative definition of the situation than are others. We turn next to a consideration of some of the situational factors that determine the likelihood of challenging authority; in chapter 11 we examine individual differences in the capacity and readiness to do so.

Binding and Opposing Forces

Milgram's obedience experiment illustrates the dilemma that people may face in an authority situation in which they are ordered to perform acts they find objectionable. Using this experiment as our model, we have described the difficulties in challenging authority that are built into the structure of authority situations. The context in which subordinates encounter authorities and the nature of the interaction established between them reinforce a definition of the situation as one in which the authorities are in full control and the subordinates do as they are told. Some people manage to break out of this definition, but many lack the cognitive and motivational resources to do so.

How the dilemma is likely to be resolved is very much affected by situational forces. Situations differ in the degree to which they encourage or enable individuals to challenge authority. This is evident from Milgram's research, which explored a series of variations on the baseline experiment described in the preceding section. By manipulating one or another feature of the situation, Milgram was able to demonstrate an increase or decrease in the level of obedience obtained. Similarly, within other types of authority situations, we would expect differences in the level of obedience as a function of situational variations. By the same logic, we would expect overall differences among different types of authority situations—for example, between military and nonmilitary situations, or between public and private situations.

Whether conflicts engendered by repugnant orders will be resolved through obedience or challenge of the authorities depends on the relative strength of the binding and opposing forces that characterize the situation. *Binding forces* are those features of the situation that reinforce its authority structure and hold the individual ever more tightly to a rigid definition of the situation, closing off possibilities for redefinition. The stronger the binding forces, the less freedom of movement the individual has to focus on features of the situation other than its authority structure. *Opposing forces* are those features of the situation that heighten the individual's reluctance to engage in the actions demanded by the authority. Opposing forces are extraneous to the authority structure and generally relate to the nature or the target of the action itself.

BINDING FORCES

What features of the authority situation strengthen its binding quality? One feature, on which Milgram's research provides impressive evidence (1974, pp. 59–62), is the physical closeness of the experimenter and the degree of surveillance he exercises. In the standard experiment, the experimenter sat a few feet away from the naive participant. In one of the variations, in contrast, after his initial instruction, the experimenter left the laboratory and gave his orders by telephone. In this variation, the level of obedience dropped sharply: Only 20.5 percent of the participants obeyed fully, compared to 65 percent in the baseline condition. Moreover, when the experimenter was out of the room, several participants—

although continuing in the teacher role—administered lower shocks than required by the procedure without informing the experimenter of their deviation.

The physical distance of the authority made the participant's refusal to go on a less provocative disruption of the flow of interaction than it is in the standard experiment. "Well-socialized subjects who have volunteered their services find it difficult to commit such an act under the very eyes of the experimenter, but when they can do it without the embarrassment of a direct confrontation, it is much easier" (Gamson, 1968, p. 134). The direct presence of the authority binds subordinates into the definition of the situation by reminding them of their obligations and subjecting them to the embarrassment that results from public exposure of their failure to meet these obligations. This binding factor contributes to obedience at the macrolevel as well as at the microlevel. As Gamson (1968) points out, for complex, modern societies, "the activation of commitments still depends both on the acceptance of a general obligation and on reminders of what that duty is in specific situations" (p. 134).

Another feature of an authority situation that strengthens binding forces is the salience of the perceived consequences of disobedience. When there is a clear expectation of punishment for disobedience, subordinates are less likely to consider that option seriously. The effect of punishment is not merely that it deters disobedience directly, but, as we pointed out in chapters 4 and 5, that it serves as a reminder of the subordinate's role requirements. The existence of legal sanctions for disobeying a category of demands is a clear indication that the expected actions are within the domain of obligation rather than the domain of preference. Even if subordinates believe that an order is illegal, they are less likely to challenge it if it is backed by legal sanctions because they would be exposing themselves to the risk of punishment if their belief turns out to have been wrong. Looking at broad classes of authority situations, it can be said that those endowed with the right and capacity to impose penalties have a stronger binding quality, at least at the macrolevel. In this respect, the binding forces were more powerful at My Lai than in Milgram's laboratory. At the microlevel, however, the fear of embarrassment is functionally equivalent to the fear of punishment, as we have seen. The fear of embarrassment, of course—in the form of stigmatization and isolation of dissidents as troublemakers, deviants, or traitors—is a binding force available to political authorities as much as to experimenters, airline pilots, or supervisors in the workplace.

The existence of legal sanctions is only one of the advantages that official authorities, whether in military or political settings, have over unofficial authorities. Other binding forces that tend to be more powerful in official contexts include widely recognized symbols of authority, a clearly articulated hierarchical structure, and the explicit or implicit links of authoritative demands to national policy and the national interest. All these features of official settings remind citizens of their role obligations and help bind them into an authority-centered definition of the situation.

A final example of binding forces that often have a powerful impact are the actions of comparable others. We look to others for cues in our effort to define situations and their requirements. This tendency manifests itself in the conformity in opinion and action that is typically found in periods of crisis, which are marked by strong pressures for group consensus. The appearance of consensus has an inhibiting effect on the expression of political dissent because it fosters a state of pluralistic ignorance, in which potential dissenters are unaware of one another's views and unavailable for mutual support (see Kelman, 1968, chaps. 10 and 11). As a result, alternative definitions of the situation, different from the one promoted by the authorities, are less likely to be considered within the society. At the microlevel, Irving Janis (1972) has noted the effect of pressures to maintain cohesiveness among members of decision-making groups, working closely in a crisis atmosphere, in inhibiting the expression of dissenting opinions and the consideration of alternatives. In the laboratory, Solomon Asch's classical experiments (1951, 1956) showed the powerful effect of a unanimous (pre-instructed) majority in inducing individuals to conform to its blatantly false judgments. The level of conformity was dramatically reduced, however, in one variation of the experiment in which a single group member was instructed to deviate from the consensus. Breaking the consensus, it seems, allowed participants to redefine the situation as one in which dissenting opinions were possible.

In deciding whether to obey or disobey an authority's order, people similarly look to others for cues that would help them define the situation. To the extent that others—in the immediate situation or in the larger society—obey, the definition of the situation as one requiring obedience is strengthened. Not only is the option of disobedience less likely to arise under these circumstances, but disobedience in the face of almost universal obedience exposes the individual to greater risks of punishment and embarrassment, which in themselves, as we have seen, act as binding forces. Milgram's experiments did not explore the binding effect of obedience by others directly. He did have one variation, to be discussed below, that showed the "liberating effects" on the naive participant of *disobedience* by (pre-instructed) fellow participants (see Milgram, 1965). There was no variation, however, in which participants were teamed with others who consistently obeyed.[11] We would expect that the level of obedience in such an experiment would rise relative to the baseline condition. The obedience of their peers would bind participants even more strongly into the definition of the situation as one in which there was no other acceptable alternative.

To identify the conditions under which it becomes possible for individuals to challenge the demands of authorities, we need to explore features of authority situations that reduce the strength of binding forces and thus make it easier for people to redefine the situation. One of Milgram's experiments suggests one condition under which the binding forces of authority situations may be greatly re-

11. Milgram (1964a) carried out one experiment demonstrating the effect of peer pressure on the level of shocks administered by naive research participants. In this experiment, however, the shock levels were set by the participants themselves rather than the experimenter. Thus, the experiment does not deal directly with the effect of others' *obedience* on a person's own obedience.

duced if not entirely eliminated: a condition of divided authority. In this variation (Milgram, 1974, pp. 105–07), two experimenters of apparently equal status ran the experiment jointly. At the point in the proceedings at which the learner began to protest vehemently, Experimenter I called for a halt, while Experimenter II instructed the teacher to continue. They did not argue with each other but issued a series of directly contradictory orders to the teacher. Milgram reports that some participants tried to ascertain which of the two experimenters was the higher authority, but no such information was forthcoming. All but one of the participants stopped administering shocks immediately; the remaining one stopped on the next trial. The level of obedience in this variation went down to zero, compared to 65 percent in the baseline condition. In the face of divided authority, the participants apparently chose to follow the authority whose orders they found more reasonable and more in keeping with their own preferences. They had no difficulty challenging Experimenter II since they were able to do so not only with the permission but also under the direct command of an alternative authority of equal status. These findings are thus consistent with our general point that an authority's orders are most readily resisted by recourse to an alternative authority.[12]

It is likely that divided authority reduces the strength of binding forces even in situations in which one of the authorities is clearly of higher status. In such a situation, of course, subordinates are not as free to choose the authority whose orders they find more congenial, as they were in the experimental variation just described. The mere fact that there is disagreement among authorities, however, raises the possibility of redefining the situation and gives some authoritative backing to that possibility. Disagreements within the hierarchy may also—at least in rigidly structured bureaucracies—have a delegitimating effect on the authority, which in itself weakens binding forces. A similar result would ensue if the authorities' legitimacy is reduced for other reasons—for example, because of demonstrable incompetence (Penner et al., 1973) or weakness, because of ineffectiveness in achieving collective goals, because of inequities in their management of resources, because of repeated evidence of corruption, or because of irregularities in their accession to power. The legitimacy of authorities—and of their orders—is also reduced the more obvious their breach of normal allowable behavior. This was probably a major factor in weakening the binding forces for some of the men under Lieutenant Calley's command.

So far we have looked at characteristics of the authorities that might reduce the binding forces in the situation they control and make it easier for subordinates to challenge their orders. There is another set of situational factors that may contribute significantly to weakening the binding forces: the opportunities the setting provides to subordinates to redefine the situation through direct communication

12. In this connection, we assume that binding forces become weaker the less closely an individual is tied to the particular chain of command and obedience. Thus, as noted in chapter 1, the most striking act of defiance at My Lai was committed by Hugh Thompson, a man not directly under Lieutenant Calley's command. The massacre also came to light through the insistence of a man who was not even present, Ronald Ridenhour.

and collective action. Such opportunities were, of course, not available to the participants in Milgram's baseline experiment who had to face the authority alone (except for the presence of the learner who, as the victim or target of the subordinate's action, stood apart from the experimenter-subject confrontation). One of the variations of the obedience experiment (Milgram, 1965; 1974, pp. 116–21), to which we have already alluded, suggests how the presence of fellow subordinates may reduce the binding forces of the situation. In this variation, three participants—two of whom were confederates of the experimenter's—shared the role of teacher. The critical element was that these fellow participants chose (by preinstruction) to disobey. At the point at which the learner began his vehement protest, one of the confederates announced that he would no longer participate. Four trials later, the second confederate withdrew. Throughout, the experimenter insisted that the experiment had to continue and turned over the tasks abandoned by the confederates to the naive participant. In this variation of the experiment, only 10 percent of the participants continued to obey to the end compared to 65 percent in the comparable baseline condition.

Several factors are mentioned by Milgram that probably contributed to the dramatic decline in obedience in this experiment. The successful challenge to the experimenter's authority, of course, contributed to his delegitimation, which in itself reduced the strength of binding forces emitted by him. The most important effect of the confederates' disobedience, however, was probably in providing the cognitive and motivational conditions that allowed the participant to redefine the situation in which he found himself. The defection by the confederates reinforced his own misgivings and helped him conclude that the experimenter's orders were indeed illegitimate. Furthermore, the confederates served as models. They demonstrated that it was possible to say no—which may not even have occurred to participants boxed into the definition of the situation—and that such a reaction was not outlandish under the circumstances. The confederates' initiative reduced the participant's fear of embarrassment and of other negative consequences of disobedience. If there were to be any negative repercussions, the participant could now expect group support for his defiant act. The burden of disrupting the smooth flow of interaction was shared; in fact, the flow of interaction had already been disrupted and the situation had already been redefined by the others. In addition to weakening the binding forces in the situation by all these means, the disobedience by the confederates subjected the participant to stronger opposing forces against continued administration of the shocks. Up to that point, the participant's responsibility for hurting and possibly damaging the learner was diffuse, since he shared it with the other teachers. With their defection, however, the responsibility was entirely his. In addition, the confederates' disobedience introduced social pressure to conform to the majority. Failure to follow suit not only placed him in the position of the deviant but also implied that he was less compassionate and courageous than his peers.

Although highly suggestive, this variation of the obedience experiment had one shortcoming: It did not illustrate the role of communication and collective action directly. Rather, it created a new situation for the participant by exposing him to a staged scenario of disobedient peers. What Milgram observed, then, was the participant's individual response to these new circumstances. An intriguing later study (Gamson et al., 1982) provides direct observations of the role of collective action in redefining a situation and promoting successful challenges to illegitimate authority. In this study, groups of six to ten volunteers each participated in what was described as a group discussion of community standards under the auspices of a fictitious organization called the Manufacturers' Human Relations Consultants (MHRC). The discussion, which was videotaped, focused on the case of a service station manager whose franchise was revoked by his parent oil company on the ground that his immoral life-style (living with a woman to whom he was not married) violated community standards and made him unfit to represent the company. The manager claimed that the company in fact acted against him because he had publicly criticized its gas pricing policy, and he sued the company for breach of contract and invasion of privacy. Presumably, MHRC was a research organization collecting information about community standards relevant to the court case.

It gradually became apparent that MHRC was in fact trying to produce evidence in support of the oil company's claim and that the coordinator was seeking to gain the groups' complicity in this effort. None of the thirty-three groups that participated in the study actually believed that the manager should have been terminated because of his life-style, as became evident in their initial discussions. Yet the coordinator asked various members to espouse that position in the taped discussions and asked all the participants to support this view in final statements. At the end he asked the participants to sign affidavits agreeing to MHRC's use of the tapes, giving the organization the right to edit them and submit them to the court. There was a strong implication that the tapes would be edited to support the oil company's claim and that the participants' statements disapproving of the manager's life-style—which they had made only at the coordinator's specific request—would be presented as their true opinions.

In contrast to the Milgram experiments, the Gamson et al. study showed a high level of disobedience. In about half the groups, all the participants refused to sign the affidavit at the end; in an additional quarter of the groups, the majority refused to do so. There were various other acts of rebellion at earlier points in the proceedings, and, in a sizable proportion of the groups, plans to take future action against the MHRC were devised. The probability of successful rebellion was higher in groups whose members' views on the issues heavily favored the station manager over the oil company and in groups that contained individuals with skills and experience in organizing for group action. Where these favorable conditions were present, it became possible to utilize the opportunities for communication and collective action to counteract the binding forces of the authority situation. Questions, protests, and acts of defiance by some members served as examples for others and raised the possibility of redefining the situation. Exchange of views among the members helped them to articulate their misgivings about the situation, to reinforce each other's doubts, and to share their interpretations of what was happening and their ideas about how to respond. Out of this process, they were able to develop a shared redefinition of the situation as one that was illegitimate. In the language of Gamson et al., they adopted a collective *injustice frame* in lieu of the *legitimating frame* that had guided their initial behavior in the situation. The new framework provided the justification for disobeying the authority's demands and for mobilizing collective action to that end. Mobilization of collective action required, among other things, the development of a sense of group loyalty and the exertion of some degree of pressure toward conformity within the group.

Gamson et al. provide a detailed illustration and analysis, at the microlevel, of the potentialities of collective action in counteracting the binding forces of authority situations and mounting an effective challenge against authority. The sharing of information and interpretations within a group makes it possible to break out of the definition of the situation as one requiring obedience and to develop an alternative collective definition of the situation as unjust and hence illegitimate. Disobedience then becomes a justified collective response to unjust authority. The group support not only provides the ideological basis for disobeying but also reduces the risks of stigmatization and punishment that disobedience by an isolated individual entails. In sum, collective action helps overcome the cognitive obstacles to challenging authority by creating an alternative definition of the situation; it helps overcome the motivational obstacles by transforming disobedience from a deviant to a socially supported act and by distributing the burden of disrupting the social order.

OPPOSING FORCES

The likelihood that authority will be challenged increases not only with the weakening of binding forces but also with the strengthening of forces in opposition to the particular actions ordered by authority. In the types of authority situations on which we have been focusing—situations in which a subordinate is commanded to hurt or harm another person—opposing forces may arise from the nature of the relationship between the subordinate and the victim and from the moral implications of the action being ordered. Destructive obedience, as we proposed in our discussion of sanctioned massacres and other crimes of obedience in chapters 1 and 2, often becomes possible because of situational conditions that weaken the usual moral inhibitions against violence and other forms of harm doing.

One of the situational factors affecting the strength of opposing forces that was explored in Milgram's obedience experiments was the closeness of the victim to the teacher as he administered the shocks (Milgram, 1974, chap. 4). In the baseline condition the learner was in an adjoining room, although his complaints could be heard clearly through the wall. In one variation, the victim was placed in the same room, a few feet away from the teacher, thus becoming visible as well as audible. Under these conditions, the level of obedience dropped from 62.5

percent in the comparable baseline condition to 40 percent. In a further variation, the victim again sat near the teacher. At the point in the proceedings in which he began to protest vehemently, he tried to avoid the shocks by refusing to place his hand on the shock plate. The experimenter ordered the teacher to force the victim's hand onto the plate. In this variation, then, obedience required physical contact with the victim as the shocks were being administered. Under these conditions, the level of obedience dropped further, to 30 percent. The findings suggest that as the victim moved closer to the teacher, opposing forces to the act of shocking him increased in intensity.

As long as victims are out of sight, it is easier to forget that there are real human beings who are being harmed by one's actions. Thus, it is easier to kill people by dropping a bomb on a distant target or pushing a button at a missile-launching station than it is to kill them face to face. When the learner became visible in the obedience experiments, the teacher was less able to deny that a real human being was suffering and more likely to react empathetically to him. Furthermore, as the victim moved closer—and particularly in the variation in which the teacher actually held down his hand—the relationship between the teacher's own action and the learner's suffering became clearly evident. Opposing forces to an action increase to the extent that we see ourselves as *personally causing* the harmful consequences of that action. (See also chapter 8.)

Psychological distance from the victim has a similar effect to physical distance in reducing the strength of opposing forces. When victims are dehumanized—by a variety of means, some of which we mentioned in chapters 1 and 2—the moral restraints against killing or harming them become less effective. Groups of people who are systematically demonized, assigned to inferior or dangerous categories, and identified by derogatory labels are readily excluded from the bonds of human empathy and the protection of moral and legal precepts. Opposing forces are also reduced when the actors themselves have just gone through the experience of intense anxiety, frustration, or stress, or when their own group suffers from a pervasive sense of victimization. Under these circumstances, the capacity for compassion with others and for recognizing them as victims of one's own actions tends to be reduced and it becomes easier to dehumanize them and to follow orders that entail their victimization.

The strength of opposing forces generated by closeness of the victim is likely to vary from situation to situation. In general, we would expect these opposing forces to be weaker in My Lai than in Milgram's laboratory. The victims of military actions are, almost by definition, dehumanized when they are placed in the category of enemy. The point is brought out clearly by Lieutenant Calley's statement, cited in chapter 1: "I did not sit down and think in terms of men, women, and children. They were all classified the same, and that was the classification that we dealt with, just as enemy soldiers" (Hammer, 1971, p. 257). To be sure, Lieutenant Calley's stark formulation may not be typical, but the concept of enemy itself carries dehumanizing implications. The Vietnamese were further dehumanized by the application of racial and ideological labels to them. Furthermore, the men at My Lai had undergone experiences of severe frustration, deprivation, and stress, and had recently lost comrades to Viet Cong ambushes. Thus, their actions were affected not only by a diminished capacity for compassion for their victims but also by an identification of the victims with the Viet Cong, who inspired both fear and a desire for revenge.

In the obedience experiments, in contrast, there were no particular reasons for dehumanizing the victim—at least initially. He was a pleasant man, in the same general category as the participant, and, most important, he became the victim only by chance. As far as the naive participants were concerned, they might well have been sitting in his chair themselves if they had drawn the other piece of paper. Thus, they had reason to empathize with him. Interestingly, some of the participants deprecated the victim *after* they began and continued to administer shocks to him—blaming the victim's stubbornness or stupidity for the predicament he was in. Devaluation of the victim in this case served to reduce their own sense of guilt and allowed them to maintain their belief in a just world (Lerner, 1970, 1971, 1980). This reaction illustrates the way in which the act of victimization itself may contribute to derogation and even dehumanization of the victim, thus further reducing the strength of opposing forces.

Although, on the whole, it seems clear that the opposing forces were stronger in Milgram's laboratory than in My Lai, there is one respect in which the reverse may have been true. In My Lai, there was no doubt in the soldiers' minds that they were killing their victims. In the obedience experiments, on the other hand, it is quite likely that most of the participants—although believing that the shocks caused pain to the learner—did not really believe that they were causing permanent damage. This belief—supported by the laboratory setting and the experimenter's statements and demeanor—probably helped weaken the opposing forces that might otherwise have exercised moral restraint. (See also Mixon, 1971.)

In describing the variation of the obedience experiment in which the teacher had to hold down the learner's hand in order to make sure that he was receiving the shock (Milgram, 1974, p. 34), we pointed out that opposing forces are strengthened by perceived personal causation of the victim's suffering. In this variation, the participants could not easily fail to notice that the pain experienced by the learner was a direct consequence of their own action. Another one of the experimental variations (Milgram, 1974, pp. 121–22) illustrates the reverse of this proposition: the weakening of opposing forces as personal causation becomes more ambiguous. In this variation, the shocks were administered by a man playing the role of another participant. The naive participant performed subsidiary tasks, which contributed to the experimental proceedings but did not require him actually to depress the lever on the shock generator. Under these conditions, 92.5 percent of the participants cooperated to the very end. In interpreting this finding, it should be noted that obedience in this variation was probably enhanced not only by the participant's ability to distance himself from the consequences of the action but also by the example set by his fully obedient partner.

In a related experiment, using the Milgram obedience paradigm, Kilham and

Mann (1974) simulated a bureaucratic hierarchy by dividing the teacher's role among two people: a "transmitter" and an "executant." In one variation the naive research participant was placed in the transmitter role and a confederate performed the executant role; in another the reverse procedure was followed. The transmitter informed the executant when a shock had to be administered to the learner and what voltage level was to be used, but did not administer the shock directly. Kilham and Mann found a significantly higher level of obedience among transmitters than among executants. It appears that their greater distance from the act and their intermediate position in the hierarchy—between the authority who issued the orders and the executant who actually pressed the lever—reduced the strength of the opposing forces.[13]

Opposing forces to destructive obedience are often weakened by the participants' ability to avoid seeing the connection between their own actions and the destructive consequences of those actions. The Nazi extermination program was carried out by a vast bureaucracy in which many functionaries—from Adolf Eichmann down to junior clerks—sat at desks, shuffled papers, arranged train schedules, and carried out a variety of other tasks without having to consider the final product of their efforts. The perception of personal causation was reduced not only by the dissociation of each functionary's contributory acts from the human consequences of those acts but also by the diffusion of responsibility within the bureaucracy. The more people are involved in an action, the less likelihood that any one of them will see herself or himself as a causal agent with moral responsibility (Latané and Darley, 1970; Latané, 1981).

More generally, the routinization processes that are so characteristic of bureaucratic organizations contribute to the weakening of opposing forces. Insofar as actions become routine, mechanical, and highly programmed, the actor can carry them out without making decisions about them or considering their larger implications. The discrete acts can be divorced from the total product to which they are contributing and thus stripped of their moral meaning. Furthermore, as actions are routinized, they become integrated into one's job and normal parts of one's daily work. Normalization, again, helps to dissociate the performance of the task from its meaning in terms of the human consequences it produces. In this respect, opposing forces to actions that involve the taking of human lives are likely to be weaker in military contexts—not only in the field but also in the offices in which such actions are planned and coordinated. In a military context, such actions can more readily be assimilated to the normal functions and tasks of the organization and hence are less likely to bring opposing forces to the fore.

Finally, the strength of opposing forces can be expected to decline when individuals are so absorbed in group action that they become deindividuated—that is,

---

13. Kilham and Mann (1974) also varied the gender of the research participants. In half of their groups all three of the participants—transmitter, executant, and learner—were males; in the other half they were females. The level of obedience was significantly lower among female teachers (in both of the two roles). As we pointed out in note 5, Milgram (1974) found no gender difference in level of obedience, but in his research the *victim* was always male, even when the teacher was female.

lose their awareness of themselves as independent actors and their capacity to regulate their behavior according to personal standards (see Zimbardo, 1970; Diener, 1979; Prentice-Dunn and Rogers, 1980). Deindividuation increases the difficulty in challenging authority when obedience takes place in the context and with the support of a group enthralled by the authority. The practice of unquestioning obedience itself contributes to deindividuation. Destructive obedience, facilitated by the processes of authorization, routinization, and dehumanization, has the effect of reducing individuals' capacity and will to act as independent moral agents, concerned with the human consequences of their actions. Thus, these processes weaken opposing forces to destructive obedience not only directly but also indirectly by the reverberating effects they have on the actors.

Conclusion

Authority situations differ in their likelihood of eliciting obedience, depending on the interplay between binding and opposing forces. Yet, whatever the strength of these forces in a given situation, individuals differ in their reactions to authority demands. Some individuals may disobey even when the binding forces are compelling; others may obey even in the face of powerful opposing forces. A major process intervening between the nature of situational forces and the way an individual handles the conflict generated by destructive orders from legitimate authority is that individual's conception of personal responsibility for actions taken under superior orders. Our remaining theoretical analysis will, therefore, focus (a) on the process of attributing responsibility in authority situations (chapter 8) and (b) on the sources of individual differences in the attribution of responsibility and, ultimately, in the readiness to obey or disobey (chapter 11). Before proceeding with the theoretical argument, however, we turn to some of our empirical findings that bear on people's reactions to authoritative demands, on their ability to challenge such demands, and on the role of binding and opposing forces in the process.

7 | Attitudes and Norms about Obedience: Public Reactions to the My Lai Massacre

In the preceding chapter, we discussed the obstacles to challenging authority that arise in authority situations, at the macro- and micro-levels. We then focused on some of the situational forces that increase and decrease people's willingness and capacity to mount such challenges. The difficulty that people experience in challenging authority stems from an interaction between the pressures they face in the authority situation and the personal dispositions they bring to that situation: their general attitudes toward obedience to authority and their perception of the norms that govern behavior in authority situations.

We have already pointed out (in chapter 3) that strong social norms in support of the duty to obey are deeply rooted in Western tradition. These norms have generated widespread attitudes in favor of obedience in hierarchically structured authority situations—attitudes that consider obedience the expected, necessary, and right response. Individuals differ, of course, in the strength of these attitudes and perceived norms, relative to competing attitudes and norms that might predispose them to disobey orders, either in general or under particular circumstances—for example, when they find the behavior ordered to be morally objectionable.

Some empirical evidence on the nature and distribution of attitudes and perceived norms about obedience in the United States can be drawn from a national survey we conducted in 1971 (first reported in Kelman and Lawrence [Hamilton], 1972a, 1972b; Kelman and Hamilton, 1974). The research began with our observation of the American public's outcry, in April 1971, against the conviction of Lieutenant Calley for the My Lai massacre and the life sentence he originally received. The massive negative reaction to the conviction has been called the greatest public response to any trial in American history (DiMona, 1972). An examination of the attitudes behind this reaction can help illuminate the phenomena discussed in chapter 6: the reluctance to challenge superior orders and the tendency to obey without question.

It is important to stress that the survey data to be reported in this and later chapters refer to people's attitudes and their views of social norms regarding obedience—their conceptions of authority and responsibility as manifested in their reactions to specific crimes of obedience. We do not focus directly on action—on the conditions under which people actually obey or disobey orders to engage in destructive behavior. This type of research has the advantage of allowing us to ask questions about prominent national events, such as My Lai or Watergate, and even to hark back to the Nuremberg trials. It also avoids the ethical dilemmas confronting experiments in which research participants are induced to engage in destructive behavior (see discussion of these ethical issues by Baumrind, 1964; Milgram, 1964b; Kelman, 1968, 1972; Crawford, 1972; and the chapters by Warwick, Macklin, and Elms in Beauchamp et al., 1982). It does, however, set limits on the kinds of conclusions we can draw.

One cannot assume a simple, direct relationship between reaction and action, as the extensive literature on attitudes and behavior makes evident (see, for example, Ajzen and Fishbein, 1977; Deutscher, 1973; Hill, 1981; Kelman, 1974a, 1978, 1980; Liska, 1975; Schuman and Johnson, 1976; Wicker, 1969). People's statements about what they would do or about what one ought to do in a My Lai–like situation do not necessarily correspond to what they would in fact do in such a situation. When people respond to hypothetical questions, they are not fully aware of the power of the situational forces that may shape their action. Moreover, they often yield—consciously or unconsciously—to the tendency to present themselves in a favorable light. Thus, it would be unwarranted to infer from our survey what proportion of Americans would have participated obediently in the My Lai massacre, or who would have obeyed and who disobeyed.

Nevertheless, our survey does have a bearing on action. The data give us a better understanding of people's attitudes toward obedience, of the social norms that they consider to apply to authority situations, and of the ideological frameworks within which they view these issues. These conceptions form a large part of the psychological context within which people act in an authority situation. They are not to be interpreted as indicators of action, but they certainly are important determinants of action. To be more specific, attitudes and perceived norms help mediate the effects of situational and social-structural factors on the behavioral outcome of obedience or disobedience.

The National Survey

The public outcry that accompanied the 1971 conviction of Lt. William Calley for his role in the My Lai massacre was noteworthy for the sheer number of Americans involved, for the apparent intensity of their feelings, and for the diversity of their social origins. Different population groups who often disagree on public issues—young and old, rich and poor, black and white, male and female—

could all find reasons to disapprove of Calley's conviction. Views on the Vietnam War, which might ordinarily have been expected to predict opinions about a wartime massacre and subsequent trial, predicted little. Hawks and doves alike could each find reasons to disapprove (or, for that matter, to approve) of Calley's trial. Just after the conviction, 79 percent of the respondents in a Gallup telephone poll registered their disapproval, whereas only 9 percent approved—a powerful national consensus. A cartoon of the times captured the national spirit: a hard hat and a hippie, each demonstrating with "Free Calley" signs, simultaneously exclaiming, "What are *you* doing here?"

What *were* they all doing here? What were the sources of their reactions? What did the reaction say about American views of obedience to authority? We became convinced that the My Lai massacre and Calley trial represented a fascinating page in the history of destructive obedience as much because of the public response as because of the factual and legal record. The public outcry over Lieutenant Calley's conviction suggested the strength of norms favoring unquestioning obedience, at least in military settings. We felt, therefore, that a study of public reactions to the Calley trial might shed light on the causes of destructive obedience. It might reveal who thought obedience was right, even in My Lai, and what made it right in their eyes.

Our strategy for finding answers to these questions was a national sample survey. Immediately after Lieutenant Calley's sentence was announced on March 31, 1971, we began to make preparations for such a survey. We approached the task with two somewhat conflicting goals. First, we wanted the survey to be sufficiently thorough to provide insights about norms of obedience. Second, we wanted to go into the field quickly, in order to capture public reactions before the issue had faded. Choices concerning the sample and items reflect compromises between these two goals.

THE SAMPLE

It took several weeks to develop the interview schedule, to run it through several pretests (both local and national), and to make the necessary revisions. The pretesting, the drawing of the sample, and the interviewing were carried out for us by a polling firm, the Roper Organization, and its national staff. The period from initial construction of the questionnaire to completion of the interviews lasted just over two months, an unusually short time span. The actual interview period was May 28 to June 12, 1971.

We decided to use a block quota sample of the U.S. population, eighteen years of age and older. Blocks of housing units were drawn randomly nationwide, but interviewers then used quotas to select respondents within each block. Quotas were set for sex of respondents on each block, and for age of respondents across the interviewer's overall assignment, to correspond roughly to the population distribution by sex and age. Such samples do not represent the U.S. population precisely; for example, they overrepresent people who are more likely to be found at home, compared to what would be obtained from a strict probability sample.

But the relative speed and inexpensiveness of a block quota sample made it the method of choice. In all, 990 interviews were obtained.

THE ITEMS

Questionnaire items covered five general categories. The lead-in to the survey included items about the respondent's sources of news of the world, about how closely he or she followed the news, and two important filter questions: First, how closely had the respondent followed the Calley trial? Second, if the answer was "not very closely," had it been followed at all? Those who responded negatively were given a restricted version of the interview.

After these filter questions, all respondents (*including* those who claimed no knowledge of Calley) were asked two hypothetical items, which are the central focus of this chapter. These concerned respondents' thoughts about whether "most people" would follow orders and shoot in a My Lai–type situation and whether they themselves would do so. These two items were adapted from questions in an earlier Louis Harris poll. If the respondent had claimed no knowledge of the trial, the interviewer then skipped to the last two sections of the interview, which dealt with the Vietnam War and demographic information, without asking questions about the Calley trial per se.

The main body of the survey covered two categories: attitudes toward the trial and evaluations of Calley's actions at My Lai. The first category included questions about the respondents' attitude toward the trial itself, Lieutenant Calley's sentence, and the trial's impact on American life, as well as some questions about two historical precedents (the Nuremberg and the Yamashita trials). The key issues in this section—whether respondents approved or disapproved of the trial and the *reason* they felt that way—will be the central focus of chapter 9. The second category explored respondents' views of the *actions* involved in the My Lai massacre and in other war situations. This category included the two hypothetical questions described just above; items focusing on the actions at My Lai itself; and items that probed possible justifications for Calley's actions.

The types of questions asked included both standard fixed choices, such as "agree/disagree" items, and a number of open-ended probes, generally asking the respondent's reason for giving a particular answer to the fixed-choice items. For example, if respondents said they would follow orders and shoot in the hypothetical situation, we asked them why. Or if they thought Lieutenant Calley should have refused to follow orders, we again asked them why. Answers to the open-ended questions will be brought into the discussion whenever they can help clarify respondents' views.[1]

The key components of the interview, then, were attitudes toward the trial, attitudes toward the acts at My Lai, and demographic factors that might predict

1. The codes of answers to the open-ended questions went through several revisions. To check on the reliability of the final categories, a sample of one hundred interviews was coded by a second coder. Average agreement between coders was above 80 percent.

these opinions (such as the respondent's age, sex, and education). Important, but less central, were respondents' attitudes toward the Vietnam War. In all tables, in this and later chapters, questions are grouped by conceptual similarity rather than by the order in which they appeared in the survey.

PRESENTATION AND ANALYSIS OF DATA

The main tool for data analyses was simple cross-tabulation of opinions by other opinions and by demographic predictors. The tables we present here almost always eliminate any "don't know" responses and are repercentaged accordingly. This strategy was adopted because the "don't know" answer was typically a small fraction of responses that produced very unequal-sized categories if it was included. Our fundamental interest also lay in patterns of stable, "real" opinion. Typically, the removal of "don't knows" slightly inflates the significance of relationships between opinions. As will soon be evident, however, these relationships are generally so strong that they are significant no matter how they are analyzed.

We always tested relationships between items for their statistical significance. A statement that a relationship was significant usually refers to the chi-square test of association between variables. A statement about the strength of a relationship typically refers to the statistic gamma. (Gamma ranges from -1 to $+1$, signifying perfect negative and perfect positive relationships, analogously to the Pearson r for correlations. However, gamma cannot be interpreted in terms of explained variance; see Mueller et al., 1978.) Statistical detail can be given short shrift here because patterns of response were so clear that in most cases the human eyeball is the main "tool" needed for understanding them. We hope that the relatively heavy reliance on it makes the argument more accessible to readers.

In testing group differences in response to open-ended probes, it was necessary to take account of the fact that respondents could give more than one answer to any given "why." Comparisons are therefore made for each possible answer category within each question, coded as "chosen" versus "not chosen." Given the large number of statistical tests made, we consider any response differences as significant only if they are both statistically significant and at least 10 percent in absolute size.

VALIDITY OF THE SURVEY: PUBLIC INFORMATION AND INTEREST

If we wish to draw conclusions about the nature and sources of attitudes and norms regarding crimes of obedience in the U.S. population, we must address the question of validity of our survey data. An important limit to this validity was the public's degree of knowledge about and interest in Lieutenant Calley and My Lai.

What may seem to have been an overwhelming public outcry according to news stories might have been the outcry of only a particularly advantaged, disadvantaged, or involved segment. Even the apparent *direction* of opinion differences could have been misread by focusing on an activist segment. Attitudes about the Vietnam War serve as an example of this potential error (see Rosenberg et al., 1970). The earliest and most extensive antiwar sentiment was found among black, female, and working-class Americans, not among college students. The activism of some college students, especially at elite colleges, led to a misleading image of antiwar sentiment. Opinion in a given direction may also be meaningless if it reflects little interest or involvement for the average member of the public. A survey respondent may have "held" an opinion largely because he or she was prodded to express one (Converse, 1964, 1970; see review of "don't know" responses and "non-attitudes" by Schuman and Presser, 1981).

Thus, if it turned out that a large proportion of our sample was unfamiliar with or unconcerned about the Calley trial, our conclusions could not be generalized to the population at large. We therefore examined our respondents' level of knowledge and interest, in order to gain greater confidence in the breadth of the population to which our findings applied and the depth of feeling on the issue they represented. The results of this analysis are presented in appendix A.

Briefly, we found a remarkable degree of public information about the Calley trial. Ninety percent of our sample reported that they had at least heard of the trial. The degree of interest in the trial—based on reports of how closely respondents followed it in the news—was related to two clusters of demographic and attitudinal variables. First, both knowledge of and interest in the trial were greater among groups higher in socioeconomic status and sophistication in public affairs, as indexed by educational attainment and other demographic variables. Second, responsiveness to the trial was related to a package of variables—including military experience, sex, region of residence, and attitude toward the Vietnam War—that seemed to be tied to military experience or sympathies. We propose that the first set of factors primarily affects cognitive processes—how people think about the issues—whereas the second affects motivational processes—experientially based identification with the defendant.

The two demographic packages will remain a continuing theme in our analyses. At minimum, these distinct sources of interest serve notice of the trial's unusual appeal. In the interplay between the social-structural/cognitive predictors and the military-related/motivational predictors lies much of the fascination of American responses to the trial of Lt. William Calley. We shall see that these two sets of variables are also related to people's responses to hypothetical questions about a My Lai–like situation, to which we turn next.

Would You Shoot? Taking the Role of the Subordinate

Early in the interviews that followed Lieutenant Calley's conviction, we directly assessed whether people felt obedience was right in a situation like My Lai. After we inquired whether respondents had heard of the Calley trial—and before asking any questions about the trial—we presented them with the following situation:

What do you think *most* people would do if they were soldiers in Vietnam and were ordered by their superior officers to shoot all inhabitants of a village suspected of aiding the enemy, including old men, women, and children? Do you think *most* people in this situation would follow orders and shoot them, or do you think most people would refuse to shoot them?

What do you think *you* would do in this situation—follow orders and shoot them, or refuse to shoot them?

Why (would you follow orders and shoot them/would you refuse to shoot them)?

The distribution of responses to the two hypothetical questions provided the most dramatic findings of this survey. In response to the first question, 67 percent said that most people would follow orders and shoot and 19 percent said they would refuse to do so. When asked what they themselves would do, 51 percent said they would follow orders and shoot and 33 percent said they would refuse (see table 7.1).

To us, the "desirable" answer to the second question would clearly be "refuse to shoot." If most respondents had seen that as the socially desirable response, they could easily have given themselves the benefit of the doubt and picked it, since this was, after all, a strictly hypothetical question. The fact that only 33 percent picked this response suggests that many respondents felt that the socially correct reaction was to follow orders. In saying that they would follow orders, they were

Table 7.1 Relationship between Two Hypothetical Questions

		What would most people do?			All Respondents
		Shoot	Don't Know	Refuse	
	Shoot	453	27	9	489 (51%)
What would you do?	Don't Know	89	57	11	157 (16%)
	Refuse	102	58	161	321 (33%)
All respondents		644 (67%)	142 (15%)	181 (19%)	967 (100%)

Note: The cell entries in this table represent the number of respondents (N) (not percentages). Use of the raw numbers here makes it easier to follow our discussion of the relationship between the two variables. In the column and row headed "All Respondents" we give the percentage of each response in the columns (answers to the question about what "most people" would do) and rows (answers to the question about what "you" would do), respectively, in parentheses below the corresponding N. Column and row percentages each sum to 100% (with some rounding error). The association between the two variables is statistically significant at $p \leq .0001$, which means that the probability of obtaining this result by chance is equal to or less than 1 in 10,000. In subsequent tables, we do not present detailed information about tests of significance. Unless stated otherwise, it can be assumed that any tabulated association between variables is significant at least at the level of $p \leq .01$—that is, that the probability of obtaining the result by chance is equal to or less than 1 in 100.

not necessarily admitting to moral weakness or expressing an indifference to human life. Those who gave this response were probably as moral as anyone else in normal interpersonal relationships. These principles of everyday morality, however, did not apply in their view in situations of legitimate authority. In such situations, for many people, a different set of moral principles applies. The obligation to obey supersedes such moral principles as the injunction against killing that would govern other situations. For them, in short, following orders—even if that means shooting unarmed civilians—is the normatively expected, the required, indeed the right and moral thing for the good citizen to do.

The normative nature of this response becomes clear when we look at the cross-tabulation of the two questions, presented in table 7.1. Of those who said that they would follow orders and shoot, almost all (453 out of 489, or 93 percent) assumed that most people would follow orders and shoot. In other words, they seemed to be saying that, in following orders to shoot, they would only be doing what was expected and required—and what, indeed, everyone else would do under similar circumstances.

The response to the two hypothetical questions contrasts sharply with the responses obtained by Milgram (1974, chap. 4) when he asked people to predict how they themselves and others would act in an obedience experiment. As we reported in the preceding chapter, his respondents all said that they would disobey in the experiment he described and they predicted that only a very small proportion of participants would go all the way. Thus, they vastly underestimated the amount of obedience that actually occurred, perhaps because they could not imagine, from the description of the experiment given to them, how compelling the authority structure of the laboratory can be. In contrast, our respondents—asked to imagine a military situation—seemed to be very conscious of its compelling authority structure and to perceive the social norms as strongly favoring obedience. Thus, unlike Milgram's respondents, they predicted a high level of obedience and a majority told us that they themselves would obey.

It may well be that our respondents in fact overestimated the amount of obedience. After all, there were quite a few instances of avoidance or refusal of orders in My Lai (see chap. 1). Perhaps people are so conscious of the powerful structure of the military situation and the norms of obedience governing it that they underestimate the strength of opposing forces that might come into play, such as revulsion against killing defenseless old men, women, and children. For this and other reasons, one cannot assume that the respondents who said that they would shoot would actually do so if they found themselves in such a situation. We are inclined to believe that many of those who said they would follow orders might in fact refrain from shooting when confronted by the competing forces that operate in a real-life setting. What we *can* say is that, in terms of their cognitive and ideological orientation, a large proportion of the U.S. population at the time viewed the killing of civilians under orders to be an appropriate and normatively expected response.

To gain some perspective on the precise distribution of responses obtained in this study—particularly the figures of 51 percent saying that they would shoot and 33 percent that they would refuse—we can compare these figures to the distributions obtained in two other studies. Just before the end of the Calley trial, the Louis Harris Organization posed an almost identical question to a national sample. Of the respondents in that survey, only 43 percent (compared to 51 percent in our sample) claimed they would follow orders and shoot; 41 percent claimed they would refuse, and 16 percent didn't know. A second study, conducted in April 1971 by Leon Mann (1973) with an Australian sample, used a question similar to that asked by Harris. There a lower 30 percent said they would follow orders in comparison to 57 percent who claimed they would refuse and 13 percent who didn't know. Mann's sample was not representative of the Australian population, however, and his analysis of the sample's characteristics suggests that the 30 percent figure underestimates the level of claimed obedience in the Australian population at that time. Thus it seems fair to conclude, as Mann did, that an ideology of unquestioning obedience to orders is held by a large percentage of Australians and is not a strictly U.S. response to My Lai.

The fact that a larger percentage of respondents in our survey indicated they would follow orders and shoot, even in comparison to the Harris survey, may be accounted for by two differences in the way the question was posed. First, it was worded somewhat differently in the two surveys. In particular, the choices presented to respondents by Harris were: "Would you follow orders and shoot them or would you be more right to refuse?" Addition of the words "would you be more right to" probably gave an added degree of moral weight to the "refuse" response in the Harris poll and increased its social desirability. Second, in the Harris poll the question "what would you do?" was asked outright, whereas in our interview, it was preceded by the question about what "most people" would do. Since two-thirds of our respondents had just told us that most people would follow orders and shoot, establishing "follow orders" as the statistically normative response, it may have been easier for them to choose the same response for themselves. Both the wording and the context of our question, as compared to the Harris question, probably increased the psychological availability of the "follow orders" option.

The increased percentage of claimed shooters in our sample suggests that such responses are fragile, in the sense that they may be affected by the timing or the wording of the question. One should not, therefore, give too much weight to the exact percentages obtained. Whether the proportion is 51 percent or 43 percent, it is still the case that a large segment of the American public seemed to subscribe to the idea that they and others should follow orders unquestioningly. The questions about what "most people" would do and what "you" would do represent an intriguing analogue to My Lai. Chapter 1 indicated that it is not fully clear what orders Lieutenant Calley received before My Lai. The men under his command, however, faced essentially the situation described in the questions above. Public opinion in the wake of the Calley conviction revealed that most

Americans could seemingly put themselves in the shoes of a subordinate at My Lai. It further revealed that most of them thought most Americans would commit a war crime if they were in those shoes (and, in lesser numbers, that they themselves would).

In our original report of these data (Kelman and Hamilton, 1974), we analyzed them by comparing respondents who said they would personally shoot and those who said they would refuse. It is possible, however, to analyze responses to the two questions—what "most people would do" and what "you would do"—in combination. Such an analysis provides more information about respondents' conceptions of obedience, and it may aid our understanding of the nature and extent of respondents' identification with the defendant. It is also important to address how such judgments are related to other attitudes—including, of course, approval versus disapproval of the trial—and whether they can be predicted by the same demographic factors that predict interest in the trial. Therefore, we now examine combinations of answers to what "most people" would do and what "you" would do.

THE MAJORITY VERSUS THE SELF

People who answered that "most people" would shoot were very likely to say that they themselves would do so. Conversely, the minority who predicted that most people would refuse overwhelmingly said that they would personally be refusers. Even those who said "don't know" to the first item tended to say the same to the second. The statistical association between the two questions was powerful (gamma = .83, standard error = .02).

Inconsistent responses to the two items can be important. A substantial minority (102 people) said that *most people would shoot*, but that *they would personally refuse* to shoot. (This minority would be even more substantial if we included the 58 individuals who responded "don't know" about most people, but indicated that they were personally inclined to refuse. In keeping with other analyses, however, we follow the more conservative rule of counting responses as inconsistent only if a definite yes to one question is combined with a definite no to the other.) Most striking is the fact that almost no one—only 9 people out of nearly 1,000—said that *most people would refuse* but that *they would personally shoot*.

If we consider that a question about "most people" and a question about what "you" would do are both ways of assessing the norms governing the situation, two points emerge. First, the power of what might be called moral congruence asserted itself: "If most would shoot, I would"; "If most would refuse, I would." It is not clear which of these was chicken and which egg, but it is clear that respondents tended to see "most people" and self as behaving consistently. This congruence indicates that both obedience and disobedience can lay claim to being moral positions—norms—from the standpoint of substantial segments of the public.

Second, the relative sizes of the inconsistent groups are revealing. The "most would/I wouldn't" and "most wouldn't/I would" response combinations both constitute personal divergences from the norm. Only the former, however, was conceivable to the vast majority of people when they responded to a question about killing civilians, an act that normally would violate moral standards. Those who said that they would shoot presumably did so because they believed that they ought to obey orders—in fact, that they would have no choice but to shoot. Under the circumstances, they had every reason to expect that "most people" would do the same. For those who said that they would refuse, in contrast, it was still plausible to imagine that other citizens would not react in the same way. They seem to have assumed the existence of a choice, acknowledging that others might differ from them in how they would exercise it.

Even a "don't know" response to either question has interesting implications. A substantial number, 58 of the 142 respondents who "didn't know" what *most* people would do, then said that they would personally refuse to shoot. Perhaps to respond "don't know" to a question like the "most shoot" item is a polite way of saying that one disagrees with the majority or that one does not care what the majority will do.

Combining responses to the hypothetical questions yields three groups of respondents that are of theoretical interest and of sufficient size for statistical analysis (see table 7.1). At one extreme are the 453 respondents whom we shall call the Consistent Shooters—those who said that most people would shoot and that they themselves would also shoot. At the other extreme are the 161 Consistent Refusers, who thought that most people would refuse and that they themselves would refuse. In between is the one clearly inconsistent group of any size in our sample—the 102 respondents who said that most people would shoot, *but* they themselves would refuse. We will refer to them as Deviant Refusers. In our analyses of how these three modes of response relate to various attitudinal and demographic items, we treated them as a single variable, "shoot-refuse," with the Deviant Refusers in the middle. Our discussion of these findings, however, will typically focus first on the two consistent groups, and then consider ways in which the Deviant Refusers are distinguishable from Consistent Refusers, on the one hand, and Consistent Shooters, on the other.

NORMS ABOUT OBEDIENCE AND ATTITUDES TOWARD
MY LAI AND THE CALLEY TRIAL

Respondents' reasons for *why* they would personally shoot or refuse to shoot make at least a promising beginning for grasping the meaning of "shoot-refuse" answers. When asked to state their reasons for following orders and shooting, Consistent Shooters offered three most frequently: that "orders are orders" and a soldier has no choice but to obey (42 percent), that soldiers must shoot for self-protection (22 percent), and that failure to follow orders is punishable (21 percent). They were probably realistic in suggesting a mix of obligation, compulsion, and fear as motives for following such orders. Consistent Refusers similarly offered, at greater than 10 percent frequency, three reasons for refusing to shoot: the action would be immoral, inhuman, murder (37 percent); the victims are inno-cent, so there is no reason to shoot them (44 percent); and "I couldn't get myself to do it" (14 percent).

Deviant Refusers can be directly compared with Consistent Refusers on this item, since each group was asked why they would personally refuse to shoot. In fact, the two groups cited the same three reasons with the greatest frequency (over 10 percent). They differed significantly, however, in the frequency with which they offered two of these answers. Whereas 44 percent of Consistent Refusers gave the argument that killing would be unjustified, only 29 percent of Deviant Refus-ers offered that response. Conversely, 24 percent of Deviant Refusers, in contrast to only 14 percent of Consistent Refusers, gave the reason that "I couldn't get myself to do it." These two differences, although not large, suggest that the basis for refusal was more rational/legal among Consistent Refusers and more emo-tional or personalized among Deviant Refusers.

Attitudes toward My Lai Actions. Further evidence of differences unfolds when we turn in table 7.2 to the relationship of "shoot-refuse" to attitudes about Lieutenant Calley's actions in My Lai. Here we tabulate "shoot-refuse" against a series of other items, with the findings presented in skeletal form (that is, just the percentage of respondents choosing one selected option for each item is shown). This abbreviated presentation is designed to provide the reader with a rapid over-view of a series of highly interrelated responses.

Item A shows that attitudes about whether Lieutenant Calley should have fol-lowed orders to shoot were, not surprisingly, closely linked to answers to the two hypothetical questions. Consistent Shooters were highly likely to say Calley should have carried out orders to shoot and Consistent Refusers highly likely to say Calley should have refused. No significant differences between the groups emerged on an open-ended follow-up probe for their reasons for thinking that Calley should have followed orders or refused. Thus, for example, if a Consistent Shooter took the unusual stance of saying Calley should have refused, the reasons offered were indistinguishable from those offered by a Consistent Refuser who said the same things.

The responses of Deviant Refusers to this item clearly fell between the extremes of the other two groups. There is no doubt that they regarded Calley's action to have been wrong (see item B). But it may be that many of them were reluctant to impose their own standards on him, since they perceived following orders to be the normatively expected response—what most people would do in such a situa-tion.

Item B shows another powerful difference, this time in the respondents' overall evaluation of Calley's action. This question offered multiple response options, as suggested in the table's summary, rather than a yes/no or agree/disagree dichotomy. The actual wording of the question was as follows:

> To sum this all up, which one of these four statements comes closest to your own opinion about Lt. Calley's actions? (HAND RESPONDENT CARD)

Table 7.2 "Shoot-Refuse" as a Predictor of Attitudes toward Lt. Calley's Actions

Items	Consistent Shooters (Most Shoot, I Shoot) (%)	Deviant Refusers (Most Shoot, I Refuse) (%)	Consistent Refusers (Most Refuse, I Refuse) (%)	All Respondents (%)
A. Assuming it is true that Calley received orders to shoot, what should he have done? (Carry out/Refuse)				
Carry out	94	42	11	70
B. Overall opinion of Calley's action (Right/ Wrong, but hard to know/ Wrong, illegal/ Wrong, immoral in any case)				
Right	53	8	4	36
C. Calley's actions were justified if people he shot were Communists (Agree/Disagree)				
Agree	64	13	12	45
D. Calley's actions were justified because better to kill some S. Vietnamese civilians than risk lives of American soldiers (Agree/Disagree)				
Agree	76	26	21	58
E. In World War II it would have been better to kill some German civilians than risk lives of American soldiers (Agree/Disagree)				
Agree	83	42	33	66
F. In terms of rights and wrongs, how do Calley's actions compare with bombing raids that also kill Vietnamese civilians? (Similar/Different)				
Similar	75	62	41	66

Note: The total number of respondents in these "shoot-refuse" categories was 716, distributed unevenly, with 453 responding as Consistent Shooters, 102 as Deviant Refusers, and 161 as Consistent Refusers. Because "don't know" responses were omitted and because some items were not answered by all respondents, the Ns for the items listed in this table and in table 7.3 range from 562 to 658. All chi-square tests of association were significant at $p \leq .01$.

a. What he did was right and was what any good soldier would do under the circumstances.
b. What he did was wrong, but it was hard for him to know what was right or wrong in that kind of situation.
c. What he did was wrong and was a clear violation of what a good soldier acting under the military code would do.
d. What he did was wrong and violated principles of morality, regardless of what the military code is.
Don't know

Given these options, Consistent Shooters were likely to say that Calley's actions were right, Consistent Refusers that they were wrong. Thus, again respondents' evaluations of Calley's actions at My Lai were straightforwardly related to their assessments of their own and others' actions in a My Lai–type setting. Deviant Refusers fell between the other two groups, although they were much closer to the Consistent Refusers than to the Consistent Shooters.

Items C, D, and E were designed to probe the extent to which respondents were prepared to justify Lieutenant Calley's actions by placing his victims in an ideological or racial category that defined them as somehow less than human, or "fair game." Dehumanization of the victim or the enemy has, of course, been a central concept in various theories of mass murder and the legitimation of evil (see chap. 1; see also Sanford and Comstock, 1971). To many respondents the concept of "Communists" (item C) may have also included the notion of armed and dangerous guerrillas, some of whom could be women and children; this inclusion would presumably justify Calley's actions on the basis of self-defense. Justification that involved South Vietnamese civilians (item D) more unambiguously tapped dehumanization, racism, or both. In order to check out in a crude way the possibility that a racial element was involved, we asked a parallel item about German civilians in World War II (item E).

All three justifications were powerfully related to "shoot-refuse." Consistent Shooters were highly likely to justify Calley's actions if the victims were Communists (item C) or if there were a trade-off between South Vietnamese and American lives (item D). They were consistent in also agreeing that German lives should have been sacrificed in World War II rather than risk American lives (item E). On all three items, Consistent Refusers rejected these rationales for killing.

On each of these three items, the Deviant Refusers, though falling between the other two groups, were again much closer to the Consistent Refusers than to the Consistent Shooters. Basically, it can be said that—when it comes to judgments of the morality of Calley's actions—the Deviant Refusers were simply Refusers. They seem to have differed from the Consistent Refusers in their basis for these judgments: They were less likely to see the issues in strictly legal terms—perhaps because, unlike the Consistent Refusers, they considered their own claimed refusal to be more a matter of personal choice than normative necessity.

The final item in table 7.2 sheds further light on the nature of the Deviant Refusers' reaction. It also brings us to the question of responsibility, the central theme of the next few chapters. Item F asked whether, from a moral point of view, there was any analogy between Calley's actions and bombing raids. Consistent Shooters were more likely to see Calley's actions as similar to bombing raids and Consistent Refusers more likely to see them as different.

From their responses to our open-ended questions about why they came to their respective conclusions, we can infer the meaning of "similar" and "different" for the two groups. Consistent Shooters tended to see Calley's actions and bombing raids as similar because both served the same military purpose. Consistent Refusers tended to see the two as different because Calley deliberately shot his victims, whereas the killing of civilians in bombing raids was unintentional. Thus, the Consistent Shooters seem to have absolved Calley of responsibility because he was acting under military orders; they did not expect the individual to make judgments about the morality or legality of particular orders under these circumstances. For the Consistent Refusers, on the other hand, military personnel remain personally responsible even when they are acting under orders. They therefore focused on intentionality of the action, which is a critical criterion for holding a person responsible for its outcome.

Deviant Refusers were relatively close to Consistent Shooters in seeing Calley's actions as similar to bombing raids. They differed, however, in their reasons for coming to this conclusion. Deviant Refusers who described Calley's actions and bombing raids as similar tended to offer the reason that both kill innocent civilians. Thus, whereas Consistent Shooters considered both actions similarly justified, Deviant Refusers considered them similarly unjustified. Those Deviant Refusers who saw Calley's actions as different from bombing raids tended to give the same reason for this view as the Consistent Refusers: the difference in intentionality. However, the fact that many more of the Deviant Refusers focused on the similarity between Calley and bombardiers—and the reason they cited for this view—again points to the way in which they differed from the Consistent Refusers. Their concern was less with the issue of legal responsibility than with their personal repugnance against killing innocent civilians.

Attitudes toward the Calley Trial. Turning to questions about the trial per se, as summarized in table 7.3, we see that item A shows a predictable pattern of opinions concerning whether Lieutenant Calley should have been brought to trial. Consistent Shooters were likely to disapprove of the trial and Consistent Refusers likely to approve. Deviant Refusers were, once again, much closer to the Consistent Refusers, with a majority expressing approval of the trial.[2] Reactions to Calley's sentencing (item B) were also predictable. Consistent Shooters seemingly

---

2. We also offered a choice of possible reasons the respondent might approve or disapprove of the trial. These reasons, which serve as the focus of chapter 9, can be broadly categorized as dealing with either *responsibility* for one's actions in a chain of command, *antiwar* sentiments, or concern with *military* honor and morale. The relationship between "shoot-refuse" and reasons for possible *disapproval* of the trial was not significant. However, there was a significant relationship of "shoot-refuse" to reasons for *approving* of the Calley trial. Consistent Shooters who happened to approve of the trial tended to do so for military-related reasons, while Consistent Refusers were likely to have approved for responsibility-related reasons. Deviant Refusers chose both responsibility-related and antiwar rationales for approving.

Table 7.3 "Shoot-Refuse" as a Predictor of Attitudes toward Lt. Calley's Trial and Sentence, and Related Trials

Items	Consistent Shooters (Most Shoot, I Shoot) (%)	Deviant Refusers (Most Shoot, I Refuse) (%)	Consistent Refusers (Most Refuse, I Refuse) (%)	All Respondents (%)
A. Should Calley have been brought to trial? (Approve/ Disapprove)				
Approve	20	54	65	35
B. Calley's sentence was (Fair/ Too harsh)				
Fair	7	26	46	18
C. Was it right or wrong to convict German officers at Nuremberg for war crimes ordered by superiors? (Right/ Wrong)				
Right	34	61	68	45
D. Should American officers be convicted for war crimes ordered by superiors? (Should be/Should not be)				
Should be	16	51	66	32
E. Was it right or wrong to convict Yamashita for actions of his men that he did not order? (Right/Don't know/ Wrong)				
Right	25	40	27	27
F. Should American generals be convicted for war crimes they did not order? (Should be/ Should not be)				
Should be	23	39	34	28
G. Reaction to draft boards who said they will suspend drafting men until Calley's sentence is reversed: (Approve/Disapprove)				
Approve	54	50	31	48

Note: For information about Ns and levels of significance, see note to table 7.2. Two exceptions to this information apply to item E: "Don't know" responses were included in the analysis of this item (see text); and the chi-square for this item was significant only at $p = .025$.

put themselves in Calley's shoes and considered the sentence too harsh. Consistent Refusers, on the other hand, were much more likely to describe the sentence as fair. On this item, the Deviant Refusers were halfway between the two consistent groups. The pattern here is the same as that observed in answers to the question about what Calley should have done (item A, table 7.2) and our explanation is similar: Although the Deviant Refusers clearly regarded Calley's action to have been wrong, many of them may have been reluctant to judge him harshly, since they saw obedience to orders as the normatively expected response. Moreover, as we have argued, they were less inclined than the Consistent Refusers to formulate the issues in terms of legal responsibility.

Another trial-related question in the interview asked who should have been tried for the My Lai massacre. It is not presented in table 7.3 because its options do not allow for any ready summary in dichotomous "yes" or "no," "agree" or "disagree" terms. As respondents heard it:

So far our questions have just been concerned with Lt. Calley's trial, but there has been a lot of argument over whether or not higher officers should also be tried for what happened at My Lai. With which of these four statements do you agree? (HAND RESPONDENT CARD)

a. Lt. Calley should have been tried *and* higher officers (including generals) should *also* have been tried for what happened at My Lai.
b. Only Lt. Calley should have been tried.
c. Only higher officers should have been tried.
d. Lt. Calley should *not* have been tried and higher officers should also *not* be tried.
  Don't know

Among these options, the two middle ones were rarely chosen. The two extremes—"neither" and "both"—revealed differences among "shoot-refuse" categories. A 46 percent plurality of Consistent Shooters asserted that neither Calley nor higher officers should have been tried, in contrast to 14 percent of Consistent Refusers and 11 percent of Deviant Refusers. The response that *both* Calley and higher officers should have been tried was favored by 64 percent of Consistent Refusers, in contrast to 40 percent of Consistent Shooters. Interestingly, Deviant Refusers endorsed this position even more strongly than Consistent Refusers: 77 percent of this group said that *both* Calley and superiors should have been tried. This difference suggests that Deviant Refusers were particularly sensitive to joint responsibility for a crime of obedience. In keeping with their view that obedience to orders is normatively expected, they overwhelmingly believed that those who give illegal orders should be tried along with those who follow them.

Items C through F in table 7.3 show the relationship of "shoot-refuse" to historical precedents in military law. Responses to these precedents should be viewed with caution, if only because the questions were asked after the Calley items. Most respondents probably realized that their consistency was being put to the test. Some may have said that the Nuremberg and Yamashita convictions were wrong solely because they had previously criticized the Calley trial's outcome; others may have used the "don't know" option to avoid open inconsistency.

For the Nuremberg precedent regarding obedience to superior orders, we supplied respondents with more detail about the historical situation than the summary in table 7.3 provides:

> After World War II, German officers were tried by the Allies in Nuremberg. A good many of them were found guilty of committing war crimes, even though they had been ordered to perform the acts by their superior officers. Do you think it was right or wrong to convict these German officers for war crimes even though they were carrying out the orders of their superiors?

Item C shows that in reacting to the Nuremberg Principle of *individual responsibility*, Consistent Shooters were very *unlikely* to agree with convicting German officers; Consistent Refusers were their virtual mirror-image opposites. The percentage of Deviant Refusers favoring conviction was only slightly less than that of Consistent Refusers.

We then asked a follow-up, parallel item about whether "American officers should or should not be convicted for war crimes, even though they were carrying out the orders of their superiors" (item D). As we expected, there was a tendency to give Americans some benefit of the doubt in comparison to Germans, but this tendency was observed differentially across groups. Consistent Refusers were likely to advocate trying Americans to virtually the same degree as Germans. But the willingness of Consistent Shooters to advocate trials—which was low to begin with—dropped even further when the defendants were American officers. Deviant Refusers also showed a drop but, with a majority still favoring a trial, remained much closer to the Consistent Refusers than to the Consistent Shooters.

A different story emerges in items E and F with the case of General Yamashita and an American parallel. Here the legal issue is *command responsibility*, the military tradition of respondeat superior: "let the superior answer." Again we provided substantially more context for respondents than the table indicates:[3]

> Some people seem to feel differently about different wars depending on the causes, circumstances, and ways they are fought. After World War II, Japanese General Yamashita was tried by the United States because men under his command had committed war crimes. It was decided that General Yamashita *was responsible* for his men's actions, even though he did not directly *order* those actions, and he was convicted. Do you think it was right or wrong to convict General Yamashita for the actions of his men even though he did not order those actions?

As we shall elaborate in chapter 8, this principle of command responsibility is not quite the opposite or inverse of individual responsibility. But it is clearly *different* from it; it is based on a commander's role obligations rather than on any deeds performed. The issue in the specific question is whether a commander is to be held responsible for the actions of his men even if he does not authorize them.

---

3. The item about General Yamashita and its follow-up were in fact asked before the Nuremberg items, but reversal of order in this presentation facilitates discussion of responsibility.

In view of the question's length, its difficulty, and the relative obscurity of the Yamashita case in comparison to Nuremberg, a high rate of "don't know" responses was to be expected. This percentage was in fact so high (30 percent of the total sample) that we retained "don't know" when percentaging the item, as table 7.3 indicates. Here, Consistent Shooters—who rejected individual responsibility for actions under orders (Item C and its follow-up)—also rejected command responsibility for those who give orders. Consistent Refusers, who accepted individual responsibility for actions under orders, rejected command responsibility at a similar rate, suggesting that the two forms of responsibility indeed differ. Deviant Refusers, in this case, favored conviction significantly more often than either of the other two groups. Thus, they stand out in affirming command responsibility here, just as they stood out in advocating that higher officers, in addition to Calley, should have been tried for the My Lai massacre.

A follow-up search for inconsistencies was also carried out with the Yamashita case by asking (item F) if the respondent thought that "American generals should or should not be convicted when *their* men commit war crimes, even though they did not directly *order* these acts?"[4] Consistent Shooters were more willing to reject responsibility for Americans than were Consistent Refusers. Deviant Refusers, once again, were the most likely to advocate command responsibility.

It appears that the two principles of individual and command responsibility neither add up to any literal 100 percent nor add up to a simple continuum of orientations to obedience. Consistent Shooters essentially rejected accountability in the situation for *all* participants, not just for the subordinates with whom they might be presumed to identify. A Consistent Shooter, we assume, adopts a frame of reference in which the focus lies on a subordinate's role-based motive: obedience to authority. Superiors, in this framework (as we shall argue in chapter 8), may escape responsibility either because they have their own role-based excuses or because they lie too far up a chain of causes to bear any clear link to the crimes produced. We may contrast this picture with that for Consistent Refusers, who were the sternest advocates of individual responsibility for subordinates in the Nuremberg items. They seem to have been adopting a frame of reference (again, to be elaborated in chapter 8) whereby individual responsibility for subordinates is assessed on the basis of normal moral judgment, which considers consequences and intentions. Thus they were harsh in the case of officers who personally and intentionally committed war crimes, but relatively lenient in the case of General Yamashita, because the issue was not intentional action.

For Deviant Refusers, as we have noted, intentionality was not the central

---

4. Pursuing the sources of inconsistency, we also asked open-ended follow-up questions of all respondents who either *approved* of the trial in the foreign cases (Nuremberg and Yamashita) and *disapproved* for Americans, or the reverse. The open-ended answers of the former group, the apparently self- or nation-serving respondents who would try Germans or Japanese but not Americans, proved uninformative. (These self-serving reasons might be described as "we won," "they attacked," "just different," or "don't know.") The latter, antinationalistic, group was so small as to be unanalyzable.

issue. Thus, they were more lenient than the Consistent Refusers toward Lieutenant Calley and other officers who acted under orders, even though they found the actions themselves morally repugnant. On the other hand, they were the group most inclined to set a stringent standard of behavior for commanders. Laying blame at the top of hierarchies can follow from a very traditional view of authority, since it can be a literal application of the ancient doctrine of respondeat superior. But it can also follow from a critical view of the authority hierarchy itself, when citizens hold it responsible for a policy they consider flawed. Respondents who felt the Vietnam War to be at fault for the My Lai massacre could adopt what looks like respondeat superior as a way of rejecting the authorities' legitimacy in waging the war. We suspected Deviant Refusers of feeling this way about Vietnam; other items below will shed further light on this possibility.

The final item in table 7.3 (item G) introduces an interesting ambiguity of meaning. The threat by draft boards to suspend drafting men until Calley's conviction was reversed was a conservative or promilitary protest; at the same time, however, such action would have produced a draft stoppage—an antimilitary effect. Table 7.3 indicates that Consistent Shooters more often approved and Consistent Refusers disapproved of this threatened action. Deviant Refusers, on the other hand, approved at almost the same rate as Consistent Shooters. Not surprisingly, though, the two groups differed in the reasons they cited for their approval. The reason offered by a large majority of Consistent Shooters was that men should not be drafted and then punished for doing their duty in Vietnam. As a protest, this action probably epitomized their sense of betrayal and their feeling that draftees—in the wake of the Calley conviction—were being placed in a double-bind situation. As some respondents put it: "You're damned if you do and damned if you don't." In contrast, the Deviant Refusers—and the Consistent Refusers who joined them in approving the threatened action—did so largely out of opposition to the war or the draft or because they felt the action might encourage a reevaluation of policies.

Correlates and Predictors of "Shoot-Refuse" Responses

We now turn to the problem of understanding and predicting the patterns of "shoot-refuse" answers in the context of respondents' other beliefs and identities. We concentrate on respondents' underlying attitudes toward the Vietnam War and their membership in differing demographic groups.

VIETNAM WAR

Positions on "shoot-refuse" might be expected to vary with respondents' views of the Vietnam War itself: Willingness to shoot and to believe that others would do so is probably consistent with support for the war. This need not mean that support for the war per se causes willingness to shoot; it might mean the reverse, that the respondent who is willing to follow orders and shoot becomes willing to

Table 7.4 Relationship of "Shoot-Refuse" Responses to Vietnam War Attitudes

Items	Consistent Shooters (%)	Deviant Refusers (%)	Consistent Refusers (%)	All Respondents (%)
A. Self-identification				
Hawk	37	8	16	28
Middle of road	34	31	31	33
Dove	30	61	53	39
All respondents (%)	63	15	22	100 (602)
B. Most important reason				
Hawkish	43	19	24	35
Dovish	57	81	76	65
All respondents (%)	62	15	23	100 (616)

Note: The table is percentaged with the column variable "shoot-refuse" as the independent variable, as we are focusing on it descriptively. We make no assumptions about actual causal priority. As in tables 7.2 and 7.3 "shoot-refuse" consists of combinations of responses to what "most people" would do in a situation like My Lai and what "you" would do. Self-identification responses exclude the "don't know" category. The rationales offered for Vietnam War views, as described in the text, were combined into five hawkish versus five dovish reasons on a priori grounds; two intermediate reasons, rarely chosen, were excluded from this analysis. The overall N appears in parentheses below the 100% figure. Both the row and the column labeled "All respondents" sum to 100% (with some rounding error), so that the N for any given row, column, or cell can be calculated as needed.

support a war or a promilitary policy. It can also mean that both support for the war and willingness to shoot follow from a more general orientation, such as militarism. Whatever the mechanism of cause and effect, it is plausible to expect the respondent who says "shoot" to be more favorable to the Vietnam War and the respondent who says "refuse" to be less favorable.

Table 7.4 presents key attitudes toward the Vietnam War. (Responses to specific policy questions, not tabulated here, distinguished only weakly among "shoot-refuse" groups; broad self-identification as a liberal or conservative or political party identification also failed to distinguish among groups.) The first item refers to general self-identification; the second is based on a set of more specific rationales for the respondent's views of the war. It appears, first, that self-identification as a hawk, at the late date of 1971, was associated with being a Consistent Shooter, and self-identification as a dove, with Consistent or Deviant Refusal. Deviant Refusers were, if anything, the most strongly dovish group. Item B contrasts the groups in terms of their choice of one of five dovish statements as the most important reason for their opinions about the war versus one of five hawkish statements.[5] Consistent Shooters again stood out in offering hawkish reasons, and Deviant Refusers again emerged as somewhat more dovish than Consistent Refusers. It is plausible that "shoot-refuse" responses did not *cause* answers about Vietnam, or the reverse, but that both dovishness about the war and refusal—especially Deviant Refusal—on these hypothetical questions reflected more general independence or perceived deviation from authority.

DEMOGRAPHIC FACTORS

Table 7.5 presents key demographic predictors of the "shoot-refuse" combination. These address the fundamental questions: What predicted being a Consistent Shooter? A Deviant Refuser? A Consistent Refuser? Here the table is percentaged, in conventional fashion, with the demographic factors (columns) as the independent variables.

The first panel presents a familiar predictor: educational attainment. Higher levels of education reduced the probability of being a Consistent Shooter. An especially large gap appeared between those who had a high school education and those whose education extended beyond high school. Once again, as noted in our summary above of who followed the trial (see also appendix A), we see some indication that respondents' judgments were governed by whatever it is that education indexes: social position, cognitive sophistication, or both.

Other indicators of social position (not tabulated) yielded the same general results. Of the respondents who were employed, those in lower-status occupations (such as skilled blue-collar work) were disproportionately represented among the Consistent Shooters, whereas those in higher-status occupations (such as professional fields) were disproportionately represented among the Refusers and particularly the Deviant Refusers. The association between socioeconomic status (based on interviewer ratings of the quality of respondents' homes and furnishings) and the "shoot-refuse" responses followed the same pattern, but fell short of statistical significance.

The middle panel in table 7.5 combines the results for two significant demographic predictors of "shoot-refuse," respondents' sex and military experience, by separating males with and without military service into distinct categories. Both sex and military experience were significantly related to "shoot-refuse" when analyzed separately, as they had been to interest in the trial (see appendix A). In this

5. Twelve specific rationales for opinions about the Vietnam War were presented; an open-ended option for respondents to offer their own reason did not generate any categories of any size. Respondents were asked which they agreed with, which had influenced their views, and which they felt was most important in shaping their views of the war. Our a priori categorization of five reasons as dovish, five as hawkish, and two as ambiguous, was borne out by the patterns of their intercorrelations on the "agree with" question. Dovish items included relatively pragmatic rationales ("The war is hurting the American economy") as well as idealistic ones ("This is an immoral and destructive war"). Similarly, hawkish items included the more pragmatic ("If South Vietnam falls to the Communists, other countries in Asia will soon go Communist, too") and the idealistic ("We should fight to preserve democracy when it is threatened").

Table 7.5 Predicting "Shoot-Refuse" Responses from Demographic Variables

	Education				Sex/Military Experience				Region of Residence		
Shoot-Refuse Response	Low (<12) (%)	Medium (12) (%)	High (13+) (%)	All Respondents (%)	Female (%)	Male-No (%)	Male-Yes (%)	All Respondents (%)	South/ Midwest (%)	Northeast/ Far West (%)	All Respondents (%)
Consistent Shooters	71	67	50	63	58	64	73	63	71	58	63
Deviant Refusers	10	13	21	14	19	13	7	14	11	16	14
Consistent Refusers	19	20	29	23	23	23	20	22	18	26	23
All respondents (%)	35	34	31	100 (708)	51	24	25	100 (711)	42	58	100 (716)

Note: The overall N appears in parentheses below the 100% figure. The demographic variable *education* is a straightforward categorization of years of schooling; *sex/military experience* combines these two variables to yield three categories: females, males with no military service, and males with service; *region* categorizes the respondent's place of residence into the broad groupings indicated.

more succinct summary we have conservatively included in the female category the nine females with military experience. The combination variable highlights the fact that males who had not had military service stood in a roughly intermediate position between females and males with military experience. Females were least likely, and males with military experience most likely, to adopt a Consistent Shooter pattern of response. The linear trend across categories suggests some contribution of general sex-role socialization, in addition to military experience, to the creation of Consistent Shooters.

It is interesting to note in table 7.5 that the increasing tendency to adopt the Consistent Shooter stance as one moves from females to males with military experience is not matched by a decreasing tendency to adopt the Consistent Refuser stance. The proportion of Consistent Refusers is very similar across the three groups. The difference among the groups shows up only in the proportion of *Deviant* Refusers. That is, females were most likely and males with military experience were least likely to adopt a Deviant Refuser pattern of response. Thus, the effect of sex and military experience seems to have been primarily on the emotional readiness to follow orders to shoot innocent civilians rather than on the cognitive assessment of legal responsibilities.

Region of the country, the right panel of table 7.5, plays a predictive role that is also consistent with its influence on trial information and interest. Respondents from the South and Midwest were more likely to fit the Consistent Shooter pattern. They were less likely to be Refusers of either variety.

A final predictor, the respondent's religious affiliation, is not tabulated here because its effect was slight and its causal role was conceptually unclear. Respondents were categorized into the nominal groupings of Catholic, Protestant, and "other" (Jewish, other, or none). In simple two-way analyses, Protestants were inclined to be Consistent Shooters; Catholics were represented in each response category roughly in proportion to their representation in the sample; and religious "others" were distinctively inclined to be Refusers, especially Deviant Refusers. Religious affiliation, however, was related to education, as we shall explore in greater detail in chapter 9. Religious "others" were particularly well-educated. In the present case, an analysis that looked at religion's effects *with education controlled* left no results of significance, but the small and uneven sizes of categories in such an analysis made it inconclusive in our view. The safest summary of the impact of religion on "shoot-refuse" is probably that it *might* have played a role in these decisions, but its role was obscured by the similar role of educational attainment.

Checks on Validity. The question of the "reality" of religion's effect leads us to close with a review of the validity of other demographic findings. It is important to ask systematically if any of the relationships discussed are *spurious* (where one "effect" is actually caused by some other variable) or *interactive* (where the effect of one predictor depends on the presence of, or a particular "dosage" of, another).

For example, is the apparent effect of region spurious: Is it due to regional differences in the number of people who have had military experience? Or do region and military experience interact: Does military experience have special meaning or honor in the South, accentuating its tendency to produce Consistent Shooters? Here and in chapter 9 we restrict such analyses to two-way combinations of predictors, where we can be confident that enough respondents filled the categories to provide reliable data. (For example, we might have been able to calculate theoretically the response of a rural southern or midwestern Jew, but our sample had none.)

For "shoot-refuse," each predictor was still significant with other variables controlled one by one. For example, the effect of education held for both men and women, and the effect of military experience held across regions of the country. Further, no interactions of demographic factors emerged; each variable's relationship to "shoot-refuse" held to a similar extent *within* categories of other demographic variables.

Conclusions

Public reactions to the My Lai massacre—or, more specifically, to the actions of Lieutenant Calley and his men in My Lai—support the analysis in chapter 6 of the cognitive and motivational obstacles to challenging authority. The attitudes toward obedience held by a large proportion of the U.S. population suggest that they would find it difficult to resist the expectation of obedience built into authority situations, particularly in the context of military combat. When asked to put themselves in the shoes of Calley or his men, a majority of our respondents predicted that they would follow orders and shoot. Nearly all of these respondents assumed that most people would do the same, which implies a perception of social norms as heavily supporting obedience in this situation. We do not know, of course, what these individuals, whom we called Consistent Shooters, would in fact do if they found themselves in such a situation, but it seems reasonable to assume that they would not find it easy to break out of the definition of the situation as one requiring obedience. They saw no choice; as many of them told us, "orders are orders."

Clearly, however, not everyone considered obedience inevitable in the hypothetical situation we described. Just as many of the men under Calley's command found ways of refusing or evading his orders, so many—a third—of our respondents predicted that they would refuse to shoot. Not surprisingly, the Refusers in our sample were disproportionately (though by no means exclusively) drawn from the higher-status segments of the population. The strongest predictor of the "refuse" response was educational attainment, which represents both position in a stratified society and cognitive sophistication about one's world. Education and status increase people's access to the informational, organizational, and material resources that can help them recognize the availability of options and afford the risk of disrupting the social order. As we pointed out in chapter 6, awareness of options and willingness to disrupt are the psychological conditions underlying people's ability to redefine the authority situation.

The distinction between the two subgroups of Refusers, the Consistent and the Deviant, helps us focus on different ways in which people may manage to redefine authority situations. Harking back to the preceding chapter's discussion of binding and opposing forces, we propose that, among Consistent Refusers, the primary basis for rejecting the nonchoice definition of the situation was the relative weakness of the binding forces, whereas among Deviant Refusers it was the relative strength of the opposing forces. The Consistent Refusers seemed to believe that the norm of obedience did not apply to My Lai or to the hypothetical situation presented to them presumably because orders to shoot unarmed civilians are illegal. They probably recognized a normative duty to disobey under such circumstances and thus did not feel bound by a definition of the situation as one in which obedience is required. Moreover, they assumed—wrongly, it would seem, at least as far as their hypothetical judgments are concerned—that most people share their interpretation. The Deviant Refusers, in contrast, seemed to believe that the norm of obedience does apply and that most people would feel bound by it. Despite this belief, however, they said that they would personally refuse to obey an order to kill civilians because the action would be immoral and they would simply not be able to "get themselves to do it." They broke out of the nonchoice definition of the situation because they found the actions called for so repugnant that they were prepared to violate the norm of obedience.

Consistent and Deviant Refusers could also be distinguished in terms of the two psychological conditions we postulated as underlying the ability to redefine an authority situation. Of course, we know only what our respondents said and not what they would do. We can speculate, however, that Consistent Refusers would more readily meet the cognitive condition for redefining an authority situation: They seemed to have an awareness and an ability to conceive of alternative definitions of the situation and interpretations of its requirements. They may have been, therefore, less enthralled by the definition proffered by the authorities and the binding forces that sustained it. Deviant Refusers, on the other hand, may more readily have met the motivational condition: At least some of them seemed to be prepared to disrupt the established social order and, presumably, suffer the consequences. They may, therefore, have been more responsive to opposing forces, even at the risk of social opprobrium. Active resistance to illegitimate authority, of course, is generally a collective process. We can well imagine that, in such a process, Consistent Refusers and Deviant Refusers would each make unique contributions to the redefinition of the situation and the decision to resist.

What Consistent and Deviant Refusers had in common was that they subscribed to the principle of individual responsibility for a crime of obedience. They both differed in this regard from Consistent Shooters, who seemed inclined to absolve Calley and others of responsibility for crimes committed under orders.

From Consistent Shooters' responses to some of the open-ended questions we can infer their view that soldiers cannot be expected to make judgments about the morality or legality of actions they are ordered to perform and that it is unfair, therefore, to hold them responsible for the consequences of such actions. Consistent and Deviant Refusers both rejected this view, as can be seen from the distribution of responses to a series of attitude questions on which the two Refuser subgroups clearly stood apart from the Consistent Shooters.

The two Refuser groups differed from each other in their precise approach to the question of responsibility. The Consistent Refusers were inclined to be more legalistic in their approach. They tended to assign responsibility in authority contexts strictly on the basis of the intentionality of the action—the criterion for judging responsibility in ordinary crimes. Thus, although they were relatively severe in judging Calley, who intentionally killed civilians, they seemed reluctant to hold bombardiers personally responsible for the unintended deaths of civilians during bombing raids, or to assert command responsibility of superiors for actions they did not specifically order. The Deviant Refusers, in contrast, were inclined to approach responsibility by reference to the nature of the action being judged and its human consequences, rather than the strict criterion of intentionality. Thus, they tended to be less severe than Consistent Refusers in judging Calley because they understood the dilemma he was in; but they were more willing to assign responsibility to bombardiers and commanders whose actions contributed to the deaths of innocent civilians, even though they may not have caused these deaths intentionally or directly. The approach of the Deviant Refusers is reminiscent of what Gilligan (1982) has called a "different voice" in moral reasoning, characteristic of women, which emphasizes caring and compassion more than abstract principle. It is interesting, therefore, that females in our sample were significantly more likely than males to be Deviant Refusers (but not Consistent Refusers).

Although the fine differences between the two subgroups of Refusers in their approach to individual responsibility are of great theoretical and social interest, what they had in common is central to our continuing analysis of crimes of obedience. Both recognized individual responsibility for such crimes, in contrast to the Consistent Shooters, who tended to reject this principle when applied to actions under orders. It appeared to us, as we contemplated the results of the 1971 survey, that these sharply divergent orientations of Refusers and Shooters pointed to the basic, underlying issue in people's judgments of the Calley trial and crimes of obedience more generally: their conceptualization of responsibility in situations governed by authority. Furthermore, we assume that people's views of responsibility have an important bearing on how they are likely to behave in authority situations. At the very least, the way they attribute responsibility to others should be related to the way they attribute responsibility to themselves in their own encounters with authority—not only ex post facto, in evaluating their own actions, but also in the authority situation itself, when they try to decide how to act.

For a more systematic discussion of the role of responsibility, therefore, we present in the next chapter a framework for distinguishing different conceptions of responsibility in authority situations. In chapter 9, we return to the 1971 survey, to examine specifically how different conceptions of responsibility—as distinguished by our framework—help to organize public reactions to crimes of obedience. Chapter 10 presents findings from a second survey, which was designed to test and confirm ideas about responsibility derived from the earlier work.

8 | Responsibility in Authority Situations

Who is responsible for a crime of obedience? This chapter reviews general determinants of responsibility and links alternative conceptions of responsibility to the likelihood of obedience in situations governed by authority.

Responsibility is an issue throughout social life, not just in the encounter between subordinate and authority. Responsibility refers to a decision about *liability for sanctions based on some judgment rule*. Sanctions are usually negative but can include rewards as well as punishments. The inputs to a responsibility decision according to our model are the violated rule itself, the actor's deeds, and the expectations of others regarding what the actor should do (Hamilton, 1978b).[1] That is, actors are judged, and judge themselves, on the basis of both what *was* done (causes) and what *should have been* done (expectations). Psychologists studying responsibility judgments have tended to focus on the first aspect, causality. Sociologists have tended to focus on the second, expectations. As social psychologists, we see both elements as critical to understanding responsibility judgments; in this chapter we hope to illustrate that lawyers, linguists, and philosophers are likely to support this conviction. In the context of situations governed by authority, we shall argue that focusing on one side of this responsibility equation versus the other is tantamount to two different definitions of the situation; one definition encourages and justifies disobedience, whereas the other supports and affirms obedience. Therefore we begin by considering these alternative elements of what it means to be responsible.

Attributions of Responsibility

A major concern of modern social psychology has been to account for causal judgments in everyday life. This interest is usually

1. The discussion in this chapter draws extensively on Hamilton's earlier article.

labeled "attribution theory."[2] Several distinct theories in fact share a focus on causal judgments or attributions. (See Jones et al., 1972, or Harvey et al., 1976, 1978, for some approaches sharing this interest.)

Social psychologists use the term *attribution* for a reason. In everyday English, we say "to what do you attribute your success (or failure, or whatever)?" when we want to know the cause or causes on which the person primarily focuses. An attribution is a lay person's explanation. Such explanations can arise in two kinds of circumstances. First, an observer can simply be puzzled about what happened; he or she wants to know *why* it happened. Second—and probably more frequently—an observer may feel good or bad about what happened and want to know who or what should receive the praise or blame. The first issue is purely causal. The second is more than that. When praise or blame, reward or punishment, come into consideration, the question becomes one of responsibility linked to causality. Modern attribution theories have tended to lump these two issues together (but see Fincham and Jaspars, 1980; Hamilton, 1980; Shaver, 1985).

The work of Fritz Heider (1958) provides the basic framework for psychological attribution theories as well as a specific model for psychologists' study of responsibility attributions. Heider's general attribution framework rests on the "naive analysis of action" by individuals. According to Heider, people want to make the world a stable and predictable place. Thus they try to understand both what is stable in the environment (the "dispositional qualities" of objects) and what causes changes in that environment.

To make attributions regarding stable properties and causes of change, people analyze the causes of action into two basic categories: forces from people acting in the environment and forces from the environment. An individual's "personal force" is a combination of power, or *ability*, and of *trying*: of what a person is able to do and tries to do. Trying itself is composed of intention (*what* the person tries to do) and exertion (*how hard* he or she tries). In any given situation, when we see a person act we need two inputs in order to decide that the action was personally caused. We must be able to infer that the person was trying and that the person was capable of performing the act in question ("can"). Heider's concept of "can" is what ability allows under existing environmental conditions. Thus when we see a person paddling hard to cross a river in a canoe against the current, we make a very different inference about the cause of reaching the other side from the one we make when we see a canoe blown across by the wind (see Shaver, 1975, for this illustration).

2. In addition to the sources cited in the text of this and earlier chapters, recent works related to attribution of responsibility include the following: Brickman et al. (1975), Fincham (1985), Fincham and Jaspars (1983), Fincham and Shultz (1981), Harvey and Rule (1978), McGraw (1985), Semin and Manstead (1983), Shaw and Iwawaki (1972), Shaw and Reitan (1969), Shultz and Schliefer (1983), and Shultz et al. (1986). Works that focus more specifically on the question of children's ability to understand subjective elements in moral judgment include Darley and Zanna (1982), Ferguson and Rule (1982), Hamilton et al. (1988), Karniol (1978), Keasey (1978), Lickona (1976), Rest (1983), and Sedlak (1979).

Heider's framework for causal judgments is a simple one. There are two fundamental kinds of attribution—to persons and to environment. Further, there are two fundamental qualities to look for in the person—power, or skills, and evidence of trying to produce the effect. Two major attribution models developed since Heider, those by Jones and Davis (1965) and by Kelley (1967), can be seen as elaborations of this basic scheme. Jones and Davis's primary concern is inference to stable properties of the individual once personal causation has been determined. Kelley's primary concerns are to elaborate on the environmental context and to capture the weighing of evidence by the ordinary perceiver.

How does this causal model relate to responsibility? Heider argued that if adults are to assign responsibility to a person for an event, they need to infer personal causality from the actor. Intention and exertion are key inferences, for Heider argued that people are held more strictly responsible for intentions and exertions than for abilities. Ultimately, attribution of personal responsibility is a trade-off between personal and environmental factors. The more influence is attributed to environmental factors, the less clearly the person can be held responsible.

Heider offered a brief account of possible stages in how responsibility is judged. Numerous psychological studies of responsibility attribution are indebted to a mere two pages of his book (1958, pp. 112–113). Heider's model sounded developmental, partly because he credited Piaget (1932/1965) for its genesis. Piaget's model of moral development included two broad levels or stages: the earlier "morality of constraint" and the later "morality of cooperation." In judging responsibility, Piaget argued that the younger child focuses on the objective consequences of action, but that the older child turns toward a focus on the subjective intent of the actor as the primary concern. Heider expanded these insights into a five-level model, summarized in table 8.1. The table shows the labels that were later placed on these levels (by Shaw and Sulzer, 1964), Heider's definitions of the levels, and comparable legal categories. We shall turn to the legal categories later when considering the sociological side of our own model.

Taken as a model of the development of responsibility attributions, Heider's scheme argues that the very young child is essentially unwilling or unable to consider intent per se. As the child develops, the differences between degrees of intent become more salient. Finally, in the mature adult, intent is traded off against the strength of environmental forces. Developmental studies comparing children's judgments of responsibility with those of adults have provided some support for the model. Younger children assign more responsibility at lower levels and differentiate levels less than do adults (Fincham and Jaspars, 1979; Harris, 1977; Shaw and Sulzer, 1964); however, even young children prove capable of employing information about actors' subjective states (for example, Darley et al., 1978). Such evidence does not support a "strict" developmental stage model, in which each level or stage would supersede prior stages (see Kohlberg, 1969, 1984). Of course, there is no indication that Heider intended the model as a strict developmental one, and these results are consistent with a looser version of how responsibility attribution develops.

Table 8.1 Heider's Stages of Responsibility Attribution, Their Definitions, and Corresponding Legal Categories

Level[a]	Definition	Approximate Legal Equivalent
I. Association	A person is "held responsible for each effect that is in any way connected with him or that seems in any way to belong to him" (Heider, 1958, p. 113).	Vicarious responsibility
II. Commission	Anything "caused by [a person] p is ascribed to him. Causation is understood in the sense that p was a necessary condition for the happening, even though he could not have foreseen the outcome however cautiously he proceeded. . . . The person is judged not according to his intention but according to the actual results of what he does" (p. 113).	Strict liability
III. Foreseeability	Here "p is considered responsible, directly or indirectly, for any aftereffect he may have foreseen even though it was not a part of his own goal and therefore still not a part of the framework of personal causality" (p. 113).	Negligence
IV. Intention	At this stage "only what p intended is perceived as having its source in him" (p. 113).	Criminal responsibility
V. Justification	In this final stage "even p's own motives are not entirely ascribed to him but are seen as having their source in the environment." The "responsibility for the act is at least shared by the environment" (p. 114).	Legal justifications, excuses, mitigations of III or IV (e.g., duress)

Source: Reprinted from Hamilton, 1978b, by permission of the publisher
[a]Labels initially applied by Shaw and Sulzer (1964).

A second area of research in responsibility attribution that owes a debt to Heider concerns responsibility for accidents. A number of investigators have used judgment of responsibility for an accident to explore effects of the perceiver's biases on attribution. These biases tend to be less rational factors such as defensiveness caused by identifying with the perpetrator, or a need to believe that the world is a just place where people get what they deserve (for example, Shaver, 1970; Walster, 1966; see also Lerner, 1980, and review by Burger, 1981). Accidents have seemed an ideal arena to explore such issues precisely because the role of personal causation is quite unclear. Unfortunately, the results of such studies have often been contradictory or ambiguous (see review by Vidmar and Crinklaw, 1974).

In suggesting a possible reason for this confusion, Fishbein and Ajzen (1973) clarified Heider's model. They argued that two dimensions are really at issue: the cognitive sophistication of the observer or judge (developmental level) and the complexity of the situation (the *situation's* level). The developmental studies themselves indicated that stories can be constructed to exemplify each level. Fishbein and Ajzen pointed out that some of the confusion in the accident studies might be caused by the uncertainty of experimental participants about the responsibility rule (that is, level) they were supposed to apply to the inherently ambiguous stimulus situation in order to determine responsibility.

The proper interpretation of accident studies is not our central concern. Rather, they exemplify recent uses of the Heiderian model in psychological research. In considering responsibility in situations governed by authority, however, we became uneasy with this model. It did not seem to explain the forces in the authority-subordinate relationship very well. We voiced this unease in an early publication of our national survey data (Kelman and Lawrence [Hamilton], 1972b). Thinking about the 1971 study helped us in developing the model for responsibility attribution presented here. Therefore, when we present data consistent with this model in the next two chapters, readers should keep in mind that our approach was largely *formed* in reaction to the first study we report and *tested* in the second.

A Role-based Conception of Responsibility

It is now time to consider carefully the legal analogues of Heider's levels as presented in table 8.1. Each of the first four Heiderian levels has a legal analogue which is a set of rules for determining responsibility. *Association* responsibility in the legal realm can be found in vicarious liability rules, such as regulations that tavern owners are responsible for the serving of liquor to minors by anyone on the premises, with or without the owner's knowledge or consent. *Commission* responsibility is represented in strict liability rules, such as the provision of workers' compensation for industrial accidents regardless of the company's good intentions or ability to prevent the occurrence of the accident. *Foreseeability* responsibility is found in both civil and criminal statutes concerning negligence. *Intention* responsibility—what Heider and other adults commonly call "full" responsibility—is typical criminal responsibility for an intended act (mens rea, or "guilty mind"). Finally, *justification* is a conglomerate of the legal categories of mitigation, justification, and excuse, all of which reduce or eliminate foreseeability and intention responsibilities.

At each of the first four levels, it is perfectly intelligible for the legal system to ask jurors whether or not a defendant is responsible according to the set of rules. It is equally intelligible for jurors to decide that the defendant is not responsible enough. It is just as possible to be *fully* association responsible (given the appropriate case) as it is to be *fully* intention responsible (given the appropriate, but different, case). Each rule is a distinct basis for judging responsibility, although they differ in the level of intentional involvement by the person being judged.

But do judgments of real adults by real adults depend on levels of personal causation alone? In a word, no. The first four Heiderian levels incorporate increasing degrees of intentionality, yet the law calls forth judgments of guilt from adult jurors in cases representing all four. And the consequences of these rules at the lower levels need not be trivial. Chapter 3 noted that, under the doctrine of respondeat superior ("let the superior answer"), vicarious responsibility can lead to a judgment of death against a commanding officer in the military. It did so in the post–World War II case of General Yamashita, which figured in our survey. What these four legal rule sets reflect is consideration of the actor's deeds in the context of the actor's role. Any actor, behaving badly enough and intentionally enough, can be liable under intention-responsibility rules. But only certain actors in certain roles and behaving in certain domains may be liable according to association-responsibility rules. Thus legal association responsibility can rest exclusively on roles in the absence of any causal connection; legal intention responsibility, on deeds in the context of general undifferentiated norms that apply to all actors. The intermediate rule sets show intermediate emphasis on the two.

Legal rules need not fully reflect or be reflected in everyday life. Yet law codifies the moral rules of a society by indicating how wrongdoing is defined, how specific instances of wrongdoing are assessed, and how wrongdoing is to be punished. It appears that liability for formal legal sanctions is determined by socially learned rules that incorporate both what the accused did and what the accused was supposed to do: the expectations of others for a person in the accused's role or position. Liability for informal sanctions may be determined similarly.

Although law defines formal rules, language determines the limits of what can be talked about under the rules and how it can be discussed. Thus it is also useful to look at the English language for evidence about what responsibility means. If we find that speakers of English use the term *responsibility* to refer to each of the components of our model, it at least suggests that the model reflects how English speakers think about responsibility. In dictionary definitions, *responsibility* is primarily taken to refer to liability for punishment or reward (more commonly, punishment). H. L. A. Hart (1968), a legal philosopher, has also conducted a linguistic analysis of the concept of responsibility that makes liability for punishment its central meaning. Hart notes, however, that *responsibility* can be used to refer simply to causality. "What was responsible for X?" can often be translated as "What caused X?" Thus to speak of responsibility may mean to speak of causation alone, without implying anything in particular about sanctions or even about intentions. (See also Critchlow, 1985; Shaver, 1975, 1985; Shaver and Drown, 1986.)

Hart's linguistic analysis includes another major use of the term *responsibility* which he labels "role responsibility." He defines it as follows: "Whenever a person occupies a distinctive place or office in a social organization, to which specific duties are attached to provide for the welfare of others or to advance in some ways the aims or purposes of the organization, he is properly said to be responsible for the performance of these duties, or for doing what is necessary to fulfill them" (1968, p. 212). According to Hart, to speak of the "responsibilities of office," of "responsible behavior," or of a "responsible citizen" is to speak in terms of the obligations or expectations attached to roles.

Responsibility clearly has multiple meanings in English. But these three meanings correspond to elements of our model: expectations for what one should do (Hart's role responsibility), perceptions of what one actually does (causal responsibility), and evaluations of whether the outcome merits punishment or reward (liability responsibility). In an actual decision about responsibility, these three meanings fit together, since both roles (expectations, obligations) and deeds (acts, their consequences, and their intentionality) determine sanctions. This combination need not be additive. The expectations of a social role may color how a person's actions are perceived. Furthermore, actions are evaluated against a backdrop of what should have been done. Evaluations may differ for people in different social roles. Therefore the model suggests that "roles × deeds = liability for sanctions," rather than "roles + deeds = liability for sanctions."

A person's *liability* for praise or blame, punishment or reward, typically depends on how deeds stack up against expectations. That is, all social roles include liability for failing to do what one should. From society's point of view this "should" is an *expectation*; from the actor's point of view it is an *obligation*.[3] If expectations for what ought to be done are met, a relatively neutral evaluation can be anticipated. When they are met consistently or thoroughly, mild positive evaluation might ensue. This is the nuance of responsibility in which we refer to the

3. We pointed out in chapter 5 that all citizens have a citizen role, whether it is inculcated via rules, roles, values, or a mix of these; here we wish to stress the parallel point that all roles have expectations and obligations. (As the text indicates, what is an expectation from society's viewpoint is an obligation from the individual's viewpoint.) What differs between roles is the *type and timing* of these expectations/obligations. For example, we shall argue that authoritative or high-prestige positions involve diffuse, forward-looking expectations that are difficult to monitor for behavioral compliance. However, we stress that expectations/obligations and sanctions for failing to live up to them are inherent in all roles. Chapter 5 indicated that *role* orientation referred to the centrality of role and not its exclusive relevance to that mode of integration. Similarly, we see the likelihood of the individual's stressing obligation per se in judging responsibility to be greatest for those whose responsibility concern is *reliable performance*. In chapter 11 we suggest that this view of responsibility is likely to be associated with identification with authorities: that is, role orientation.

reliability of a responsible citizen or responsible worker. When someone exceeds expectations, fulfills what seem to be high and internally generated standards, goes "beyond the call of duty"—this is the stuff of which praise is made. When someone falls below the line—by failing to live up to the standards of home, school, motor vehicles bureau, job, society—this is the stuff of everyday spankings, civil suits, and prison terms.

The next key piece of the puzzle is to clarify how being in different social positions leads to the application of different responsibility rules. This will lead us to the relative positions of authority and subordinate in a crime of obedience.

If "roles × deeds = responsibility," then just what effect do different social roles have on the rules for assessing responsibility? Looking at the legal analogues to Heider's stages in table 8.1, it appears that different criteria are used for certain role positions. When actors occupy these roles, lower levels of intent or personal causation are required before a judgment of responsibility is made. We need to ask how these responsibility standards may be related to hierarchies of authority and subordination.

The idea that authority produces variation in rules for responsibility is suggested by the fact that Hart's (1968) original discussion of role responsibility was framed in terms of bureaucratic obligations; in addition, his first illustration of role responsibility involved a sea captain, who stands at the top of a chain of command. For present purposes it is vital to be able to compare the presence and extent of authority in different situations. Authority is a universal characteristic of social structure. Preceding chapters emphasize, however, that modern (rational-legal) authority is predominantly either bureaucratic or professional in nature: resting on bureaucratic control, professional expertise, or both. We shall use the status or prestige of an occupation as a convenient summary of these two types of authority. The highest-status jobs are high in professional authority (such as a physician) or bureaucratic authority (such as business ownership or top managerial position). Medium-status jobs may involve some professional training or bureaucratic control (such as sales or clerical positions). Low-status jobs tend to require little formal training and typically involve being ordered or supervised by another (such as a factory operative or manual laborer). Higher-status jobs require more education and return more income. The issue is whether they are judged according to different standards of accountability.

The relation of role to responsibility can conveniently be considered in terms of the timing of accountability. *Blame* for failing to meet expectations, judgment that current performance is *reliable*, and being *charged with* the responsibilities of high office can be seen as past, present, and future "tenses" of responsibility, since they refer to falling behind, meeting, and being assigned societal expectations for performance. Although we should again stress that all roles embody expectations and obligations, roles differ in their breadth and in the extent to which future burdens are meant and imposed. (See also note 3.) That is, social roles of differing status embody different mixtures of these "tenses" of responsibility. Low-status jobs are conceived of and administered in terms of compliance with explicit job standards. Feedback typically comes in the form of after-the-fact punishment for deviations from these standards or rules. Medium-status jobs involve a web of expectations and positive or negative feedback focused on reliable current performance. High-status jobs—ones with major role "responsibilities" in Hart's sense—entail expectations that the occupant will meet diffuse and internalized expectations for both action and, potentially, overseeing the actions of others. (See also Fox, 1974; Kohn, 1977; and discussion of socialization patterns below.)

Past, present, and future tenses of responsibility can also be distinguished by reference to a morality of duty versus a morality of aspiration (Fuller, 1969). A morality of duty focuses on punishment after the fact for failures to perform according to minimal standards set forth previously. Criminal sanctions in the common law exemplify a morality of duty. Indeed, since it is always possible for role occupants to fail to live up to minimal standards, a morality of duty is applicable to role performances at all status levels, whether or not they fall within the bounds of what is legally actionable. A morality of aspiration focuses on the achieving of good deeds, on striving for praiseworthy performance above the average rather than avoiding blameworthy performance below the average. This orientation tends to be characteristic of moral and religious systems of thought rather than legal ones. A system of law can call on people to avoid wrong, but can hardly compel them to do right.

The treatment of higher-ups in responsibility allocation blends these two moralities. All roles involve liability for what is done relative to what one is expected to do. But higher-status individuals—whether professional or bureaucratic in authority—tend to be subject to diffuse standards for their action at future time points; it is expected that they oversee the action of others; and they are supposed to exercise such qualities as good judgment, caution, and control. To *omit* these sometimes ill-defined activities is to fall below the standards of the social role, to render oneself liable for sanctions. When societal expectations are diffuse and call for high levels of foresight, as we have argued may be true of high-status roles, then formal standards of accountability become strict.

Perhaps the most extreme version of such liability rests on the obligation to oversee the actions of others. This is the doctrine of respondeat superior, as we saw in earlier discussion of military law. Military law is but one of the places where respondeat superior may be relevant. For example, the discussion in chapter 2 of President Nixon's responsibility for Watergate reflected a similar consideration. He was politically and legally liable for what his subordinates did whether he made it happen or only allowed it to happen. The unlucky tavern owner with whom we introduced the notion of civilian vicarious responsibility is another such case. Parents can share in this sort of liability on the basis of their supervisory role over children. It is clear who can be treated legally according to vicarious liability doctrines: superiors in hierarchies of authority and subordination. Such superiors are thus held to more "primitive" Heiderian standards, the adult world's association responsibility. But this obviously does not mean that society is less moral in how it treats superiors. Instead, it reflects the fact that different roles are treated according to different standards of accountability. To sum up: Authority is associated with relatively strict liability for relatively diffuse expectations.

Similar issues appear in somewhat diluted form in the expectation that professional authorities advise or guide others' actions. Doctors are expected to try to cure patients; lawyers to represent clients; teachers to teach students. Even psychologists in their laboratories have a web of obligations toward research participants, complicated by potential conflict between scientific advance and participants' well-being. In all of these professional relations, the "subordinate" is expected to take the advice or follow the instructions of authority. The authority, in turn, is liable for loss of control over the situation.

Stringent standards of liability need not, however, be accompanied by stringency in sanctioning. Bureaucrats and professionals may be normatively bound to higher, diffuse, and forward-looking standards, but there is an escape hatch involved in such standards. Just as it may be difficult to say when they have been met, it is correspondingly difficult to say when they have been seriously violated. High-status jobs are accompanied by expansion of autonomously controlled time; such jobs are characterized by diffuse, occupant-controlled boundaries between work time and time off. Deadlines may be correspondingly occupant-controlled or flexible, such that there is more time before one is called on the carpet for nonperformance. And the standards themselves are in part the inherently slippery ones of a morality of aspiration, such that we are more comfortable in praising clear achievement than in blaming failure. What higher-status roles thus guarantee is increased freedom of action rather than improved behavior by actors. The powerful may eventually hang, but in the meantime they are given a great deal of rope.

Responsibility for Crimes of Obedience

In view of the differences in obligations, deeds, and liability among roles in the social hierarchy, the key problem is what happens to responsibility when a subordinate and a superior together produce a crime of obedience. Who is responsible for such a crime? How responsible? On what basis? We shall address these questions in terms of authorities and subordinates who are arrayed in explicit chains of command (Hamilton, 1986).

THE ROLES OF AUTHORITY AND ACTOR IN A CHAIN OF COMMAND

Assignment of responsibility in a chain of command is more difficult than in the case of single individuals who commit misdeeds. It is difficult because role expectations and physical causation are differentially distributed in the chain and because they provide competing bases for responsibility in these circumstances. Thus we shall argue that responsibility in such chains need not be attributed to authority *or* subordinate, but can be attributed to authority *and* subordinate, for different reasons.

Social-scientific theory suggests that when one person causes another to act, the deed is "justified" and the actor's responsibility reduced or even eliminated (Heider, 1958). The law's more venerable treatment of these problems is similar. The law also emphasizes the search for voluntary human actors and "justifies" acts whose source is external: "Actions which are less than fully voluntary are assimilated to the means by which or the circumstances in which the earlier action brings about the consequences" (Hart and Honoré, 1959, p. 71). When one person's action is caused by another, psychology and law agree that the actor's responsibility is assimilated or absorbed by the party causing the action. This assimilation is not complete, however. As Hart and Honoré (1959) emphasize, there are linguistic, logical, and legal differences between direct voluntary action on the one hand and causing another to act, or interpersonal causation, on the other. For example, "Tom shot Harry" is not the same as "Tom caused Dick to shoot Harry." Responsibility for interpersonal causation tends to be divided rather than falling entirely upon an initial voluntary actor in a causal chain.

Direct physical coercion or duress is perhaps the clearest case in which most responsibility would be transferred to another person who instigates an action. But authorities are not mere coercive forces. An authority certainly has power over a subordinate; but given the right to command or instruct, an authority typically assumes that its commands will be obeyed because they ought to be obeyed. One side consequence of this assumption is that an authority need not and does not monitor obedience to the extent that a coercive agent does. Subordinates' obedience, in turn, inevitably involves *interpretation* of orders, even in the military context. The course of battle rather rarely follows the precise orders set out by leaders. Instead, at each step along the line, orders are taken, interpreted, sometimes misinterpreted, and then sometimes ignored. (See Keegan, 1976, on Agincourt, Waterloo, and the Somme; or Tolstoy, 1957, on the Battle of Borodino.) To attribute a particular military victory to a particular leader is often a serious error in strictly causal terms; to attribute a disaster or loss to that leader is equally erroneous.

Of course, responsibility involves more than causation. An authority is expected to oversee subordinates in return for interpersonal control over them; it is part of the role. (See also Hamilton and Sanders, 1981, 1983.) Causation and expectations need not, however, fit together neatly in a chain of command to produce an overall responsibility "score." Causal responsibility is *shared* between authority and actor. Subordinates physically produce effects that the authority interpersonally causes. Role expectations are *reciprocal* rather than shared. The subordinate's duty is to carry out orders while the authority's reciprocal obligation is to oversee subordinates. Staying within the bounds of normal role behavior is usually sufficient to keep a subordinate out of trouble. It is part of the implicit contract between authorities and subordinates that the authorities are liable for outcomes produced by their orders in exchange for the subordinates' obedience of these orders. If an authority's instructions exceed normative bounds, however, the subordinate is caught in a dilemma: faced with doing wrong either by carrying out the directive or by disobeying it.

How, then, is the subordinate likely to frame the problem when faced with potentially illegitimate orders? The moral account of the action that will probably be given, especially by the subordinate inclined to obey, involves role expectations. These are likely to be expressed, and felt, as obligations: "It's your duty to follow orders"; "The experiment had to go on." In Mills's (1940) terms, the "vocabulary of motive" used to persuade self or others that the action was appropriate is quite literally a vocabulary of role-based *motives* behind the action. (See also Scott and Lyman, 1968.) The rare actor who resists authority's demands, in contrast, is likely to focus on the foreseen *consequences* of obedience: on innocent persons killed, other experimental participants harmed, and the like. The actor who focuses on role-based motives, on the demands of the subordinate role, is using a frame of reference that stresses role expectations over actions as determinants of sanction. The subordinate who focuses on an act's consequences and draws inferences from them to the responsibility of the actor is engaged in the sort of responsibility attribution portrayed in Heider's (1958) model: One observes what a person did, makes inferences about intentionality of the action, and assigns blame accordingly. In this frame, the "oughts" involved are general ones that can apply to all actors equally.

In short, a subordinate in a hierarchy of authority inevitably has two alternative frames of reference available in response to orders. These frames invoke two different bases, or models, of responsibility in the situation: role obligations, on the one hand, and deeds physically caused, on the other.

A further problem in determining responsibility in chains of command is that authority hierarchies rarely stop at two. Superiors are under someone else's command; bosses have bosses. At each point in such a chain, complications are added. Suppose there is a policy-making superior who gives orders to subordinates. These subordinates in turn give orders to *their* subordinates. The policymaker therefore has liability based on role responsibility, in Hart's sense, for all outcomes throughout the chain. If the bottom-rung subordinate committing a deed-as-ordered has any liability, it is based on causal responsibility. In between lie chains of interpersonal causation running down the hierarchy from policymaker to intermediate authorities and from them to subordinates. These chains include interpretations of orders made by the intermediate authorities.

The problem that is exacerbated in an extended chain of command is the logical connection between policy and execution. Orders become minipolicies or grand policies as one moves up a chain of command, and a policy is logically of a much more general nature than a specific order or the actions carried out in response to it. One may ask, for example, what the causal relationship is between a search-and-destroy policy and a My Lai massacre; it may not be immediately clear that the general policy implies the specific outcome. Conversely, it is not always easy to tell whether a policy has been executed, because one must take the inductive steps back up from all of the small effects produced to the general effect intended. What is *intended* by the policymaker is the general effect. It is only the general effect for which both causal and role elements make the policymaker responsible.

Chains of command entail a moral and legal paradox: The greater the range of outcomes for which a superior can be held responsible on grounds of what was expected, the weaker the evidence becomes that the superior is causally responsible for any given outcome.

The two responsibilities of superior and subordinate are not truly the reciprocal suggested by the ancient notion of respondeat superior. Instead, when authoritative orders exceed legitimate boundaries, subordinates whose excuse of superior orders is rejected tend to be judged on their degree of personal causation. Superiors tend to be judged on their degree of role responsibility—perhaps in part because the greater the superior's role responsibility, the less clear any specific causal responsibility is likely to be. War crimes judgments at Nuremberg and in the case of General Yamashita are consistent from this point of view. The Nuremberg decisions focused attention on a subordinate's room for personal causation and stressed the independent status of each subordinate. These judgments can be seen as a ringing affirmation that orders do not remove personal causation from subordinates' acts. The Yamashita decision, on the other hand, focused attention on respondeat superior: the traditional, diffuse expectation that the superior is the party to answer for all outcomes.[4]

The nonreciprocal "responsibilities" of authority and subordinate and the different nuances of meaning that the term *responsibility* takes on for each may explain certain otherwise anomalous findings about responsibility allocation in the Milgram (1974) experiments. Theoretically, Milgram emphasized the ceding of responsibility to the experimenter as a key to the obedience of research participants; he even argued that the resulting "agentic state" had evolutionary significance. Our discussions of the Milgram studies have also emphasized a trade-off in responsibilities, an implied contract between the parties. Yet when research participants were asked afterward about who was responsible for what happened, they took on a substantial amount (though not a majority) of the responsibility themselves, even when they had obeyed the experimenter (Milgram, 1974; Mantell and Panzarella, 1976). We suggest that to a research participant, a post-hoc question about relative responsibility may be ambiguous, given the multiple meanings of the term. For example, actors are quite aware of their causal role in administering shocks; they may see themselves as "responsible" research partipants; and they may think the experimenter is ultimately liable if things go wrong.

We would differentiate the positions of obedient and disobedient research participants, or other subordinates, primarily in terms of their model of responsibility,

4. Kirschenbaum (1974) makes a similar point about the separate responsibilities of superior and subordinate from the perspective of Jewish law. Depending on the circumstances, either the superior or the subordinate may bear sole responsibility for a crime of obedience, or both may simultaneously bear full responsibility for it. In other words, respondeat superior does not replace or diminish the individual soldier's responsibility for the consequences of his deliberate actions, and vice versa. An interesting nuance in Kirschenbaum's analysis is that the responsibility of superiors increases when they have reason to expect that their subordinates will most probably carry out the actions they order— for example, in a military situation, where subordinates "are trained to unswerving loyalty and instant obedience" (p. 190).

which derives from the framework into which they place their actions in the situation. A model that focuses on role-based motives and obligations implies obedience, whereas a model that focuses on actions and their consequences calls for disobedience. Thus the obedient actor might say, "I was responsible for moving the switch," or "I was fulfilling my role obligation to the experimenter." The disobedient actor might say, "Of course I was responsible for hurting that person; that's why I stopped." The critical difference lies in these two actors' frameworks for understanding responsibility in the situation.

Thus our original question in this chapter—who is responsible for a crime of obedience?—has no clear single answer. The superior is an interpersonal cause of what happens, and the subordinate is a physical cause who also has a role obligation to obey. The superior is expected to show foresight and oversight, to the extent of being potentially answerable for all outcomes. These responsibilities only appear to be additive. They can also multiply. The subordinate may be seen as responsible on "Nuremberg grounds" while the superior is responsible on respondeat superior grounds: the subordinate because of deed, the superior because of role. If responsibility can multiply, it can also disappear. The subordinate, the clear physical cause, may be excused because of superior orders. This role-related excuse may then pass up the chain of command until a higher-up can effectively claim, "But that is not what I meant." Depending on the case and the number of steps in a chain of command, we might find that the subordinate is blamed, that the superior is blamed, that both are blamed, or that neither is blamed. What we can be confident about is that the *bases* of blame may differ and should rest on the trade-off between roles and deeds (Hamilton, 1978a).

We assume that human discomfort at assigning responsibility becomes greater as one moves away from direct physical contact. We therefore expect allocation of blame to gravitate toward the physical causation end of a chain of command. The balance of responsibility is such, however, that it might be more comfortable if one could find an actor who both physically participated and also gave orders: deeds committed and obligations violated by the same person. Such may be the secret of the one conviction out of thirty court-martial proceedings for the massacre at My Lai; Lt. William Calley was such an actor.

The complexity of the balance between role-based and deed-based responsibility in chains of command can further our understanding of responsibility allocation problems in all bureaucracies, not just the military command chain. So-called corporate crimes, illegal or immoral acts perpetrated by or in the name of corporations, have proved elusive to study, to understand, and to prosecute in part because of the chains of command that characterize such crimes. Responsibility regularly becomes lost in the ways we have described above. For example, two recent books on corporate crime present quite different pictures of responsibility depending on the level of analysis and focus in the corporate hierarchy (see Ermann's 1985 review of these works). Clinard (1983), interviewing retired middle managers, finds them willing to use a "superior orders" defense—"I was just following orders" from corporate bosses. In contrast, Vaughan (1983), in analyzing the organizational underpinnings of corporate crime, finds that very often top managers do not know or are not sure "what happened." Our analysis suggests how and why responsibility can be defended against by all the members of the corporate chain of command. The defenses simply shift from a denial of personal causation, at the top, to a denial of initiative at the bottom of such hierarchies. Perhaps everyone is responsible, but in ways different enough to diffuse and defuse anyone's liability.

DIVERGENT VIEWS OF THE SUBORDINATE'S RESPONSIBILITY

When subordinates are confronted with potentially illegitimate orders from their superiors—when they find themselves in a situation that might well become a crime of obedience—judgments of responsibility become complex, both for subordinates themselves and for outside observers. Such situations create a tension between the subordinates' role responsibilities and their causal responsibilities, both in their own eyes and in the eyes of outside judges. On the one hand, their role obligations, often backed up by the authorities' power to impose sanctions for failure to meet these obligations, invoke the duty to obey. On the other hand, the harmful nature of the actions they have been ordered to perform invokes the duty to disobey. In response to this dilemma, as we have noted above, subordinates—and observers—could adopt a model of responsibility focusing on role-based motives or a model focusing on the consequences of the act. We would expect systematic differences between subordinates themselves and outside observers—including members of the public—in their tendency to adopt these alternative models.

The expectation that subordinates and outside judges would tend to adopt different models of responsibility is based on research suggesting that certain general attributional differences exist between actors and observers. Actors emphasize situational or role-related reasons for behavior, especially where outcomes are negative. Observers instead tend to focus on the actor as a cause (Jones and Nisbett, 1971; Nisbett and Ross, 1980; Ross, 1977). Each group of perceivers must resolve a dilemma. Should one focus on the blameworthy consequences of action and hold the actor responsible? Alternatively, should one focus on the actor's motives, including an obligation to obey, and deny that the action is blameworthy? Actors in crimes of obedience should find it easier to account for their actions in terms of role-based motives, perhaps never leaving or even questioning that framework. Observers are more likely to treat the actor as a proximate and personal cause of observed consequences.

Authorities themselves frequently act as observers or judge of crimes of obedience. Their training and position serve to reinforce the tendency of observers to focus on consequences and thus blame the subordinate for following illegitimate orders. That is, authorities are trained to show higher levels of independent judgment as well as to know the "official" version of what subordinates should do (for example, not follow illegal orders). Presented with a clear-cut case of illegitimate orders, they may therefore more readily blame the obedient subordinate than would others, such as that actor's fellow subordinates. Authorities judging a crime of obedience may in effect use a standard of independent judgment against those to whom this independence is least available: subordinates.

Not all observers adopt a "consequences" model, however, nor do all actors in the subordinate role adopt a "motives" model. In fact, as far as observers are concerned, the data from our own research, reported in the last chapter, suggest that only a minority of respondents (the Consistent and Deviant Refusers) were prepared to judge Lieutenant Calley in terms of the consequences of his actions. A much larger proportion (the Consistent Shooters) seemed to identify with Calley and adopt a motives model in judging his behavior. The observers, in this case, seemed to be attributing responsibility in much the same way as actors would be expected to do.

We are ready to return to our survey data now to examine specifically how people assign responsibility for a crime of obedience. We shall use the distinction, drawn in this chapter, between two models of judging responsibility—one based on consequences and the other on motives—to organize the data presented in the chapter that follows.

Time and *Newsweek* featured the same subject and nearly the same headline on their covers of April 12, 1971. *Time* showed a portrait of William Calley with the headline, "Who shares the guilt?" *Newsweek* superimposed a photo of Lieutenant Calley over one of Ron Haeberle's photos of the dead along a trail at My Lai (see chapter 1). Its headline was: "The Calley verdict: Who else is guilty?" All the evidence of public reaction at the time can be boiled down to a single message: The Calley trial was a drama of shared responsibility for a crime of obedience.

We noted in chapter 7 that American reaction to the conviction of Lt. William Calley was intense, and that opposition to the verdict flowed from many sources. But it is not yet clear what such intensity implies about the normative supports that make people available as participants in such crimes. In this chapter we focus on *why* respondents approved or disapproved of the trial. We first report basic patterns of approval versus disapproval and differentiate respondents' reasons for holding each position. Then we turn to detailed comparisons between what we felt to be the core opinion groups on the Calley trial: those for whom the issue, pro or con, was responsibility.

The Calley Trial: Approval, Disapproval, and Their Bases

Early in the questionnaire, after probing for respondents' information about the trial and asking about a My Lai–like hypothetical situation (see chapter 7), we asked those who had heard something about the trial for their opinion of it:

> There has been a good deal of discussion about whether or not Lt. Calley should have been brought to trial in the first place. Considering what you have seen, heard, or read, do you approve or disapprove of Lt. Calley having been brought to trial?

Overall, 34 percent (301) of the respondents approved of the trial, 59 percent (522) disapproved, and 8 percent (68) didn't know. These figures represented a definite shift from earlier surveys. For example, a Gallup telephone poll taken just after the conviction reported 79 percent disapproval and 9 percent approval. There were at least two factors contributing to this discrepancy.

First, at the time the Gallup poll was taken, the media were filled with reports of intense emotional reactions against the trial. The national consensus seemed to be entirely in the direction of disapproval. Only later, when Captain Daniel (the prosecutor in the Calley trial) sent a strong letter to the president and various prominent figures spoke out in defense of the trial, was the appearance of negative consensus broken. By the time our survey was conducted, it can be presumed that negative reactions had cooled off to some degree and that the image of a totally one-sided consensus had dissipated.

Second, the wording of our question differed from the Gallup poll's. We asked about Lieutenant Calley's having been *brought to trial.* Gallup, on the other hand, asked about reactions to his having been *found guilty of premeditated murder.* A person could, of course, approve of the former without approving of the latter. The Gallup question was also more likely to pick up negative reactions to the sentence per se, which was considered to be too harsh even by many who approved of the trial itself.

Our question wording was similar to (and in fact adapted from) that used by the Becker Research Corporation in a telephone poll conducted in Massachusetts within a few days after the conviction. In this poll, 67 percent disapproved of Lieutenant Calley's having been brought to trial and 27 percent approved. Thus immediate reaction by Massachusetts residents was intermediate between Gallup's results and ours. In our sample residents of the Northeast (including Massachusetts) were *less* inclined to disapprove of the trial than our national sample as a whole. Differences between Becker's Massachusetts poll and our later national sample seemed, therefore, to reflect opinion changes over time. Overall, it is plausible that the less extreme national disapproval shown in our study reflected some true moderation in opinion from the intense and largely one-sided reaction of early April 1971.

PREDICTING APPROVAL VERSUS DISAPPROVAL

Certain demographic variables encountered in chapter 7 also differentiated between trial approvers and disapprovers: factors that indicate "cognitive sophistication" or social-structural position. Approving of the trial was significantly linked to higher levels of education, socioeconomic status, and occupational prestige, and to urban rather than rural residence. Thus even more of these indicators of sophistication or position were linked to opinion of the trial than figured in earlier discussions of trial interest or "shoot-refuse" responses (see appendix A and chapter 7). Approval was also linked to region of residence, which in chapter 7 we suggested might signify emotional identification with Lieutenant Calley, and to religious affiliation, whose meaning as a predictor we found in chapter 7 to be unclear. Residents of the Northeast and Far West were more inclined to approve of the trial, as were those whose religious affiliation was "other" (Jewish, other, or none). These associations with simple approval or disapproval of the trial were generally not strong, and certain cleavages that one might expect to find—such as differences based on sex or military experience—were notably absent.

Key attitudes and self-descriptions, also associated with views of Calley's trial, seemed to represent more emotional sources of interest in the trial or its defendant. For example, both self-identified political conservatives and self-proclaimed hawks on the Vietnam War were more likely to disapprove of the trial. But again, relationships were not very powerful. A series of questions on Vietnam policy choices were *not* significantly related to opinion of the Calley trial. The general picture that emerges from looking at trial approval/disapproval is one of a broad consensus in the direction of disapproval, weakly predictable from standard demographic sources. Even at the relatively late date of our survey, a large proportion of Americans simply disapproved of the Calley trial.

REASONS FOR APPROVING VERSUS DISAPPROVING

Opinion polls by other researchers in 1971 found similarly weak links between demographic and attitudinal factors and trial opinion, but they did not ask about the respondent's *reasons* for approval or disapproval. Because these reasons seemed a good way to assess whether My Lai represented a crime of obedience in American eyes, we concentrated on them in an attempt to build a systematic picture of American reaction to the trial.

After respondents indicated their general opinion about the trial, they were asked to think about why. First, respondents were asked whether they *agreed with* various reasons for approving or disapproving of the trial. The reasons we presented, listed in table 9.1, seem to have captured the major bases for opinion about the Calley trial.[1] Respondents were given an opportunity to add their own reasons, but very few took advantage of it. Additional reasons also tended to be idiosyncratic and did not suggest new categories. If they agreed with more than one reason, trial approvers and "don't know" respondents were then asked to indicate which reason for approving was the most important; disapprovers were similarly asked to choose the most important reason for disapproval. Our analyses use the "most important" reasons for approval as obtained from *both* approvers and those respondents who initially said "don't know." Restricting analysis of reasons solely to approvers yields substantially identical conclusions. The table shows the percentages of respondent groups who agreed with each reason and who chose each as "most important."

Many respondents agreed with more than one reason. Each reason received at

1. Since the climate of opinion at the time suggested that a "don't know" answer was closer to approval than to disapproval, those who initially said "don't know" were asked reasons for trial approval first and reasons for disapproval second. They were asked about their "most important" reason for approval, rather than disapproval, under the same assumption that they probably leaned toward approval.

Table 9.1 Attitude toward Calley Trial

Reasons	Agree with (%)	Most Important (%)
FOR APPROVAL[a]		
a. Even a soldier in a combat situation has no right to kill defenseless civilians and anyone who violates this rule must be brought to trial.[b]	53	27
b. The trial helps to make clear the immorality and cruelty of the Vietnam War and of the way we are fighting it.	45	20
c. To preserve its honor, the army has to bring to trial anyone accused of breaking its rules of warfare.	45	14
d. The trial helps to put across the important idea that every man must bear responsibility for his own actions.	48	17
e. Many other U.S. soldiers have been tried for crimes in Vietnam; it would be unfair to let Lt. Calley off without a trial.	40	8
f. None of these or don't know.	14	13
Total		99
		(368)
FOR DISAPPROVAL		
a. It is unfair to send a man to fight in Vietnam and then put him on trial for doing his duty.	83	45
b. The trial keeps us from facing the real issue: what's wrong is the war and the way it is being fought, not just the actions of an individual soldier.	43	9
c. The trial is an insult to our fighting men and weakens the morale of the U.S. Army.	64	11
d. The trial used Lt. Calley as a scapegoat: one young lieutenant shouldn't be blamed for the failures of his superiors.	67	15
e. Many other U.S. soldiers have done the same kinds of things as Lt. Calley; it is unfair to single out one man and put him on trial.	69	15

Continued on next page

Table 9.1—*Continued*

Reasons	Agree with (%)	Most Important (%)
f. None of these or don't know.	3	<u>5</u>
Total		100
		(510)

[a]The question about most important reason for approval was asked of both those who responded "approve" (34%; N = 301) and those who said "don't know" (8%; N = 68) regarding their attitude toward the trial. The question about most important reason for disapproval was asked only of those who responded "disapprove" (59%; N = 522). Small discrepancies in the N between the trial attitude item and the reasons result from the fact that a few respondents offered their own, uncodable reasons.
[b]Italicized items are those used to identify assert-responsibility (AR) and deny-responsibility (DR) subgroups discussed in the text.

least 40 percent agreement, and the various reasons for both approval and disapproval were highly intercorrelated. The patterning of reactions becomes clearer, therefore, when we examine responses to a forced choice: the "most important" column in table 9.1.

Among the reasons for approving of the trial, the most frequently chosen was *a*, which essentially affirms the individual soldier's responsibility for killing defenseless civilians. A related item, *d*, is a more general and abstract statement of individual responsibility. Taken together, the two items dealing with responsibility account for a plurality (44 percent) of responses about "most important" bases for approval. Smaller proportions of reasons for approval reflect opposition to the war (item *b*) or aspects of the integrity of the military (item *c*, concerning the honor of the army, or item *e*, focusing on equity in its treatment of soldiers).

Parallel items were offered as choices for those disapproving of the trial. The clearly dominant reason chosen as most important, item *a*, again deals with responsibility. Respondents choosing this item indicated that they considered it unfair to hold Lieutenant Calley responsible for what occurred in the course of performance of his duty. Similarly, item *d* reflects concern with allocation of responsibility but emphasizes the issue of where responsibility should rest in the hierarchy of command. Together, these reasons account for 60 percent of the disapprovers. A small number of respondents picked item *b* as their most important reason, indicating disapproval of the trial on the grounds of opposition to the war. Other respondents focused on the implications of the trial for the military: that it may weaken army morale (item *c*) or constitute an inequity in the treatment of soldiers (item *e*).

News stories had suggested that American reactions to the trial flowed from multiple sources. The options we provided as reasons reflected this expected diversity, and the responses we obtained confirmed it. Approval and disapproval of the Calley trial cut across dimensions one would normally expect to be relevant. Opposition to the war seemed to lead some people to approve of the trial and others to disapprove; concern with the integrity of the military sometimes led to approval and sometimes to disapproval. To make sense out of the public reaction, we therefore separated respondents into subgroups whose approval or disapproval of the trial involved clearly different reasons.

We first divided approvers and disapprovers into three subgroups each, according to the item chosen as the most important reason for their opinion: (1) those who approved or disapproved because of their different conceptions of how responsibility should be allocated—that is, who chose either *a* or *d* as the most important reason; (2) those who approved or disapproved because of their opposition to the war—that is, who chose reason *b*; and (3) those who approved or disapproved because of their concern with the integrity of the army—that is, who chose either *c* or *e* as the most important reason. These six subgroups were formed on both logical and empirical grounds. We combined those reasons (*a* with *d*; *c* with *e*) that fit together in terms of the focal concern reflected and were highly intercorrelated (on the "which do you agree with" question).

Because the respondents concerned with responsibility (the *a/d* approvers or disapprovers) composed the most numerous subgroup, the question remains whether responsibility was conceptually as well as numerically the dominant American response to the trial of Lieutenant Calley. Table 9.2 presents opinions by the three subgroups of approvers (left panel) and of disapprovers (right panel) on several key questions.[2] The *a/d* respondent group in each panel is labeled "responsibility," the *b* group "antiwar," and the *c/e* group "army." Subsequent discussion and tables will refer to the approvers on responsibility grounds as the AR group (for *a*ssert individual *r*esponsibility) and the disapprovers on responsibility grounds as the DR group (for *d*eny individual *r*esponsibility).[3]

The left side of table 9.2 indicates that differences between ARs and the other

2. Note that the totals for these collapsed subgroups are not identical with the totals from each separate subgroup added together. This results from the presence of a small number of respondents who could not decide on one "most important" reason. When the reasons they could not decide between formed one of the collapsed subgroups (*a* and *d*; *c* and *e*), they were coded as belonging to that group even though they could not be coded as favoring either of the included reasons taken individually.

3. Suedfeld et al. (1985) have recently developed scales to distinguish specific from diffuse responsibility ascription. "Specific" ascription is literally attribution of responsibility to any specific individual. "Diffuse" responsibility attribution, in contrast, consists of rejecting individual responsibility (for example, in favor of "the system"). The present DR-AR distinction with regard to hierarchies of actors is a different one. DR-AR differences concern allocation among individuals within hierarchical chains. Although responsibility may be effectively "lost" in such chains, the loss occurs because responsibility is being spread among numbers of individuals. The closest parallel to the Suedfeld et al. diffuse responsibility in our analysis is found in antiwar reasons for approving or disapproving of Calley's trial. These reasons, presented in table 9.2, express the idea that individual participants per se are not responsible but the war or war effort (the system) is.

Table 9.2 Responses to Selected Other Items by Groups Differing in Their Reasons for Approving or Not Approving of Calley Trial, 1971

Items	Reasons for Approving of Trial			Reasons for Disapproving of Trial		
	Responsibility (%)	Antiwar (%)	Army (%)	Antiwar (%)	Army (%)	Responsibility (%)
A. What would *most* people do [in a My Lai-type situation]? (Follow orders and shoot/Refuse to shoot)						
Follow orders	46	76	79	85	87	90
B. What would *you* do in this situation? (Follow orders and shoot/Refuse to shoot)						
Follow orders	22	34	61	68	75	80
C. Assuming it is true that Calley received orders to shoot, what should he have done? (Carry out/Refuse)						
Carry out	27	46	72	65	78	86
D. In terms of rights and wrongs, how do Calley's actions compare with bombing raids that also kill Vietnamese civilians? (Similar/Different)						
Similar	41	72	47	62	76	73
E. Reaction to draft boards who said they will suspend drafting men until Calley's sentence is reversed (Approve/Disapprove)						
Approve	18	43	36	54	50	62

Note: The total number of respondents among approvers was Responsibility = 165, Antiwar = 135, and Army = 74, and Army = 80 (see text for explanation of these labels). Among disapprovers, Ns were Army = 135, Antiwar = 46, and Responsibility = 306. Because "don't know" responses were omitted and because some items were not answered by all respondents, the N for items A – E ranges from 259 to 284 approvers and from 412 to 449 disapprovers. All chi-squares for approvers were significant at $p \leq .01$; among disapprovers, the only significant relationship appears in item C (again $p \leq .01$). (As in chapter 7, all tabulated relationships can be assumed to be significant at $p \leq .01$ except where stated otherwise.)

approver groups were occasionally striking. Items A and B, the pair of hypothetical questions featured in chapter 7, revealed that ARs were dramatically less likely than other approvers to say either that most people would shoot in a My Lai–type situation or that they themselves would shoot. ARs also asserted that if Lieutenant Calley received orders to shoot, he should not have carried them out (item C). Antiwar approvers were intermediate between the ARs and the army approvers in responding to these items. But items D and E illustrate that this responsibility-antiwar-army linearity did not always hold. In comparing Calley's actions to bombing raids, antiwar approvers stood out in judging the two to be morally similar. Antiwar approvers were also more favorable than other approvers to draft boards that were threatening to suspend the draft until Calley's sentence was reversed. On these latter two items the antiwar approvers looked, or sounded, rather like chapter 7's Deviant Refusers. (Indeed, to an appreciable extent Deviant Refusers tended to pick antiwar reasons, as note 2 in chapter 7 indicated.)

The right panel illustrates that subgroups of disapprovers were much less distinguishable from one another. The only significant subgroup difference concerned whether Calley should have shot if ordered. Item C shows that DRs stood out in asserting that Calley *should* have carried out orders. In contrast, on related items (items A and B) DRs were not significantly more likely than other disapprovers of the trial to respond "follow orders."

Across an array of trial-related items, illustrated by those presented in table 9.2, responsibility was the conceptually as well as numerically dominant issue. The AR and DR groups regularly anchored the polar extremes of opinion with the other four groups somewhere in between. In some comparisons, the percentage distributions of army approvers actually resembled those of the disapprovers, while antiwar disapprovers resembled approvers. Most often, the four other subgroups simply obscured the sharp differences between the AR and DR groups. It is as if, in judging the Calley trial, a responsibility orientation represented a "signal"—a core position from which other opinions followed. Concern with the war or with the integrity of the military represented "noise"—deviations from the numerically *and* conceptually dominant core of opinion. We therefore concentrated on these core responses as a way of clarifying the normative meaning of crimes of obedience.

Before turning to detailed analysis of AR and DR groups, it is important to take note of how results might differ if all ten "most important" reasons were analyzed separately. In fact, separate analyses of reasons for approving confirmed that respondents choosing *a* as their most important reason answered trial-related items very similarly to those choosing *d*. Combining these two subgroups did not introduce any distortions. On the other hand, among the disapprovers, those choosing *a* were more extreme about various trial-related questions than those choosing *d*. Therefore differences shown in the rest of the chapter would be even *greater* if comparisons were based only on those respondents who approved or disapproved for reason *a*.

Two Conceptions of Responsibility in Authority Situations: Responsibility Assertion and Denial

We can expect many potential differences in trial-related attitudes between the AR and DR groups, given their divergent conceptions of responsibility in the situation in which Lieutenant Calley found himself. It is helpful to pause a moment to flesh out the picture of what each responsibility orientation may mean. The DR group presumably subscribed to the view that the individual soldier should not be held responsible (or solely responsible) for his actions in combat. They saw the soldier as someone who is subject to orders. In terms of the theoretical discussion in the last chapter, they should be viewing My Lai from the standpoint of a soldier's *motive*, in that the demands of the subordinate role form the motive—and justification—for actions within it. Thus the trial seemed unfair to them. At the very least, they would argue, Calley's superiors should also have been brought to trial.

In contrast, AR respondents apparently believed that individual soldiers must be held accountable for what they do in combat situations. This position does not necessarily imply that the individual must take responsibility for governmental or military policies. Probably only a minority of the AR group held to that view. The basic position of the AR group was what we have called a focus on *consequences*: on the deed committed and on the actor's personal causation of that deed. Such a position entails applying the usual standards of morality and attribution of responsibility. It assumes that a situation involving legitimate authority is not beyond the normal bounds of individual morality. Thus the AR group held Calley responsible because his direct, intended action caused the killing of defenseless civilians.

To explore this interpretation, we pulled out the two responsibility groups— DR versus AR orientation—for a more detailed set of comparisons. As might be expected from the preceding table, sharp differences between these responsibility orientations were found on virtually every item related to the Calley trial. Tables 9.3 and 9.4 summarize DR and AR views on key items about Calley's actions in My Lai and his conviction. Only for a very few items in the entire survey were DR-AR differences not statistically significant. The tables do not include responses to open-ended questions. As in chapter 7, answers to these questions will be discussed whenever they can help clarify respondents' views. Differences will again be considered noteworthy only if the DR-AR gap is both statistically significant in cross-tabulation and 10 percent or larger in absolute size.

ATTITUDES TOWARD MY LAI ACTIONS

Table 9.3 highlights the large differences in the way DRs and ARs saw Lieutenant Calley's actions at My Lai. Items A-C reproduce the responses shown in table 9.2, but directly compare the two groups whose focus is responsibility. DR and AR respondents stood in stark contrast to each other in their belief that shooting civilians is normative and in their willingness, hypothetically, to participate in

Table 9.3 Responsibility Orientation as Predictor of Attitudes toward Lt. Calley's Actions

Items	Deny Responsibility (%)	Assert Responsibility (%)	Total Sample (%)
A. What would most people do [in a My Lai–type situation]? (Follow orders and shoot/Refuse to shoot?)			
Follow orders	90	46	78
B. What would you do in this situation? (Follow orders and shoot/Refuse to shoot)			
Follow orders	80	22	60
C. Assuming it is true that Calley received orders to shoot, what should he have done? (Carry out/Refuse)			
Carry out	86	27	68
D. Overall opinion of Calley's actions: (Right/Wrong, but . . ./ Wrong, illegal/Wrong, immoral)			
Right	54	3	32
E. Calley's actions were justified if people he shot were Communists (Agree/Disagree)			
Agree	61	11	42
F. Calley's actions justified because better to kill some S. Vietnamese than risk lives of American soldiers (Agree/Disagree)			
Agree	76	20	55
G. In World War II it would have been better to kill some German civilians than risk lives of American soldiers (Agree/ Disagree)			
Agree	82	33	64

Continued on next page

Table 9.3 —*Continued*

Items	Deny Responsibility (%)	Assert Responsibility (%)	Total Sample (%)
H. In terms of rights and wrongs, how do Calley's actions compare with bombing raids that also kill Vietnamese civilians? (Similar/ Different)			
Similar	73	41	64

Note: The total number of DR respondents was 306; for AR respondents, N = 165. Ns for specific items in this table and in table 9.4 ranged from 383 to 468 (DRs plus ARs). All DR-AR differences were significant at $p \leq .01$. Percentages for the total sample include respondents who gave reasons other than the DR or AR choices.

such shooting. For DRs, most people would shoot, they themselves would shoot, and Calley should have shot; for ARs, most people would not follow orders and shoot, they personally would not, and Calley should not have done so. Item D indicates that for a majority of DRs, but an almost invisible minority of ARs, Calley did the right thing.

Items E, F, and G were designed to probe the extent to which respondents were prepared to justify Calley's actions. DR respondents, apparently feeling that Lieutenant Calley's actions were right and that they would have acted similarly, were understandably ready to accept justifications for those actions. Fewer ARs agreed with justifications of Calley's actions on the basis of victims' being Communist (item E) or on the basis of the relative worth of South Vietnamese and American lives (item F). In absolute terms AR respondents were more likely to condone the killing of German civilians in World War II (item G) than the killing of either Communists or South Vietnamese civilians by Lieutenant Calley; but they still differed significantly from DRs in the level of acceptance of this rationale.

The final item in table 9.3, which asked respondents to compare Calley's actions and bombing raids that also kill civilians, helps to bring out sharply the difference in the meanings of the two responsibility models. DR respondents usually viewed Calley's actions as *similar* to bombing raids. When asked why they were similar, DRs' responses reflected their particular orientation to the question of Calley's responsibility: Intentional causation in the normal moral sense is irrelevant, since Calley—like the bombardier—was operating under the constraints of legitimate authority. The two acts were similar in that they both occurred in the line of duty. That minority of AR respondents who described the two actions as similar tended to base their choice on different reasons. Significantly more often than DR respondents, they described Calley's actions and bombing raids as similar because both involved the killing of innocent civilians or because both were morally "wrong." Thus the ARs' reasons for responding "similar" were unlike those offered by the DRs. For the DRs, Calley's actions and bombing raids were similar because both served the same military purpose or both were carried out under orders.

A majority of ARs saw the actions as different. When asked why, they explained that the killing of civilians in bombing raids is unintentional (even if predictable), whereas Calley's actions involved intentional and deliberate killing of civilians. Thus, in distinguishing Calley's actions from bombing raids, the AR respondents suggested their reason for holding Calley responsible: They assigned responsibility on the basis of intentional action, and Calley was clearly an intentional actor in My Lai. Since it is far less clear that bombardiers are intentionally causing the deaths of innocent civilians, most AR respondents would probably absolve them of responsibility. The issue of intentionality was also the reason most commonly cited by the minority of DRs who responded "different," but ARs offered it significantly more often. On the other hand, DRs who asserted that Calley's actions and bombing raids were different were more likely than ARs to respond descriptively, simply saying that the two involved different kinds of actions.

ATTITUDES TOWARD CALLEY'S SENTENCE

Table 9.4 presents differences between DRs and ARs in their views of the sentence Lieutenant Calley received and of the conviction of military officers in related cases.

The first item in the table shows that, whereas half of the ARs found Calley's sentence to be fair, almost no DRs concurred in this view. (The answer "too light," also a possible response to this question, was selected by less than 1 percent of respondents and was deleted from the percentage base.) The fact that many ARs found the sentence too harsh may indicate that for some respondents higher authorities at least shared the blame; it may also reflect their judgment that the situation in which Calley found himself—a guerrilla war with unwritten rules and indefinite goals—was highly ambiguous.

An additional item, not tabulated, asked respondents to decide who should have been tried for My Lai: Lieutenant Calley and higher officers, just Calley, just higher officers, or neither. (See chapter 7 for the exact wording of the question.) On one hand, very few respondents said that *only* Calley should have been tried for the deaths at My Lai; even among ARs only 6 percent selected this option. It appears that Calley's actions were not perceived as highly deviant from typical behavior in that role or situation—even by ARs. On the other hand, few respondents asserted that *only* higher officers should be tried; even among DRs, only 18 percent chose that option. Most respondents, and the vast majority of ARs, said that *both* Calley and higher officers should have been tried (89 percent of ARs versus 31 percent of DRs). Conversely, DR respondents were much more likely than the AR group to say that *neither* Calley nor higher-ups should have been tried (by 51 percent to 3 percent). We would argue that DRs were not necessarily saying that nothing wrong happened at My Lai, or that no one deserved blame. Instead, some of them may have felt that it was impossible to assign blame to anyone clearly enough to justify a legal trial and conviction. Therefore, answers

Table 9.4 Responsibility Orientation as a Predictor of Attitudes toward Lt. Calley's Sentence and Related Cases

Items	Deny Responsibility (%)	Assert Responsibility (%)	Total Sample (%)
A. Calley's sentence was (Fair/Too harsh)			
Fair	4	50	16
B. Was it right or wrong to convict German officers at Nuremberg for war crimes ordered by superiors? (Right/Wrong))			
Right	29	78	47
C. Should American officers be convicted for war crimes ordered by superiors? (Should be/Should not be)			
Should be	12	77	33
D. Was it right or wrong to convict Yamashita for actions of his men that he did not order? (Right/ Don't know/Wrong)			
Right	21	34	26
E. Should American generals be convicted for war crimes they did not order? (Should be/ Should not be)			
Should be	19	41	27
F. Reaction to draft boards who said they will suspend drafting men until Calley's sentence is reversed (Approve/Disapprove)			
Approve	62	18	46

Note: For information about Ns and significance levels, see note to table 9.3.

to this question reinforce the theoretical possibility, discussed in the previous chapter, that crimes of obedience can leave a responsibility vacuum.

In short, individual responsibility and command responsibility together can add up to 200 percent responsibility, as they did for many ARs; or to 0 percent responsibility, as they did for many DRs; or (presumably) to anything in between. With disturbingly high frequency, joint responsibility for the My Lai massacre added up to zero in the public's eye.

Items B through E refer to legal precedents, described in detail in chapter 7.

DR respondents appeared reluctant to conclude that it was right to convict German officers at Nuremberg (item B) or, to an even greater extent, their hypothetical American counterparts (item C). Similarly, DRs were about equally disinclined to advocate conviction for General Yamashita (item D) and for potential American counterparts (item E). AR respondents firmly advocated convictions in the German case (item B) and were almost perfectly consistent in their responses about American officers acting under orders. ARs took a considerably weaker stance toward convicting General Yamashita (item D) and toward upholding command responsibility as a principle that applies to Americans. Nevertheless, AR respondents were significantly more prone to convict in the Yamashita case than were DRs, who seemed reluctant to convict anyone. And AR respondents were if anything *more* stringent about command responsibility for American generals than they were in the case of General Yamashita. The overall pattern of AR responses indicated an absence of self-serving or nation-serving responses—a striking consistency in judgments made about "them" and "us." This pattern is reminiscent of chapter 7's Consistent Refusers; it is not surprising, because ARs to a large extent *were* the Consistent Refusers.

The fact that DR-AR differences were more striking on the issue of Nuremberg and its American counterpart than on the Yamashita issue is understandable in our model of the two groups' responsibility judgments. For ARs, we argue, responsibility attribution is characterized by a focus on actors' personal causation of observable consequences. The Yamashita case, however, evoked command responsibility: respondeat superior. Presumably, many AR respondents did not accept or did not fully agree with this principle, finding it difficult to attribute responsibility to superior authorities in the absence of clear-cut personal causation. On the other hand, AR respondents strongly approved conviction of both Germans and Americans for war crimes carried out under orders, where it is clear that the crimes themselves were directly and intentionally caused.

Across these legal precedents and their American analogues, DR respondents were disinclined to convict anyone. Their objection on Nuremberg-related items is hardly surprising, since these questions are directly related to the issues raised by the Calley trial; yet they also rejected, in larger proportions than the AR group, the conviction of General Yamashita and of American generals on the basis of command responsibility. This again suggests a potential void in which no one is left responsible, a void consistent with our earlier contention that individual and command responsibilities are separable issues.

The final item in table 9.4 refers to the refusal of a few draft boards to conscript men as a protest against the Calley sentence. This action represented a form of civil disobedience toward which DRs were obviously more inclined than ARs on the average. This finding is interesting in its own right, since DR respondents appeared otherwise oriented toward "law and order" and unwilling to defy legitimate authority. When asked why they approved, DRs responded overwhelmingly because "draft boards should not be drafting men who will be sent to Vietnam and then punished for doing their duty." Sixty-two percent of DRs (versus 29 percent of ARs) gave this reason, which echoes the original reason *a* for trial disapproval (see table 9.1). In contrast, of the small number of AR respondents who approved of the draft boards' actions, one-third did so because they opposed the draft (in contrast to 11 percent of DRs). DR and AR respondents did not differ in their reasons for *disapproving* of the boards' actions, agreeing that such actions were illegal, irresponsible, or inappropriate.

We have already alluded to the concept of betrayal or double-bind in chapter 7, when discussing the reactions of Consistent Shooters. This concept seemed to be a powerful undercurrent in both the most popular reason (*a*) for trial disapproval itself and in DR respondents' reasons for approving of civil disobedience by draft boards. Both reflected, in our view, a sense of betrayal—a feeling that the understanding, the tacit contract, under which men were being drafted and sent to Vietnam had been violated by the Calley trial. The trial, they felt, placed them in a double-bind, in which—in the words of many DR respondents—"you're damned if you do and you're damned if you don't."

TWO DEFINITIONS OF THE AUTHORITY SITUATION

DR respondents, who would deny a subordinate's responsibility for a crime of obedience like My Lai, and AR respondents, who would assert individual responsibility in the face of superior orders, reacted to other questions with great consistency. For DRs, most people would shoot, they would shoot, Calley should have shot, and what Calley did was right or understandable. They were prepared to accept various justifications for his action, and they saw it as similar to bombing raids that also kill civilians. DRs saw Calley as a soldier doing his duty. For ARs, most people would refuse to shoot, they would refuse, Calley should have refused, and his actions were wrong. They were not prepared to accept justifications for his actions, and they saw it as different from bombing raids in which the killing of civilians is unintentional. They insisted on Calley's individual responsibility in terms of the usual moral standards. ARs' differentiation between Calley's actions and bombing raids also suggests that the concept of individual responsibility has distinct limits. Most ARs, it seems, did not expect individuals to take responsibility for governmental or military policies in which they participate and for the unintended consequences of such policies. They held them responsible only for the direct and intended consequences of actions in which they are able to exercise some personal choice.

Overall, the DR and AR groups seemed to be operating in terms of different definitions of the situation in which Calley found himself and of the hypothetical situations we presented to them. Of the two terms linked together in some questions, "follow orders and shoot," the DR group seemed to focus on the first, "follow orders," and the AR group on the second, "shoot."

For the DR group, the definition of the situation centered on a soldier's obligations to a legitimate authority. The individual in this situation is merely carrying out actions of which someone else—the superior who gives the orders—is the author. DRs made a sharp distinction between authority situations and normal interpersonal relations. In an authority situation, obedience is normatively expected ("most people would follow orders") and the right thing to do ("what any good soldier would do under the circumstances"). Since people have no choice in the matter ("orders are orders"), they should not be held responsible for the consequences of their actions. To do so, as was done in Calley's trial and conviction, is unfair.

The AR group, in contrast, apparently defined the situation in terms of personally caused negative consequences. In such a definition, the individual is knowingly performing actions that result in the killing of unarmed men, women, and children. ARs saw some continuity between authority situations and normal interpersonal relations (without necessarily being unaware of the unique features of the authority situation). Because the usual standards of morality and criteria for assessing responsibility apply, Calley's action could not be considered either normal or right. It violated moral principles and it was proper to hold him responsible for it.

In short, for the DR group the action performed was carrying out orders; for the AR group it was killing people. A crime of obedience is not a paradox to most observers. It resolves itself into a consistent image: either obedience or crime.

Predicting Responsibility Orientations

Responsibility orientations logically represent intervening variables: They intervene between other specific attitudes that they help to organize or predict (dependent variables) and causal factors (such as demographic characteristics). We have treated the DR-AR distinction thus far as an independent variable predicting other attitudes. Now we turn to examine how responsibility orientation itself may be predicted or understood.

Our survey responses included a number of clues to how and why people might arrive at DR or AR positions, in the form of questions about the Vietnam War itself as well as about individuals' demographic characteristics. In table 9.5 we sift from these questions a set of key predictors or correlates of being a DR or AR respondent in this survey. For the sake of consistency, percentages for each item are computed across rows, with the row variable considered to be the independent variable, although we view Vietnam War attitudes as a correlate rather than a cause of responsibility orientation.

In the light of the multiple reasons for Americans' interest in the Calley trial, for their "shoot-refuse" responses, and for their approval or disapproval of the trial, it was plausible that responsibility orientations would be related to views of the Vietnam War. Attitudes about the war, however, were only weakly linked to DR-AR. Specific hawkish and dovish reasons for opinions about the war, which had significantly related to "shoot-refuse" responses in chapter 7's analyses, showed the same trend in differentiating between DRs and ARs, but not significantly. Analyses also indicated that a whole array of Vietnam policy items did not predict DR-AR differences. Item A in table 9.5 shows the only significant relationship of this sort: Hawks were more likely to be DRs, whereas self-declared doves tended to a

Table 9.5 Predicting Responsibility Orientation from Vietnam War Attitudes and
Demographic Variables

Predictors	*Responsibility Orientation*		*All Respondents (%)*
	Deny Responsibility	Assert Responsibility	
A. Vietnam War self-identification			
Hawk (%)	77	23	27
Middle of road(%)	67	33	33
Dove (%)	55	45	39
B. Religion			
Catholic (%)	61	39	28
Protestant (%)	70	30	60
Other (%)	49	51	12
C. Region			
South/Midwest (%)	76	24	42
Northeast/Far West (%)	57	43	58
D. Place of residence			
Rural (%)	77	23	16
Urban (%)	63	37	84
E. Education			
Low (<12) (%)	74	26	31
Medium (12) (%)	68	32	38
High (13+) (%)	52	48	31
F. Social class			
Low (%)	70	30	69
High (%)	51	49	31

Note: In this table, the row variables are treated as the independent variables, so that
percentages add up to 100 for each row designating a particular demographic or self-identification category. Thus, for example, hawks break down into 77% DRs and 23% ARs,
whereas among doves the comparable percentages are 55 and 45. The total number of DR
respondents was 306 (65%); the total number of ARs 165 (35%). Overall Ns for specific
predictors ranged from 394 (item A) to 471 as a function of occasional missing data. In
item A, self-identification excludes "don't know" responses.

greater extent to be ARs. Apparently to call oneself a dove meant to define oneself
as part of the opposition to the government, to adopt the stance of critic. The fact
that such a self-definition was associated more often with AR responses is consistent with other elements in this orientation toward personal responsibility.[4]

DEMOGRAPHIC DETERMINANTS

Item B, respondents' religion, bears an overall relation to responsibility orientation that parallels its link to trial approval/disapproval. What appears distinctive
is that a religious identification other than Christian—including Jewish and

---

4. General liberalism-conservatism was unrelated to DR-AR differences.

none—was associated with an AR orientation. Protestants were if anything the religious group most inclined toward a DR stance, but follow-up tests showed that they did not differ significantly from Catholics.

Item C shows that respondents' region of residence significantly differentiated between DRs and ARs. Residents of the South or Midwest were predictably inclined to be DRs; those living in the Northeast or Far West were more likely to take an AR position. In addition, respondents who were rural as opposed to metropolitan residents were significantly more likely to hold a deny-responsibility orientation (item D).

Education and social class (items E and F) are also familiar variables. The relationship of education to responsibility orientation is no surprise. Evidence of prior studies and our own theoretical understanding of responsibility judgments both suggest that to be in, or to be trained for, a position of authority may lead to an assert-responsibility orientation (see chapters 8 and 11). Item E indicates that this was indeed the case. Markers of such position and training include, in addition to greater education, higher social class or more prestigious occupation. Such other markers of high position showed consistent results. Interviewers assessed social class by rating (on a ten-point scale) each respondent's home and durable household items. For presentation in table 9.5, we divided the respondents into two social-class categories: "low," which can be thought of as lower-middle-class, working-class, and poor respondents, and "high," which corresponds to upper-middle-class and upper-class respondents. Item F shows that respondents who were rated as high on this measure were significantly more likely to be ARs. (Dividing the sample into three, four, or five groupings produced the same pattern of difference between lower and higher groups, with higher standing always significantly associated with an AR orientation.) In addition, higher occupational prestige tended to show the same pattern.[5]

Finally, a variety of other demographic variables did *not* significantly predict responsibility orientation. These included respondents' sex and military experience—variables that figured importantly in chapter 7—as well as respondents' race and age.

As was true in chapter 7, two types of demographic factors or forces seemed to contribute to responsibility orientation. The division did not precisely follow the line suggested in that chapter, however. There we contrasted social-structural position and/or cognitive sophistication, indexed by education, with emotional identification. Some of the contributors to identification, such as sex, military experience, and a range of Vietnam War views, are notably missing from the current

---

5. The failure of occupational prestige to reach significance might seem surprising, given the relatively powerful relationships for education and social class. However, the pattern of results was consistent. Professional or managerial occupation predicted an assert-responsibility orientation. The lack of significance can be accounted for by two factors. First, we used a crude nine-category scheme based on the census categories for coding open-ended responses about occupation; hence collapsed groupings based on these were also crude. More important, data about occupation were recorded only for respondents themselves, excluding housewives and students. The reduced N in itself accounts for the nonsignificance.

picture. Instead, it seems more accurate to describe the predictors of DR versus AR views as, first, elements of social-structural position (such as education, social class, or occupational prestige) and, second, whatever cultural or subcultural norms about authority and responsibility may be imparted by one's religion, region of residence, or place of residence.

VALIDITY OF PREDICTORS

It is important to ask whether these demographic variables are all true predictors of responsibility orientation. Some variables may actually be surrogates for others in the simple zero-order relationships shown here. For example, the apparent effect of region might be due to a correlated variable like urban residence, or the reverse. Predictors may also interact with one another, making it necessary to consider them in combination to get an accurate picture. We therefore tested all two-variable combinations of predictors from among the five variables that were significant in the two-way (zero-order) analyses (education, social class, region, urban versus rural residence, and religion), plus occupational prestige. Combinations of more than two predictors tend to be unreliable owing to the very small Ns or empty cells that result. The most important statistically reliable interaction is presented in table 9.6.[6]

Table 9.6 Predicting Responsibility Orientation from Education and Religion Combined[a]

| | Religion[b] | | | All |
Education	Catholic	Protestant	Other	Respondents
Low (<12)	44	18	33	26
Medium (12)	34	31	27	32
High (13+)	40	43	77	48
All respondents	39	30	51	

[a]Entries are the *percent* AR for each group. For each category or cell, the percentage giving the DR response can be calculated by subtracting the figure shown from 100%. Overall N (ARs plus DRs with data for religion and education) = 457.
[b]Strength of relationship between education and DR-AR ranges from gamma = −.05 for Catholics, through gamma = .37 for Protestants, to gamma = .60 for religious "others" (Jewish, other, none).

6. The tabulated interaction was also significant when log-linear analysis (BMDP4F; see Dixon, 1983) was used. The three-way relationship among education, religion, and responsibility orientation was significant in a saturated model that included just these variables; the necessity of including it in the model was tested and confirmed by adding a fourth variable (age) and deleting the term for the relation among education, religion, and responsibility orientation. In addition to this interaction, each social-status variable—education, social class, and occupation—also interacted with the others in predicting DR-AR differences. In each case the form of the interaction was that effects of a given social-status variable were stronger in higher categories of the other two. We do not dwell on these interactions because they do not affect basic predictions about main effects of these variables.

It is useful to stress, first, what did *not* happen in these analyses. None of the predictors was spurious; all of them, controlling in turn for each of the others, predicted DR versus AR orientations. Second, the cultural variables (religion, region, and place of residence) were relatively "noninteractive" either with each other or with social position variables. Region of the country did not interact with any other variable. The pattern for urban residence was basically the same as that for region; a possible interaction of place of residence with religion is difficult to assess because the sample included no DRs or ARs who were both rural residents and religiously Jewish, other, or none. (The entire national sample included only five such individuals.) Any effects of urban residence and religion are inevitably confounded. With these "nots" in mind, we turn to table 9.6's interaction between education and religion as predictors of responsibility orientation. Percentages in this three-way table refer to the percentage of respondents holding the AR position.

There are two ways to describe the education-religion interaction. Focusing on education, one can say that it was among respondents who have more than a high school education that the most dramatic religious differences in AR tendencies appeared. Focusing on religion, the interesting finding was that for Catholics there was no effect of education on responsibility orientation. In contrast, there was a strong linear effect for Protestants and an even stronger effect for religious others (Jewish, other, none). Catholics and Protestants were fairly similar in their average DR versus AR tendencies. Yet it made a great deal of difference how educated the Protestant was; it made no difference how educated the Catholic was. The religious "other" group stood out from both Catholics and Protestants in its average tendency to respond as ARs, but this was at least in part because these "others" were more educated.

Religions, as social groups, provide members with powerful cognitive frameworks and motivations for adhering to these frameworks. They build ethical subcultures among members. These ethical subcultures, communities of understanding about right and wrong, can do two things that affect responsibility orientations. They can and must provide a baseline set of standards against which secular authority is to be judged. As noted in chapters 3 and 6, religious authority has long served as a rationale for disobedience to secular authority in the Western world. Religious ideologies—like all ideologies—also provide cognitive frameworks for interpreting new information. Catholic ideology, by this standard, appeared here to be relatively encapsulated. Instead of "allowing" education to produce its usual effect of increasing the assertion of individual responsibility, Catholicism predisposed adherents to a position about obedience regardless of whether they held sixth grade or graduate school diplomas. It is important to note, however, that not all Catholics agreed about the stance to be taken—whether to obey or to refuse—presumably because they interpreted the church's position differently. What Catholics shared was that their choices were relatively independent of their levels of educational attainment.

Overall, education provides alternative ways of viewing the world, compared to those held by authority, as well as alternative sources of power vis-à-vis authority; across levels of education, Catholicism appeared to offer an alternative ethical subculture with regard to the issue of obedience to secular orders.

Conclusions

The findings reported in this chapter can help us account for the massive public outcry against the trial and conviction of Lieutenant Calley. In doing so, they can also help us understand the role that different conceptions of personal responsibility play in people's susceptibility to destructive obedience.

Understanding American reaction to the Calley trial requires going beyond questions about approval and disapproval of the trial. On each side of this issue, positions were apparently held on the basis of responsibility considerations, antiwar sentiment, or concern with morale or fairness in the army. The core reasons, both numerically and conceptually, were those involving responsibility. One body of opinion approved of the trial on grounds of individual responsibility for immoral acts even in wartime, whereas another body of opinion disapproved on grounds that the individual is not responsible for acts under the push of orders or the imperatives of duty. These assert-responsibility and deny-responsibility stances significantly separated the sample on virtually every other item related to the trial or to Calley's action.

RESPONSIBILITY ASSERTION AND DENIAL

The essence of the AR stance appeared to be the acknowledgment that authority has limits, that choices and judgments are always needed, and that normal moral standards can be applied in situations governed by authority. DRs appeared to view authority very differently, and therefore felt betrayed—quite understandably—by the Calley trial and conviction. In their interpretation, a situation like My Lai becomes a double-bind, a no-win situation for a subordinate, if that subordinate can be blamed for following orders as well as for refusing to follow them. DRs clearly regarded shooting civilians when ordered to do so as the normatively expected response and evaluated Calley's action in these terms. No doubt they saw following orders in a combat situation as a soldier's moral obligation, just as surely as the ARs considered it a moral obligation to take responsibility for one's actions despite the military setting.

Although the range of individual responsibility was obviously wider for AR respondents than for DR respondents, some answers also indicated that even for AR respondents the concept of individual responsibility had distinct limits. For example, in differentiating between Calley's actions and bombing raids, ARs held individuals responsible only for the direct, intended consequences of actions in which they seemed able to exercise personal choice. This limit is similar to the standard requirement of mens rea, "guilty mind," in criminal prosecutions (see chapter 8). ARs were also reluctant, in responding about who should go on trial for My Lai and in reacting to legal precedents, to invoke a superior's command responsibility for unintended consequences. Under the appropriate circumstances, the AR respondent—like the DR respondent but for different reasons—might judge subordinates *or* their superiors innocent of a crime of obedience.

We argue that in assessing a crime of obedience, people generally focus either on the crime or on the obedience, but not on both. The reactions of AR and DR respondents to My Lai and the Calley trial were so different as to seem almost a reaction to different events. We come back to our discussion in the last chapter of alternative ways of looking at a situation like My Lai: one that stresses the obedient *motives* of the subordinate versus one that stresses the possible *consequences* of obedient action. When one follows orders to shoot, for example, the *follow orders* part refers to the motive and the *shoot* evokes the consequence. It appears to us as if DR respondents, in denying responsibility, were seeing Calley's action as the following of orders—through a filter of motives. It appears that AR respondents, in asserting responsibility, were seeing the action as killing civilians by shooting them—through the anticipation of consequences.

Can we identify what leads one individual to see a situation through the definition provided by the authority of the moment, and what leads another to see the same situation through an independent definition or perspective? The beginnings of an answer to this question can be found in the relationship of the DR and AR orientations to two groups of demographic variables.

First, being a DR or AR was linked to social position. Lower social class, education, or occupational standing predicted a more pliant stance toward orders from above, as expected. Seemingly the elements of social position represented material and cognitive resources that allowed individuals to assert the actor's independence and individual responsibility in an authority situation.

Second, being a DR or AR was linked to cultural or subcultural norms about authority, which seemed to differ as a function of region of residence, place of residence, and religion. Region and place of residence had straightforward effects: Southern or midwestern and rural respondents took a more obedient, DR, stance. Religion had more complex effects. On the average, religious "others" were likely to be ARs. Catholics were almost as likely as Protestants to offer DR responses on the whole. For Protestants, however, as well as for religious "others," the proportion of DR responses was inversely related to education, whereas among Catholics less educated respondents were no more likely to be DRs than their more highly educated coreligionists. We speculated that this result may have reflected the Catholic church's traditional role (described in chapter 3) as an alternative source of authority in secular conflict.

EXPLAINING THE PUBLIC OUTCRY

We know from our survey that DRs formed the largest subgroup of Americans who disapproved of the Calley trial. It seems reasonable to propose, therefore, that this segment of the population contributed significantly to the strong expressions of indignation and dismay in the wake of Calley's conviction. It is likely that DRs, at least initially, set the tone for the national response because the conviction spoke directly to their own condition. Given their conception of individual responsibility in relation to legitimate authority, the Calley conviction created a deep sense of confusion, anxiety, and anger in this large segment of the population.

Basically, it seems, DRs see themselves—and average citizens in general—as having no choice when confronted with official orders, particularly in the domain of foreign and military policy. They may or may not like a policy—and by 1971 most of them neither liked nor understood the war in Vietnam—but this does not reduce their obligation to abide by it. Thus, presumably, they allowed themselves to be drafted for Vietnam, encouraged their sons to accept the draft, and did whatever they were told was required of them.

To some extent, this attitude may be related to a sense of powerlessness—a feeling that they are "pawns" rather than "origins" (deCharms, 1968) in the society, who have neither the right nor the capacity to determine national policy. Such a feeling would be consistent with the demographic characteristics of the DRs, who tend to be lower in education and social class. Thus, the realities of their lives—the jobs they hold, their positions in society, the resources available to them—in fact limit their opportunity to take independent action and influence the policy process. Also, there is a greater likelihood that people with lower socioeconomic backgrounds have been socialized to obey the rules and stay out of trouble, rather than to develop a sense of ownership of the system, a feeling that they can shape and evaluate policies (see chapter 11). The DRs' feeling that they have no choice but to obey is not necessarily linked to a sense of powerlessness, however. It may also be derived from a strong identification with power, which leads to a view of obedience as a moral duty overriding any other moral considerations that might arise. We shall have more to say about these two possible motives behind the DR orientation in chapter 11.

We propose that for DRs the relationship between citizens and political authorities is based on an implicit contract, whereby the citizens—out of necessity, rooted in their own powerlessness, or out of a sense of duty, rooted in their identification with the power hierarchy—relinquish control to the authorities. They agree to obey without question, at least in the domain of grand national policy. In return, however, the authorities are expected to accept full responsibility for the consequences of such obedient actions. Thus, while the individual citizens abandon their freedom of choice, they are also liberated of personal responsibility for any untoward outcomes of their actions and the guilt these might engender. This contract is reminiscent of the contract between experimenter and research participant that we described in our discussion of Milgram's research.

If we assume that DRs operate in terms of this kind of contract, we can understand their reaction to the Calley trial and conviction. Calley, in their view, was fulfilling his part of the bargain—obeying orders, doing what he had to do. But when things went sour, the authorities—who presumably gave the orders—

turned around and held him personally responsible for the consequences. From the DRs' perspective, this decision represented a violation of the contract and a betrayal by the authorities.

This account assumes that DRs by and large identified with Calley—a reasonable assumption, particularly in view of some of the demographic characteristics of DRs. One must keep in mind that Calley was not a typical officer and that most people perceived him as an ordinary soldier. He became an officer only because of personnel shortages at the time. He was not particularly bright, had limited education, had failed in most of his undertakings, and was short—unlike the stereotype of a proper officer. Many DRs must have felt (and indeed told us) that they would have done what he did in the situation. In fact, in their own way, they had "obeyed questionable orders" by supporting the war despite their increasing misgivings about it. Calley's conviction left them confused because it placed them, no less than him, in a double-bind situation. On the one hand, they risked being penalized and feeling morally delinquent if they refused to obey; but now, they were told, they also risked being penalized and branded as morally delinquent if they did obey. It is not hard to understand why they felt betrayed.

FURTHER QUESTIONS ABOUT RESPONSIBILITY ORIENTATIONS

The DR and AR patterns flesh out the theoretical distinctions between motive-based and consequences-based orientations to responsibility developed in the preceding chapter. These two patterns clearly provide a useful conceptual handle for explaining public reactions to the Calley trial and for organizing different approaches to the issues raised by the trial. The DR-AR distinction was significantly related to many other attitudes: Responsibility orientation served as a filter through which people interpreted these events. DR-AR responses were also related to a number of demographic variables. Thus, there is reason to believe that this distinction can help us understand how people react to crimes of obedience in general and—by inference—how they themselves might act in authority situations. We must always keep in mind, of course, that there is no perfect correspondence between what people say and what they do.

Several questions arise if we want to build on the DR-AR distinction—and the two models of responsibility attribution they represent—in our further exploration of crimes of obedience. First, how stable are these reactions? We identified them in relation to a specific case which, at the time of the 1971 survey, had only recently been at the center of public attention and the focus of a heated, emotion-laden debate. It would be helpful to know whether these patterns still emerge clearly when people react to events at a greater temporal and emotional distance. Second, how general are these reactions? We identified them in relation to a crime of obedience in a military setting, in which the authority hierarchy is most rigidly structured and the norms of obedience are especially strong. It would be important to see to what extent these reactions generalize to crimes of obedience in other settings. Finally, how do we account for differences in the approach to responsibility adopted by different individuals? Here it would be useful to explore broader psychopolitical orientations that may be related to both the demographic predictors and AR versus DR responses.

In order to investigate some of these questions, we undertook a second survey, to be presented in the following chapters. Chapter 10 focuses on our findings regarding the stability and generality of the DR-AR patterns. Findings about individual differences are reported in chapter 12—after a discussion, in chapter 11, of various theoretical formulations of this issue.

10 | Assertion and Denial of Responsibility: The Generality of Reactions to Crimes of Obedience

In examining American reactions to My Lai and the Calley trial in 1971, we found that responsibility—whether asserted or denied—seemed to be an organizing core for opinions about this crime of obedience. In 1976 we set out to replicate and extend the 1971 survey in order to test whether this basic finding about responsibility would still hold at a time when Americans' visceral reaction to the trial and conviction of Lt. William Calley had faded. We wanted to see, moreover, to what extent responsibility orientations generalize across crimes of obedience and whether people's demographic characteristics would mold these orientations in the same way they did in the earlier survey. We also sought to test the effects on conceptions of responsibility of political orientations via rules, roles, and values. In the present chapter we describe the 1976 survey and assess whether the basic results from 1971 were indeed replicated and generalized to other crimes of obedience. Findings on the effects of political orientations appear in chapter 12.

The Boston Survey

To determine the reliability of patterns such as the DR versus AR orientations to responsibility, it would have been preferable to have a national sample again as we had in 1971. Insufficient funds dictated otherwise. The survey was therefore restricted to the Boston area (the Standard Metropolitan Statistical Area, or S.M.S.A.). We shall argue below that this restriction of the second survey actually offers a stringent test of the generality of our results. First, however, we briefly outline methodological improvements we sought in this second survey.

The two basic improvements involved the range of crimes of

obedience studied and the set of questions posed about responsibility for their occurrence. As we do not think such crimes occur only in military settings, or even only in bureaucratic ones, it is important to test the generality of responsibility orientations across incidents as well as over time and locale. We also wanted to expand the ways in which we asked about responsibility.[1] This is necessary because the DR-AR distinction was geared quite specifically to the My Lai incident and because it captured only a subset of reasons for respondents' views.

In addition, we attempted to fill certain logical gaps from the first survey. One gap concerned the meaning of responsibility assertion, for we never directly asked in 1971 whether the respondent thought that Lieutenant Calley had received orders to act as he did. As we have interpreted it, a true AR position represents the assertion of the actor's responsibility *in the presence of* actual or probable orders. A second gap concerned the relationship between crimes of obedience and "ordinary" crimes. We interpreted responses to My Lai on the assumption that judgments of these two types of crimes differ fundamentally from each other. In particular, our interpretation of the DR orientation—which denies the responsibility of the actor for the crime—certainly does not imply any general tendency of DRs to be "soft on crime"; if anything, it suggests the opposite. However, we had not tested the validity of this assumption.

The 1976 survey therefore covered a range of crimes of obedience, assessed responsibility judgments in more than one way, added a direct question about whether Calley had received orders, and included items about other crimes.

THE SAMPLE

In February and March of 1976 the Survey Research Program of the University of Massachusetts, Boston, conducted the follow-up survey. The survey instrument included a face-to-face interview of approximately forty-five minutes and a mail-back questionnaire, estimated to take a similar length of time to complete. Given its efficiency and lower cost, quota sampling at the block level was the method of choice, as in 1971. We had an original goal of 400 interviews, composing a quota sample of the Boston S.M.S.A. Of this number, 391 interviews were completed. (The goal for total interviews was not met because some blocks were essentially non-English-speaking.) Respondents were selected by probability sampling methods to the block level. Quotas for sex, race, and age were used within blocks. Blacks were oversampled for purposes of a companion study described below by overrepresenting blocks that were at least 20 percent black in the 1970 census; fifty blacks were interviewed. The final sample included a balanced spread of sexes and age groups.

1. Statistics presented in this chapter are slightly more complicated than those encountered thus far since the variables include some continuous measures of responsibility attribution. In addition to the familiar tests for significance of cross-tabular data we will therefore use parametric statistics as needed. Like chi-square, these can always be interpreted in terms of the probability that the result happened by chance. (For example, $p < .01$ still means a probability of less than 1 in 100 that the occurrence was by chance.) Cross-tabular associations can again be assumed significant at $p < .01$ unless stated otherwise.

Approximately half of both the face-to-face interview and the mail-back questionnaire dealt with crimes of obedience. The other half of each instrument consisted of evaluations of everyday crimes and related issues, such as attitudes toward capital punishment and perceived safety from crime. These items were part of a separate but conceptually related study (Hamilton and Rotkin, 1979; Hamilton and Rytina, 1980). We will draw on them in discussing the relationship between judgments of a crime of obedience and judgments of other crimes.

As in the prior study, the main interview led people into the task with a question about following the news. General views about the Vietnam War were then probed; wording of questions used in 1971 was changed to reflect the passage of time. Estimates of respondents' extent of information about the Calley trial followed next. Given the time lag since the event, we decided not to exclude respondents who claimed to be uninformed from subsequent sections of the interview, as we had done in 1971. We then asked whether the respondent thought Lieutenant Calley had been ordered to kill Vietnamese civilians or not.

Key questions from the 1971 survey were replicated. These core items concerned whether "most people" would shoot; whether "you" would shoot; trial approval versus disapproval; reasons for each position; and whether Calley "should" have shot if ordered. An open-ended query about why the respondent would shoot or refuse was also included, and the same categories were used to code responses as in the earlier survey. In lieu of the earlier question about the fairness of Calley's sentence, we asked a question about the appropriate punishment for him, which presented a range of possible penalties. This change seemed necessary in view of the national sample's overwhelming rejection of Calley's original sentence, as well as the reduction in the sentence Calley actually served. We also asked for respondents' evaluation of various actors' *relative responsibility* for My Lai (see below for wording). Finally, instead of replicating once-topical items like the refusal of draft boards to draft men or the similarity of bombing raids to My Lai, we asked respondents to evaluate conscientious objection to the war and amnesty for draft resisters and deserters, issues that were more current. The half of the survey dealing with ordinary crimes intervened at this point, before items about Watergate and hypothetical crimes of obedience.

Additional crimes of obedience. The Watergate scandal provided examples of crimes of obedience in a civilian, political bureaucracy. Watergate questions first probed the respondent's trust in various sectors of government—the executive, the Supreme Court, and local government. The trust items were modified from standard Louis Harris poll queries on trust in government. In parallel with the new Calley item, we then asked if respondents believed the Watergate burglars were acting under orders or not. Subsequent items paralleled prior ones about Lieutenant Calley: whether the burglars should have carried out orders, whether most people would have carried out the burglary, and how responsibility for the Watergate burglary should be divided. We did not ask whether "you" would have carried out the burglary; at the time this item seemed likely to show little variation while entailing the possible cost of offending respondents. We also modified the item on what most people would do—providing options of "most people" versus "only some people" or "very few people," rather than a dichotomous choice—in the hope of increasing variance of response. After these items about the Watergate burglary itself, we inquired about dividing up responsibility for the cover-up.

Two hypothetical situations were then presented to respondents. Both incidents portrayed professional authorities acting in a bureaucratic capacity: issuing instructions to someone to do something to a third party. One was a case of a nurse on hospital duty who received telephone orders from a doctor to administer what turned out to be a drug overdose. The scenario was adapted from an experiment by Hofling et al. (1966)[2] and was presented to respondents as follows:

> A nurse on hospital duty was telephoned by a doctor on the hospital staff. He asked her to give one of the patients a dose of a drug that was not on the approved list for that patient. When she reminded him that, according to hospital rules, such requests had to be made in writing, he said that he was just leaving for the hospital to examine the patient and would write out the form on arrival, but that he wanted the drug to take effect by the time he arrived. When the nurse went to get the drug from the cabinet, she found that the dosage the doctor had asked for was twice the amount listed on the bottle as the maximum daily dosage.

After presenting the situation, we asked what the nurse should have done (since there was no already established ending); what "most people" would do; what "you" would do; whether the nurse would have any legal responsibility if the drug was administered with negative effects; and how responsibility should be divided between the nurse and the doctor. The new question about legal responsibility was included because no real-world analogue such as the Calley trial or the Watergate hearings was available.

The second case presented the Milgram (1974) experiment (discussed extensively in chapter 6) in a hypothetical version. It took the Milgram scenario up to the point at which the "learner," mentioning his weak heart, begins to scream and demands to be released:

> Mr. Jones volunteered to be in a psychology experiment. On arriving at the laboratory, he got the promised payment of 5 dollars and was assigned the job of giving electric shocks to another volunteer every time the man made a mistake on a learning task. The

---

2. In their original study Hofling et al. reported a high rate of obedience by nurses. A replication by Rank and Jacobson (1977), however, found a much reduced level of obedience when conditions were more typical of hospital settings—the drug in question was one familiar to the nurses (Valium), and the nurses had an opportunity to consult with others about dosage. We agree with Miller's (1986) analysis that the divergent outcomes of these two studies illustrate the impact of situational factors on obedience. In the replication both the nurses' familiarity with the drug and their opportunity to consult bolstered their relative level of information or expertise; consultation, in addition, lends social support. In the terms of chapter 6, a subordinate's own professional expertise strengthens the opposing forces that lead to challenging authority; social support for disobedience weakens the binding forces that tie individuals into the authoritative definition of the situation.

instructions were to gradually increase the strength of the shock as the experiment wore on. After a while the other man began to scream, said that he had a weak heart, and asked to be released. Mr. Jones turned to the experimenter and asked him what to do. The experimenter instructed him to disregard the other man's screams and to go on with the experiment.

Questions included whether the teacher should or should not go on, whether "most people" would go on, whether "you" would go on, whether the teacher would have any legal responsibility in the event of a heart attack on the part of the learner, and how responsibility should be divided between experimenter and teacher.

Demographics. Several modifications were made in the demographic items from the prior study. In 1971 one of the key components of social standing, social class, was derived from an interviewer "grading" of house and household items. Such an index has limitations. It combines the impact of income (without actually recording it) with educationally related or occupationally related tastes. It also represents a subjective evaluation of this unclear combination on the part of the interviewer. Therefore in the Boston study a pure income measure was chosen instead. Respondents were asked to indicate to which of fifteen income groups their family belonged (in terms of gross 1975 family income). This question about income category was selected in preference to one about exact income because respondents are generally reluctant to divulge exact figures even if they are able to do so.

The 1976 survey also recorded occupation for heads of household in an improved manner. A set of open-ended and closed questions was used to enable coding of occupation via the Duncan Socioeconomic Index (Duncan, 1961), which yielded finely differentiated occupational categories. Respondents' educational attainment was an open-ended question with responses coded into six categories (later collapsed into three). Overall, the elements of social position were available in the follow-up survey in a more clearly separated form than they had been in the earlier study.

Other demographic variables, such as the respondent's age, sex, race, and military status, were coded in substantially the same fashion as in 1971.

Mail-back instrument. At the end of the interview, respondents were asked to fill out a mail-back questionnaire. They were told that they would receive five dollars for doing so. With this incentive presumably boosting the response rate, an unusually high proportion—81 percent—of mail-backs was returned (314 of the 391 respondents). The first segment of the mail-back called for judgments about crimes of various types, as part of the companion study. Then followed 117 attitude items, including a series of previously established attitude scales, as well as our own political orientation and attachment scales, randomly interspersed. The previously developed items, included for their relevance to attitudes toward authority and responsibility, were McClosky's (1958) conservatism scale (9 items); 10 items from the traditional moralism scale (Gold, Christie, and Friedman, 1976, p. 17), a derivative from Richard Christie's earlier efforts to devise a balanced measure of authoritarianism; and 12 items from Collins's (1974) version of internal-external control (see also Rotter, 1966). Our new scales were intended to test whether broader orientations toward political authority might underlie responsibility judgments. All scales are discussed in chapter 12.

DIFFERENCES BETWEEN THE 1971 AND 1976 SURVEY POPULATIONS

Generalizations that can be drawn from any comparison between the 1971 and the 1976 surveys are clearly limited by the differences between the populations they sampled: the U.S. population at large versus the population of a single metropolitan area. Differences in the demographic characteristics and the baseline attitudes of the two samples must be taken into account when we compare the pattern of relationships between variables found in the two studies. We therefore compared the two samples on key demographic and attitudinal items. We also included in the comparison the subsample of respondents from the Northeastern region in the 1971 survey, who can provide an approximate indication of how a Boston sample might have responded in 1971. This comparison helps in teasing out the extent to which attitude differences between the 1976 Boston sample and the 1971 national sample are due to stable regional differences as opposed to changes over time.

The results of the comparison are presented in Appendix B. Briefly, we find that the Boston sample differs from the national sample in level of educational attainment and in religous composition, as well as in baseline attitudes. For example, the majority in the 1976 Boston sample approved of the Calley trial, most often on the basis of an AR stance, and indicated that they would refuse to shoot in a My Lai–like situation. In contrast, the majority of the 1971 national sample, as we have seen, disapproved of the Calley trial, usually on the basis of a DR stance, and gave Consistent Shooter responses. The differences appear to be due to attitude changes during the five years intervening between the two surveys rather than to broader regional differences, although they are no doubt also a function of some of the demographic characteristics of the Boston area, such as the higher average level of educational attainment in its population.

We conclude from our comparison that the differences in baseline attitudes— the fact, for example, that the Boston sample included a much larger proportion of ARs than the national sample—would not affect our theoretical conclusions if the 1976 data replicated the *pattern* of relationships between responsibility orientations and other variables. In fact, it would add strength to these conclusions by showing that the same pattern asserts itself in two surveys that differ not only in time and place, but also in opinion baselines. We turn now to the findings on responsibility orientation in the Boston survey and the pattern of its relationships to other variables.

Replicating Responsibility Orientations

We begin the test for generality by assessing whether 1976 items concerning My Lai and the Calley trial had the same relationships to one another as were seen in chapter 9. The investigation of responsibility orientations uses both the DR-AR dichotomy based on people's reasons for approving or disapproving of the Calley trial, which was the central tool for the analysis presented in chapter 9, and a measure based on relative allocations of responsibility among the parties to a crime of obedience. The key theoretical issue in these analyses is whether we again observe the same patterning of responsibility orientations to crimes of obedience in relation to other attitudes.

MEASUREMENT

Interviewers asked whether the respondent approved or disapproved of Lieutenant Calley's having been tried for My Lai, using retrospective wordings where appropriate. Then they asked respondents to choose one reason (from among sets of five reasons for approval or for disapproval) as the most important basis for their opinion. The five reasons for each opinion reproduced, with a change in wording to past tense, the choices from the 1971 survey in their original order of presentation (see table 9.1). These reasons were later divided, as in the national survey, into three groups: a responsibility category consisting of two reasons, an antiwar category consisting of one reason, and a military category consisting of two reasons concerning the morale or honor of the military.

Two reasons for approving of the Calley trial, presented in positions *a* and *d*, captured individual responsibility assertion: the AR position. As in 1971, these were the most popular category of reasons for trial approval (N = 113 ARs out of 219 approvers). The corresponding reasons, *a* and *d*, for trial disapproval constituted the DR position of denial of the subordinate's responsibility; they represented the most popular category of disapproval reasons (N = 81 DRs out of 137 disapprovers).

In addition, the relative responsibilities of participants in the military chain of command were assessed as follows. The issue was introduced by noting, "It's not always easy to decide who is responsible for events like My Lai. Let us say that the total amount of responsibility for the My Lai killings is 100%. How would you divide up that 100% among the following people?" Respondents were then handed a card (which was also read to them) that included six choices, worded as follows: "the President and other foreign policy makers, top generals in the Pentagon, Lt. Calley's superior officers in the field, Lt. Calley, men under Lt. Calley," and an optional category, "others (Who?)," to be specified by the respondent.

The crucial responsibility attribution is that to Lieutenant Calley. Dividing the sample into those who assigned Lieutenant Calley *no* responsibility versus those who assigned him at least *some* responsibility captures the concepts of responsibility denial versus assertion. It represents the concept of denial of responsibility rather literally and stringently. A none/some dichotomy has certain advantages for our analyses, including the greater number of respondents who answer the question (compared to the DR-AR dichotomy, which is based on subsets of disapprovers and approvers) and the possibility of comparing responsibility allocations across incidents of crimes of obedience. Therefore analyses below use both the original DR-AR dichotomy and dichotomous responsibility allocations constructed for each situation.

THE DR-AR DICHOTOMY

A first question is whether DR and AR orientations again represented core orienting views with regard to the My Lai massacre and Calley's trial. We compared groups formed on the basis of *why* they approved or disapproved of the trial. Respondents' reasons for their opinions were first grouped into responsibility-related versus antiwar versus army-related reasons, yielding six groups paralleling those in the original study. Table 10.1 presents the six groups of reasons in relationship to other key items. As before, the small "don't know" category was removed from the percentage base throughout the analyses to clarify comparisons. These results can be compared to corresponding findings from the national survey that were presented in table 9.2.

Responsibility orientations, again the most popular reasons for trial opinions, seemed once again to organize responses to other questions. Item A shows that DR respondents were the group most likely to say that most people would follow orders and shoot in a situation like My Lai, although they did not differ significantly from other disapprovers. In contrast, AR respondents were the group most likely to say that most people would *refuse* to shoot, and they differed significantly from other approvers in doing so. Items B and C reveal the same pattern for other issues: whether the respondent would shoot or refuse and whether Calley should have shot or refused to shoot.[3]

---

3. Responses to the "most shoot" and "you shoot" items themselves also replicate the findings from the 1971 survey. The 1971 findings based on these items and their combination, it will be recalled, were the central focus of chapter 7. The comparable findings from the 1976 survey will be briefly summarized here. There were striking differences between the 1976 survey and its national predecessor in the marginals, the overall percentages offering each answer. Table 10.3 shows that among those who held an opinion in 1976, 62 percent thought that most people would shoot, similar to the national figure earlier; but 66 percent asserted that they would personally refuse to do so, in contrast to the 51 percent majority of 1971 respondents who thought they would shoot. But at the same time, the *pattern* in which the responses are linked appears intact. Respondents who said that most people would shoot tended to say that they would do so, and respondents who said that most would refuse were highly likely to say they would refuse (gamma = .80).

In addition, the three major groups of respondents—Consistent Shooters, Deviant Refusers, and Consistent Refusers—were again distinguishable on demographic and attitudinal grounds. Refusers, especially Deviant Refusers, were more likely not to have served in the military, and there were trends for Refusal and especially Deviant Refusal to occur more frequently among females, more educated respondents, and those aged twenty-five to thirty-four. Consistent Shooters were more likely to be Catholic. Finally, there was some attitudinal evidence that Deviant Refusers were especially opposed to the Vietnam War. Such group differences were generally more slight than in 1971, but patterns of response were consistent with results of the national survey.

Table 10.1 Responses to Selected Other Items by Groups Differing in Their Reasons for Approving or Not Approving of Calley Trial, 1976

Items	Reasons for Approving of Trial			Reasons for Disapproving of Trial		
	Responsibility (%)	Antiwar (%)	Army (%)	Antiwar (%)	Army (%)	Responsibility (%)
A. What would *most* people do [in a My Lai–type situation]? (Follow orders and shoot/Refuse to shoot)						
Follow orders	42	62	59	62	75	82
B. What would *you* do in this situation? (Follow orders and shoot/Refuse to shoot)						
Follow orders	10	33	25	56	48	64
C. Assuming it is true that Calley received orders to shoot, what should he have done? (Carry out/Refuse)						
Carry out	13	34	30	77	70	80

Note: The total number of respondents among approvers was responsibility = 113, antiwar = 57, and army = 49 (see text for explanation of these labels). Among disapprovers, Ns were antiwar = 13, army = 43, and responsibility = 81. Because "don't know" responses were omitted and because some items were not answered by all respondents, the N for items A – C ranges from 193 to 211 for approvers and 119 to 131 for disapprovers. Differences among approvers were significant at $p \leq .01$ for items B and C and at $p = .04$ for item A; no differences among disapprovers were statistically significant.

This internally consistent pattern replicates the findings of chapter 9. Bostonians' DR and AR orientations again represented opposite extremes among the rationales for opinion about Calley's trial. Adhering to a responsibility orientation appeared to organize responses to an array of other items. And the AR position was again more distinguishable from other approval reasons than was the DR position from other disapproval reasons. In the remaining comparisons, we treated DR and AR views as a single dichotomous variable. All analyses with this variable include those respondents who picked reasons *a* or *d* for trial approval or disapproval. The variable is coded DR-AR to reflect increasing assignment of responsibility to the subordinate. Statistically, the variable contrasting the DR and AR groups is always strongly related to other My Lai items.[4] Table 10.1 illustrates how other reasons for approving or disapproving of the trial can mask these sharp DR-AR differences when the sample is considered as a whole.

Trial Interest and Other Views. It was also important to ask what levels of interest or information DR and AR groups were bringing to bear on their judgments of trial-related issues. We did this by examining DR-AR differences in reporting remembrance of My Lai and in thinking that Calley was in fact ordered to act as he did there. The first of these questions is roughly comparable to a 1971 item about how closely the respondent followed the trial. The second is our new question about whether or not Calley received orders.

In 1971 the DR group expressed greater interest in the trial (although not significantly so). But by 1976 the AR respondents claimed to recall My Lai better (at $p = .03$). Some 42 percent of ARs as opposed to 27 percent of DRs claimed to remember My Lai "very well." Boston DR-AR differences, however, involved remembering "very well" versus "fairly well," not a gap that indicates disturbing differences in levels of interest or information about the trial.

The question about whether Calley was or was not ordered to kill civilians at My Lai directly tested respondents' information. The response options included saying that Calley was ordered, that he was not ordered, or that it was not clear whether he was ordered. This last response option is a risky one in a survey, since it could have been used by unsure respondents as a "safe" answer. It was also the most nearly *correct* answer, however, as best we could ascertain from accounts of the incident, trial testimony, and the court-martial verdict. Significantly more ARs (17 percent compared to just 5 percent of DRs) did say that Calley was *not* ordered, but not in large numbers or by a large margin over the DR percentage. The groups showed a parallel difference in their tendencies to say it was "not clear" (the most accurate answer): 54 percent of ARs versus 42 percent of DRs.

---

4. On the key items listed in Table 10.1, the association of DR-AR to choice of response is as follows: For the question about what most people would do, gamma = .72 (82 percent of DRs said "shoot," and 58 percent of ARs said "refuse"). For the question about what respondents themselves would do, gamma = .88 (64 percent of DRs said "shoot," and 90 percent of ARs said "refuse"). For the question about what Calley should have done, gamma = .92 (a symmetrical 80 percent of DRs said he should have followed orders and 87 percent of ARs said he should have refused).

Finally, DRs were predictably more convinced that orders were definitely given (53 percent versus 29 percent of ARs). These differences do not negate our interpretation of AR responses, since the large DR-AR gaps on other items cannot be accounted for by ARs' greater disbelief that Calley received orders.[5]

As indicated above, the 1971 question about the fairness of Calley's sentence was replaced in 1976 by an item that presented a range of possible choices of punishment for Calley and asked respondents to select the most appropriate one. The new item produced a similar pattern of responses: light punishments by DRs, relatively heavy punishments by ARs. As was true in the earlier survey, many AR respondents were relatively lenient, even to the point of favoring a more lenient punishment than the one Calley actually received; nevertheless, ARs selected a wide range of punishments. DR respondents, in contrast, overwhelmingly chose no punishment at all (72 percent) or probation (24 percent) in lieu of any incarceration. Most striking was the relative willingness of the two groups to go beyond Calley's time served (three years) or his eventual sentence after appeals (ten years). No DR respondents advocated severe sentences (on our scale, punishments in the range between fifteen years and the death penalty), but 37 percent of ARs chose punishments in this range.

A pair of questions concerning conscientious objection and amnesty for draft resisters was also included to assess respondents' more general views of authority and obedience. In Boston a majority even of DRs (51 percent) indicated that it was right to refuse to fight in Vietnam on grounds of conscience, but 78 percent of the AR group responded this way, a significant difference. An open-ended probe about why it was right or wrong to refuse to fight yielded no significant differences by our criterion of a 10 percent minimum gap between the two groups' choices. On the more policy-oriented issue of amnesty for draft resisters, the groups also divided significantly. Two-thirds of ARs approved, but 62 percent of DRs disapproved, of amnesty. These findings were consistent with our argument that ARs stressed individual conscience, but they also showed the DR-AR differences to be a matter of degree.

Judgments of Other Crime. The Boston survey provided an unusual opportunity to examine the relationship between judgments of crimes of obedience and judgments of other crimes. For the purposes of another study (see Hamilton and Rotkin, 1979; Hamilton and Rytina, 1980), it included a large number of questions about crime and punishment in general. We are therefore able to see whether DRs and ARs differed in their responses to some of these questions.

We indicated earlier that a DR orientation does not imply a tendency to be lenient toward crimes in general, but in fact suggests the opposite. The apparent contradiction in attitudes toward crimes of obedience and crimes where legitimate

---

5. Cross-tabulations of DR-AR differences for key opinion items were also done separately for those respondents who thought Calley *was* ordered versus those who either said it was *unclear* or thought he was *not* ordered. DR-AR differences remained highly significant regardless of the respondent's belief about Calley's orders.

authority is defied was epitomized in one of the slogans adorning demonstrators' placards shortly after Calley's conviction in 1971: "Hang Manson, free Calley!" Such slogans may seem illogical: Why kill one murderer and release the other? (Charles Manson was a cult leader recently convicted for murder.) But this slogan had a deeper psycho-logic. It asked that one person whose heinous acts involved gleeful defiance of authority and conventional society be killed, and that another person who killed scores of people, but who supported and obeyed authority, be spared. The slogan's two parts reflected a common perspective on the issue of upholding authority. We have argued all along that crimes of obedience are dilemmas about authority and responsibility. Such a slogan was a further reminder that authority is central to understanding such crimes.

A person who advocates harsh punishment for one crime can usually be expected to do likewise for others. In addition, persons who favor the death penalty tend to be more punitive; they are inclined to punish capital and noncapital offenses more harshly and even to convict offenders more often (see Jurow, 1971; Cowan et al., 1984). In turn, favoring capital punishment has been shown to be associated with authoritarianism, a personality syndrome one of whose elements is punitiveness toward deviants (for example, Hamilton, 1976; Vidmar and Ellsworth, 1974). If responses to crimes of obedience proved to be different from— even the inverse of—reactions usually inspired by crimes, we would have a fuller understanding of the psychological roots of denial versus assertion of responsibility in situations governed by authority.

We measured respondents' specific inclinations to punish offenders for fourteen hypothetical crimes (administered in the mail-back questionnaire)[6] and, in the main interview, asked two attitude questions about capital punishment. One question probed the respondent's general attitude toward the death penalty and the other asked what the respondent would personally do on a jury if death was a possible penalty. The respondent therefore had repeated opportunities to advocate relatively lenient or harsh punishments for other instances of lawbreaking, most of which were serious crimes, as well as two different ways of expressing approval or disapproval of the death penalty.

Responses to ten of the fourteen vignettes about these other crimes showed a

---

6. Vignettes describing these hypothetical crimes included experimental variations in the crimes, not relevant for our present purposes. Their general form is illustrated here for the least serious offense, with variations indicated by brackets:

The defendant was a 23 year old [black/white] [male/female].

Circumstances: The defendant had been working as a teller in a bank for several months. One week when (s)he was short of money, (s)he took an envelope that was deposited in the bank's automatic 24-hour deposit window. The envelope contained $50 in cash.

The defendant was charged with $50 larceny.

For brevity, we concentrate on these vignettes rather than abstract crime labels (such as "manslaughter"), which were also presented. The vignettes represented a more vivid stimulus and therefore probably elicited a more reliable response. Results for abstract offense labels showed the same pattern of associations.

significant relationship to DR-AR orientations. In each case, DRs on the average advocated *more* severe punishment than did ARs. Responses to the remaining four vignettes were unrelated to the DR-AR dichotomy. Furthermore, both general approval of capital punishment and willingness to use it as a juror were significantly correlated with being a DR. In short, statistically speaking it was true that those most likely to "free Calley" were also most likely to "hang Manson"—and the reverse.

The Calley case, then, stood out as unlike other serious crimes. The response to his case was obviously more than a response to his actions per se. He admitted killing people. The response seemed to flow from the authority setting in which he acted. It was, after all, the authority of superior orders that in Calley's eyes provided a legal and moral justification for acting as he did. Responsibility orientation, as measured by the DR-AR response, clearly captured the differences in people's response to the authority situation.

RESPONSIBILITY ALLOCATION IN HIERARCHIES

The military chain of command is important both for examining the overall pattern of how people allocate responsibility in such a crime of obedience and for the differences in attribution we can expect between DR and AR respondents. Table 10.2 presents the average responsibility attributed to actors in the My Lai chain of command—first by DR respondents, then by AR respondents, and finally by the total sample. (This sample average need not fall precisely between the

Table 10.2 Relationship between Responsibility Orientation and Average Percent Responsibility Assigned to Various Actors for My Lai Killings

	Responsibility Orientation		
Actors	Deny Responsibility (%)	Assert Responsibility (%)	Total Sample (%)
President and other makers of foreign policy	27	14	19
Top generals in Pentagon	27	15	20
Lt. Calley's superior officers in field	38	38	40
Lt. Calley	6	26	15
Men under Lt. Calley's command	2	7	5
Others	0	0	1

Note: Hotelling's T^2 for overall difference between means for DR versus AR $= 51.4$, degrees of freedom (d.f.) $= 6, 184$; $p < .0001$. Responsibility allocation totaled 100% across actors. The DR and AR groups also differed significantly in their allocation of responsibility to each specific actor (or group of actors) except "Lt. Calley's superior officers in field" and "others."

DR and AR scores, since the overall sample includes respondents who held anti-war or army-related reasons for their views about the trial.) Each respondent's allocation was supposed to sum to 100 percent.

The choices provided to respondents went the full distance up the chain of command to the president as commander in chief. Theoretically and practically, however, we expected that most responsibility would stick close to the criminal deed. Anyone, regardless of his or her responsibility orientation in our terms, might find it easiest to assign responsibility to the physical cause of an effect or to immediately available interpersonal causes (see chapter 8). We included the full chain of command among the choices in order to observe which respondents would follow responsibility up the hierarchy and how far they would do so.

The overall pattern for the sample was consistent with a trade-off between top-down responsibility based on role obligations and bottom-up responsibility based on physical causality. Less than half the total responsibility was allocated to the president and other creators of the policy of search-and-destroy and to the top generals who were the first step in implementation of the policy. Overall responsibility peaked with Calley's superior officers in the field, who were allocated 40 percent of the total. Such officers represented the last point upward in a chain of command where face-to-face knowledge or participation was likely to occur. Calley, in contrast, was allocated only 15 percent of total responsibility; men under his command were allocated only 5 percent; and potential "other" targets for responsibility were virtually unmentioned.

Table 10.2 shows that the DR-AR gulf extended to the attribution of responsibility, as expected. DR and AR respondents differed both from the overall sample and from one another in theoretically appropriate ways. Each group assigned slightly *less* responsibility to Calley's immediate superiors than did the sample as a whole. Responsibility allocation by DRs shifted further upward toward superior officers with role obligations. Allocation by ARs shifted downward toward subordinates who were physical causes. The two groups differed significantly from each other in their overall pattern of responsibility attribution. They differed in the allocations made at the top of the chain of command, where DRs assigned significantly more responsibility to policymakers and generals. And they differed in attributions at the bottom of the chain of command, where ARs assigned more responsibility to Calley and to men under his command. Thus the responsibility attributed to Calley for the My Lai killings was consistent with our theoretical arguments about what the DR and AR orientations mean.

The allocation of responsibility as summarized in table 10.2 brings into relief the DRs' emphasis on role requirements and the ARs' emphasis on direct causation in assigning responsibility. The DRs demonstrated their role-based approach by assigning both less than average responsibility to Calley and his subordinates, presumably because their roles require them to obey, and more than average to top officials, presumably because their roles make them accountable for the execution of their policies. The ARs, on the other hand, were relatively oblivious to role considerations, both at the top and at the bottom. They assigned more than average responsibility to Calley and his men, presumably because they directly and intentionally caused the killings, and less than average to top officials, presumably because they were not directly involved in the actions at My Lai. We thus have further evidence for the limitations in ARs' conception of individual responsibility noted in chapter 9.

We have already suggested that one particular division in the attribution of responsibility is close to the DR-AR distinction: the gap between *no* responsibility assigned to the subordinate and the assignment of *any*. Below we use such a dichotomy (*no* responsibility versus *some* responsibility) constructed from raw percentages of responsibility attributed. It is hardly surprising that this dichotomy for responsibility attribution to Calley is powerfully related to DR-AR orientation. Among DRs, 76 percent assigned *no* responsibility to Calley, whereas 73 percent of the ARs assigned him at least *some* responsibility. These DR-AR differences were again consistent with DRs' theoretical emphasis on role obligations versus ARs' emphasis on physical causes. The general form of this responsibility dichotomy between none and some has the advantage that comparable analyses can be conducted for the other situations included in the survey.

The conceptual fit between responsibility orientation and responsibility attribution was not perfect, however. The DR and AR orientations were direct responses that expressed agreement with statements we saw as embodying responsibility denial versus assertion. In contrast, a respondent might assign zero responsibility to Calley for a number of reasons other than a deny-responsibility orientation. Such a view could follow from antiwar sentiment ("the war's at fault"), from concern with military honor and morale ("support our fighting men," or "they all did it," or both), or from other reasons not even represented in our survey. The same indeterminacy held for assignment of "some" responsibility to Calley: Reasons other than responsibility per se could lie behind the assignment of either some responsibility or none. In addition, the criterion of zero responsibility represented a stringent test of the concept of responsibility denial.

The lack of a perfect conceptual fit between responsibility orientation and attribution is reflected in the relationship between responsibility assignment to Calley and the full set of reasons for trial opinions. In fact, the three subgroups of Calley trial approvers—ARs, antiwar, and army—did not differ significantly from one another in allocation of responsibility to Calley. The AR group's 73 percent assignment of some responsibility was nearly equaled by the antiwar approvers' 70 percent; it was even relatively close to the army approvers' 61 percent assignment of some responsibility to Calley. The three subgroups of disapprovers did differ significantly (at $p = .02$), but DRs were not the distinctive group. Instead, DRs and those who disapproved for reasons of army morale or honor registered identical 76 percent assignment of zero responsibility to Lieutenant Calley. Antiwar disapprovers were distinctive, assigning zero responsibility to Calley only 38 percent of the time. (This was one of those occasions when an antiwar reason led to a cross-over in which antiwar disapprovers responded more like approvers.) Thus to assign *some* responsibility did not automatically mean a respondent chose AR reasons.

Correspondingly, to assign *no* responsibility did not mean that the respondent chose DR reasons. DR-AR orientation and the none/some attribution dichotomy were imperfectly overlapping measures of what responsibility means in a setting governed by authority.

Crimes of Obedience in Other Settings

Given all the turmoil surrounding American reactions to My Lai, it is easy to forget that the incident and the trial represented but one encounter with illegitimate authority. Since we obviously hope it was an atypical encounter, we must also explore similarities and differences among other incidents involving authority. We do so by turning to respondents' judgments across a range of situations where a crime of obedience had occurred.

We have compared items of similar content and wording across the incidents presented in the survey. The incidents included the Watergate burglary and cover-up, representing misuse of bureaucratic authority in a political setting, and the subject-experimenter and nurse-doctor hypothetical situations described above, representing misuse of bureaucratic authority in professional settings. Key items were whether "most people" would carry out the act in question; whether "you" would do so; whether the actor "should have done" so; and the constructed dichotomy of zero/some responsibility attributed to the subordinate.

For the burglary itself, responsibility was divided among the following: former President Nixon, Mr. Nixon's closest advisers (such as Mitchell, Haldeman, Ehrlichman), the subordinates of those advisers, the people who actually carried out the burglary, and "others (Who?)," an optional category. Questions about the burglary itself were followed by relative responsibility allocation for the cover-up. This item was introduced by noting: "After the Watergate burglary was discovered, elaborate efforts were made to cover up the involvement of the White House. Let us say again that the total amount of responsibility for the cover-up is 100%. How would you divide up that 100%?" The card handed to the respondent included the following categories: former President Nixon, Mr. Nixon's closest advisers, the subordinates of those advisers, the clerical staff (such as secretaries), and the optional "others (Who?)" category.

For the hypothetical authority incidents the question about relative responsibility was worded: "How would you divide up 100% of the responsibility for what happened between the nurse and the doctor/between Mr. Jones and the experimenter?" These items did not require a card.

To have a consistent terminology across situations we will refer to questions as "most do," "you do," "should do," and "responsibility assignment." Since the wording of questions varied across situations, we did not test statistically for differences in the incidence of responses; we simply present percentages of a given response to the relevant question in each case. We did, however, test for patterns of association among responses to different situations.

ATTITUDE TOWARD THE ACTION

Table 10.3 presents answers to the "most do," "you do," and "should do" questions. Concerning what most people would do, the projected level of obedience dropped from an overall average of 62 percent for My Lai to 31 percent for the Watergate burglary, 24 percent for the hospital incident, and 17 percent for the hypothetical experiment. Concerning what the respondent would personally do, the already low 34 percent projected obedience for a My Lai–like situation dropped to virtually nil for both the nurse and research participant hypothetical situations. ("You do" was not asked for the Watergate burglary.) And "should do" responses dropped from 43 percent asserting that Calley should have obeyed at My Lai through 24 percent favoring obedience in the Watergate burglary to near-unanimous rejection of obedience in both the hypothetical stories involving authority in professional settings.

Some of these patterns of response are very lopsided—in statistical terms, skewed—compared to an even 50–50 difference of opinion. This stacks the deck against finding statistical associations among the items, since mathematically one cannot find associations *between* items unless there is variation in responses to each of them. But we found significant relationships among the "most do," "you do," and "should do" items in spite of these skewed distributions of opinion. Half of six possible associations among the different "most do" items were significant by chi-square test: the associations between the "most do" response for My Lai and the Watergate burglary, between the Watergate burglary and the hypothetical experiment, and between the two hypothetical situations. Respondents who said most people would obey (or refuse) in one of these incidents were significantly more likely to say most would obey (or refuse) in another. Such associations were weaker for "you do," where only one of three possible relationships was significant (between the two hypothetical incidents). Answers to "you do" questions, however, were the most severely skewed, with virtually everyone in some cases claiming they would refuse to obey. Linkages among the "should do" responses were as strong as those for "most do." Again half of the six possible linkages were significant by chi-square test: My Lai and the Watergate burglary, the Watergate burglary and the hypothetical experiment, and the two hypothetical incidents. Those who thought it right to obey (or refuse) in one setting thought it right to obey (or refuse) in others. Within incidents, answers were also internally consistent. That is, those who said most would obey always tended to say they would obey and that the subordinate should obey, and vice versa for refusal.

ALLOCATION OF RESPONSIBILITY

Relative responsibility allocation among participants in the chain of command differed substantially across the incidents. For example, responsibility in both Watergate questions was more top-heavy than that for My Lai (see table 10.2 above). President Nixon was assigned 42 percent of overall responsibility for the burglary and 56 percent for the cover-up. But this is comprehensible, since evidence of at

Table 10.3 Comparison of Responses across Crimes of Obedience

Items	Calley at My Lai (%)	Watergate Burglars (%)	Nurse Giving Overdose (%)	"Teacher" in Hypothetical Milgram Study (%)
A. What would most people do? (Obey/Refuse)[a]				
Obey	62	31	24	17
B. What would you do? (Obey/Refuse)[a]				
Obey	34	—	4	3
C. What should actor have done? (Obey/Refuse)[a]				
Obey	43	24	3	3
D. Percentage responsibility assigned to subordinate[b] (None/Some)				
None	46	46	19	18

[a]Question wording varied slightly depending on act being referred to—e.g., "follow orders and shoot" versus "follow instructions and administer the drug." In addition, the query for the Watergate burglary asked whether "most people," "only some," or "very few" would have carried out the burglary. For comparative purposes here the latter two categories have been combined as the "refuse" response. Also, the "what would you do" question was not asked for the Watergate burglary.
[b]Subordinates' responsibility items refer to assignment of responsibility to Calley for the My Lai incident, to the burglars for the Watergate burglary, to the nurse for the drug-administration hypothetical case, and to the "teacher" in the Milgram experiment (described as a hypothetical incident involving "Mr. Jones" and "the experimenter").

least guilty knowledge on the part of the president, if not guilty action, was widely available to the American public at that time (see chapter 2). In view of the importance of causality in ordinary responsibility attributions, as discussed in chapter 8, it is likely that citizens are both willing and able to use causal evidence against any actors in a command chain, but such evidence is usually unavailable against higher-ups. Respondents' greater willingness to assign blame at the top of the Watergate chain, compared to their judgments about My Lai, may simply have reflected the presence of evidence that tied higher-ups causally to the outcome in the case of Watergate.

Responsibility allocation in professional hierarchies also differed dramatically from that for My Lai. On the average, the nurse received 64 percent of the responsibility for the hospital incident and Jones received a similar 61 percent of responsibility for the laboratory incident. The allocation of greater responsibility to subordinate actors in professional situations was consistent with respondents' previous denials that they themselves or other people would act obediently in such settings. However, since allocation was being made between two—rather than among four or five—participants, respondents may have been assigning the actor more responsibility as much because of *how* the question was asked as because of *what* was asked. We cannot tell for certain here why the shorter chains of command for authority in professional settings led to more responsibility allocation to subordinates.

RESPONSIBILITY ASSIGNMENT

We compared the relative responsibility of the subordinate across incidents using the responsibility-assignment dichotomies (none/some to each subordinate). The key subordinates in the Watergate incidents were participants with clear evidence of having physically caused the crime or having opportunity to do so: the burglars and the clerical staff. The subordinate in the professional incidents was automatically identified by the story: in the hospital incident, the nurse; in the Milgram analogue, Jones, the "teacher." Comparing these incidents for the tendency to assign or not assign the subordinate any responsibility at all shows that these attributions fell into line with other answers. If an act was something the respondent thought that most people would do, that he or she would do, and that people should do, it was ignored or treated lightly in assessing responsibility—and vice versa. As shown in table 10.3 (item D), just over half of all respondents assigned *any* responsibility to either Calley or the Watergate burglars (54 percent in each case). In contrast, 81 percent assigned at least some responsibility to the nurse and 82 percent to Jones in the professional situations.

Respondents' consistency in attributing responsibility across situations can be tested by use of these none/some attribution variables, given their comparable wordings and relatively balanced response distributions. Table 10.4 summarizes the statistical associations among all responsibility dichotomies: My Lai responsibility allocation (DR-AR), included for comparative purposes; responsibility assignment to Calley; and the responsibility-assignment items for other incidents.

Table 10.4 Interrelations among Responsibility Orientation and Responsibility Assignment across Situations: Gamma Statistics[a]

Items	Orientation Deny/Assert	Calley, Zero/Some Responsibility	Watergate Burglars Zero/Some	Watergate Secretaries Zero/Some	Nurse Zero/Some	Jones Zero/Some
Orientation	—					
Calley	.78	—				
Burglars	.50	.75	—			
Secretaries	.02[b]	.33	.78	—		
Nurse	.56	.44	.38	.50	—	
Jones	.38[c]	.39	.40	.41	.85	—

[a]Gamma is a measure of strength of association that ranges from + 1 (perfect positive) to − 1 (perfect negative). All associations were significant at $p \leq .01$ by chi-square test except where noted.
[b]Chi-square not significant.
[c]Chi-square significant at $p \leq .05$.

Significant relationships appear throughout the table, and they are sizable. Responsibility assignment to Calley performs quite well as a measure of responsibility denial versus assertion. Its relationships with other responsibility-assignment items parallel the findings for the DR-AR variable and are generally stronger. Thus, to say that a subordinate should have some responsibility for one incident implies at least some responsibility for a corresponding (subordinate) actor in another incident. To say none implies none.

Another way of looking for general trends in the attribution of responsibility across crimes of obedience is to form indices that use all relevant items in some sort of summary score. This is usually an average, sometimes a weighted average as in factor scores (see chapter 12). We formed indices of average responses across situations for all responsibility-assignment items; we also did so for the raw responsibility attributions to subordinates (expressed in percentages). Neither index performed better than the pair of individual items about My Lai: responsibility assignment to Calley and DR-AR. These individual items were as closely related to attitude items and to demographic predictors as were the scales. The indices' lack of predictive power may reflect their low reliability; for example, the six-item index using the responsibility dichotomies in table 10.4 had a relatively low Cronbach's alpha of .64. We concluded that the core items—DR-AR and responsibility assignment to Calley—were superior to the indices for exploring the predictors of responsibility judgments.

Predicting Responsibility Judgments in Crimes of Obedience

We turn now to the possible roles of demographic factors such as the respondent's social standing and religious identification in producing responsibility orientations. On the basis of the 1971 study, we predicted in chapter 9 that more educated or higher-status respondents would be inclined to an AR orientation, and we speculated that religion and education might interact, so that Catholics would be relatively insulated from the impact of education on responsibility judgments.

To be consistent with earlier analyses, we used categorical versions of the demographic variables below. Each of the three status variables was collapsed into a trichotomy (low/medium/high). Religion was analyzed as a dichotomy (Catholic/ non-Catholic) rather than a trichotomy (Catholic/Protestant/Jewish, other, none) as in 1971 because of the smaller sample size in the Boston study. We again tested for significance of associations using chi-square and report gamma statistics for strength of association.

The three status variables showed a clear pattern of relationships across responsibility orientation and attribution. More education, more income, and more prestigious occupation were associated with the assert-responsibility stance and with attribution of some responsibility to Calley. Education proved the most powerful and consistent of these predictors. For DR-AR orientation, cross-tabular analyses showed that education was a highly significant predictor, income was a marginally significant predictor, and occupation was not a significant predictor. Relationships of the status variables to responsibility assignment to Calley were stronger, with education again the most powerful predictor. Education strongly predicted assigning Calley some responsibility. Occupation was also significant, but income was not. No significant pattern of interactions among the status variables emerged (in contrast to 1971; see chapter 9, note 6).

In general, it is predictable that the different measures of social status would be related to one another. Here, the interrelationships were not overwhelmingly large. (Using the continuous versions of each variable, correlations were $r = .26$ between education and income, $r = .47$ between education and occupation, and $r = .38$ between income and occupation.)[7] Below we concentrate on education, since it was the most powerful predictor of responsibility judgments and was measured in the most comparable fashion across the surveys. The final key demographic variable, religion, was also related to education (although not to income or occupation). Non-Catholics were more likely to be highly educated (correlation of .24 between education and the Catholic/non-Catholic dichotomy). This dichotomy was significantly linked to both DR-AR orientation and responsibility assignment to Calley, with Catholics more inclined to a DR stance and an attribution of no responsibility.[8]

RELIGION AND EDUCATION

More interesting than differences in average judgment of responsibility among religious groups was the question of an interaction between education and religion. Would the effects of education on responsibility judgments depend on the individual's religious affiliation, as we unexpectedly observed in 1971? We explored this three-way linkage among religion, education, and opinion for both DR-AR and responsibility assignment to Calley. DR-AR orientation did not show any interaction between religion and education. Table 10.5, however, shows that responsibility assignment to Calley—the attribution of some responsibility to him versus none—was related to religion and education at least somewhat interactively. The association between education and responsibility attribution was significant for non-Catholics but not for Catholics, and the strength of association varied accordingly (gamma = .55 for non-Catholics, .27 for Catholics). This

7. The Pearson r statistic for correlations expresses the extent of positive or negative linkage between two variables in a range from perfect positive $(+1)$ to perfect negative (-1). Correlations and other parametric statistics are also always evaluated in terms of the likelihood that the result would happen by chance.

8. One difference emerged between this and the prior study in the basic relationship of religion to the responsibility measures. In 1971, it was religious "others" who were distinctive in their average responsibility orientations, and they tended to be ARs. In Boston, while Catholics tended to be DRs, *both* Protestants and "other" religious groups were inclined to be ARs. What differs in Boston, then, is the average response of Protestants. Inasmuch as there may be many differences between Boston-area Protestants and Protestants nationally, we are not inclined to make much of this difference. What it chiefly does for our present purposes is to reinforce our decision to group Protestants and "others" together into a Catholic versus non-Catholic religious dichotomy.

pattern is similar to the one observed in the 1971 national survey (see table 9.6), but not as powerful.[9] The interesting finding in the earlier survey was that for Catholics—in contrast to Protestants and especially religious others—education had no effect on responsibility orientation. In this survey education did have an effect on Catholics' responsibility judgments (measured by responsibility assignment rather than DR-AR), although it was weaker than in the case of non-Catholics and fell short of statistical significance. The most striking finding in Table 10.5 is that highly educated Catholics differed from other highly educated respondents in being less likely to assign Calley any responsibility at all.

Conclusions

This chapter replicated and extended the earlier survey's study of responsibility in authority hierarchies. First, crucially, patterns of denial versus assertion of a military subordinate's responsibility (DR-AR) appeared stable over time and samples. DR and AR orientations still emerged and still dominated the way respondents viewed the Calley trial. We extended the study of responsibility orientations to look further at the military *chain of command* and other hierarchies of authority and subordination. Overall, we found that the highest average attribution of responsibility was directed at low-level superiors, in whom role obligations and personal causation converge. People focused blame on those of whom more was expected *and* who were or might be physically involved in the crime. DR and AR respondents also diverged in allocating responsibility: DR respondents emphasized blameworthiness of top superiors, whereas AR respondents emphasized that of subordinates. DR respondents pointed up, and AR respondents down, the chain of command in assessing responsibility. In addition, we developed an alternative to the DR-AR measure by dichotomizing judgments into the attribution of *no* responsibility versus at least *some* to Calley. This measure was strongly related to DR-AR—DRs assigned none, ARs assigned some—but it could be adapted to the other crimes of obedience covered in the survey.

9. Log-linear tests for the significance of the interaction, paralleling those reported in chapter 9, showed a borderline three-way relationship among religion, education, and responsibility assignment to Calley ($.10 > p > .05$). One possible contributor to the weakness of the religion-education link is the presence in Boston of a new significant predictor: respondents' age. Respondents who were aged thirty-five or less tended to assign Calley some responsibility to a greater extent (66 percent attributing "some") than respondents aged thirty-five to forty-nine (54 percent "some") or those over fifty (40 percent "some"). In addition, age interacted with education and, to a lesser extent, with religion. The impacts of both those variables on responsibility attribution were stronger in the thirty-five-and-under respondent group. It appears that younger respondents in Boston were more sensitive to issues of authority and responsibility. We prefer not to stress age differences, as we are confident of neither their meaning nor their generality. In 1971 the peak AR orientation was shown by those aged twenty-five to thirty-four, but the age effect was not significant in this much larger sample. Such differences clearly deserve further exploration. In the present case they may help to account for the restricted impacts of the other key variables.

Table 10.5 Predicting Responsibility Assignment to Lt. Calley from Education and Religion Combined[a]

| | Religion[b] | | All |
Education	Catholic	Non-Catholic	Respondents
Low (<12)	32	32	32
Medium (12)	51	51	51
High (13+)	54	76	69
All respondents	47	61	

[a]Entries are the percent of each group assigning *some* responsibility to Calley. For each category or cell, the percentage who assigned *no* responsibility to Calley can be calculated by subtracting the figure shown from 100%. Overall N (those with data for religion, education, and responsibility assignment to Calley) = 365.
[b]For Catholics, strength of relationship between education and responsibility assignment to Calley is gamma = .27. For non-Catholics, this gamma = .55.

Possible *situational differences* in responsibility allocation were an important focus of the survey. We included judgments of crimes of obedience in different authority-subordinate relationships within and across official (relatively coercive) versus professional (relatively voluntaristic) settings. Responses about Watergate, a crime in the context of political bureaucracy, tended to be intermediate between answers about My Lai and answers about wrongdoing in professional settings—whether the issue was responsibility attribution, what most people would do, or what people ought to do. Respondents were relatively consistent in their answers within and across situations. Items about My Lai, however, appeared to be the most powerful and robust measures of responsibility assertion and denial. We suspect that the power of questions about a crime like My Lai is due to relatively widespread understanding among citizens of the *coercive* pressures authority can bring to bear in the military setting as well as the normal *obligation* to obey once one has entered that setting. In short, if there is ever an implicit contract between subordinate and authority—an exchange of obedience for protection from liability—we think that the military setting is a likely place to find it and a likely place for the citizenry to know about it.

In sum, the findings of the Boston survey lend further support to the distinction between the two conceptions of individual responsibility in authority situations proposed in chapter 8—one focusing on roles and their motives, the other on acts and their consequences. The DR and AR patterns identified in the earlier survey, which correspond to these two conceptions, proved to be relatively stable and general in the follow-up study. Responsibility orientation appears to be an important filter in people's reaction to authority and readiness to obey destructive orders. Moreover, the 1976 survey replicated earlier findings about the demographic predictors of responsibility orientation. In particular, the various markers of social position—education and, to a lesser extent, income and occupation—were found to be related to DR-AR response and to responsibility asignment. An interaction between education and religion emerged again, although it was not as strong as in the earlier survey.

Educational attainment and other demographic variables clearly help to account for individual differences in response to authority situations. Their effects may also be linked to broad political orientations, such as the three distinguished in chapter 5: rule, role, and value orientation. For example, people's position in the social structure may incline them toward one or another of these orientations, which may in turn determine the way they relate to authorities and their orders. Differences in political orientation may also derive from more general personality dispositions. One of the purposes of the 1976 survey was to explore the effects of rule, role, and value orientations on conceptions of responsibility in authority situations. We shall discuss the relevant findings in chapter 12. First, however, chapter 11 presents a framework within which these findings can be understood.

11 | Individual Differences in Conceptions of Authority and Responsibility

The institutional and situational forces that operate in authority relationships make it exceedingly difficult for subordinates to challenge the demands of their superiors, as we argued in detail in chapter 6. It does not follow, however, that authority situations are so overwhelmingly powerful that subordinates are inevitably caught up in the superiors' definition of their role obligations. Individuals differ in how they assess authority situations and their responsibilities within them.

With regard to actual behavior in such situations, we know from the experiences of Nazi Germany, of My Lai, of Milgram's laboratory, and of many other instances of obedience to unjust and destructive authority that, no matter how powerful the situation may be, individuals differ in how they react to it. There were many men and women in Nazi-occupied Europe who risked their lives—and many who lost them—by rescuing Jews or defying the authorities in other ways. At My Lai, as we have seen, the level of obedience to Lieutenant Calley's orders was far from complete. As for the obedience experiments, the dramatic demonstration of obedience often leads observers to forget that more than one-third of the participants in the baseline condition defied the experimenter. To be sure, subordinates cannot ignore the socially prescribed definition of the situation, and, at the very least, they experience intense conflict when an authority orders actions that they find personally repugnant. But people differ in how they resolve that conflict. Some remain completely boxed in by the definition of the situation, whereas others are able to break out of it.

In the preceding three chapters we distinguished two conceptions of responsibility in authority situations. Which of these conceptions is likely to prevail depends, in part, on situational factors, such as the binding and opposing forces described in chapter 6. But within any given situation, individuals differ in their view of responsibility. These individual differences, in turn, are closely linked to differences in the conception of the authority itself. Although there is no simple or direct correspondence between attitudes and actions, these views of authority and responsibility together clearly have a bearing on people's readiness to challenge authority and their tendency to obey or disobey.

Differences in how people conceive of authority and responsibility, how they resolve conflicts about obedience, or how they judge the actions of others confronted by such conflicts can be traced to differences in social position, in personality characteristics, and in political orientation. We shall discuss each of these individual-difference variables in turn. The discussion of the first set of variables will take as its starting point our own finding, reported in the preceding chapters, of a consistent relationship between social position and attitudes toward crimes of obedience. We shall then turn to a brief discussion of several personality variables and a fuller description of the three types of political orientation—rule, role, and value orientation—first introduced in chapter 5. Data on the relationship of the three orientations to conceptions of authority and responsibility will be presented in the next chapter.

Social-Status Variables

In both of our surveys, social position—particularly as indexed by educational attainment—proved to be the strongest predictor of responsibility attribution, as well as of "shoot-refuse" responses. The more highly educated respondents, for example, were consistently more likely to assert individual responsibility for actions under orders and to indicate that they would refuse to shoot civilian villagers if ordered to do so. It would be a serious mistake, however, to view the role of social class in deterministic terms. High status in no way ensures resistance to unjust authority, nor does low status preclude it, as historical and sociological evidence demonstrates. It would be similarly misleading, in our view, to reduce the obedient stance of a DR, for example, to a characterological shortcoming such as high authoritarianism (Adorno et al., 1950), a personality syndrome often mistakenly attributed to the working or lower classes (see Jackman, 1973, for a discussion of this issue).

To locate the problem in a particular social class would be unwarranted for several reasons. First, of course, none of the differences observed for our measures of status or class was truly large. Yes, more educated or higher socioeconomic status respondents were more likely to be ARs than their less educated or lower-status counterparts—but not by much. In the national survey, for example, we encountered differences of 22 percent for education and 19 percent for status in a sample of nearly a thousand individuals. These differences are significant but not overwhelming. Therefore to describe the DR orientation as a uniquely working-class or lower-class phenomenon does not square with the empirical results. Many ARs can be found among lower-class respondents and many DRs in the higher classes. Thus, there are obviously other sources of responsibility orientation and the tendency to obey or disobey, apart from social class.

Second, there is no logical or empirical reason for interpreting the social-class differences that we did find in broad characterological terms. It is more parsimonious to account for these differences in terms of the situations in which different population groups find themselves. As a result of their societal positions, of the socialization experiences by which they are typically prepared for these positions, and of the realities of their daily lives, lower-status respondents, compared to their educated middle-class counterparts, are less likely to have the means, the skills, and the opportunities to act as responsible agents vis-à-vis national policies, particularly in the domain of foreign policy. Furthermore, their relationship to an actor like Lieutenant Calley is different from that of the educated middle- or upper-class individual, given the closer correspondence in position. It is easier for such respondents to see themselves in his shoes.

Third, in drawing the implications of the observed effects of social class, we must put these findings in a larger perspective. To view availability for crimes of obedience as a lower-class phenomenon is to ignore the central part that higher-status and highly educated actors play in producing such crimes. In their roles as decision makers, as executive officers, and as upper-echelon subordinates, they devise the policies, give the orders, and often enthusiastically obey the orders that culminate in crimes of obedience. Thus, any analysis implying that crimes of obedience result from the moral deficiencies of the lower classes misses the social-structural realities within which these crimes take shape.

In short, the relationship of social status to responsibility denial or assertion should be understood in its situational context. It reflects differences in the life chances and daily realities of citizens of differing classes, rather than differences in their psychological maturity or moral sensitivity. But the relationship does exist, and it appears to be systematic and stable, although the associations are not strong. How can this relationship be best summarized and interpreted?

Evidence suggests that individuals higher in socioeconomic status, educational attainment, and occupational position are more likely to possess the cognitive skills and motivational orientations required to adopt a "consequences" model of responsibility and to challenge authority. It appears that the socialization, life experiences, and actual life situations of people who occupy higher positions in the social structure predispose them to take a more active, questioning stance toward authority and its demands than those occupying lower positions are likely to take. Melvin Kohn (1977; Kohn and Schooler, 1983), who has conducted some of the most extensive empirical work substantiating this relationship, summarizes the argument thus:

> The essence of higher class position is the expectation that one's decisions and actions can be consequential; the essence of lower class position is the belief that one is at the mercy of forces and people beyond one's control, often, beyond one's understanding. Self-direction—acting on the basis of one's own judgment, attending to internal dynamics as well as to external consequences, being open-minded, being trustful of others, holding personally responsible moral standards—this is possible only if the actual conditions of life allow some freedom of action, some reason to feel in control of fate.

Conformity—following the dictates of authority, focusing on external consequences to the exclusion of internal processes, being intolerant of nonconformity and dissent, being distrustful of others, having moral standards that strongly emphasize obedience to the letter of the law—this is the inevitable result of conditions of life that allow little freedom of action, little reason to feel in control of fate.

Self-direction, in short, requires opportunities and experiences that are much more available to people who are more favorably situated in the hierarchical order of society; conformity is the natural consequence of inadequate opportunity to be self-directed. (Kohn, 1977, p. 189)

In Kohn's analysis, occupational experiences that facilitate self-direction—which are more common in higher-status occupations—foster a more self-directed view of self and society in general, resulting in greater willingness to make independent judgments even in authority situations. By contrast, the constricting job conditions typically experienced by people in lower-status occupational positions encourage them to follow authoritative demands both on and off the job. Occupational opportunities are related to educational qualifications, which in turn are affected by family income and social class. Education also contributes independently to self-direction because it helps in the development of the analytical ability, intellectual flexibility, and breadth of perspective required for challenging the authority's definition of the situation.[1]

Family background, in addition, has a direct impact on socialization for self-direction. Middle-class parents attempt to inculcate in their children such values as autonomy and "responsibility"—which are aspects of self-direction—whereas working-class parents are more likely to emphasize respect for rules (see also Kerckhoff, 1973). The transmission of social class across the generations is in part the transmission of values and orientations toward work, including different views of responsibility accompanying one's work.

Roles that differ in status differ in their sanctions for nonperformance, as we suggested in chapter 8 in reviewing differences in responsibility across roles. To avoid overt wrongdoing, one usually needs nothing more than to comply with rules. Internal agreement with those rules is not at issue. This approach characterizes low-status, subordinate roles. To fulfill many role expectations, one may need to identify with the role in order to find out what peers and superiors define as "oughts" as well as "ought nots." This approach characterizes intermediate-status roles. Enacting diffuse expectations in an extended time frame, unsupervised by others, may be easier when one has internalized values with which this enactment is consistent. This approach characterizes authoritative roles. The differences in approach to sanctioning across roles—with differential emphases on the role occupant's compliance to rules, identification with roles, or internalization of values—have direct implications for the orientation to responsibility the role occupant is likely to adopt.

1. Milgram (1974, p. 205) reports that, at least in his first series of experiments, the better-educated participants were more likely to defy the experimenter than the less educated.

Higher occupational status and educational attainment are also likely to enhance both the expectation and the reality of control over one's own life and influence on public policy. In the first place, policies are more likely to reflect the interests and values of higher-status groups. In those instances in which members of these groups find a policy objectionable, they can more readily draw on their connections and resources to exert influence on the policy process. In view of these expectations and experiences, they are more likely to see themselves as independent agents in the society, able to take a more active stance vis-à-vis the authorities they encounter. Furthermore, they are closer to and hence less awed by authority. They may be authorities themselves in certain areas of their lives or have realistic aspirations to attaining authority positions; they have more contact with people in authority and greater access to them, and are more likely to count such people among their relatives, friends, or personal acquaintances. Challenging authority, therefore, is an act that they can more readily envision and that may strike them as less disruptive of the social order. Finally, when they mount a challenge, higher-status individuals have more financial, institutional, and cognitive resources to take effective action. Thus a challenge to authority may be more freely made by a higher-status member of society, and this challenge is more likely to succeed.

Under normal circumstances, higher-status citizens may be less likely to challenge authority because they do not often find themselves in subordinate roles where conflict with authority about obedience may arise. Our analysis of the socialization and life experiences of those in high versus low social positions suggests that *when placed in the same situation*, higher-status individuals are more likely to mount challenges to the authority's definition of the situation than are lower-status individuals. Lower-rung subordinates in a chain of command are unlikely to have received any training or encouragement in this direction. Therefore those who are most in need of a normative counterweight are least likely to find it psychologically available. Those to whom it is most obviously available are usually the authorities themselves.

In general, social-structurally based differences among observers of authority situations are likely to parallel those already suggested in considering the effects of stratification among actors. For example, the observer's own socialization and experiences should affect whether an independent normative stance is available or acceptable. The markers of social standing in America—education, occupation, and wealth—all facilitate taking an independent normative stance.

Personality Variables

Conceptions of responsibility and readiness to challenge authority may also be related to a number of broad psychological dispositions, which, in turn, may be related to social-status variables. For example, let us postulate "self-direction" as a general personality orientation, which is conducive to an AR stance vis-à-vis orders from authority. Such a personality orientation may be more prevalent in the middle class than in the working class because of the class differences in socialization patterns suggested above. Thus, the relationship between social class and DR-AR responses could be explained by class differences in self-direction: If social class is related to self-direction and self-direction is related to DR-AR responses, then social class should be related to DR-AR. This would not necessarily mean, of course, that the relationship between class and DR-AR is *entirely* explained by self-direction; social class may have a variety of other consequences that link it to responsibility attribution, a number of which we discussed in the preceding section. Nor would it mean that the relationship between self-direction and DR-AR is always traceable to social class; self-direction may have a variety of other sources independent of class standing.

Among general personality dispositions that have been identified and measured, the one that appears most directly related to an independent stance vis-à-vis authority is personal efficacy or competence (see Bandura, 1977; Douvan and Walker, 1956; White, 1959). A sense of efficacy implies that the individual feels both able to make personal judgments about what is required, even in an authority situation, and capable of launching an effective challenge to an authority's demands. Various measures of a related concept, political efficacy, have been used to predict political participation since it was introduced in early voting research (see Campbell et al., 1954). Whether people possess a sense of personal or political efficacy, in turn, is likely to be related to their perceptions of the primary determinants of their life experiences: whether they see themselves as "origins" or "pawns" in human relations (deCharms, 1968) and whether the perceived locus of control of their fate is primarily internal or external (Rotter, 1966). Those who lack efficacy, see themselves as pawns, or see control as external tend to react passively to authoritative orders rather than proceed on the assumption that they can redefine situations through their own actions.

The sense of efficacy and control is likely to be related to a person's social position, with high efficacy and internality more characteristic of those high in occupational status, social class, and education. Social position, however, is but one determinant of these personality dispositions. Whether individuals emerge with a strong or a weak sense of personal efficacy is undoubtedly affected by a variety of conditions in the environment in which they grow up and are socialized that are quite independent of social class.

A personality construct that directly taps reactions to authority is authoritarianism, which has most often been measured by the F-scale, where F stands for fascism (Adorno et al., 1950). Since a submissive, uncritical attitude toward authorities is one of the components of the authoritarian syndrome, high authoritarians can be expected to follow orders without challenge. If the F-scale is interpreted as indicating narrow perspective (Kelman and Barclay, 1963), a high F-score would again be expected to predict greater obedience, in line with Kohn's (1977) view of breadth of perspective as a determinant of self-direction. Consistent with these expectations, Elms and Milgram (1966) found a significant difference in authoritarianism (F-scores) between obedient and defiant participants in the

Milgram obedience experiments. Another factor that seems to differentiate between obedient and defiant participants in these experiments is moral development as measured by Kohlberg (1969, 1984). In a small study of undergraduates who participated in Milgram's pilot research, Kohlberg (1969) found that individuals at his highest stage of moral reasoning—one that rejects conformity to others or to law and order in favor of personal conscience—were more likely to disobey than those at lower moral stages.

In our view the personality configurations that incline an actor to obey or disobey in an authority situation and those that incline an observer to condone or condemn obedience are fundamentally the same. We therefore included measures of some of the personality factors mentioned above in our Boston survey in order to check whether they show the expected relationship to observers' attribution of responsibility for crimes of obedience. Specifically, we included a measure of internal versus external locus of control (see Rotter, 1966) and a measure of authoritarianism derived from the original F-scale (Gold et al., 1976), in the expectation that perceived external control and high authoritarianism would both predict a DR stance toward crimes of obedience.

We included measures of locus of control and authoritarianism in the survey because of the importance of these concepts in the history of personality research. But the primary focus in our search for the psychological foundations of individual differences in reaction to authority was on the three types of political orientation introduced in chapter 5. These orientations, compared to authoritarianism or locus of control, are more directly relevant to the phenomenon we are trying to explain and are based on finer distinctions. We return, therefore, to our discussion of rule, role, and value orientations, with the specific purpose of using these concepts to account for individual differences in conceptions of authority and responsibility, and in behavior in concrete authority situations.

Rule, Role, and Value Orientations

Since crimes of obedience often occur in political contexts, in hierarchies governed by the state, we might improve on the prediction of individual differences by use of a measure of political ideology. Our distinction among rule, role, and value orientations to political authority is likely to be more closely connected to behavior or judgment vis-à-vis political authority than general personality characteristics or demographic variables. In turn, we see these orientations to political authority as systematically linked to demographic and personality factors, such as those discussed in the preceding sections. They can therefore help us trace how individuals occupying particular positions in society and characterized by particular personal dispositions relate themselves to the political state; and how the nature of this relationship, in turn, shapes their reactions to the specific situations in which they encounter authority.

The discussion of the three orientations below treats them as *ideal types*, which do not necessarily manifest themselves in the pure form in which they are presented. Such ideal types are reifications that serve to clarify the distinctions among the orientations. It is important to recall that, both in theory and in practice, the orientations are not mutually exclusive. People's orientations may differ in relation to authorities in different spheres of their lives. Even within a single sphere— the political sphere, for our purposes—they may vary at different times and occasions. And even at the same time, different orientations may coexist or alternate. Nevertheless, we assume that these political orientations are sufficiently distinct and stable to have some explanatory power.

As noted in chapter 5, the three orientations refer to three components of the political system through which citizens may be bound to it and integrated in it. They represent three processes by which the legitimacy of the state is generated, assessed, and maintained in the eyes of individuals. Each orientation, therefore, has distinct implications for the way in which those who subscribe to it relate themselves to political authorities. It is necessary to develop a fuller picture of these patterns of citizen-authority relations in order to predict differences among them in the likelihood that individuals will challenge unjust or destructive authority in a specific situation. Table 11.1 summarizes the defining characteristics of each of the three ideal types of relation between citizen and political authority, and some of the social and psychological tendencies associated with each.

The distinctions among the orientations can be cast, first, in terms of their views of the implicit contract that defines the reciprocal relationship between citizen and government: what the citizen has a right to expect from the government and what the government has a right to expect from the citizen in return. The first two rows of the table indicate that both these sets of expectations tend to be minimal for rule-oriented citizens. They see it as their task to follow the rules: to respect authorities' demands, do what is required of them, and stay out of trouble. In return, they expect the government to uphold the rules and thus protect their basic interests and ensure societal order. They support policies that contribute to their sense of security within the rules. Role-oriented citizens, who identify with the nation and are involved in their roles within it, have a higher set of expectations. They want to be and to perceive themselves as good citizens who meet their role obligations by actively supporting the government and faithfully obeying its demands. In return, they expect the government to uphold the integrity of their roles by ensuring high status for the nation, from which they derive vicarious satisfaction, and relatively high personal status for themselves. They support policies that contribute to enhancing their sense of status within their roles as national citizens and their other roles in the society. Value-oriented citizens are committed to the government because they share the cultural and institutional values on which they believe the state to be founded. They see it as their citizen obligation to take an active part in formulating, evaluating, and questioning national policies. Their view of the citizen role requires them to support policies that are in keeping with what they see as the society's fundamental values, but to oppose policies that violate these values—even to the point of civil disobedience. They expect the government to pursue policies that uphold and reflect these fundamental values.

Table 11.1 Characteristics and Correlates of Three Types of Political Orientation

	Rule Orientation	Role Orientation	Value Orientation
Expectation from citizen	Follow rules; avoid trouble	Meet citizen obligation to obey and support the government	Take active part in formulating, evaluating, and questioning policies
Expectation from government	Uphold rules; assure security and order	Uphold roles; assure national and personal status	Uphold values; pursue policies reflecting national principles
Participation in duties	Passive: minimal compliance (as necessary to protect interests)	Supportive: active part in carrying out policies	Evaluative: active part in formulating and assessing policies
Participation in benefits	Minimal: subsidiary and service roles; tenuous integration; low level of education and occupation	Moderately high: active role in conducting society's affairs; comfortable integration; middle level of education and occupation	High: role in ownership and management of system; integration in establishment; high level of education and occupation
Socialization process	Compliance	Identification	Internalization
Role of morality in citizen action	Moral principles irrelevant	Moral obligation to government overrides personal morality	Personal moral principles must enter into consideration
Role of morality in state action	Moral principles irrelevant	Special set of moral principles applies	Moral principles fundamental
Level of moral reasoning	Preconventional	Conventional	Postconventional
Nature of support to government	Compliant	Reliable, enthusiastic	Firm but conditional
Conditions for protest	Threat to security	Threat to status	Threat to values
View of responsibility	Liability to sanctions for nonperformance	Reliable fulfillment of role obligations	Internalized standards for evaluating consequences of action

These different sets of expectations imply different patterns of participation in carrying out the duties of citizenship, spelled out in the third row of table 11.1. Participation by the rule-oriented tends to be passive. They generally comply to the degree necessary to protect their interests—to ensure access to the resources to which their citizenship entitles them and avoid penalties for breaking the rules. Participation by the role-oriented tends to be far more actively supportive. They identify with the state and are emotionally and instrumentally involved in their societal roles. They are, therefore, concerned with meeting their citizen obligation by giving substantive support to national policies, taking an active part in carrying out such policies, and conducting the everyday business of the society. Finally, the value-oriented citizens conceive their citizenship duties as requiring active participation not only in carrying out national policies but in formulating and evaluating such policies.

There are interesting parallels between the three patterns of participation that we postulate for the three orientations and Walzer's (1970) distinction among different types of citizenship. Although Walzer distinguishes three kinds of citizenship (pp. 226–28), the first of these, the *oppressed citizen*, does not correspond to our trichotomy, which focuses essentially on different types of integration into the political system and different ways of assessing and accepting its legitimacy. His second type, however, the *alienated citizen*, is reminiscent of rule orientation. This type of citizen "receives whatever protection the state provides," but "does not participate at all in political life. . . . He thinks of the state as an alien though not necessarily a hostile force, and he wants only to live in peace under its jurisdiction. He is bound to those actions necessary for the safety of the social life he shares" (p. 226). Walzer then goes on to describe "another kind of alienated citizen . . . who participates in political life but only in ways that fit the ideology, not in ways that fit the ideal, of citizenship. That is, he is active in essentially trivial ways. . . . The *alienated citizen (2)* is not self-made, but a product of the system and its ideology. He is unlikely to experience conflicts of obligation, and for this reason he is widely regarded as a 'good' citizen. If the state stands over him as an alien force, he does not know it; he thinks it is his own" (p. 227; emphasis added). This subtype is clearly reminiscent of role orientation. Finally, Walzer's third type, the *pluralist citizen*, is reminiscent of value orientation. This type of citizen "receives protection and shares in ruling and being ruled, not in spite of his plural memberships but because of them. Citizenship (as a moral choice rather than a legal status) is possible only if there are other groups than the state within the state, and it is fully accepted only by joining other groups along with the state. This means that at any given moment, citizens fall into one of two categories. They belong to groups that are actually making claims against the state, and then they *may* be obligated to disobey its laws. . . . Or, the citizens belong to groups that are not putting forward such claims . . . and then they are simply bound . . . to obey the laws they help in making" (p. 227). The implication of pluralist citizenship that the individual evaluates state actions on the basis of independent criteria is consistent with our idea of internalization. The internalized values against which our value-oriented citizen measures state actions are, of course, anchored in and shared with groups other than the state to which the individual belongs.

Levels of participation in societal benefits, as seen in the fourth row of table 11.1, are likely to parallel the participation in duties. What we propose here are not elements of the definition of the three orientations but hypotheses about empirical relationships—about experiences and attitudes we expect to be associated with the orientations. Rule-oriented citizens are likely to be performing subsidiary and service roles within the society rather than taking charge of its institutions; accordingly, the benefits available to them are relatively limited and their integration is tenuous. They probably do not see themselves as having adequate control over their own fates, let alone being able to influence national policy. They are likely to be relatively low in social class, educational attainment, and occupational status or prestige. Role-oriented citizens, in contrast, are likely to be actively involved in conducting the daily activities of the institutions through which the society carries out its affairs. The benefits the society makes available to them are moderately high, and they are fairly well established and comfortably integrated. In the stratification of society they are likely to belong to the lower middle or small entrepreneurial class and to be average in educational attainment and occupational prestige. Value-oriented citizens, finally, are likely to play a role in the management and decision making of social institutions. Their benefits are high and they are securely integrated as part of society's establishment. They probably see themselves as sharing in the ownership of the society and in the responsibility for running its affairs. Typically, they belong to the upper middle class, are highly educated, and hold high positions in the occupational hierarchy.

The predominant process by which individuals are socialized into occupational and other roles is also expected to differ among the orientations, as the fifth row of table 11.1 indicates. Here we refer to the likelihood with which the three processes of social influence—compliance, identification, and internalization—are brought to bear in training individuals for positions in society.[2] Rule-oriented socialization emphasizes compliance, an influence strategy that uses direct punishments and rewards to alter a person's behavior. This pattern can at times result in "undersocialization" from society's point of view; its reliance on actual or potential surveillance to achieve adherence to rules may reduce the stability of the social

2. As detailed in chapter 5, the three orientations are derived from and coordinated with the three processes of influence. This relationship suggests some propositions about the dynamics of the three orientations. One type of proposition refers to the social influence processes whereby individuals acquire these different orientations. Thus, we are proposing here that a socialization process that emphasizes compliance is conducive to rule orientation, one that emphasizes identification, to role orientation, and one that emphasizes internalization, to value orientation. A second type of proposition refers to the predominant influence process that marks the relationship of the individual to political authorities in each of the three cases. Thus, in our discussion above of the patterns of participation in citizen duties characteristic of the three orientations, and in our discussion below of the nature of the support provided to government policies, we propose that rule orientation is conducive to automatic but minimal compliance, role orientation to a high level of involvement rooted in identification, and value orientation to the evaluative approach associated with internalization.

order. Role-oriented socialization emphasizes identification, an influence strategy that appeals to the person's desire to maintain a self-defining relationship to another person or a group. This process represents the most reliable and powerful mode of socialization into citizenship. Value-oriented socialization emphasizes internalization, an influence strategy that seeks to alter behavior by demonstrating the congruence of the proposed change with the person's own values or central beliefs. Internalization may result in "oversocialization" from the point of view of social control, since a person socialized via values applies independent standards to govern action.

The different patterns of participation in duties and benefits suggest that, in many respects, the three orientations fall on a continuum. Actual or perceived responsibility for running the affairs of the society and depth of integration into the society increase from rule to role to value orientation. In one respect, however, role orientation stands out from the other two. In both rule and value orientation the individual may take an outsider's perspective toward authority—in part because of undersocialization in the one case and oversocialization in the other. Thus rule-oriented individuals may stand apart in that they see authority as a distant force, outside of themselves, with which they, as pawns, must come to terms. Value-oriented citizens take the stance of outside observer in judging how well authorities live up to what they, the citizens, regard as the society's fundamental values. Role orientation, on the other hand, involves a fundamentally more interactive relationship to the authorities. Role-oriented individuals tend to be caught up in the workings of the authority structure. They have a stronger sense of belonging to the society than the rule-oriented and therefore become behaviorally and emotionally more involved in its operations. At the same time, they have a weaker sense of ownership of the society than the value-oriented and therefore feel less able to stand in judgment over the authorities. These differences have important implications for reactions in concrete encounters with authority.

Related to the differences in socialization and in the stance toward the authority structure are divergent views of the role and meaning of morality in the political sphere. The next two rows of table 11.1 indicate that, for the rule-oriented, moral principles are largely irrelevant both to the actions of the citizen in an authority context and to the actions of the state in pursuit of its primary purposes: ensuring public order and national security. This view has a cynical overtone. The state cannot afford the luxury of concerning itself with higher principles, and individuals can be expected to do only what they must in order to stay out of trouble. For the role-oriented, special moral principles apply to the citizen in relation to the state as well as to the state itself. The morality of obedience—the obligation to obey and support the government—at the level of the individual citizen and the duty to pursue the national interest at the level of the state both override standard moral considerations. Finally, for the value-oriented, principles of personal morality continue to govern the behavior of individuals as citizens, and adherence to moral principles is fundamental to the legitimacy of state action. Actions by and on behalf of the state may not always conform precisely to the expectations that govern personal relations, but they have to be chosen and evaluated with reference to standard moral principles.

In their view of the role of moral principles and in their relationship to authority more generally, the three orientations are reminiscent of Kohlberg's (1969, 1984) three levels of moral development, summarized next in the table. (See also Tapp, 1987.) We do not, however, conceive of the three orientations as developmental stages in any strict sense of the term. Rule orientation corresponds roughly to Kohlberg's preconventional level of moral reasoning, where the choice of right action is based on considerations of punishment or instrumental satisfaction. Role orientation corresponds to Kohlberg's conventional level, where the judgment of what is right focuses on meeting others' expectations or doing one's duty to maintain the social order. And value orientation resembles Kohlberg's postconventional level, where moral judgment is based on orientation to a social contract or the utility of action for the greater good (Kohlberg's stage 5), or on adherence to personal conscience in the service of universal ethical principles (stage 6).

Under normal circumstances, we do not expect systematic differences among orientations in readiness to support the government and adhere to its authoritative demands. Rule-, role-, and value-oriented citizens all typically accept the legitimacy of the political system. Thus, when a legitimate authority issues an explicit and seemingly appropriate order, all three types of citizens are inclined to obey—for their own reasons and in their own fashion. They are likely, however, to differ in the *quality* of their support of government policies, as summarized in table 11.1. Rule-oriented citizens can be expected to provide the most automatic support, but it tends to be of a compliant sort: They do what is necessary and no more. The role-oriented provide the most reliable and enthusiastic support, reflecting their identification with the state and the citizen role. The value-oriented are likely to provide the greatest long-run support to a society that adheres to its principles. But their support in any given case is conditional since they tend to make their own judgments of the appropriateness of official policy.

These differences in the quality of support translate into differences in the ability and readiness, under exceptional circumstances, to challenge authority's definition of what must be done. When an apparently legitimate authority orders actions that the individual would normally consider morally unacceptable, the ensuing conflict is resolved differently for each political orientation. Value-oriented individuals can more readily break out of the authority's definition of the situation, since they see the citizen role as including an obligation to evaluate and to question. They are also more likely to have the cognitive skills, motivational inclinations, and material resources needed to challenge authority. In contrast, both rule- and role-oriented individuals are less likely to challenge authority under these circumstances, but for different reasons.[3] This does not mean that we view

3. In an earlier article (Kelman and Lawrence [Hamilton], 1972b), we made a rather different prediction of the effects of role orientation—or what we then called (following Kelman, 1969) role-participant integration. Since writing that article, we developed scales to measure the three political

rule and role orientation as never allowing for dissent or even disobedience. Citizens of both types are likely to protest when they feel that their contract with the authorities—as they perceive it—has been violated and their basis of integration in the society is threatened. For example, the rule-oriented may protest policies that constitute threats to their security, whereas the role-oriented may be sensitive to threats to their status. But when confronted with the dilemma of a legitimate authority ordering them to perform morally objectionable acts, both groups are inclined to obey without challenge.

Responsibility in an authority situation therefore takes on different nuances for each of the three orientations. We postulate a linkage between each orientation and one of the many meanings of responsibility discussed in chapter 8; these are summarized in the last row of table 11.1. In the view of the rule-oriented individual, the authority-subordinate contract calls for compliance by the subordinate with authoritative demands: adherence to the rules and regulations in the interest of staying out of trouble. This view of responsibility focuses on *sanctions* for breaking rules. For the role-oriented individual, the contract with authority involves the subordinate's identity; responsibility focuses on *fulfilling role obligations* as part of living up to this identity. For the value-oriented individual, responsibility is a matter of *independent judgment*, self-direction based on internalized standards. These standards apply whether the value-oriented citizen is acting under authority or, as may often be the case, *as* the authority.[4]

The three orientations imply differences in readiness to challenge authority and in conceptions of responsibility vis-à-vis authority that can enrich our understanding of how authority dilemmas are framed. Thus far we have suggested that obedience versus defiance, and the condoning versus the condemnation of obedience, can be understood in terms of two different psychological frameworks that individuals may adopt in viewing the authority situation and in determining the responsibility of subordinates within such a situation. The authority situation, we have proposed, can be seen through two filters. Through one, the actions of subordinates are judged relative to the requirements and obligations of their roles in the situation. The focus in assessing their responsibility is on the role-based *motives* for their actions. Through the other filter actions are judged independently

---

orientations and explored the relationship of these measures to attitudes toward crimes of obedience, as part of the research reported in chapters 10 and 12. The profile of the role-oriented that emerged from our scaling effort differed in content and emphasis from our original conception of this pattern. Moreover, role orientation—as in fact measured—showed a different relationship to obedience attitudes than the one predicted on the basis of our earlier formulation of the concept. As a result of these empirical inputs, we have revised our conception of role orientation and our expectations about its attitudinal and behavioral consequences. The formulation presented here reflects these changes. It should be viewed, therefore, not as a prediction of the findings reported in chapter 12 but—to a considerable degree—as a product of these findings.

4. In chapter 8 we noted that the obligations of different roles themselves vary such that the roles more characteristically held by the value-oriented are likely to embody more diffuse and aspirational standards of performance than the roles held by the rule- or role-oriented.

of the authority relationship, according to standards of morality and propriety that would apply in any setting. The focus in assessing subordinates' responsibility is on the anticipated *consequences* of their actions. We have argued that individuals who see the authority situation in terms of role-based motives tend to be bound into an obedient stance (and to excuse obedience by others), whereas those who assess the consequences of action independently tend to choose disobedience (and to condemn obedience by others) when the authority's demands are illegitimate. The findings of our two surveys support this analysis by revealing two distinct patterns of reaction: a DR pattern, reflecting an approach to assessing subordinates' responsibility based on motives, and an AR pattern, reflecting an approach based on consequences. These two patterns appear replicable and generalizable, and are consistently related to demographic variables, on the one hand, and to attitudes toward crimes of obedience and their punishment, on the other.

How then does our distinction between the three types of political orientation relate to these two filters for viewing authority situations with their two approaches to assigning responsibility (DR versus AR) and their two presumed behavioral outcomes (obedience versus disobedience)? How can it extend our analysis of conceptions of authority and responsibility as they affect commission and judgment of crimes of obedience? As far as value orientation is concerned, it should clearly be associated with an AR stance and its focus on the anticipated consequences of action. The hallmarks of value orientation—support for political authority at a level of internalized values and willingness to evaluate policies and orders against that independent criterion—imply precisely the kind of assertion of personal responsibility in the face of authoritative orders that the AR approach represents. Value orientation should impel an individual in the direction of disobedience if and when an obedient act is seen as violating central values or a disobedient act is seen as embodying them. The concept of value orientation adds another dimension to the "consequences" approach to attributing responsibility by linking that approach to a broader political orientation and its particular formulation of the citizen role. In doing so, it illuminates one—though by no means the only—motivational base for an AR stance and for an independent posture toward authority.

As far as the distinction between rule and role orientation is concerned, it helps us refine the analysis of role-based motives by considering the two orientations as variants of this view of responsibility. Behaviorally, both rule- and role-oriented individuals are likely to obey authority, as we have noted; but motivationally and cognitively, rule orientation and role orientation imply different role-based motives. They represent two paths to the same, obedient, outcome.

The rule-oriented can be said to obey out of a sense of *powerlessness* in the situation. Their role-related "vocabulary of motives" emphasizes "I had to do it" in the service of avoiding punishment. They tend to see themselves as pawns who lack the capacity to challenge authoritative demands and who cannot afford the risks that such a challenge would entail. Rule-oriented citizens might be tempted to disobey if they thought they could get away with it. When there is a high probability of penalties for disobedience, however, rule orientation impels people in the direction of obedience.

The role-oriented, in contrast, can be said to obey out of a sense of *obligation* to the authority. Their role-related vocabulary of motives emphasizes that "it was my duty to do it" as a good citizen. Obedience in this case is not just a necessity, but a good in its own right. It does not arise primarily out of a feeling of power-lessness, but out of identification with those in power and a desire to share this power vicariously. Even when the role-oriented are quite removed from the sources of power they are, as we have argued, caught up in the authority structure and unable to step outside of it. For the role-oriented the risk of punishment is a secondary issue, since they act out of a sense of duty rooted in the morality of obedience. They would probably be tempted to disobey only if they had support for doing so from an alternative authority with equal legitimacy. Under most cir-cumstances, role orientation impels people in the direction of obedience. Obedi-ence among the role-oriented may in fact extend over a greater range of situations than among the rule-oriented, who tend to be bounded by the limits of surveil-lance.

In short, both rule and role orientations have the effect of binding subordinates to the authority's definition of the situation unless they have clear indications from reliable alternative sources that disobedience is safe or acceptable. Both orienta-tions provide what we have called role-based motives for obedience. But these motives are different, and the inability to extricate the self from authority's de-mands flows from different sources.

Conclusions

Social-status variables can be expected, on theoretical grounds, to account for some of the individual differences observed in response to authority situations. The findings of our two surveys support this expectation, although we spelled out various reasons for interpreting these findings with considerable caution.

In the bulk of this chapter, we explored some of the psychological foundations of individual differences in attitudes and behavior toward authority. We focused in particular on our theoretically derived distinction among three types of political orientation—rule, role, and value orientations—whose images of the contract between citizen and state center, respectively, on compliance to rules, identifica-tion with the citizen role, and internalization of societal values. We proposed that, in assessing personal responsibility, value-oriented citizens would be more likely to focus on the consequences of actions and, accordingly, that they would be more inclined to challenge authority. In contrast, both rule-oriented and role-oriented citizens would be less inclined to challenge authority, adopting two different vo-cabularies of role-based motives to justify obedience: for the rule-oriented, the *necessity* to obey, arising from a sense of powerlessness, and for the role-oriented, the *obligation* to obey, arising from identification with the powerful state and with the citizen role.

We also hypothesized an association between the three orientations and indicators of social status, such as educational attainment, occupational prestige, and level of income. Thus, rule orientation is likely to be more characteristic of working-class or tenuously integrated individuals, role orientation of members of the middle class, and value orientation of those in positions of authority and control. In a general population, educational achievement, insofar as it provides a degree of internal authority and structurally produced independence, should be conducive to higher value orientation in contrast to rule and role orientations. Thus, the three political orientations may represent psychological variables that mirror the effects of social status on attitudes and behavior vis-à-vis authority.

The three orientations may also be linked to general personality dispositions, such as perceived locus of control or authoritarianism, that may themselves be associated with response to authority situations. Moreover, our three-way scheme, by postulating two distinct motives for the inclination to obey, may improve on the dichotomies between internal and external control or origin and pawn within which the psychological foundations of obedience have often been discussed. The distinction between rule orientation and role orientation can also be viewed as a refinement of the concept of authoritarianism in that it separates two facets of authoritarianism: one more reactive, the other more proactive.

We have already mentioned that our Boston area survey included measures of rule, role, and value orientations, as well as of several other individual-difference variables. We are now ready to return to a discussion of that survey. The next chapter describes the way in which the three orientations (and other psychological variables) were assessed in the Boston survey and how they related to responsibility orientations. We stress that the data to be presented in chapter 12 should not be viewed as tests of the hypotheses discussed in this chapter. For one thing, we do not have the kind of data that would allow us to test the entire array of relationships postulated in our discussion of the three types of orientation. Furthermore, as mentioned in note 3, our current formulation of the three patterns was partly influenced by the results of the measurement efforts and the data analyses presented in the next chapter. Thus, the data to which we now turn should be viewed not as a formal test of a conceptual model but as an initial and rather limited illustration of the usefulness of our distinctions in organizing a set of empirical findings.

12 | Rules, Roles, and Values: Three Orientations to Authority

One of the purposes of the Boston area survey, as noted in chapter 10, was to explore the effects of rule, role, and value orientations on conceptions of responsibility in authority situations: to assess the extent to which these orientations predict whether a person will deny or assert personal responsibility for crimes of obedience. Accordingly, we developed scales to measure these three orientations. Questions pertaining to these scales, as well as other measures of individual differences, were included in the mail-back questionnaire that respondents in the 1976 survey were asked to complete. In this chapter, we describe the various measures of individual differences used in the study, including the orientation scales developed as part of our own research. We then present the findings on the relationship of rule, role, and value orientation to demographic factors, on one hand, and to responses to the Calley trial, on the other.

Measuring Individual Differences

PERSONALITY CONSTRUCTS

Authoritarianism has been an extensively used—and abused—social-scientific concept since the publication of the landmark work *The Authoritarian Personality* (Adorno et al., 1950; see Samelson, 1986). The authors argued that the personality syndrome, authoritarianism, includes the display of such diverse traits as intolerance of ambiguity, social and sexual conventionality, stereotyping, and superstitiousness; the core trait is a tendency to submit to authority and dominate subordinates. Adorno described authoritarianism's central traits of dominance and submission with a German word meaning "bicyclist's personality": "Above they bow, below they kick" (cited in Greenstein, 1969, p. 103). The authors' *F*-scale, the most commonly used single measure of authoritarianism, boasts at least two book-length methodological and conceptual critiques (Christie and Jahoda, 1954; Kirscht and Dillehay, 1967).

The authoritarianism literature has been plagued by problems in format and wording of items, as in the original F-scale, where the authoritarian response to each item is also the "agree" response. The most common problem results from yea-saying—some respondents' tendency to say yes no matter what the content of the item (see Schuman and Presser, 1981). To correct for such a bias, Richard Christie, one of the early methodological critics of authoritarianism research, undertook various efforts to develop a balanced scale with equal numbers of items for which disagreement represents the authoritarian response and items for which agreement does so. The traditional moralism scale (Gold et al., 1976, p. 17), a derivative of these earlier efforts, is described by the authors as a measure of right-wing authoritarian proclivities that is "a conceptual descendant of the original California F-scale" (p. 16). We used ten of the twelve items of the traditional moralism scale, half phrased positively and half phrased negatively, to assess how authoritarianism contributes to understanding crimes of obedience. Sample items with which the traditional moralist would agree include "Police should not hesitate to use force to maintain order" or "The right to private property is sacred." Sample items with which the traditional moralist would disagree include "People ought to pay more attention to new ideas, even if they seem to go against the American way of life," and "A problem with most older people is that they have learned to accept society as it is, not as it should be." In their own summary description of the scale, the authors state that traditional moralism "taps a conservative, status quo view of society, emphasizing traditional values about the worth of hard work, antipathy to new ideas, and the necessity of maintaining order—by the use of police force if necessary" (Gold et al., 1976, p. 25).

Because of the multitude of scales for authoritarianism or similar measures, and because the traditional moralism scale had not been tested extensively at the time of our survey, we selected an additional established scale that was expected to overlap with authoritarianism: McClosky's (1958) conservatism scale. Typical items from this nine-item scale include "I prefer the practical man any time to the man of ideas" and "If you start trying to change things very much, you usually make them worse." All of this scale's items were worded so that agreement signified conservatism. We expected conservatism to be correlated with the traditional moralism scale: that high conservatism would be associated with high traditional moralism (authoritarianism) and the reverse. We had no basis for expecting any specific differences in the performance of the two scales. A careful reading of the two sets of items, however, reveals a difference in tone that will help explain some of the findings to be discussed below. Although both scales measure conservatism, the items in the conservatism scale favor the status quo largely on pragmatic grounds, whereas the traditional moralism items favor the status quo largely on moralistic grounds.

Chapter 11 pointed to the possible relevance of a second broad personality construct, which concerns perceived control over one's outcomes. This is often described as a dimension from internal to external control (Rotter, 1966) or a distinction between seeing the self as origin versus pawn (deCharms, 1968). Since more work has been done in developing scales for the distinction between internal and external control than for the origin-pawn concept, we concentrated on the former. The basic distinction between internality and externality refers to whether the individual feels personally able to control outcomes or feels that outcomes are externally controlled. Several investigators have subdivided the original distinction, largely in acknowledgment of the multiple ways in which a person can be externally controlled; luck and Big Brother are both external, but they have very different impacts on one's life (see Gurin et al., 1978). For our survey we selected six of the internal and six of the external items analyzed by Collins (1974); these represent both personal and political control. More personally oriented items include "Sometimes I feel that I don't have enough control over the direction my life is taking," an external item, or "People's misfortunes result from the mistakes they make," an internal item. Politically oriented counterparts include "This world is run by the few people in power, and there is not much the little guy can do about it" (external), and "By taking an active part in political and social affairs the people can control world events" (internal).

It seemed to us that an assert-responsibility (AR) approach psychologically corresponded to internality, or, alternatively, an origin perspective, and that a DR approach resembled externality, or a pawn perspective. Such a distinction might be as relevant as authoritarianism to understanding crimes of obedience; at a minimum, it draws on different social-scientific roots and different assumptions. Internality and externality, for example, emerged from studies of social learning and are quite compatible with "cognitive," "economic," or "rational actor" models or schools of social psychology. This stands in contrast to the Freudian roots of the authoritarian syndrome.

POLITICAL ORIENTATION AND ATTACHMENT

The key scales tested in the Boston survey were our own. Chapter 11 indicated that, although we felt both authoritarianism and internal-external control were relevant, we thought distinctions derived from our model of social influence and legitimacy should be more refined and more directly linked to reactions to political authority. Specifically, our framework suggested that a person's orientation to authorities or political systems via *rules*, *roles*, or *values* should be related to judgments of crimes of obedience. In addition, we created scales for political attachment—*sentimental* versus *instrumental*—that cross-cut the political orientations and that represent two fundamental sources of perceived legitimacy of political authority (see chapter 5, including table 5.2).

Three issues arose. First, could we develop psychometrically adequate scales for these concepts? Second, would the contemplated scales add to or improve on older scales—such as those measuring authoritarianism, conservatism, or perceived locus of control? And third, would such scales be significantly linked to key attitudinal responses? For example, would they predict DR-AR judgments? Below we present an abbreviated account of this scale development, some of which occurred during pretest studies before the Boston survey; further data gathering occurred after the survey was completed.

Initial Scale Development. We set out in 1974 to create items that might tap political orientation, attachment, and their combination. Scale development was done in collaboration with Frederick D. Miller and later also with John D. Winkler. We began by generating a pool of 221 items designed to tap attachment and orientation to political authority. An early round of data gathering, in which respondents each received half of the items, included 104 Harvard undergraduates and 196 residents of the Boston area, sampled by mail. After analysis of this first round we reduced the number of items to 110, discarding some that produced little variation in response. A second round of data gathering used diverse samples of Boston area and Suffolk County, Long Island, residents (N = 197). After analysis of these data some items were dropped as inadequate, some were modified to improve question wording, and a few new items were drafted.

At the outset of the Boston survey we had developed a final pool of 86 items tapping orientation and attachment. Of these, a small number had been adapted from other relevant scales by Bloom (1974), Ferguson (1942), or Milbrath (1968). To this pool we added the measures of traditional moralism, conservatism, and internal-external control discussed earlier, bringing the item total to 117. Items were then arranged in random order; each was presented in a seven-point Likert-type format, asking for degree of agreement or disagreement. This set of attitude items was included in the mail-back portion of the study rather than in the main interview because of its length. The number of respondents (N) in this chapter's analyses is therefore 318, not 391. Just as our overall quota samples are less representative than a probability sample, this mail-back subsample is unrepresentative in still further ways. But the fact that our mail-back questionnaire had a very high response rate, over 80 percent, helped ensure that enough members of key population groups remain for comparisons.

The large number of attitude items needed to be reduced to more general summaries or indicators of the concepts involved. For those readers who are unfamiliar with analysis of these kinds of questions, we offer a brief road map of the steps taken. The major technique was factor analysis, the most commonly used method for reducing large numbers of items to conceptual summaries (see Cooley and Lohnes, 1971; Harman, 1976). A factor is a *dimension*. It is created from a set of items by drawing a best-fitting straight line through the data. Each item has a "loading" on a factor: a positive or negative association with the dimension. Those items that come closer to the line that defines a factor will have loadings of larger absolute value. If, for example, internal and external control really form a single scale, the twelve items of this type (half internal, half external) would yield a single factor when analyzed. And if internal and external answers were really opposites, one set of items would relate positively to the factor and the other set would relate negatively. Under those circumstances this factor would represent a dimension of internality-externality. Some sets of items may require several factors—linear summaries—to capture the variation they contain. For example, we expected that our orientation items would reveal rule, role, and value factors.

When factors are identified by means of the common principal-components technique, they are independent of one another: uncorrelated. Uncorrelated factors are geometrically orthogonal (at right angles) to each other. Obtained factors are also often rotated in space to another uncorrelated arrangement that makes the factors more interpretable—more conceptually clear and distinct. Here we carried out these commonly used factor-analytic operations: principal-components analyses with varimax rotations of the orthogonal factors. We also carried out a series of cluster analyses, a different analytic technique that identifies clumps rather than dimensions of items in space (see, for example, Andenberg, 1973); none of the results from different variations of this technique was more compelling than the factor results reported here.

Separate analyses of orientation and attachment items yielded three orthogonal factors in the first analysis and two in the second.[1] The three orientation factors appeared to represent rule, role, and value orientation and the two attachment factors similarly represented instrumental and sentimental attachment. Other researchers' scales were each factor-analyzed separately. These results and their relationships to our scales will be discussed further below.

Analysis of Political Orientation Scales. The orientation scales presented below were derived inductively. Empirically, what we saw was one factor that emphasized compliance with rules, one factor that emphasized the citizen's role obligations, and one factor that emphasized the citizen's own values. It therefore appeared that at some level we had succeeded. However, some items that we originally thought would represent one concept—one factor—instead loaded with another. One systematic difficulty was that items we intended to be negatively loading ("disagree") value items instead emerged as positively loading rule or role items. Altogether, the scales derived from the factor analysis did not correspond completely with our original conceptualization of the orientations (see chapter 11, note 3). Had the correspondence been closer, we could have felt confident that the scales measured our theoretical concepts. In view of the imperfect match, our confidence in the meaning of the scales depends on the degree to which their relationship to other variables is consistent with theoretical expectations. Any opportunity to replicate the factor structure, demonstrating reliability for the empirically derived factors, also becomes correspondingly more important.

1. The goal of our factor analyses of orientation items was to develop, as closely as possible, distinctive or "ideal-typical" measures of the rule, role, and value constructs. In our initial analyses, the choice of number of factors to rotate was a relatively open one. As is often the case, a relatively restrictive analysis could have been made, employing one factor only; alternatively, quite minor factors could have been retained. The choice of three factors as a break point was made primarily for theoretical reasons, although it also represented a mathematically reasonable choice. Since subsequent analyses pruned items that did not clearly distinguish among the three factors, a three-factor solution became the clear empirical as well as theoretical choice.

Table 12.1 presents the individual items that make up the rule, role, and value scales, along with their factor loadings. Items with larger loadings contributed more to the factor than items with small loadings; theoretically, they are closer to the concept the factor is measuring. The table's items and its three-factor structure survived a series of prunings of the item set as principal-components analyses were conducted for a successively shrinking number of orientation items. Criteria for retaining an item through this pruning were that it load with an absolute value of .400 on a final rotated factor and that it *not* load above .300 absolute value on any other factor. The loadings in table 12.1 refer to the orthogonal factors extracted from a varimax rotation of the final principal-components solution. The first factor extracted was actually the role factor, then the value factor, and finally the rule factor, although the value factor explained the least variance.

Mathematically speaking, the scales in table 12.1 are not the most powerful combinations of orientation items in the data set. Instead, the items that showed the highest communality—the highest intercorrelations with other items—were typically items that spanned the rule and role factors. Such items may correlate well with each other, but they do not discriminate between integration via rules and roles. Since our task was to do just that, we discarded such double-loading items. Of the items that remain in the final set of twenty-five, one falls just short of our .400 criterion; it was retained because it was above the criterion when analyzed in all larger sets of items and always loaded distinctively on its factor.

The reliabilities (Cronbach's alpha) of these resulting scales were mixed. Alpha, calculated for complete cases on each scale, was a sizable .87 for the role scale and .79 for the rule scale. The value scale had a lower reliability of only .64; although disappointingly small, this is perhaps not a surprising result in light of the small number of value items that survived pruning. We shall explore below the extent to which the value scale taps the construct we sought, but we cannot at present recommend it for use by others.

The face validity of the scales is relatively high and their content is varied, at least for the rule and role factors. Most rule items seemed to cluster around a few themes: Government has power, which it must use to ensure basic security—physical and economic—and to maintain public order. It cannot afford the luxury of worrying about higher values or moral principles. The task of citizens is to obey—to do what is required of them and stay out of trouble. Anything else would invite anarchy. Most role items, in contrast, emphasized obligation to obey and to participate: Good citizens do their part in upholding national symbols, national strength, and prosperity. They respect authority; they obey the law, which is a sacred institution; and they give unconditional, enthusiastic support to government policies, regardless of personal values. These items have the feel of identification with the government, whereas the rule items clearly have the feel of compliance.

Even the scanty array of items tapping value orientation had some variability in themes. The person agreeing with value items was asserting an active, questioning, even protesting stance toward government and authority, and expected the

Table 12.1 Items and Factor Loadings for Scales of Rule, Role, and Value Orientation[a]

Items	Loadings
A. Rule orientation factor	
The most you can expect the government to do is to see to it that all citizens are able to earn a living and be safe.	.639
If you have doubts about an official order, the best thing is to do what is required of you, so you will stay out of trouble.	.590
One reason for supporting the U.S. government is that anarchy will result if there are too many critics.	.559
In matters involving the national interest, we cannot apply the same moral principles that we follow in everyday life.	.510
The government must sometimes set constitutional principles aside in order to deal with problems of the modern world.	.501
The best politicians are ones who get things done, no matter what compromises they have to make.	.500
The real symbols of a country are its strength and power, not its abstract ideals and goals.	.486
As I see it, the basic purpose of law is to keep people from committing crimes.[b]	.462
If you have doubts about obeying an official order, the best thing to do is to follow the consensus among people like yourself.	.448
America no longer has a responsibility to take in the world's "tired and poor"; we need to take care of Americans first.	.389
B. Role orientation factor	
A good American is one who is prepared to do his part in carrying out government policies.	.680
I feel an obligation to support the government even when its policies disagree with my values.	.667
A good American always respects authority and obeys the laws.	.659
I feel that I should pay taxes because the government must have money to keep America strong and prosperous.	.639
In a democracy, military service is part of the obligation to support the country that every eligible citizen should be happy to meet.	.617
One should obey one's government, even when it means going against one's principles.	.616
The most valuable contribution an individual citizen can make is to give active support to government policies.	.613
I can think of many situations in which I would stop supporting the government.	−.605
The law is more than the enactments of Congress: it is a sacred institution.[c]	.495

Continued on next page

Table 12.1 *Continued*

Items	Loadings
Once a law is enacted, people are obligated to obey it, even if it discriminates against certain groups.	.449

C. Value orientation factor

I feel obligated to protest both vigorously and publicly if the government does something that is morally wrong.[d]	.663
The most valuable contribution an individual citizen can make is to maintain an active and questioning approach toward government policies.	.575
The most important thing the government can do is to see that the basic rights and freedoms of all citizens are protected.	.492
Citizens have a responsibility to take an active stand against government policies that violate the Bill of Rights.	.473
I expect a good citizen to be politically aware and active all year long, not just around election time.	.469

[a]Factor analysis of these items using principal components revealed three factors explaining 36.4% of the variance and two additional factors with eigenvalues less than 1.0. Loadings reported here come from a varimax rotation of the first three factors. The sole negative loading occurs for an item intended to elicit a "disagree" response.
[b]Item drawn from scale by Bloom (1974).
[c]Item drawn from scale by Ferguson (1942).
[d]Item modified from scale by Milbrath (1968).

government to protect the rights and freedoms of the citizenry. However weak the scale, it captured a third view of authority. The pattern of interrelationships among items and scales also suggests that disagreement with both rule and role orientations represented value orientation, over and above that aspect of it picked up by its own scale.

Our confidence that these orientation scales measured what we sought is increased by the fact that a later study produced the same basic factor structure among Detroit adults (Kelman, Miller, Hamilton, and Winkler, 1977). Replication strengthens the argument that these factors represent the theoretical constructs in question.

Analysis of Political Attachment Scales. Scales for instrumental and sentimental political attachment, theoretically orthogonal to the three orientations, were a second goal of the scaling effort. As we had hoped, two factors captured the pattern of responses. After rotation, every item that we expected to be instrumental loaded on an instrumental factor; and every item that we expected to be sentimental loaded on a sentimental factor. (Items sometimes loaded on both.) We were especially pleased that the instrumental scale was balanced: Half the items were ones with which the respondent was meant to agree and half were items with which we intended disagreement.[2] Cronbach's alpha was substantial for both scales: .81 for the instrumental and .88 for the sentimental scale. As table 12.2 indicates, the scales had substantial face validity. The instrumental scale captured respondents' commitment to America as a country whose institutions work in ensuring democracy, justice, and equity, and which has given them economic benefits and the opportunity to get ahead. The sentimental scale emphasized unswerving loyalty to the country, pride in its power, and respect for national symbols like the flag and the anthem.

In developing the original pool of items for the attachment scales, we wrote items expressing each type of attachment by way of rules, roles, and values—in other words, representing each of the six cells of table 5.2. However, the sentimental and instrumental scales that emerged from the factor analysis did not represent the three subtypes in balanced fashion. Items that were intended as instrumental items of a rule type loaded on the sentimental factor as well as the instrumental; conversely, items that were intended to be sentimental items of a value type loaded on the instrumental factor as well as the sentimental. Both these groups of items, therefore, were dropped from the final scale versions. We cannot be sure what this implies for the concepts involved. It may be that attachments and orientations simply are not independent. The orientations and attachments, as described in chapter 5, were conceived as cross-cutting, but we had no specific expectation that this cross-cutting relationship would be one of complete independence between the constructs. Thus, the observed pattern is not inconsistent with theoretical understandings of the concepts. If sentimental attachment—as measured—amounts to a global, unconditional loyalty, then value-oriented items would indeed be underrepresented, as they express conditional attachment. Similarly, if instrumental attachment is thought of in terms of degree of integration into a system of resource distribution, then rule-oriented items would be underrepresented, as they express the most tenuous instrumental linkage.

Unfortunately, this failure to achieve balanced representation for different types of orientations across attachments, while consistent with a view that the constructs

2. This scale was used to make a correction for acquiescence (yea-saying). The correction eventually devised by Richard Hogan involved three basic manipulations of the balanced instrumental attachment scale. First the respondent's supposed disagree answers were reversed (subtracted from 8), summed, divided by the number of responses of that type, and the result subtracted from the sum of agree answers divided by the number of responses of that type. This step yields the difference in intensity of answers to the positive versus negative items. Respondents who answered less than half of the 8 items in question were deleted from analysis, leaving $N = 311$. Each respondent's mean difference was then expressed as a deviation from the sample's mean difference. (That is, the sample's observed average judgment was used instead of presuming zero difference between the positive and negative sets of items.) The respondent's deviation from the sample mean became that individual's measure of acquiescence (that is, scores above the sample mean represented yea-saying and scores below the mean represented nay-saying, relative to the sample as a whole). The final step, correcting for acquiescence, involved taking each scale to be corrected, regressing it on the individual's acquiescence measure, and saving the residual as the new scale value for that individual. The residual variable, by definition, is orthogonal to acquiescence as we measured it.

Table 12.2 Items and Factor Loadings for Scales of Instrumental and Sentimental Attachment

Items	Loadings
A. Instrumental attachment factor	
I don't feel that I benefit particularly from the freedom of choice that our economic system is supposed to provide.	−.648
The American system has given me excellent opportunities to improve my position in life.	.647
Democracy is just an empty word that has very little to do with the way our society is really organized.	−.631
I find it hard to think of this country as the land of opportunity.	−.606
What I like about this country is that I have as good a chance as anyone else to get the kind of job I am qualified for.	.530
Even though there are occasional injustices, I feel that our judicial system is basically capable of assuring justice to all citizens.	.504
A person without connections can't feel sure that his rights will be protected.	−.462
Our political institutions provide no foolproof guarantees against abuse, but I feel that they are fundamentally sound.	.462
B. Sentimental attachment factor	
I am bothered that so many people nowadays don't show proper respect for the American flag.	.832
I always support my country, even if I feel that it may be wrong.	.776
I cannot think of any circumstances under which I would stop supporting America.	.741
As an American, I take great pride in our armed forces.	.702
It doesn't matter to me if someone wants to sit while the Star Spangled Banner is being played.	−.686
Americans who criticize their government in front of citizens of other nations are acting against the best interests of their country and its people.	.667
I get personally upset at people who criticize the government in times of national crisis.	.538
It is personally important to me to know that America has great influence on the world scene.	.499
I feel that there are times when it's perfectly all right for people to disobey the government.	−.414

Note: Principal-components factor analysis of these items revealed two factors that together explained 42.5% of the total variance. Loadings reported in this table come from the varimax rotation of these factors. Negative loadings represent "disagree" items.

are genuinely nonindependent, has multiple interpretations. The overlapping scales could also be reflections of underlying common causes, such as education or social class; for example, being in an educational or economic elite might cause both feelings of instrumental attachment and tendencies to be politically integrated via values. Or, finally, we may simply have failed to develop an adequate pool of items to tap all six combinations of the orientation and attachment constructs. Below we attempt to be sensitive to this ambiguity in interpreting relationships of the attachment scales to other items.

In evaluating the performance of the orientation scales, we considered how they related both to one another and to other relevant scales. First, we considered the adequacy of the other scales as revealed through factor analyses.

Factor analyses of items representing conservatism, traditional moralism, and internal-external control revealed mixed results. Principal-components analysis of conservatism items yielded a straightforward single factor solution in which all nine items loaded satisfactorily. Traditional moralism, although it also yielded a one-factor principal-components solution, was not well balanced. Items intended to elicit agreement had loadings of substantially higher absolute value than items with which high traditional moralists were expected to disagree. Not surprisingly, traditional moralism's reliability (alpha) was a low .57. Finally, in keeping with Collins's (1974) finding of multiple factors, internal-external control was not a single scale. The analysis yielded two scales: a two-factor solution that rotated into a purely internal factor and a corresponding external factor. We decided to use separate internal and external control scales in all analyses so as to capture these independent elements.

Data Preparation. For comparisons between scales we moved to a more conservative measure of the concepts by using *scale* scores rather than factor scores. Use of a scale score gives an unweighted average of items. On the one hand, this scoring procedure loses information about the relative power (loadings) of items and may result in correlations among scales even though the corresponding factor scores were orthogonal. On the other hand, any factor scores are unique to a given data set, and almost any practical use of the scales beyond this study would employ scale scores. Therefore scale scores were preferred here as relatively more generalizable measures of the concepts, although the scales were not statistically independent as they would be in their factor form. In the analyses a high score on the scale always indicated adherence to the concept being measured. (Scores on negative items, for which the disagree response taps the construct, were reversed.)

Analyses described thus far refer to factor scores, all of which were calculated on complete cases. That is, respondents must have answered all items being analyzed in order to be retained in the factor analysis. A second step in preparing for comparisons across scales was to be more inclusive of respondents who had missing data on some scale items. We chose to take the conventional approach of substituting the sample mean as the value for an item when an individual had missing data, making it possible to compare performances of scales using the same number of respondents across analyses. Requiring that all cases be complete across all items, in contrast, would sharply cut the size of the data set. All scale correlations and other analyses below are therefore based on the full N of 318 mail-back questionnaire respondents.

Intercorrelations among Scales. Table 12.3 presents the intercorrelations of our scales with one another and with the established scales: conservatism, traditional moralism, and internal and external control (scaled separately). The simple zero-order correlations of the scales are shown here ($N = 318$).[3]

Looking first at the relationships among our orientation and attachment scales, it is apparent that the uncorrelated factors provided by the varimax rotations were artificially independent. For example, table 12.3 shows a sizable correlation of .47 between rule and role orientations *when they are expressed as scale scores* rather than factors. Orientation via compliance and orientation via role obligations were associated in our respondents' minds. This association is consistent with our argument that the orientations need not be mutually exclusive and that, indeed, individuals often have multiple reasons for performing a given act. The feelings that one *has* to, and that one *ought* to, behave obediently toward political authority are empirically and conceptually linked. There are two interpretations for the table's weak negative associations of value orientation with the other two orientation scales. The small size of the associations may have been a function of the weakness of the value scale itself; but the association of value with rule and role may be a true negative, as we noted above. It is perhaps most accurate to say that our rule and role scales strongly tapped compliance and identification, including the *absence* of a value stance; the value scale, in contrast, only weakly represented that stance in a positive way. We can safely consider only the rule and role scales to be reliable measures of the concepts they were intended to measure.

Similar overlap is evident between the instrumental and sentimental scales. As rotated factors, these were orthogonal—uncorrelated—but table 12.3 shows a sizable correlation (.43) between their scale scores. There is, of course, every reason theoretically to expect this association. That is, the two forms of attachment are conceived of as mutually reinforcing and likely to move in tandem, such that to be highly committed in one way implies being highly committed in the other.

The pattern of relationships between orientation and attachment is of greater substantive interest. We shall concentrate on rule-role comparisons in light of

3. For each relationship two correlations were in fact calculated, here and in subsequent analyses. The first, reported here, involves the raw scale-scored variables; the second used the scale score corrected for acquiescence as described in note 2. The latter correlation represents in our view a less contaminated measure of scale content; however, it is necessarily specific to our own sample given the nature of the correction. Since the correction made little difference empirically, we do not present the correlations of corrected variables.

Table 12.3 Intercorrelations of Orientation Scales, Attachment Scales, and Other Scales

Scales	Orientation			Attachment		Other Scales			
	Rule	Role	Value	Instrumental	Sentimental	Conservatism	Traditional Moralism	Internal	External
Rule	—	.47	-.11	-.10	.44	.71	.33	.19	.35
Role		—	-.07	.52	.83	.52	.62	.41	.01
Value			—	-.05	-.05	-.02	-.14	.20	-.18
Instrumental				—	.43	-.04	.37	.39	-.42
Sentimental					—	.47	.37	.37	.04
Conservatism						—	.40	.29	.31
Traditional moralism							—	.37	-.12
Internal								—	-.18
External									—

Note: Scales are averages of item ratings. All missing data for individual items are replaced by the sample mean for the item; thus $N = 318$, the number of individuals responding to the mail-back questionnaire. All correlations are significant at $p \leq .01$ except the following: correlations of .11 to .14 are significant at $p \leq .05$; correlations of .10 or less are not significant.

these scales' greater reliability relative to the value scale. The biggest correlation anywhere in this table—the greatest similarity of scales—is the .83 association between role orientation and sentimental attachment. The role-oriented person was sentimentally attached, and vice versa. This may in part reflect the sentimental scale's composition, which was solely rule and role items. It is also theoretically reasonable that sentimental attachment, as loyalty, should be at a peak among role-oriented respondents; value orientation implies conditional attachment and rule orientation implies more tenuous integration. One of the table's biggest differences in relationships is also found among the orientation-attachment intercorrelations: There was no significant link between being rule-oriented and being instrumentally attached, but there was a sizable ($r = .44$) tendency for the rule-oriented respondent to be sentimentally attached. Methodologically, this result is consistent with the absence of rule items in the instrumental attachment scale. This absence of rule items, of course, may also reflect a fundamental inconsistency or weak tie between rule orientation and instrumental attachment, as we have already noted.

The right side of table 12.3 shows how other researchers' scales related to the orientation and attachment scales. McClosky's conservatism overlapped strongly with our rule scale; it both correlated highly with it and related to other scales in similar ways. Traditional moralism overlapped with the role scale, correlating with it highly and showing similar associations with other items. The separate scales for internal control and external control were modestly negatively correlated with each other and differed substantially in their relationships to other scales. Internal control was related to everything. That is, the respondent who professed to be internally controlled professed to be everything else, including value-oriented, *except*, of course, being externally controlled. External control was positively related to rule orientation and conservatism. It showed a substantial negative correlation with instrumental attachment, smaller negative associations with value orientation and traditional moralism, and no relationship with role orientation or sentimental attachment.

These correlations of the new scales with older measures that tap authoritarianism and individuals' sense of control offer some preliminary insights into the scales' meanings. It appears that rule and role orientations may represent two variants, faces, or forms of authoritarianism, at least if one takes seriously the parallels between these two scales and the conservatism and traditional moralism scales, respectively. Rule orientation represents compliance with power; role orientation, obligation to obey authority. It appears likely that value orientation taps a sort of anti-authoritarianism, internal control, or both.

Orientations to Political Authority and Demographic Factors

We continued to explore the meaning of the three orientations and the differences between them by asking which demographic groups tended to score high on each scale. For sociological purposes this amounts to asking what causes the scale scores. In this analysis we will simply examine which demographic variables relate to which scales; we will not try to establish causal precedence among these variables—that is, which demographic factors are the most potent predictors.

All demographic variables were converted into quantitative dimensions, which made it possible to compute coefficients of correlation between each of these variables and each of the scales. Table 12.4 presents the correlations of the orientation scales, as well as the attachment scales, with most of the demographic variables from the survey. The respondent's sex was omitted because males and females never differed significantly on any scales. We included in the table only those variables that correlated significantly with one or more of the scales. We will summarize first the relationships for the orientations, keeping in mind that value orientation, a weak scale, can be expected to have few significant correlates. We will then turn briefly to the attachment scales.

Scales for rule and role orientation showed certain similarities in their potential social causes. One genuine constant was education. More educated respondents were more likely to disagree with both rule and role items to an equivalent extent. A second constant was religion, with Catholics significantly more likely to be high on both scales than non-Catholics. But many relationships differed to at least some extent for the two orientations. Being older was significantly associated with both rule and role orientation, but the correlation was substantially stronger for role orientation. High rule orientation was more strongly associated with being in a low-status occupation than was true of role orientation. Rule orientation was also significantly linked to being both poor and black, whereas role orientation was not associated with either of these variables. High rule scores were correlated with Democratic party identification, whereas role advocacy tended to be associated with Republicanism. In addition, agreement with role scale items was significantly linked to military service and home ownership; both these variables were unrelated to rule scores. The general profiles of these two orientations are distinctive, despite the many overlapping associations. Respondents high in rule orientation were more likely to be young, low in income and occupational status, black, and Democratic, and less likely to own their homes and to have had military experience, than those high in role orientation. Both such respondents were relatively uneducated and likely to be Catholics. Thus, relatively speaking, the profile of the rule-oriented suggests a working-class or tenuously integrated individual, whereas the profile of the role-oriented suggests a member of the lower middle class.

The only significant correlate of value orientation was age, with older respondents more value-oriented, although the correlation was considerably lower than that between role orientation and age. The *lack* of correlation between value orientation and education was consistent with expectations, at least in contrast to the high negative relationship of education to the other two orientations. That is, comparison across scales suggests that respondents high in value orientation were likely to be better educated on the average than respondents high in the other two orientations. Similarly one can conclude, on the basis of comparisons across

Table 12.4 Demographic Correlates of Orientation and Attachment Scales

Demographic Variables	Orientation			Attachment	
	Rule	Role	Value	Instrumental	Sentimental
Age (in years)	.15	.50	.13	.31	.47
Education (6 categories)	−.40	−.40	.02	−.05	−.42
Income (15 categories)	−.15	−.08	−.01	.08	−.07
Occupational status (Low/Medium/High)	−.25	−.12	−.02	.12	−.10
Religion (Non-Catholic/Catholic)	.26	.26	−.10	.11	.34
Race (Black/White)	−.16	.04	−.02	.22	.08
Military experience (No/Yes)	−.03	.13	.04	.19	.11
Own home? (No/Yes)	.02	.19	−.08	.24	.22
Political party (7 categories, from Strong Democrat to Strong Republican)	−.17	.10	−.01	.18	.05

Note: Correlations use scale scores (averages) in which missing data are replaced by the sample mean for that variable; the baseline N for these and all analyses involving scales is 318, the number who returned the mail-back. Occasional missing data on demographic items yield slightly varying Ns for individual correlations above. Demographic variables were coded according to natural units (e.g., age) or in the direction expected to be associated with higher attachment (e.g., "own home," no/yes). All correlations with an absolute value of .15 or larger are significant at $p \leq .01$. Correlations of .11 to .14 are significant at $p \leq .05$. Correlations of .10 or smaller are not significant.

scales, that respondents high in value orientation were less likely to be Catholic or to be low in occupational status than those high in rule or role orientation. Unfortunately, the absence of associations between value orientation and demographic variables can also be explained by the weakness of the scale.

The relationships of demographic variables to instrumental and sentimental attachment also showed interesting convergences and divergences. Respondents' age and home ownership were related to greater attachment of both varieties. Neither attachment scale was significantly related to income. Catholicism was strongly related to sentimental attachment and weakly related to instrumental. Conversely, military service was strongly related to instrumental attachment and weakly related to sentimental. But the scales differed in that high instrumental attachment was associated with being white and Republican; sentimental attachment was correlated with neither of these variables. Similarly, instrumental attachment was correlated with being in a high-status occupation, whereas sentimental attachment tended to be associated with low occupational status. Sentimental attachment was associated with lower education; instrumental attachment was uncorrelated with education. In both cases, attachment seemed to mean having a stake in the society, having roots. But instrumental attachment was greater among those who may have had more resources to which to attach themselves and who, in general, were closer to the various centers of influence and prestige within the society. Sentimental attachment apparently reflected a more diffuse emotional investment, characteristic of people who clearly have a stake in the society but belong to more peripheral demographic categories.[4]

ORIENTATIONS VERSUS OTHER SCALES

The pattern of interrelationships among the various scales has shown that McClosky's conservatism scale was strongly associated with rule orientation and closely resembled rule orientation in the way it related to other scales. On the

4. One obvious question concerns the relative strengths of the different demographic variables in predicting orientation and attachment. We carried out regression analyses in which predictors were considered in combination. It is important to note that findings may be unstable when correlated variables are analyzed together without specific expectations about their performances. When scale scores were regressed on the full set of demographic variables from table 12.4, value orientation showed no changes in predictors and the attachment scales showed slight changes. (For sentimental attachment, home ownership was no longer significant; for instrumental attachment, home ownership and occupational status were insignificant.) Predictors that dropped below significance for role orientation were occupational status and military experience. Those that dropped out for rule orientation—where results differed most from the simple correlations—were age, income, political party preference, and occupation (leaving education, religion, and race). In some cases the elimination of a predictor from significance indicates that the original correlation was suspect (spurious). Thus it is easy to understand why home ownership might drop out of equations that include income and age. But in some cases it is difficult to say which result is more "real." The occasional insignificance of income and occupational status—in equations that include income, occupational status, and education—may reflect random fluctuations in the size of correlations rather than true differences in the variables' predictive power. Given all these considerations, the text simply presents the separate correlations rather than making assumptions about the causal priority of the variables.

other hand, the traditional moralism scale was strongly associated with role orientation and closely resembled role orientation in its relationship to other scales. These findings raise questions about the distinctiveness of our rule and role scales and the extent to which they measured the same dimensions tapped by these other more established scales. Thus it is important to address systematically how different—if at all different—the conservatism and traditional moralism scales were from the rule scale, the role scale, and each other in their demographic correlates.

Conservatism differed little from rule orientation; traditional moralism differed little from role orientation; and the conservatism and traditional moralism scales differed relatively little from each other in their demographic correlates. Some of the established scales' relationships to demographics, such as their correlations with education and religion, were similar to those observed for rule and role orientations. Among the variables that had differentiated between these two orientations, conservatism and traditional moralism repeated the patterns of difference for income, occupational status, military service, home ownership, and political party membership. Conservatives on the McClosky scale were relatively low in income and occupational status, lacked military service, and were Democrats. Traditional moralists were homeowners. Two factors that had separated rule and role orientations did *not* significantly differentiate conservatism and traditional moralism: race and age.

One approach to dealing with these overlaps is to stress differences between the newly developed rule and role scales and the scales of conservatism and traditional moralism, especially improvements provided by the new scales. For example, the orientation scales could be constructed with orthogonal factor scores, and using such scores in the analysis increased the sharpness of the differences presented here. But we think it is more honest, and more interesting, to take seriously the substantial overlap in results and presumably the similarity in meaning among our own and the more established scales.

We do *not* think the rule scale is just an improved scale for conservatism and the role scale an improved traditional moralism scale. Instead of asking whether we have simply remeasured conservatism and traditional moralism, it is plausible to ask what it is that conservatism and traditional moralism themselves measure. It seems to us that each earlier scale assesses some element of authoritarianism—or, to be more precise, of right-wing authoritarianism (see Gold et al., 1976)—but that they differ in the particular element of authoritarianism they tap. Each scale presents one facet of authoritarianism. The conservatism scale has a flavor of cautious minimalism; the traditional moralism scale, a flavor of obligation to uphold tradition.[5] From our perspective conservatism and traditional moralism are unplanned and uncoordinated measures of, respectively, authoritarianism via rules/compliance and authoritarianism via roles/identification (see also Hesselbart

5. Focusing on the elements of conservatism tapped by each scale, one can describe McClosky's scale as primarily a measure of pragmatically based conservatism and traditional moralism as a measure of moralistically based conservatism.

and Schuman, 1976). What we have created in the rule and role scales are more purified measures of each. Further, this overlap between our own measures— which were addressed to the respondents' views of political authority—and the earlier more broadly conceived measures indicates the existence of considerable overlap between respondents' approach to authority that is specifically political and to "authority" in a more general or diffuse sense.

From this perspective the failure to create an adequate value orientation scale may simply mean that the two variants of authoritarianism are *negatively* related to value orientation as we conceive it rather than orthogonal to it. Hence those value items that survived our orthogonal analysis were relatively weak measures of the concept. This third component of the original theoretical framework therefore required special attention in the subsequent analyses. We attempted to pull out the most distinctive version of value orientation that was feasible. The simplest way to do this was to create a typology of respondents: those who scored high on rule only, those high on role only, and those high on value only. Such a typology could tease out when, if ever, value orientation is a driving force behind opinions and choices. Below we first examine how rule, role, and value orientations, as scale scores, predict key dependent variables; we then turn to the analysis of these "pure" types.

Orientations to Political Authority and Responses to the Calley Trial

In chapter 11 we described the distinct characteristics and correlates that we postulate for each of the three orientations. On the basis of these distinctions, we then presented our current formulation of how each orientation should relate to a person's approach to responsibility in authority situations and attitude toward obedience versus disobedience. We proposed that value orientation, with its relative independence from authority, should be associated with assertion of individual responsibility (that is, an AR stance) and a readiness to disobey questionable orders. On the other hand, we proposed that both rule and role orientation, for different reasons, should incline citizens to deny individual responsibility for actions under superior orders (to take a DR stance) and impel them in the direction of obedience. Differences between these orientations appear most likely where, on one hand, penalties for disobedience are made salient and surveillance is close; and, on the other hand, obligation to obey is evoked as a value in itself.

We turn first to correlations between respondents' scores on the three orientation scales and their answers to key items about obedience and resistance to military authority.[6] Table 12.5 presents these correlations. For most items in the table

6. The three orientations to political authority were expected to be linked to responses about the military setting. We also explored their relationships to the other authority situations—Watergate and the two hypothetical scenarios involving professional authorities. The three orientations were unrelated to judgments of the hypothetical incidents in a hospital and a research setting. This is an unsurprising result, both in light of the skewed responses to questions about these incidents (see chapter 10) and in light of the greater theoretical distance between the situations and orientations to political authority. However, the scales were significantly related to only one response about Watergate. (Role-oriented

rule and role scale scores moved in tandem. Value orientation generally diverged from the other scales in ways suggestive of independence from authority, assertion of individual responsibility, and readiness to disobey. But the patterns, like the scale, were weak. Only two correlations were significant at the .05 level: the association of value orientation with approval of the Calley trial and with the severity of punishment advocated for him. The overall pattern observable across rule and role scales was obedience. Both rule orientation and role orientation were associated with a tendency to disapprove of Calley's trial; to adopt a DR stance; to attribute no responsibility to Calley; to say that you would follow orders and shoot; to say that Calley should have followed orders to shoot; and to advocate no punishment or a lenient punishment for him.

Table 12.5 Orientation Scales as Predictors of Reaction to the Calley Case and Related Issues

	Orientation		
Items	Rule	Role	Value
Trial disapproval/approval	−.17	−.23	.13
Responsibility orientation (DR/AR)	−.23	−.32	.12
Calley responsibility attribution (None/Some)	−.28	−.34	−.05
What would most people do? (Shoot/Refuse)	−.14	−.03	.06
What would you do? (Shoot/Refuse)	−.27	−.24	.10
What should Calley have done? (Shoot/Refuse)	−.29	−.33	.03
Punishment for Calley? (scored None to Severe)	−.22	−.31	.12
Refusal to fight in Vietnam was (Wrong/Right)	−.16	−.41	.11
Amnesty for draft resisters? (Disapprove/Approve)	−.13	−.34	.09

Note: Orientation scale items were scored from 1 = strongly disagree to 7 = strongly agree. For consistency in presentation, dependent variables were coded so the high score indicated the assertion of responsibility or an independent stance toward authority. All correlations with an absolute value of .16 or larger are significant at $p \le .01$. Correlations of .12 to .14 are significant at $p \le .05$. Correlations of .11 or smaller are not signficant. (For responsibility orientation, the .12 correlation falls short of significance because the N is smaller in this case.)

---

respondents were distinctively likely to say that the burglars should have followed their illegal orders.) It is possible to engage in special pleading regarding the unusualness of Watergate-related acts as examples of crimes of obedience; however, the most conservative conclusion is that we have demonstrated a connection between the scales and judgments only for a clear-cut crime of obedience sponsored by the state, as in sanctioned massacres.

The divergences between the rule and role orientation scales in their patterns of correlations are themselves consistent with our understanding of the orientations. Rule orientation was significantly correlated with saying that most people would shoot, whereas role orientation was not. For a rule-oriented individual, what most people would do is important for two reasons: It helps establish what the rule is and it shows what needs to be done in order to stay out of trouble. These issues are less central to the role-oriented citizen, since they have no direct bearing on obedience to authority as a moral obligation. What counts for the role-oriented, presumably, is not so much what most people do, but what good citizens do. The two scales also diverged in the strength of their relationship to two items about resistance to the Vietnam War. High role orientation was more strongly associated with answering that conscientious refusal to fight in Vietnam was *wrong* and that amnesty should *not* be granted to draft resisters and to deserters. Role-oriented respondents could be expected to feel moral indignation toward those who "shirk" their military obligations, whereas rule-oriented respondents would be likely to view the issue more pragmatically than morally. In sum, the pattern of correlations is consistent with the interpretation of rule orientation and role orientation as two paths to the same, obedient, outcome: one based on a view of obedience as necessity, the other on a view of obedience as obligation.[7]

The correlations of scores on the other scales used in this survey with responses to the Calley trial were consistent with what we already know about the relationships among scales. Once again, the traditional moralism scale behaved very much like role orientation and the conservatism scale like rule orientation. Traditional moralism, like role orientation, was significantly associated with all the items listed in table 12.5, except the question about what most people would do, although the size of the correlation was smaller in each case. The pattern of correlations for conservatism was very similar to that for rule orientation, but again the size of the correlations (with one exception) was smaller. Traditional

---

7. These analyses leave open the possibility that relationships between the political orientations and such crucial variables as DR-AR or responsibility assignment to Calley may have been spurious. That is, because demographic factors caused both the political orientations and the responsibility judgments, they may account for the appearance of a linkage between orientations and responsibility. We therefore assessed whether the orientation scales significantly predicted the responsibility variables *when the contribution of demographic factors had been taken into account.* Education and religion were the key demographic variables in these analyses for three reasons: They had been the crucial demographic predictors in our 1971 survey, they had continued to predict both responsibility assignment to Calley and DR-AR in this survey, and they were each significant predictors of rule and role orientations with other demographics controlled (see note 4). Stepwise regressions were carried out with education and religion entered first, followed in turn by rule, role, and value orientations. The major dependent variable was responsibility assignment to Calley; the secondary one, because of its smaller N, was DR-AR. (Note that although the dependent variables were dichotomies, regression is relatively robust to this violation of its assumptions.) Rule orientation uniquely accounted for 3 percent of the variance in responsibility assignment to Calley ($p = .003$) and 2 percent of the variance in DR-AR ($p = .06$). Role orientation uniquely accounted for 4 percent of the variance in both responsibility assignment to Calley ($p = .0004$) and DR-AR ($p = .01$). Not surprisingly, value orientation made no significant unique contribution to the variance in either case.

moralism differed from conservatism, as role orientation differed from rule orientation, in showing a stronger association with the tendency to disapprove of refusal to fight in Vietnam and of amnesty for draft resisters. Conservatism differed from rule orientation, however, in showing no association with the estimate of what most people would do. In general, the pattern of correlations supports our earlier conclusion that conservatism and traditional moralism, as it turns out, seem to have been tapping the two facets of authoritarianism specifically distinguished by rule and role orientation.

The external control scale was not significantly associated with any of the items in table 12.5; all the correlations hovered around zero. The internal control scale showed the same pattern of associations with responses to the Calley trial as the role orientation and the traditional moralism scales, but the size of the correlations was consistently much lower for internal control than for the other two scales; only three of the correlations were statistically significant. The few relationships that did appear indicate clearly that the internal control scale did not tap the respondents' readiness to react to authority with some degree of independence, which is the defining characteristic of value orientation. Altogether, then, external and internal control, at least as measured by the items selected for this survey, did not show the theoretically expected relationship to conceptions of authority and responsibility in a military crime of obedience.

PURE TYPES: RULES, ROLES, AND VALUES

Identifying those respondents who were distinctively oriented in one of the three ways can help clarify the meaning of the orientations. For this reason, and in order to help tease out any possible strengths of the otherwise weak value orientation scale, we dichotomized the scale scores for each dimension. A score at or above the median value for the sample on the particular scale was designated as high and any other score as low. We then identified those respondents who were high on only one of the three scales—that is, relatively pure typifications of rule, role, and value stances. Such a distinction is most artificial and most difficult in the case of rule and role types; since these scales were substantially correlated, to be high on one implied being the same on the other. In the entire mail-back sample of 318, we were able to identify 125 pure types. Of these, only 35 were pure rule and 28 pure role, in contrast to 62 pure value types. The substantial size of the value group is to be expected, since the correlations of value orientation with the other two scales were negative. Any analysis of pure types must therefore be carried out with the caveat that distinctions between rule and role are likely to be relatively unreliable and that respondents who are pure rule or role are atypical. But any strengths of value orientation should be highlighted by such an analysis.

First we look at the make-up of the pure types—the social characteristics of pure rule, role, or value respondents. Table 12.6 summarizes significant relationships of the orientation typology to categorical versions of the demographic variables. Results are very similar to those of table 12.4, but there were fewer significant outcomes; this may be due to the smaller number of respondents when only pure types are included in the analysis. For example, item A shows a sizable relationship between type of orientation and educational attainment. The value-oriented were distinctively more educated than the other two groups. Relationships of the typlogy with occupational status and income, in contrast, were not significant. Item B presents a clear trend in religious affiliation: The proportion of Catholics declines as one moves from rule to role to value orientation. Value-oriented respondents were also more different from role-oriented respondents in this regard than the role-oriented were from the rule-oriented. Military service did not distinguish significantly among groups.

Other distinctive social characteristics for the different orientations can be observed across items C–E, which include relationships to age, home ownership, and race. As the earlier correlations (table 12.4) showed, role-oriented individuals were distinctively older. Some 44 percent of them were fifty or over, in contrast to 11 percent of rule-oriented and 13 percent of value-oriented respondents. The role-oriented were also more likely to be home owners. Pure rule types were distinctive with regard to race: Whereas the pure role type was 4 percent black, and the pure value type 8 percent black, the rule-oriented respondent group was 31 percent black. In each of these relationships the creation of pure types sharpened previously drawn distinctions and conclusions, although it drastically cut the number of cases for analysis. A demographic summary, or perhaps caricature, of

Table 12.6 Rule, Role, and Value Orientations as Pure Types: Relationship to Demographic Variables

	Pure Type			All Respondents (%)
Demographic Variables	Rule (%)	Role (%)	Value (%)	
A. Education				
(<12 years/12 years/13 + years)				
13 + years	38	19	70	50
B. Religion				
(Non-Catholic/Catholic)				
Catholic	51	43	27	37
C. Age				
(18–24/25–34/35–49/				
50 and over)				
50 and over	11	44	13	19
D. Own home (No/Yes)				
Yes	42	79	40	50
E. Race (Black/White)				
White	69	96	92	86

Note: Pure types were constructed from raw scale averages for the rule, role, and value scales. Respondents at or above the median for each were counted as "high"; a pure type was *high* on one of the scales and *low* on the other two. Numbers of respondents varied from 121 to 125 across items A–E (rule, $N = 33$–35; role, $N = 27$–28; value, $N = 60$–62). All associations were significant at $p \le .01$ except that for item B, where $p = .04$.

Table 12.7 Rule, Role, and Value Orientations as Pure Types: Relationship to Attitudinal Variables

| | Pure Type | | | All |
	Rule (%)	Role (%)	Value (%)	Respondents (%)
Items				
A. Responsibility orientation (DR/AR)				
AR	43	46	79	64
B. Calley should have (Followed orders/Refused)				
Refused	58	54	81	69
C. What would you do? (Shoot/Refuse)				
Refuse	59	78	85	76
D. What would most people do?/ What would you do?				
Consistent Shooters	42	23	10	22
Deviant Refusers	27	32	33	31
Consistent Refusers	31	45	57	47
E. Refusal to fight in Vietnam was (Right/Wrong)				
Wrong	15	64	5	19
F. Amnesty for draft resisters? (Approve/Disapprove)				
Disapprove	35	76	27	40

Note: Pure types were constructed from raw scale averages for the rule, role, and value scales. Respondents at or above the median for each were counted as "high"; a pure type was *high* on one of the scales and *low* on the other two. N ranged from 61 (item A) to 119. Associations were significant at $p \leq 01$ for items B, E, and F and at $p \leq .05$ for the remaining items.

the pure types might suggest that the rule-oriented tended to belong to the working class, the role-oriented to the lower middle class, and the value-oriented to an educated class.

Table 12.7 summarizes relationships between pure types and key questions about authority and obedience. These analyses help address our concerns about the contribution of the value scale to our understanding of the orientations; they also help sharpen the distinctions between the rule and role scales. Responses fell into three basic patterns. The first was the emergence of a distinctive value orientation when pure types were contrasted. Value orientation stood out in responses to items A and B: responsibility orientation (DR versus AR) and the question about what Calley should have done. Value-oriented respondents asserted individual responsibility and said that Calley should have refused orders, in contrast to both other groups.

A second pattern of results was a roughly linear trend in the tendency to obey, with rule orientation highest and value orientation lowest. Significant differences following this second pattern appeared in responses to the question about what the respondent would personally do (item C) and in the combination of responses to the questions about what most people would do and what the respondent would personally do—the distinction between Consistent Shooters, Deviant Refusers, and Consistent Refusers introduced in chapter 7 (item D). The question about most people by itself did not show a significant relationship here, but responses show a consistent trend: 71 percent of rule respondents said that most people would shoot versus 58 percent of pure role respondents and 47 percent of pure value respondents ($p = .10$). In general, moving from rule to role to value dramatically increased the resistance to orders that respondents said they would offer in items C and D. The movement from rule to role to value was a movement from a plurality of rule-oriented saying that "most would shoot" and "I would shoot" to a majority of value-oriented saying instead that "most would refuse" and "I would refuse." The pattern of answers was consistent with our expectation that rule-oriented respondents would show strong adherence to orders especially when punishment for disobedience is salient and surveillance is close; these features characterize the military context, especially during combat.

A third pattern could also be identified: distinctiveness for those who were purely role-oriented. This possibility was discussed earlier in terms of the activation of obedience as an obligation. A hint that role orientation is distinctive in this way, already provided by the earlier correlational analysis (table 12.5), is fleshed out in the final items of table 12.7. The crucial issues were again draft resistance during the Vietnam War (item E) and amnesty for resisters (item F). Substantial majorities of both rule and value respondents supported draft resistance and approved of amnesty. A sizable majority of role-oriented respondents rejected both. This pattern was striking both for the strength of the role response and for the different view held by the rule group. The position of role types can be understood in terms of obedience as an obligation—part of the core of role orientation as we have defined it. Citizens who fail to meet their obligations can be expected to evoke, in a role-oriented respondent, a reaction of moral indignation. The rule types' position was consistent with their orientation to authority as requiring compliance, doing what one must. In the context of an unpopular, failed policy, such as the Vietnam War, individuals who are purely rule-oriented may well regard minimal compliance as the most sensible response. They can be expected, therefore, to be less outraged by or punitive toward those who refuse to comply altogether. A situation of policy conflict or policy failure is particularly likely to reveal such clear distinctions among citizens who react to government demands on the basis of different standards: rules, role obligations, and values.

Conclusions

The goal of this chapter was to probe the social-psychological underpinnings of the different approaches to responsibility we had observed in our two surveys about crimes of obedience. We sought to identify broad orientations toward authority that would help us predict and understand the individual's reaction to a particular authority. The tools included scales for relevant psychological tendencies already devised by other researchers as well as new scales of our own. The new scales were meant to capture orientations to political authority and, secondarily, attachments to that authority as outlined in chapters 5 and 11. Our primary theoretical interest was in developing measures of rule, role, and value orientations and exploring their relationship to conceptions of authority and responsibility.

THE ORIENTATION SCALES

Our effort to develop measures of the three orientations was partially successful. Scales for orientations to authority emerged in a three-factor structure of rules, roles, and values. Of these three factors, both the rule and role scales had good reliability and face validity; but value orientation was more elusive.

The rule and role scales, in their composition and performance, fell somewhat short of our expectations, but on balance they proved themselves strong and useful. The items that survived the successive screening procedures in the course of scale development do not cover the entire range of characteristics that form part of our definitions of the two orientations. Thus, the orientations as measured reflect only part of the orientations as conceptualized. Nevertheless, each scale captures the essential flavor of the orientation it is designed to measure: the minimal expectations from the government and the correspondingly minimal compliance of the citizen in rule orientation, and the stress on the obligations and active participation of the good citizen in role orientation. The correlation between scale scores (in contrast to factor scores) on the two measures, .47, is higher than we would have liked to see it, although a correlation of this size still leaves considerable room for independent variation. Moreover, there is no theoretical reason for viewing these two orientations as mutually exclusive. Given the high correlation between the two scales, it is not surprising that their relationships to demographic variables were not as distinct as might have been expected on theoretical grounds. For example, both rule and role orientation showed a correlation of $-.40$ with educational attainment. Where the relationships did diverge, however, they revealed demographic profiles consistent with theoretical expectations. Crudely summarized, rule orientation is characteristic of relatively lower-status respondents, whereas role orientation appears to be the approach of more settled and stable citizens. If compliance characterizes a proletariat, obligation and participation are hallmarks of a bourgeoisie.

The relationships of the two orientation scales to other researchers' scales, to our attachment scales, and to demographic predictors offer a reasonably clear picture of what the new scales may contribute to a crowded literature. The most interesting patterns involved the close parallels between rule orientation and McClosky's conservatism scale, on the one hand, and role orientation and the traditional moralism scale, on the other. The parallels suggest that all four scales were tapping facets of authoritarianism: rule orientation and conservatism, a compliant, pragmatic, minimalist authoritarianism; role orientation and traditional moralism, a moralistic authoritarianism of obligation and participation rather than submission out of a sense of powerlessness. In our view these overlaps help to clarify what was being measured and need not diminish the usefulness of any of the scales in question.

There is undoubtedly room for improvement of the rule and role scales, particularly by broadening the range of the component elements of each concept that are tapped by the scales. Overall, however, these are good scales, with adequate reliability and validity. The verdict on the value orientation scale, on the other hand, is much less positive. The scale we developed is usable, but it has few items and their internal coherence is weak. Value orientation is also represented, perhaps as well, by the negative end of the rule and role scales. As noted earlier, several items that were initially intended as negatively worded value items turned out to have high positive loadings on either the rule or the role factor. Thus, the rule scale can be interpreted as a bipolar measure, with a high score representing rule orientation and a low score value orientation. Similarly, the role scale can be interpreted as a bipolar measure, with role orientation at the positive end and value orientation at the negative end.

Furthermore, although the value scale per se was relatively weak, the analysis of respondents who were pure types on each scale bolstered the distinctive meaning of value orientation. Value-oriented respondents who were also low scorers on the other scales were distinctively highly educated and likely to be non-Catholic. By contrast, both rule and role orientation tended to be associated with lower education and Catholic affiliation. Overall these demographic associations were consistent with the theoretical construct of value orientation as embodying readiness to use one's own values as independent standards for judging the demands of authority. The responses of the pure value types to the Calley trial were similarly consistent with the conceptual picture of value orientation drawn in chapter 11.

The development of a more effective value orientation scale remains a task for future research. Although we generated a large number of value items in our efforts to produce orientation scales, most of them did not survive the successive pruning procedures. A major reason for the failure of value items was that the distribution of responses to many of these items was skewed: Large numbers of respondents apparently found it easy to agree with them. Perhaps in future efforts special attention should be paid to generating items with which it is more difficult to agree, such as items in which the value-oriented response entails personal costs to the respondent (for example, statements expressing willingness to protest a morally unacceptable policy even at the risk of going to jail or being called a traitor) and goes counter to a widely accepted social norm (for example, statements expressing willingness to take or support principled actions that are unpopular or considered improper by others). The pool of value items could also be enlarged by using statements that refer to specific values. In order to avoid confounding value orientation with commitment to a particular set of values, one could follow the procedure used by Alfred Bloom (1974, 1977) in developing his measure of social principledness: asking respondents to evaluate actions of others (such as disobeying certain government orders) out of commitment to *their* particular values, whether or not those values are shared by the respondents themselves.

POLITICAL ORIENTATION AND OBEDIENCE

Whatever limitations the orientation scales may have—relatively minor ones for the rule and role scales and serious ones for the value scale—the conceptual distinctions between the three types of political orientation and their relationship to conceptions of authority and responsibility emerged clearly from the overall pattern of findings of the Boston survey. Further research can improve the scales, but for our present purposes there is sufficient empirical support for the distinctions to permit some reasonably firm conclusions about the nature of the three orientations and their relationship to obedience versus disobedience.

It appears that general orientations to political authority, as measured by our scales, were linked to individuals' advocacy of obedience or disobedience, of shooting or refusing, on Calley trial items. Responses were consistent with the theoretical picture of the three orientations drawn in chapter 11. Value orientation was related to a tendency to assert individual responsibility for crimes of obedience and to a disposition to disobey commands that violate the individual's own principles. In contrast, the rule and role scales were both associated with a tendency to deny individual responsibility and a disposition to obey authoritative orders. The similarity in performance of the scales conforms to the view of the two orientations as two paths to the same, obedient, outcome.

It may be unnecessary for many purposes to distinguish rule from role orientations, if they come down on the same (obedient) side of the issue. But our data also suggest that the individual's reason for obeying is not irrelevant. On those items on which the two scales diverged, the patterns of association were consistent with our understanding that the rule-oriented tend to regard obedience as a matter of pragmatic necessity, whereas the role-oriented are more likely to view it as a matter of moral obligation. Thus, rule-oriented respondents were more sensitive to the question of what "most people" would do, since the answer to that question suggests what they need to do in order to stay out of trouble and avoid punishment by authorities. In contrast, the issue of how to judge Vietnam War draft resisters highlights obedience as a legal or moral obligation; role-oriented respondents were distinctively harsh in judging disobedience under these circumstances. These contrasts suggest that, across situations, divergences between the logic of rule orientation and the logic of role orientation may be predictable. That is, it is possible to predict times when rule orientation will produce more obedience, or more acceptance of obedience, and times when role orientation will yield more. What is necessary to know are the elements of the situation that are likely to be perceived as coercive, hence promoting compliance among the rule-oriented, and the elements that are likely to evoke obligation, hence promoting identification among the role-oriented.

The distinctions among the orientations to political authority flesh out the meaning of responsibility in authority situations. We have argued that an individual's focus on role-based motives leads to the denial of individual responsibility in such situations, whereas focus on the action's consequences leads to the assertion of responsibility. The overall pattern of differences between rule and role orientations, on the one hand, and value orientation, on the other, is consistent with the broad distinction between responsibility denial versus assertion. But the further distinction between rule and role orientations implies that there are two paths to responsibility denial, two reasons for focusing on the actor's motives. We argue that the understanding of both actors' accounts of their situations and observers' judgments of them can benefit from drawing this distinction. Obedience can and does flow from obligation as well as compulsion—from role as well as rule orientation to authority. And the denial of responsibility for action, by actor or by observer, can flow from the feeling that the actor responded to "oughts" or to "musts." In the next chapter, we shall draw on these distinctions in the pursuit of one of our main objectives in studying crimes of obedience: the search for ideas on how to eradicate them or at least reduce their frequency.

13 | On Breaking
the Habit of
Unquestioning Obedience

A crime of obedience is an illegal or immoral act committed in response to orders or directives from authority. Just as obedience follows from authority, crimes of obedience follow from the unrestrained or wrongful exercise of authority. The reach of authority in coordinating human action has been extended by the development of modern bureaucracies and nation states. Concomitantly, crimes committed in the name of authority have become larger in their scale and more horrific in their outcome. Crimes of obedience have provided many of the twentieth century's most terrifying images—images of Holocaust victims and survivors of the Nazi death camps produced by a massive, systematic governmental program of continental scope, as well as images produced by more isolated incidents and represented by one morning's photographs of the bodies of men, women, and children strewn about at My Lai.

Crimes of obedience are decidedly not things of the past, as evidenced by our sampling in chapter 2 of several cases in the recent news. Nor are they limited to particular nations and organizations. In addition to the German, Austrian, Argentine, and U.S. cases already discussed, we might cite recent incidents involving just three out of the many other countries in which crimes of obedience have occurred. In Poland, for example, four military officers working on behalf of the Interior Ministry were convicted for the 1984 abduction, torture, and killing of Father Jerzy Popieluszko, a supporter of the Solidarity labor organization. In another of this decade's striking cases, French agents were implicated in the bombing of the Greenpeace ship *Rainbow Warrior* in New Zealand's waters, a connection the French government attempted to cover up. The bombing was apparently designed to dissuade Greenpeace from antinuclear activity at a time when the French government was preparing a nuclear test. In yet another example two Palestinians who took part in the hijacking of an Israeli bus that resulted in the death of one of the passengers were tortured and killed while in the custody of security agents. The head of the Israeli security service and nine other members admitted participation in the killings or in the incident's subsequent cover-up. Military and quasi-military examples of crimes of obedience literally cover the globe and extend across the range of human history.

Crimes of obedience also occur in civilian settings. In chapter 2 we discussed two incidents in recent U.S. history that involved criminal actions in the context of governmental bureaucracies: the Watergate scandal and the Iran-contra affair. We also described briefly the Chrysler odometer case, which illustrates a probable crime of obedience in the context of a corporate bureaucracy. Civilian bureaucracies can often provide a setting for insidious crimes of obedience that stretch the boundaries of our definition. One recent incident highlights this problem. Millions of Americans watched on January 28, 1986, as the space shuttle *Challenger* exploded, killing seven astronauts. This tragedy was compounded by the presence of a teacher among the victims; her students and other schoolchildren across the nation watched the launch and explosion. Surely this was a tragedy—but was it a crime of obedience? To the extent that the space shuttle disaster resulted from people keeping quiet, going along, not rocking the boat, and following orders when they knew better, perhaps the answer is yes.

In this final chapter we shall reflect upon the elements that make up and delimit crimes of obedience, extending the discussion of definitional issues that we introduced at the end of chapter 2. After examining differences among authority situations in the manner in which and the degree to which they lend themselves to destructive obedience, we shall focus on differences among individuals in their reactions to authority situations. We shall conclude by drawing on the distinction among rule, role, and value orientations to political authority to identify ways in which individuals can be encouraged to accept personal responsibility and take an independent view of authoritative demands. The purpose of this concluding section is to point to the types of changes in social structures, in patterns of political participation, in foci for political socialization and civic education, and in the quality of collective support systems that are needed to develop a more responsible citizenry—a citizenry prepared to apply human values and moral principles in evaluating the political authorities' policies and demands.

In sum, the overall goals of this chapter and of this book are to understand the situational forces that impel actors to obey illegitimate orders, to identify the resources individuals can draw upon in resisting such orders, and to suggest policies and strategies for turning unquestioning obedience into independent judgment.

Situational Differences in Binding and Opposing Forces

Authority situations embed differing combinations of two fundamental factors, corresponding to the two basic determinants of responsibility outlined in chapter 8 and explored in the two surveys: the roles people occupy and the deeds they perform. The first factor, related to role definitions and obligations, is the presence and clarity of a *chain of command*. This factor affects the participants' cognitive interpretations of the situation and the salience of their different motives for obeying or defying the authority. We have argued that a clear chain of command leads subordinates, and frequently observers as well, to conceive of actions in terms of role-inspired motives (such as "following orders"). The second factor, the presence of clearly identified *targets to be harmed*, is related to anticipation of the consequences of obedience. This factor affects the extent to which participants and observers accept various authoritative justifications and definitions of the situation, the type of excuses that are available for obedience, and the probability that alternative, everyday moral frameworks for interpreting the situation will occur to the participant or observer. Thus authority situations vary in the way they frame role obligations and in the way they present the goals or consequences of actions. We shall argue that differences among these situations make some authorities more likely to generate crimes of obedience; at the same time, we stress that crimes of obedience may be stubbornly resistant to eradication even in those settings where they are more rare.

PROFESSIONAL AUTHORITY

Professional relationships per se involve no chain of command, since professional authorities issue instructions to individuals who adopt recommendations on the basis of the authority's expertise. Strictly speaking, actors lack an *obligation* to obey. Professional authority situations also lack targets for purposive harm; indeed, goals often include *help* to the target (who, for example, may be intended to get well, pass French, or win a damage award with the aid of the authority). Professional authorities can, however, act in a bureaucratic capacity—instructing or ordering one party to act vis-à-vis a third party. It is in this capacity that Milgram's (1974) experimenter declared that the "experiment must go on." It is in this capacity that we see a potential for crimes of obedience in professional authority contexts.

The normal features of professional authority—lack of a chain of command and of a target of harm—do, however, color the interpretations that a subordinate may place on bureaucratic commands that emanate from such an authority. That is, situations under the control of professional authority are distinctive with regard to both binding and opposing forces. First, a professional authority has minimal official capacity to punish disobedience, even in acting bureaucratically vis-à-vis a subordinate; we have noted that subordinates tend to be bound to the situation more through the informal forces of anticipated embarrassment than through fear of formal sanctions. Second, binding forces generated by observing the conformity of others to the authority are likely to be minimal, since professional authority is in many senses more private in its enactment than is purely bureaucratic authority. And third, the subordinate, on the basis of personal experiences, usually expects the ultimate consequences to be beneficial or at worst neutral: The patient gets well, the student passes the test, the client wins the suit, the research participant advances the cause of science. Thus the actor's value preferences are unlikely to represent a salient opposing force. In short, professional authority creates an anomalous setting for the perception of potential crimes of obedience, insofar as professional authorities are characteristically unable to activate obligations to obey, unable to punish disobedience, and likely to pursue benign goals.

This anomaly is reflected in the divergent reactions of outside observers and actors to a crime of obedience generated by professional authority. As chapter 10 indicated, outside observers typically assign heavy responsibility to subordinates who obey when professional authorities make illegitimate demands on them; these observers also fail to realize that many individuals might succumb to the pressures of such a situation. Yet actors frequently do obey in such settings. In this regard, Mixon's (1971) findings in a role-play version of the Milgram experiment are noteworthy: The level of obedience that observers envision in different hypothetical scenarios of the experiment depends on how clearly the harmful consequences to the victim are presented. It appears that the weak chain of command that characterizes professional authority blinds observers to the strength of binding forces that tie the actor to the authority's definition of the situation; and the authority's normally benign goals blind subordinates to opposing forces—based on realization that a victim may be harmed—that should have been activated in the situation. Although participants tend to go along with authority on the basis of expectations that no harm will come—until and even when they realize that their blind trust has been misplaced—the outside observer is more readily able to blame the obedient actor on the basis of the actual violation of expectations that has occurred.

The key characteristics of professional authority—presumptively weak chain of command and benevolent goals—have disturbing implications for the possibility of eliminating crimes of obedience in this context. Crimes of obedience may be rare in such settings, but their very unexpectedness may encourage subordinates to succumb to illegitimate demands from professional authorities. The binding power of the authority and the consequences that ensue in the surrounding situation become evident only when the individual is already caught up in the deeds ordered. It is as if the actor is reading the wrong "script," the typical definition of a situation involving professional authority, until it becomes too late to bow out of it.

BUREAUCRATIC HIERARCHIES

The roles of participants in a variety of civilian hierarchies—corporate or governmental—can be viewed as fundamentally similar to each other, and as differing from roles in other forms of authority relations. These similarities and differences flow from the patterning of two factors: the existence of a chain of command, governing individual role obligations, and the hierarchy's treatment of targets, defining the anticipated consequences of action. Civilian bureaucracies differ from professional authority in that they include an explicit and sometimes extended chain of command. They share with professional authority the fact that their institutional goals do not typically include harm to any target groups. Embeddedness in a hierarchy of command builds the strength of binding forces, including the existence of a system of sanctions, the conspicuousness of authoritative surveillance, and the opportunity for observing others' conformity to orders.

In governmental bureaucracies, binding forces may be further strengthened by overriding loyalty to the leader and the sense of a transcendent mission, as we suggested in our discussion of Watergate and the Iran-contra affair in chapter 2. Bureaucracies are also often vehicles for routinizing potentially harmful acts, weakening the opposing forces against destructive obedience. Absence of an explicit target of harm reduces the likelihood that individual resistances, opposing forces based on acknowledgment of a victim, will be activated.

One of the difficulties of many harmful bureaucratic acts, whose consequences we might wish to describe as crimes of obedience, is that they involve at most an "oblique" intentionality on the part of actors (see Hart, 1968). That is, the actor means to do *something*; there is an action, not an accident, that occurs. Precisely *what* is meant, however, is not—or not directly—to harm someone. Many acts that social scientists characterize as corporate crimes have this element of confusion of intentions. The concept of corporate crime is a fuzzy one that need not concern us here, except insofar as many actions described as corporate crimes involve individuals in hierarchies who act in the name of or at the behest of the organization. Many corporate crimes are in fact handled legally as torts, which typically involve negligence rather than intentionality and for which civil remedies are sought (Blum-West and Carter, 1983). To the extent that corporate crimes often do not involve fully intentional harm doing, it may be more accurate to call them "corporate torts." The individual adherences to orders upon which we focus in this volume would then become "torts of obedience." Below we briefly examine the issue of less-than-intentional harm by describing two examples: Ford Motor Company's development and production of the defective Pinto gas tank, and the problems at the National Aeronautics and Space Administration (NASA) and among subcontractors in the space program that culminated in the *Challenger* disaster.

In September 1977, the magazine *Mother Jones* published an exposé of the safety record of Ford Pintos built during the 1971–76 model years (Dowie, 1977; see also Committee on the Judiciary, House of Representatives, 1980; Kinghorn, 1984; Strobel, 1980). The problem was simple: a gas tank with a faulty design that left it likely to rupture in rear-end crashes at relatively low speeds. Ford engineers had known about the problem early on; a number of suggestions for modifications were made before and after the Pinto's introduction. For Ford executives, the safety issue was pitted against the problem of the challenge of cheap imports. The Pinto was lightweight and cheap, and could carry a set of golf clubs in its trunk as long as the gas tank remained in its unorthodox and dangerous position. One of the more famous documents to come to light in the eventual investigations and trials was an explicit cost-benefit analysis of the cost of modifying the gas tank design (estimated at $11 per car) versus the payouts anticipated in connection with the deaths, injuries, and property losses resulting from continued use of the faulty, cheaper design (estimated at perhaps $200,000 per death). The memo provided striking evidence that dehumanization of victims need not be limited to military or similar contexts; in the corporate context dehumanization did not involve targeting human deaths but rather callously quantifying and dismissing those deaths.

This form of dehumanization is reminiscent of military actions in which victims are viewed as expendable rather than as direct targets of government policy, discussed in chapter 1.

Ford sold over 1.5 million of these defective Pintos. Defective product cases against corporations are not unusual, but the injuries and deaths associated with the Pinto defect led to numerous lawsuits which were far from trivial in damages claimed or awarded. One California case of a horribly burned teenager brought a jury award of $127.8 million, $125 million of which constituted punitive damages. (This award was later reduced to $3.5 million.) The Pinto defect did more: It generated the first prosecution of an American corporation for a *criminal* offense. The company was indicted in Indiana for reckless homicide and criminal recklessness in the burn deaths of three teenaged girls, but was acquitted in 1980. It had proved too difficult to trace who knew what and who meant to do what. But even in the Indiana case, the charges involved recklessness—not fully intentional harm, not murder with "malice aforethought." It was widely acknowledged that Ford Motor Company had—or intended to have—customers, not victims. In what is usually discussed as a corporate *crime*, the individual participants surely did not intend to produce the harmful outcomes that resulted.

Acts in bureaucratic contexts that are less callous than the Pinto gas tank design may nevertheless feature people who "know better" following orders for bureaucratic reasons. Instead of exhibiting oblique intentionality or criminal recklessness, these people may simply be negligent, hurried, sloppy, or overworked. If they are any of these, and are focusing on other corporate goals when they act, there can be tragic outcomes for whatever and whomever they act upon. This may be what happened to the American space shuttle program.

Literally volumes of information are available regarding the *Challenger* disaster, including the book-length report of a presidential commission (*Report of the Presidential Commission*, 1986). As of this writing, lawsuits are still pending against both the government and the contractor. There appears, however, to be general agreement on certain points in the sequence of events leading to the tragedy. First, the booster rocket's O-rings that were supposed to seal critical joints were generally problematic and were not likely to be effective under the temperature conditions of the shuttle's cold-weather launch. Second, engineers at the company making the booster, Morton Thiokol, had urged NASA not to launch on the basis of the weather conditions. Third, Morton Thiokol had reversed this recommendation, according to the presidential commission, "in order to accommodate a major customer," NASA (*Report of the Presidential Commission*, 1986, p. 104). Fourth, NASA had in any event already received earlier warnings about the O-rings. Fifth, such warnings were ignored or overruled, consistent with a general atmosphere of laxity about quality control and pressures about deadlines. Journalists have been analyzing these points for many months; historians are likely to do so for decades to come. From our point of view, a relatively early report captures a critical feature of the situation. As *U.S. News and World Report* put it the week of March 10, 1986, America's space program was "stunned by revelations that its chain of command was fatally flawed" ("NASA Falls from Grace," 1986, p. 20).

For present purposes it is not necessary, if it is even possible, to dissect precisely which scientists or bureaucrats did what at the space agency or the contractor. Events illustrate that professionals can succumb to bureaucratic hierarchy and that this hierarchy has teeth, whether it is private or governmental. Scientists and bureaucrats both at Morton Thiokol and in NASA fell victim to the imperatives of the bureaucratic hierarchy around them. This was true even of whistle-blowers like Morton Thiokol's Allan McDonald or Roger Boisjoly, who questioned the O-rings' safety. Boisjoly, the leading expert on the safety seals, had warned of dangers with the O-rings as early as mid-1985. McDonald, Morton Thiokol's liaison for the solid rocket booster project at Kennedy Space Center, arranged a January 27 teleconference in which company engineers, including Boisjoly, attempted to convince those at the launch site to cancel the launch. But at the time, each stopped short of going outside the chain of command to protest.[1] In short, nobody stepped very far out of line, and the line was that launch had to be soon. What was intended, by everyone, was presumably a safe launch; but nobody wanted to grasp the contradiction between *safe* and *soon*.

What happens in such bureaucratic settings represents an insidious variant of dehumanization of the victim. Indeed, it may be more appropriate to refer to this process as *neutralization*. When neutralized, the victim is ignored because there is no overt target; psychologically the victim is "not there" rather than dehumanized. This appears to be what occurs when, as in the space program, other bureaucratic goals compete with and overwhelm concerns about safety. In our view, neutralization is especially insidious because it obviates many of the social-psychological forces that can otherwise be drawn upon in challenging authority. Opposing forces depend heavily upon the salience of a victim and thus rest ultimately on the actor's awareness that he or she is connected to a victim.

Such bureaucratic disasters and tragedies only partially fit the definition we originally suggested for crimes of obedience: acts the larger community considers illegal or immoral. They are likely to be acts the larger community considers sloppy or sleazy or immoral *after the real consequences are pointed out*. The key factor that differentiates these bureaucratic situations from other crimes of obedience is the explicitness with which the goal involves or necessitates harm to a victim. This is the critical social-psychological, legal, and moral difference between a My Lai massacre and a *Challenger* tragedy. In short, we envision a continuum of obedient actions vis-à-vis victims—ranging from clear evidence of harm

1. When Boisjoly and McDonald did later report their concerns and describe their actions to the presidential commission, each was effectively demoted by Morton Thiokol. Pressure from the commission resulted in their reinstatements. Within a year, McDonald reemerged within Thiokol as a spokesperson for a redesigned safety seal. Boisjoly, in contrast, took sick leave, then was put on long-term disability, and eventually left the firm. He is suing Morton Thiokol for $1 billion in personal injury and damages (see, for example, Boffey, 1987; Sanger, 1987). In January 1988 the American Association for the Advancement of Science named Boisjoly a winner of its Scientific Freedom and Responsibility Award ("Whistle Blower to Get Award," 1988). These cases illustrate both the pressures that may be put on those who would blow the whistle and the wide range of individual differences in reactions that may ensue even among those who do go public with their stories.

at one extreme to well-meaning ignorance of it at the other—within which harm may be generated at authority's behest. Although we retain the term *crime* in discussing incidents across this continuum, we stress that many such bureaucratic incidents do not represent full-blown crimes in the legal sense.

We shall not elaborate at this point on crimes of obedience in governmental bureaucracies, such as the Watergate scandal and the Iran-contra affair, both because we have discussed these cases in some detail in chapter 2 and because they are not substantially different from corporate crimes with respect to the two factors on which the present discussion focuses. Governmental bureaucracies also involve explicit chains of command and their institutional goals do not include harm to any target groups. To be sure, there are important differences between the two settings. The Watergate and the Iran-contra actions took place in the context of a bureaucratic hierarchy charged with the task of pursuing the national interest and protecting national security, and were explicitly or implicitly authorized by the president of the United States. These circumstances, and the sense of personal loyalty to the president and commitment to a transcendent mission that they engendered, are likely to strengthen the binding forces present in any chain of command.[2] In some respects, therefore, such governmental bureaucracies may be in an intermediate position between hierarchies in corporate settings and those in military or social-control settings.

MILITARY AND SOCIAL-CONTROL AGENCIES

The most obvious sources of crimes of obedience are military, paramilitary, and social-control hierarchies, in which soldiers, security agents, and police take on role obligations that explicitly include the use of force. These hierarchies are the classic ones from which the term *chain of command* is borrowed; authority is bureaucratically stringent. The goals of these bureaucracies and the role definitions of actors within them in fact *require* harm to certain categories of others (such as an enemy or subversive). The sole question concerns the scope and definition of the target of harm rather than the existence of such a target. In this context authorization is explicit and backed by multiple binding forces: Sanctions are potentially severe; surveillance by authority can be strict; and others' conformity is often observable. Routinization of actions that may contribute to harming targets is characteristic of the organization. And dehumanization of victims, especially in wartime, is systematic.

It is no surprise that, as we have seen throughout this research, obedience to orders is widely expected and widely received in such settings; and crimes of obedience accompany lawful obedience. Defense and control bureaucracies differ from others in the likelihood that an actor will be knowingly connected to harm-

---

2. The Watergate and Iran-contra actions were also, at least in part, directed at specific target groups they sought to undermine: the Democratic party presidential campaign in one case, the U.S. Congress in the other. These groups were duly dehumanized, being viewed as "the enemy" or as impediments to the attainment of national security. In the main, of course, these crimes amounted to an abuse of power whose primary victims were the democratic process and hence the larger public.

ing a victim. A soldier may *feel there is no choice* but to obey, knowing what the orders entail. In contrast, the member of a civilian bureaucracy may *not know there is a need to make a choice* because the orders have no known link to a harmful outcome. Ironically, it may be easier to encourage opposing forces when the bureaucracy does not deny that there are targets; after all, we have seen that military law has a long tradition of regulation of obedience to orders, whereas civilian law struggles with even defining various forms of corporate crime.

In sum, to speak of "authority" is to oversimplify the nuances of legitimate power and subordination; to lump together all crimes of obedience may be to miss the different underlying dynamics that generate such crimes. The potential to generate crimes of obedience is a function of both the binding forces in the chain of command and the opposing forces that can be activated by the knowledge that there is a target of harm.

Individual Differences in Response to Authority Situations

CONCEPTIONS OF RESPONSIBILITY AND POLITICAL ORIENTATIONS

Situations are stages upon which actors face dilemmas of obedience. Differences among situations may drastically affect the shape of those dilemmas and the response of the average citizen to them. Within any given situation, as we pointed out above, individuals differ in how they respond to the dilemma it presents: how they resolve the conflict between binding and opposing forces. A major theoretical question that we have raised throughout this volume has been how to account for such individual differences—differences in readiness and ability to redefine authority situations, to challenge the legitimacy of authoritative demands, to disobey superior orders that appear unlawful or immoral. Answers to this question are crucial to helping us both understand the conditions conducive to crimes of obedience and prevent the occurrence of such crimes by identifying ways of breaking the habit of unquestioning obedience.

The question of who holds responsibility in authority situations proved to be a central issue in our research; it helped organize people's reactions to crimes of obedience in both surveys. In view of these findings, as well as on logical grounds, we consider it likely that subordinates' conception of their own responsibility plays an important role in their actual response to questionable orders: in their relative sensitivity to binding and opposing forces and in their tendency to obey or disobey. If we are right, then data about the correlates of responsibility denial and assertion can help us account for individual differences in reaction to authority situations. The DR and AR patterns reflect differences in approach to responsibility that are quite *specific to authority situations*. Thus, individual-difference variables that are likely to distinguish between DR and AR responses—and ultimately between obedience and disobedience—need to refer to people's general conceptions of authority, which significantly affect the way they approach responsibility in authority situations.

In both of our surveys, social position—particularly as indexed by educational attainment—proved to be the strongest predictor of responsibility attribution, as well as of answers to the questions about what most people and respondents themselves would do in a My Lai–like situation. Such demographic measures have obvious advantages as predictors of attitudes over personality or orientation scales, which often are subject to response biases and include questions similar in form (and sometimes even in content) to the questions measuring the dependent variables. Moreover, there is generally less ambiguity about the priority of demographic factors in a causal chain than there is about psychological factors. Our demographic correlates of responsibility orientation must, therefore, be taken very seriously, and we did assign them a central role in the interpretation of our findings and in our conceptual scheme.

But demographic variables such as education and class present their own problems in interpretation of the findings and in the implications to be drawn from them. There is a serious risk of overestimating the role of social class in the effort to trace the psychological foundations of responsibility orientation. It is too tempting, especially for middle-class analysts, to interpret the DR or Consistent Shooter response as a lower-class phenomenon—perhaps even a manifestation of a general personality syndrome that is class-linked, such as "working-class authoritarianism" (see Lipset, 1960). Such an analysis carries the invidious implication that the problem arises from psychological and moral deficiencies in the lower classes, which could presumably be cured by augmenting their education and enhancing their moral development.

Thus, although we assign a central role to social class in our theoretical account of crimes of obedience, we reject a deterministic view of that role. In keeping with this approach, we focused our search for individual differences on the exploration of broader psychopolitical orientations, which may well be associated with social status but also have independent sources, including general personality dispositions and worldviews rooted in personal experiences in the context of family, community, and workplace. Specifically, we drew on the distinction between rule, role, and value orientations, derived from our analysis of the dynamics of authority. We formulated these orientations as personal dispositions that might account for individual differences in conceptions of authority and responsibility and in reactions to authoritative orders.

In relating the orientations to the two approaches to responsibility in authority situations distinguished by our theoretical analysis, we pointed out that value orientation should clearly be associated with an AR stance and its focus on the anticipated consequences of action. Exercise of independent moral judgment vis-à-vis the demands of authorities is a defining characteristic of this orientation. Value-oriented citizens, therefore, should be more willing to challenge authority and to disobey orders that violate central values.[3] In contrast, both rule and role

3. Value-oriented citizens generally adhere to the rules and accept the role obligation to support and obey the authorities, but they bring independent judgment to bear on the authorities' demands, using their personal values as criteria. Individuals who share the values of the government and are in agreement with the goals pursued by national policies are not necessarily value-oriented by our defini-

orientation should be associated with a DR stance and its focus on role-based motives. Rule-oriented and role-oriented citizens should both be reluctant to challenge authority and inclined to obey, but for different reasons: The two orientations imply different role-based motives that impel actors toward the same, obedient outcome. Rule orientation disposes subordinates to obey in order to get by and stay out of trouble; they view responsibility in terms of sanctions administered for noncompliance. Role orientation leads subordinates to obey in order to do their duty and live up to authoritative expectations; responsibility is seen in terms of the obligations that adhere to the subordinate role. In short, the rule-oriented see obedience as a necessity, arising from their sense of powerlessness; the role-oriented see it as an obligation, arising from their identification with the powerful state and the citizen role.

CONCEPTIONS OF RESPONSIBILITY: NORMATIVE AMBIGUITIES

When we seek to draw the implications of our theoretical analysis and empirical findings for ways of counteracting the tendency to obey without question and promoting independent judgment in the face of authority, the obvious starting point would seem to be responsibility orientation, which has proved to be central to people's attitudes toward crimes of obedience. Thus, we might ask: How can people be encouraged to adopt an AR stance, to assess individual responsibility in authority situations on the basis of the intended consequences of action? How can they be discouraged from taking a DR stance, from evading personal responsibility by recourse to the role-related motives for action? We deem it preferable, however, to pose the policy questions not solely in terms of AR and DR stances but in terms of the political orientations that, according to our model, may underlie these different stances.[4] Such a focus, we believe, is likely to produce a set of recommendations that is not only richer but also less burdened by some of the normative ambiguities of the DR-AR distinction.

A DR stance is most readily associated with subordinates in a hierarchy; it clearly serves the interests of subordinates in that it absolves them of responsibility for the consequences of their actions. Thus, the most obvious interpretation of this pattern is one that views it as a response of the powerless within a given situation and, by extension, of the low-status segments of society at large. The demographic correlates of the DR response in our two surveys lend support to this interpretation. Indeed, in our original interpretation of the findings of the national survey (Kelman and Lawrence [Hamilton], 1972a, 1972b; Lawrence [Hamilton] and Kelman, 1973), we postulated actual and felt powerlessness as the primary sources of a DR approach. We continue to assign a central place in our

---

tion. Value orientation implies a readiness to use such shared values as criteria in the independent judgment of policies. Applying independent judgment and making support and obedience contingent on its outcome are essential features of this orientation.

4. We do not wish to imply that we have demonstrated a causal link between political orientations and approaches to responsibility. Our empirical findings show the expected associations, but they do not permit us to draw causal conclusions.

analysis to powerlessness; we view it as a key element in rule orientation, one of the two bases of responsibility denial. Overcoming the effects of powerlessness—through empowerment and the redistribution of power—is therefore one of the important features of our recommendations below for counteracting the habit of unquestioning obedience.

But our analysis of responsibility denial suggests that a sense of powerlessness is not the only source of a DR stance. Insofar as such a stance derives from role orientation, it may well characterize individuals who do not feel particularly powerless and who may in fact not be powerless: individuals who gain a sense of vicarious power from identification with the state and, in some cases, individuals who occupy powerful positions within the hierarchy. Role orientation may help account for the obedience and responsibility denial found among the high-status participants in crimes of obedience: among high-level functionaries, such as Adolf Eichmann, who saw himself as acting out of a sense of citizen duty and personal loyalty to the Führer (Arendt, 1964; von Lang, 1983); among high-level professionals, such as the doctors who played a central role in the Nazi killing projects (Lifton, 1986); and, in a very different time and context, among the high White House officials responsible for the Watergate scandal and the Iran-contra affair, who justified obedience by their overriding obligation to the president or commitment to a transcendent mission (see chapter 2). Role orientation is by no means restricted to the upper echelons; in fact, it is probably more characteristic of middle-level subordinates. But it broadens our view of responsibility denial by suggesting that such an orientation is not entirely or necessarily a product of powerlessness.

By identifying role orientation as a second potential source of responsibility denial, our analysis corrects for the inclination to treat unquestioning obedience as a lower-class phenomenon. We are *not* proposing that role orientation, in the general population, is associated with high social status. Our data do not support such a conclusion; rather, respondents high on our role orientation scale tended to be drawn from what can best be described as the petite bourgeoisie.[5] What we *are* proposing is that role orientation is not necessarily associated with low social status. Responsibility denial based on role orientation, therefore, suggests a different set of recommendations for counteracting the habit of unquestioning obedience than does responsibility denial based on rule orientation: recommendations that focus on how to deglamorize power, rather than how to overcome powerlessness, and that are directed at all levels of the organizational hierarchy and the social structure.

We have linked our third political orientation, value orientation, to responsibility assertion. Again, a focus on this potential basis for responsibility assertion, rather than on the AR stance as such, is likely to yield a broader and, from our point of view, more appropriate set of recommendations for breaking the habit of

5. Of course, the number of upper-echelon officials who are likely to be included in a representative sample of the Boston area is too small to affect the demographic profile of the role-oriented (or any other subgroup of) respondents.

unquestioning obedience. In our treatment of the different models of responsibility, we have been quite explicit about our own normative position. We have clearly preferred that subordinates take an AR, independent, stance—that they allocate responsibility on the basis of deeds and their consequences. We have also alluded, however (in chapters 9 and 10), to some possible normative limitations of the AR stance as it emerged from our two surveys.

One of the limitations of the AR perspective is that it represents a narrow, legalistic view of individual responsibility. AR respondents hold subordinates responsible for the direct and intended consequences of actions in which they are able to exercise some personal choice—using a criterion very similar to the standard requirement of mens rea in criminal prosecutions. Most ARs, however, do not expect individuals to take responsibility for government or military policies in which they participate and for the unintended consequences of such policies. Thus, they tend to differentiate between Calley's actions and the actions of a bombardier, because the killing of civilians in bombing raids, though clearly predictable, is unintentional. ARs as a group do not necessarily expect individuals to resist policies because they violate basic moral values. The AR stance is essentially a legalistic answer to a legalistic question: Should a particular subordinate be blamed? It answers that question without reference to larger policy issues or the broader legitimacy of the authority in the situation. We still prefer an AR stance toward obedience dilemmas over a DR stance because it rejects the idea that authorities must be obeyed without question under any and all circumstances. ARs expect subordinates to recognize and refuse illegitimate orders and do not allow them to transfer responsibility for their actions totally and automatically to the authorities. But the AR stance as such does not go beyond actions in response to specific orders that are "manifestly unlawful."

The relatively narrow focus of AR respondents on intended consequences of actions is also reflected in their attitude toward the responsibility of superiors. In their answers to questions about who should be tried for My Lai and about legal precedents, ARs showed reluctance to invoke a superior's command responsibility for unintended consequences. In the Boston survey, ARs tended to shift down the chain of command in assessing responsibility: They assigned more than average responsibility to Calley and his men, presumably because they directly and intentionally caused the killings, and less than average to top officials, presumably because they were not directly involved in the My Lai actions. These findings point to another normative ambiguity of an AR stance. It can be argued that to advocate an AR position regarding responsibility is self-serving for members of the elite groups in a society, just as advocacy of a DR position may be self-serving for those who are typically in subordinate positions. After all, members of higher-status groups are more likely themselves to be authorities in obedience dilemmas or to identify with the authorities. Therefore an AR orientation takes them personally off the hook by shifting blame to subordinates. This class-related bias in the AR stance would be less problematic if the authority of subordinates themselves were enhanced, as we shall recommend below. Under such circumstances, subordinates would have a realistic basis for seeing responsibility as authorities see it and there would be little normative ambiguity in encouraging them to adopt an AR model. Under present circumstances, however, one cannot ignore the possibility that an AR orientation may serve the interests of higher-status groups at the expense of those in lower-status positions.

These normative ambiguities are considerably reduced when one focuses on value orientation as a basis of responsibility assertion, rather than on the AR stance itself. Value orientation is not as susceptible as the AR position to the charge of reflecting a self-serving bias among high-status groups. To be value-oriented means to hold individuals at all levels of the hierarchy, not only lower-level subordinates, responsible for the consequences of actions and of the policies that guide these actions. Furthermore, value orientation is not subject to the criticism of narrow legalism that may be leveled against the AR view of responsibility. It is consistent, for example, with such broader challenges to authority as civil disobedience; indeed, we have argued that it is likely to foster such challenges. Of course, there is no necessary contradiction between taking an AR position vis-à-vis a particular subordinate—for example, insisting that Lieutenant Calley should have been convicted for what he did—and also making independent critical judgments of the broader authority structure—for example, concluding that the Vietnam War was wrong and should have been resisted long before My Lai occurred. These are simply different moral judgments about situations that generate crimes of obedience; the judgments refer to authority at different policy levels and may each reflect an orientation to political authority in terms of personal values.

POLITICAL ORIENTATIONS AND RESPONSES TO BINDING AND OPPOSING FORCES

We have proposed that analysis of different approaches to responsibility in authority situations has important implications for efforts to counteract the habit of unquestioning obedience. We further argued that such an analysis is likely to be most productive if we focus on the political orientations that may underlie assertion and denial of responsibility. How do these political orientations affect individuals' views of responsibility or their actual behavior when they must choose between obeying and disobeying a potentially illegitimate order? We propose that one way to address this question is to consider the relationship of political orientation to the binding and opposing forces that individuals encounter in such situations. The effect of rule as well as role orientation is to increase the impact of the binding forces. The stronger these orientations, the more likely people are to feel that they have no choice—that they are compelled or obligated to obey—and hence to deny personal responsibility for their obedient response. The effect of value orientation is to increase the impact of opposing forces. The stronger this orientation, the more likely people are to assert responsibility and to disobey.

In our effort, therefore, to map out some broad strategies for reducing the prevalence of crimes of obedience, we shall ask: How can one counteract the elements of rule and role orientation, respectively, that make people particularly sensitive to the binding forces in authority situations—that is, subject to the effects of authorization—and thus more inclined to deny responsibility and to obey without question? Conversely, how can one enhance the elements of value orientation that make people sensitive to opposing forces—that is, resistant to the effects of routinization and dehumanization—and thus more inclined to assert responsibility and to disobey unlawful and immoral orders?

Before turning to our recommendations for changing responses to authority, we need to introduce some qualifications about the nature of the three political orientations and of their relationship to binding and opposing forces. Throughout the book we have often treated the orientations as ideal types—as if three pure forms of relationship to political authority could be observed and as if individuals could be reliably distinguished on this basis. We have stressed, however, that it is in fact rare for an individual to be oriented to authority solely in one of these ways; typically individuals respond differently across situations and may even manifest more than one orientation in a given situation. Thus, it would be more accurate to conceive of the orientations as dimensions of individual attitudes rather than as typifications of individuals. This more precise formulation still treats the orientations as dispositions that individuals bring to authority situations and that account for individual differences in reaction to situational forces. The orientations can also be thought of, however, as dimensions of individual action: as situationally induced ways of responding. A particular set of structural arrangements and situational forces may be conducive to one or another orientation. Of course, insofar as individuals are exposed to that set of structural and situational conditions over time and on a regular basis, the resulting orientation will take on a dispositional character.

If we view the orientations as both dispositional and situationally induced, then their relationship to binding and opposing forces becomes reciprocal. On the one hand, political orientation may affect individuals' sensitivity to various binding and opposing forces and hence the impact these situational forces have on their response to authority. On the other hand, the binding and opposing forces in a particular situation may affect the strength of the rule, role, or value orientation that is generated in that situation and hence the nature of the individual's response. The reciprocal relationship between political orientations and situational forces is reflected in the recommendations for changing responses to authority to which we devote the remainder of this chapter.

Promoting Personal Responsibility and Independent Judgment in Authority Situations

We shall try to identify some of the broad changes in social structures, in patterns of political participation, in foci for political socialization and civic education, and in collective support systems that might reduce the tendency to respond in rule- and role-oriented fashion to illegitimate orders and enhance the tendency to respond in value-oriented fashion. We shall organize our recommendations into ways of (1) reducing the impact of binding forces by counteracting the effects of rule and role orientation, respectively, and (2) enhancing the impact of opposing forces by buttressing the effects of value orientation. The analysis will thus tend to focus on the orientations as dispositions that affect reaction to situational forces. But, in fact, many of our recommendations shall refer to changes in the situations in which individuals face authority or in the broader social structure. Such changes, in effect, are addressed directly to binding and opposing forces, which in turn may affect political orientations as dimensions of individual action and attitude. In short, we shall be proposing strategies for altering the relative strength of value-oriented versus rule- and role-oriented responses to questionable orders, and the relative strength of opposing versus binding forces in authority situations, whatever may be the causal relationship between these two sets of variables.

REDUCING THE IMPACT OF BINDING FORCES

Binding forces are those elements of the situation that psychologically tie the individual to the authority's definition of the situation. As we noted in chapter 6, binding forces are strengthened by such situational factors as direct surveillance by the authority, salience of the consequences of disobedience (in the form of punishment or embarrassment), existence of a clearly articulated hierarchical structure, presence of authority symbols, and observation of the obedience of comparable others. Both rule and role orientations have the effect of enhancing the impact of certain of those binding forces and thus holding the individual to the authority's definition of the situation.

Rule orientation increases sensitivity to binding forces out of a sense of powerlessness, whereas role orientation increases such sensitivity out of a sense of obligation. The more rule-oriented people are, the less they see themselves as having the *capacity* to challenge the authority's definition of the situation; the more role-oriented they are, the more they are caught up in the authority's definition of the situation and hence the less their perceived *right* or, indeed, their *will* to challenge that definition. Thus each orientation, for its own reason, leads to an impairment of critical judgment, a denial of personal responsibility, and a tendency to act without question according to the authority's definition of the situation. To counteract the binding effects of rule orientation, which derive from the sense of powerlessness, it is necessary to *reduce* individual citizens' distance from authority, so that they will be more familiar with it and feel more capable of judging its demands. In contrast, to counteract the binding effects of role orientation, which derive from entrapment in the authority's framework, it is necessary to *increase* citizens' distance from authority, so that they will be able to bring an independent perspective to bear on its demands.

Rule Orientation. Counteracting the effects of actual and felt powerlessness vis-à-vis authority, which characterizes rule orientation, calls for changes in social structures, educational experiences, and group supports that will contribute to the *empowerment* of individual citizens and enhance their sense of personal *efficacy*. Empowerment means having the opportunity and the right to make decisions about one's own life and to participate in decision making on public issues. Efficacy means possessing the skills, the knowledge, the material resources, and the social supports that enhance people's ability to determine their own fates and to influence public policy. The two are likely to be correlated: Empowerment increases the skills and other resources required for effective action and undoubtedly contributes to a sense of personal and political efficacy; efficacy in turn increases ability to grasp opportunities and to insist on rights to participate in decision making. Empowerment and efficacy can be linked, respectively, to the two sources of the right to command on which modern authorities typically draw: bureaucratic authority, which is based on position in the hierarchy and the coercive power associated with it, and professional authority, which is based on expertise and competence. Thus, empowerment and enhanced efficacy bring citizens closer to authority in the sense that they themselves acquire some of the elements of authority, which they can turn into means for challenging authoritative demands.

Structural changes most conducive to the empowerment and enhanced efficacy of citizens would involve the *dispersion of authority* within the society. We need to invent ways of providing for as many citizens as possible, across the entire spectrum, the opportunity to enact authority roles at some time in their lives, in some areas of their lives. In the long run, dispersion of authority implies increasing decentralization of political and economic institutions. But even within our present institutions, authority functions can be distributed more widely. In work organizations, for example, it is often possible to break down the strict hierarchical structure of the production effort into smaller, semi-independent units, thus making a larger number of authority positions available. Moreover, individuals who occupy subordinate positions in the production effort itself may be encouraged to take leadership roles in nonproduction activities, such as committees focusing on employee grievances, mutual aid, or social events. Outside of the workplace, deliberate efforts can be made by community groups, religious associations, voluntary organizations, and the like, to provide leadership roles for those who do not exercise authority in the occupational sphere—in contrast to the prevailing tendency of conferring authority on those who already exercise it elsewhere. Finally, the regular and relatively frequent rotation of leadership roles in all organizations would also contribute to the dispersion of authority.

We stress dispersion of authority because we believe personal experience in authority roles often has a liberating effect on individuals' relationship to others in that role. Those who are in authority roles in some area of their lives, or who have been in such roles, or who can realistically aspire to such roles, are more likely to take an independent stance toward authoritative orders. Moreover, with greater dispersion of authority within the society, even those individuals who do not themselves have an opportunity to enact authority roles would be more likely to know others—people like themselves, from their own circle of personal acquaintances—who are or have been in authority positions. They would thus also have greater access to authorities and opportunity to influence them. Such direct or indirect familiarity with authority would help reduce the distance between citizens and authority and make individuals feel more capable of judging and criticizing an authority's demands and interpretations. It would have the effect of demystifying authority in the sense of depriving it of its veil of mystery. Those who are relatively close to authority, and in particular those who have learned how to exercise authority themselves, are less likely to feel that the processes by which authorities arrive at their decisions and the knowledge and wisdom they bring to bear on these decisions are so mysterious that average citizens cannot penetrate them. They are less likely to feel overwhelmed and incapacitated in the face of authoritative demands. They can imagine themselves in the position of the authority and are thus aware of the ambiguities within which authorities operate and the inevitable fallibility of authoritative decisions. They know that, like themselves, authorities can be wrong.

People who have experience in authority positions or who are otherwise closer to authority can more easily come to view it as a role rather than as part of the essence of the person who happens to exercise it. In the normal course of events, they are likely to respect the authority and be prepared to obey its demands in fulfillment of their part of the social contract that defines the relationship between citizens and authorities. They are inclined to give the authority the benefit of the doubt because they view the presumption of legitimacy of authorities and their demands as necessary to the reliable, effective, and equitable functioning of societies and organizations. At the same time they feel that they themselves could be in the authority role—perhaps not in the particular situation because they lack some of the specific skills required, but certainly in other situations. Under the circumstances, they feel qualified to judge the authority's performance of the role and to evaluate, question, and if necessary challenge its definition of what is required.[6]

Dispersion of authority, then, might contribute significantly to the empowerment of citizens and enhancement of their efficacy, making them less susceptible to the binding effects of rule orientation in authority situations. Even under the best of circumstances, however, there are limits to the number of citizens who can occupy positions of political authority or community leadership. On the other hand, virtually every citizen can have an opportunity at least to share in some of the functions of authority through *participation in political decision making* at different levels. Even the most minimal form of participation in a democratic system, voting in the election of political officers, contributes to the empowerment of citizens and begins to narrow the gap between them and the authorities by underlining the principle that authorities rule by the consent of the governed. As the level of participation increases—as citizens take more active part, for ex-

6. The distinction between the role of authority and the person who enacts that role facilitates an evaluative stance for at least two reasons. First, as noted in the text, it encourages citizens to think of themselves as potential authorities and thus makes them more aware of the fallibility of authorities' judgments. Second, it reminds them that authorities also function as partisans (see Gamson, 1968, pp. 28–31), and insofar as they do, citizens are not obligated to accede to their demands.

ample, in selecting candidates for office, in debating issues, in making their views known to authorities (particularly through collective channels)—the gap between citizens and authorities is further closed.

Experience in various forms of direct or participatory democracy, even at lower levels of political organization such as the county or municipality, is especially conducive to empowerment and enhanced efficacy. Such participation may range from preparing, debating, and voting in referenda to active involvement in town meetings or popular assemblies. These various forms of participation in decision making within a particular authority context reduce the binding effects of authority and hence the tendency to respond in rule-oriented fashion in that situation. Widespread participation in different contexts, over time, should have the effect of reducing the disposition to respond in rule-oriented fashion to authority in general and thus attenuating the impact of binding forces in any given authority situation. Empowerment and the sense of efficacy are likely to be enhanced by active participation in authority functions, not only in the political sphere, but also in other areas of life—such as the workplace, the community, and even social research (see Kelman, 1972, for a discussion of participatory research). In short, the experience of participating in decision making should have an effect similar to, if less pronounced than, the effect of experience in authority roles themselves: It reduces citizens' distance from authority and thus contributes to their capacity to evaluate, question, and challenge authoritative policies and demands.

General capacity to challenge authority is increased by specific training for the enactment of authority roles and for participation in decision making in the course of an individual's socialization and education. Such training includes both cognitive and experiential components: the development of expectations that one will hold authority and actively participate in decision making, and the opportunity to experiment with gradually increasing degrees of authority and with making consequential personal and group decisions.

To a certain degree, education per se promotes the empowerment and enhanced efficacy of individuals. The negative correlation we found between educational attainment and scores on our rule (as well as role) orientation scale is consistent with this proposition. The effect is probably due in part to the role of higher education in channeling people into positions in society that involve greater levels of authority and decision-making power and preparing them for such positions. Education contributes to both the expectations and the opportunities of occupying such positions. Moreover, it provides the knowledge and skills that enhance the sense of efficacy so essential to the readiness to evaluate authoritative demands. More specifically, education expands individuals' knowledge of the contents and requirements of authority positions and, for that reason alone, enhances their perceived efficacy in dealing with occupants of such positions.[7] In sum,

---

7. A similar logic underlies the practice in some industries of acquainting workers with the jobs of other workers. The Japanese auto industry, for example, is noted for its tendency to train individuals to be generalists rather than specialists (see Cole, 1979).

education reduces the distance between citizens and authorities and helps demystify authority, both by making the authority role more familiar and accessible and by providing the tools for evaluating authority actions. Dispersion of education throughout all segments of society is thus one significant way of countering the tendency toward rule orientation in relation to authority and the widespread incapacity to challenge authority. It is also important, in this connection, to make the specific knowledge and skills that may be required to question and challenge authority demands more widely available across the society. These include, among others, legal skills, skills in community organizing, and skills in the conduct and evaluation of social research (see Kelman, 1972, for a discussion of the democratization of the research community).

Apart from increasing access to education in general and to the specific domains of knowledge and skills required to relate to authorities with a degree of independence, social change efforts must be directed to developing patterns of political socialization and civic education that are deliberately geared to empowering individuals and making them more efficacious. Both the content and process of political socialization and civic education can be designed to enhance individuals' capacity for challenging authority and to provide them with the tools for bringing independent judgment to bear on an authority's demands. Examples of educational programs directed to this end are some of the curriculum materials that have recently been developed to help students deal with the threat of nuclear war (Hemphill, 1985). In their discussion of one such curriculum at the senior high school level, *Decision Making in a Nuclear Age*, Snow and Goodman (1985) describe its purpose as empowering students by helping them confront the reality of the nuclear problem, combat their sense of powerlessness and helplessness, acquire the information necessary to their becoming active participants in the search for solutions, and explore the meaning of active citizen involvement in social change. The curriculum tries to organize the classroom itself in such a way as to foster direct student participation in decision making. Achievement of this goal depends, however, on counteracting the effects of the overall structure of the school, which may well encourage a passive attitude toward authority and an avoidance of initiative (Wilson, 1985).

Another and particularly exciting example of an educational model geared to empowerment is Paulo Freire's "pedagogy of the oppressed" (1971) or "education for critical consciousness" (1973). The prototype of his approach to adult education is a literacy training program that he and his colleagues developed for peasants in northeast Brazil. The content and process of the literacy training itself, and the group discussions in which it was embedded, were designed to encourage a critical attitude among the students at the same time as they were taught to read. Acquiring literacy became part of a process of *conscientização*, in which the participants learned to reflect on themselves and on their condition, developed critical awareness and an increased capacity for choice, and began to see themselves as active agents with a role in transforming the world. Although Freire's specific techniques were obviously designed for literacy training among an isolated, impoverished, rural population, their underlying philosophy is relevant to any educational effort aimed at counteracting passive acquiescence and unquestioning obedience to authority rooted in a sense of powerlessness.

A critical feature of any empowerment effort—whether it takes the form of educational programs, such as those pioneered by Freire, or of community organizing, or of the expansion of participatory democracy—is that it joins individuals in a collective enterprise. Membership in such an enterprise enhances individuals' feeling that they have a right to participate in decisions that affect their lives and that they have the capacity to take effective action. Moreover, the collectivity is a source of support and power that enables individuals to take a more independent stance in judging and, if necessary, challenging authoritative demands. As we pointed out in chapter 6, one of the most important factors in reducing the impact of binding forces in an authority situation is the opportunity to face authority as part of a group whose members can engage in direct communication and collective action. The backing of a collectivity can help overcome individuals' tendency to obey out of a sense of powerlessness because it reinforces their belief that a challenge to authority is feasible, it allows them to share the burden of disrupting the social order, it reduces the risks of stigmatization and punishment as a consequence of their disobedience, and it promises group support in dealing with whatever negative consequences they do incur. Thus, to reduce the impact of binding forces that arise from and give rise to rule orientation, it is necessary to develop groups and associations that are able, through collective action, to empower individuals in their challenges to unjust authority.

We have been referring so far to groups organized by individuals who share a common set of beliefs and interests that induce them to challenge a particular policy or disobey a particular demand and who join together for collective action and mutual aid. There is also a need to establish and strengthen specialized organizations that can provide some of the resources essential to individuals who challenge authorities or have to deal with the consequences of such challenges: legal aid, financial aid, counseling, political support, pressure on administrative agencies, mobilization of public support. Obvious examples are such organizations as Amnesty International, the American Civil Liberties Union, or the Central Committee for Conscientious Objectors—groups that seek to protect the rights of political dissidents, of war resisters, and others who run afoul of authorities because of their principled opposition to certain policies or practices. We also have in mind organizations established to protect the rights of individuals and groups whose condition of disadvantage—based, for example, on minority group membership, gender, age, disability, mental illness, poverty, alien status, or deviant life-style—makes them both more subject to discriminatory treatment by authorities and less capable of effectively challenging such treatment.

Role Orientation. We have proposed that the increased sensitivity to the binding forces in authority situations that is due to a role orientation arises not from a sense of powerlessness but from a sense of obligation. The role-oriented do not necessarily lack the capacity to challenge authority, but they lack the will to do so; the role of the good citizen or of the loyal subordinate does not, in their view, entitle them to question authority's orders. Role orientation represents an identification with authority that derives from individuals' attraction to the authority's mystique and allows them to share vicariously in the authority's power. As a result of this identification, individuals become entrapped in the authority's perspective and find it exceedingly difficult to extricate themselves from its definition of the situation.[8]

For most role-oriented citizens the sharing of power is largely vicarious. Role orientation, however, may also be manifested by individuals who are close to the sources of power or are even themselves in powerful positions within political or other hierarchies. Such individuals, as we noted in the discussion of several of the cases presented in chapter 2, may obey without question and often with enthusiasm to the point of committing crimes of obedience. Their sense of obligation to obey may be linked to an overriding loyalty to their leader or to commitment to a transcendent mission in which they see themselves as active partners. From their positions at or near the center of power, they too may be caught in the authority's mystique and entrapped by the authority's perspective.

To counteract the effects of entrapment by the authority's perspective, which characterizes role orientation, requires changes in social structures, educational experiences, and group supports that will ensure citizens and subordinates in bureaucratic hierarchies regular access to *multiple perspectives*, external to and independent from the authority. Exposure to alternative perspectives helps individuals increase their psychological distance from authority, thus enabling them to evaluate its demands with a greater degree of independence and, on occasion, to recognize obligations to disobey rather than obey such demands. Both empowerment and access to multiple perspectives have the effect of encouraging independent judgment in relation to authority. Empowerment does so by bringing individuals closer to authority in the sense of familiarizing them with the authority role and enabling them to think and feel more like authorities, thus enhancing their capacity to judge and challenge authority's demands. Exposure to multiple perspectives does so by distancing individuals from authority in the sense of enabling them to judge its demands from alternative standpoints, thus enhancing their capacity to make an independent choice in responding to these demands. Independent judgment requires both being close enough to authority to know what one is judging and removed enough to know that there are alternative bases from which judgments can be made. In sum, access to external alternative perspectives can counteract the binding forces that individuals may experience in authority situations by being excessively identified with authority and caught up in its definition of the situation.

8. Insofar as role orientation represents a lack of will to challenge authority, it is reminiscent of what Étienne de La Boétie (1574/1975) long ago described as voluntary servitude. La Boétie offers colorful descriptions of the ways in which the masses as well as the "tyrant's" retinue become entrapped in extending him their willing and often enthusiastic support. La Boétie's *Discourse*, however, does not explicitly postulate a sense of obligation as the driving force behind the voluntary servitude he observes.

Access to multiple perspectives, like empowerment, contributes to demystification of authority, though in a different sense. Whereas empowerment, as we argued above, helps deprive authority of some of its *mystery*, exposure to diverse perspectives deprives it of some of its *mystique:* its special aura of sanctity and transcendent value. It removes authority's actions and demands from a category beyond normal processes of evaluation and criteria of morality, and underlines the possibility of subjecting them to alternative, independent, critical standards.

Structural changes that would help reduce entrapment in the authority's definition of the situation involve the invention and institutionalization of mechanisms for bringing diverse perspectives to bear on the policy process. Such mechanisms can be seen most clearly in the context of face-to-face decision-making groups. Some of the tactics suggested by Irving Janis (1972) for reducing the tendency toward "groupthink" in policy-making bodies seem relevant here since they are designed to increase members' exposure to alternative perspectives. One set of recommendations would essentially assign members to roles that require them to take an independent perspective on the issue under consideration. In this vein, Janis proposes that "the leader of a policy-forming group should assign the role of critical evaluator to each member, encouraging the group to give high priority to airing objections and doubts" (p. 209); that "at every meeting devoted to evaluating policy alternatives, at least one member should be assigned the role of devil's advocate" (p. 215); and that after reaching a preliminary consensus, groups hold "second chance" meetings "at which every member is expected to express . . . residual doubts and to rethink the entire issue before making a definitive choice" (p. 218).

Another set of recommendations offered by Janis (1972) to counteract groupthink would introduce alternative perspectives by breaking down the boundaries of the group so as to offset its monolithic character and its insulation. Thus, he proposes that several independent policy-planning and evaluation groups be set up within the organization "to work on the same policy question, each carrying out its deliberations under a different leader" (p. 211); that "the policy-making group should from time to time divide into two or more subgroups," each meeting separately with its own chair (p. 213); that each member should periodically discuss the group's deliberations with trusted others outside of the group and bring back their reactions; and that outsiders should be invited to meetings of the policy-making group and be "encouraged to challenge the views of the core members" (p. 214).

Adoption of recommendations such as these may well reduce the probability of crimes of obedience that occur near the top of bureaucratic hierarchies, where policy is being shaped. Structural changes in the form of institutionalizing roles that require an independent perspective and breaking down the boundaries of monolithic, insulated groups can also be introduced, however, in the relationship of ordinary citizens to political authorities. Such changes would be tantamount to a redefinition of the citizen role—of what it means to be a "good citizen"—that would make people less susceptible to the binding forces that arise from and give rise to role orientation.

One necessary element in the redefinition of the citizen role suggested by our analysis is an emphasis on *dissent* not merely as a right of citizens that a democratic society must tolerate and protect but as an obligation of citizenship. To this end, it becomes important to strengthen norms that prescribe dissent—on occasion to the point of civil disobedience—when citizens are confronted with policies and orders that, from their independent perspective, they find illegal or immoral. In effect we are proposing that the prophetic function be incorporated into the role of the general citizen—a modern version of the wish expressed by Moses, "Would that all the Lord's people were prophets" (Numbers 11:29). Dissent performs the vital function of reminding people that the authority's definition of the situation may not be the only possible definition—of breaking down the authority's monopoly on determining reality. Dissent can thus counteract the binding force of an apparently unanimous consensus. By increasing people's awareness that opposing views exist within the society and may even be widespread, dissent helps overcome a state of "pluralistic ignorance," in which each individual considers "deviant" what is in fact a common or majority position. Alternative perspectives are least available in situations in which they are most needed: situations viewed as national crises that can easily become the breeding ground for disastrous policy decisions and crimes of obedience. Such situations tend to be governed by norms that strongly discourage dissent, treating it as an act of disloyalty that breaks national unity and resolve. This is precisely the context in which norms supportive of dissent as an obligation of loyal citizens must be asserted.

But what is the source of the alternative perspectives that make dissent possible? We have argued that challenges to an authority's demands generally require recourse to a "higher authority," or at least to an authority of equal status, that makes countervailing demands. This requirement suggests a second element in the redefinition of the citizen role that would increase access to alternative perspectives and help counteract entrapment in the authority's definition of the situation. Instead of being equated with exclusive allegiance to a monolithic, insulated state, good citizenship ought to be defined as fully compatible with allegiance to multiple authorities within and outside of the state. Although these alternative authorities hold sway in different domains, they can act as constraints on the power of the state. Thus, whenever citizens are confronted with demands from political authorities, these countervailing sources of authority can potentially provide alternative interpretations of the demands' legitimacy.

The idea of multiple authority is by no means novel. At the macrolevel, the principle of separation of powers between the executive, legislative, and judicial branches of the U.S. government creates checks and balances that reduce the sweep of authority of any particular branch (Kadish and Kadish, 1973). This arrangement ensures that, within the polity at large, important issues can be considered from different perspectives, representing authorities with independent and more or less equal status. In the relationship of the individual citizen to political authority, we have noted—on the basis of our own data and a variety of historical experiences—that religion is often a source of an alternative perspective based on countervailing authority. What we are proposing now goes further in incorporating the idea of multiple authority in the definition of the citizen role itself.

Our view of the citizen role is very similar to Walzer's (1970) description of the pluralist citizen. For pluralist citizens, the state is the largest or most inclusive group to which they have obligations, but it is not the only one. They have "other responsibilities, for there is no way to be a responsible citizen except to have more than one responsibility" (p. 221). It is in fact through participation in groups other than the state—such as religious organizations, labor unions, or political parties—that citizens govern themselves most actively and have a role in determining state policy. But this kind of pluralist participation has the inevitable consequence of creating, in our terms, a condition of multiple authority. "For if the business of the 'lesser' groups is not trivial, then . . . the [state] authorities . . . will lose their distinction: they will be challenged by a multitude of 'lesser' authorities 'dutifully discharging their public functions'" (p. 221). Most of the time, the pluralist citizen is not only a good citizen but an exemplary one. Indeed, citizenship as a moral choice becomes possible only by virtue of membership in groups other than the state. But if the authorities pursue policies of which they disapprove, pluralist citizens are more likely to disobey. "They are committed to 'business of a public character,' but not always the same piece of business or kind of business as are the authorities" (p. 222).

The redefinition of the citizen role that we have been proposing has direct implications for patterns of political participation that can help reduce the impact of binding forces linked to role orientation. Active participation in decision-making functions, which we stressed as a source of empowerment to counteract the effects of rule orientation, remains essential. Beyond the *scope* of participation, however, the *quality* of this participation becomes critical. Citizens must have opportunities to participate not only in carrying out government policies but also in the formulation and particularly in the evaluation of such policies—evaluation on the basis of independent criteria derived from a variety of perspectives. Such participation is more readily available to citizens through the various groups within the state—as well as groups cutting across national lines—to which they might belong. Insofar as participation in public affairs takes place in such a pluralistic context, there is greater assurance that alternative perspectives will be brought to bear on the evaluation of policy—provided, of course, that these groups do not merely function as subgroups of the state but approach state action from an independent vantage point.

Entrapment in the authority's mystique and perspective becomes less likely if individuals are systematically exposed to multiple perspectives in the course of their socialization and education, and are trained to subject authority's policies and actions to independent evaluation. To this end, it is important to include competence in making judgments and developing appropriate criteria for such judgments—including standards of morality—as a central component of citizenship education (Remy and Turner, 1979). It is also essential to assign a central role in citizenship education to the development of a global perspective (Remy, 1977), which can provide a corrective to the nationalist or ethnocentric view that so often prompts people to acquiesce in crimes of obedience.

The civic education programs that we cited earlier to illustrate the possibilities of empowerment are also designed to expose students to multiple perspectives. Thus, Snow and Goodman (1985) describe the curriculum for *Decision Making in a Nuclear Age* as a multiperspective approach. Students are encouraged to consider conflicting viewpoints carefully, to examine them critically, and to develop their own perspective out of the various viewpoints to which they have been exposed. Freire's (1971, 1973) educational model encourages his adult students to develop a critical awareness of the system that oppresses them and to recognize the possibility of alternative perspectives on their condition. They thus become better able to redefine their own relationship to authority and to see themselves as active, independent agents.

Finally, collective supports are important in reducing the impact of binding forces linked to role orientation, just as they are in overcoming the effects of rule orientation. Confronting authority with the backing of a group not only counteracts the sense of powerlessness by enabling individuals to share the burdens and risks of disobedience but also helps them extricate themselves from the authority's definition of the situation. Groups can provide individuals the alternative perspective they need if they are to decide that an authority's demand is illegitimate and redefine their obligations accordingly. Membership in groups other than the state, as we noted in the discussion of the pluralist citizen, is generally also the source of the countervailing obligation to disobey an authoritative demand that is deemed illegitimate. Thus, civil disobedience is typically a collective action. The collectivity helps create the obligations and provide the supports that make disobedience necessary and possible; and it is through collective processes that an authority situation comes to be redefined as one in which the usual norm of obedience no longer applies (see also Gamson et al., 1982; Walzer, 1970).

ENHANCING THE IMPACT OF OPPOSING FORCES

The essence of value orientation is independent judgment in the face of authority's orders. Indeed, our data suggest that high value orientation is associated with a disposition to disobey illegitimate orders and to condemn others who obey such orders. We have suggested that to a large extent value orientation may represent the inverse of rule and role orientations. Thus the recommendations we have made for reducing the impact of binding forces based on these orientations should by the same token contribute to the strength of value orientation. Insofar as empowerment and enhanced efficacy counteract the sense of powerlessness, and insofar as access to multiple perspectives counteracts entrapment in the authority's mystique and definition of reality, individuals become more capable of evaluating authority's policies and demands from an independent perspective rooted in their personal values.

It should also be clear that everything we have written about the importance of group supports in reducing the impact of binding forces linked to rule and role orientation applies directly to the strengthening of value orientation. Value orientation may sound highly individualistic in that it refers to independent judgment based on personal values. Such personal values, however, are almost invariably shared within a collectivity. It is the shared character of the values that gives an individual the sense of obligation, the standing, and the courage to act on them. Civil disobedience, for example, which is a quintessentially value-oriented action, is typically carried out in, by, and for groups. Collective processes of reframing the situation provide the basis for an individual's civil disobedience, by declaring the authority's policies and demands to be out of keeping with fundamental values. Collective support makes it possible for individuals to bear the material and psychological costs of acting on their values and increases the likelihood that such action will have an impact on the policy process. Revolt against a legal system, the extreme example of disobedience to the unjust, is an obviously collective process that also has a foundation in values (see Moore, 1978). As the anonymous motto on Thomas Jefferson's seal suggests, "Rebellion to tyrants is obedience to God." In our perspective, "rebellion to tyrants" bears a direct relationship to individual resistance to authoritative orders; and "obedience to God" can be phrased, more generally, as adherence to what the individual holds most valuable and most sacred. Thus the beliefs and values of a citizenry, although they exist in individuals, are anchored in groups, and threats to those values are likely to be met by groups.

In sum, group supports—as well as structural arrangements, patterns of political participation, and forms of civic education—that reduce the *binding* effect of authority strengthen, by that very fact, the readiness to challenge authority from an independent value base. But value-based resistance to illegitimate authority may also emerge from the relationship between value orientation and the *opposing* forces in authority situations. Opposing forces to destructive obedience are likely to arise insofar as the individual's personal values and moral standards are activated in the situation. Value orientation has the effect of sensitizing people to these opposing forces and thus enhancing their impact. Any steps that strengthen value orientation, therefore, should increase people's readiness to accept personal responsibility and to disobey when they are ordered to perform actions that they find legally questionable or morally repugnant.

In the recommendations that follow, we focus on the development and buttressing of social norms, societal practices, and situational cues that would increase sensitivity to opposing forces linked to moral values. Changes in social structures, educational experiences, and group supports need to be designed to counteract the tendency to suspend independent judgment that is so commonly found in authority situations. Put more generally, mindlessness in response to authority needs to be replaced by mindfulness—by heightened awareness, active information processing, and attention to multiple perspectives (see Langer, 1988, for a recent statement of this distinction). Sensitivity to opposing forces would be enhanced by individuals' mindful attention to the actor, to the action, and to the target of the action—that is, to themselves as responsible agents, to the meaning of the act they have been ordered to perform, and to its human consequences. For each of these foci of attention, we shall point to some of the cognitive and motivational factors that prevent activation of opposing forces and offer recommendations for overcoming their effects.

The Actor: Personal Agency. Opposing forces in response to destructive orders are likely to arise to the extent that individuals perceive themselves as personally causing harmful outcomes. The very nature of the authorization process, however, as we have seen throughout this book, is to create a sense of diminished agency in many subordinates. They often deny personal responsibility for actions taken under orders. Although it is clear that they physically carry out the act, they divorce themselves from it psychologically; they do not see themselves as causal agents. The sense of diminished agency is reinforced by the diffusion of responsibility that characterizes authority hierarchies (see chapter 8) and many other group situations (see Latané and Darley, 1970; Latané, 1981). Another psychological process that may manifest itself when people act in groups is deindividuation (for example, Zimbardo, 1970): a reduction in awareness of the self as an independent actor and hence as a personal cause of the outcome produced. The division of labor in bureaucratic organizations also makes it easier for functionaries to dissociate their own contributory act from the final outcome.

Within a given bureaucratic hierarchy, the sense of diminished agency can be countered by mechanisms that heighten individuals' attention to themselves as responsible actors. Thus, the practice of displacing responsibility up or down the hierarchy might be reduced by mechanisms of accountability that spell out the expectations associated with each position and hold individuals to them. The effects of diffusion of responsibility might be countered by keeping careful track of each individual's role in producing the organizational outcome. The effects of deindividuation can be reduced by maintaining group members' salience to themselves as separate individuals—differentiable, for example, by their dress or hairstyle, as well as by their interests and ways of thinking.

In the relationship of citizens to political authorities, as well as in the relationship of subordinates to their organizational superiors, personal agency is likely to be enhanced by the changes we recommended above in our discussion of rule and role orientations. People who feel empowered and efficacious, who have learned to judge authority from independent alternative perspectives, and who participate in public decision making from a pluralistic base are inclined to see themselves as responsible agents. As such, they are not only less immobilized by the binding forces of authority situations but also more responsive to the opposing forces generated by illegal or immoral orders.

The Action: Meaning and Context. Opposing forces to potential crimes of obedience are likely to arise to the extent that individuals are mindful of the nature and precise meaning of the action they are asked to perform and of the larger project to which this action contributes. The process of routinization, however, which is particularly prevalent in bureaucratic settings, makes it unnecessary to contemplate the meaning of the action or to attend to its implications (see chapters 1 and 6). Fragmentation of the task into small steps, routinely performed, makes it easier for actors to ignore the final product, just as division of labor enables them to forget their own contribution to that product. Moreover, the integration of criminal activities into the normal, everyday operations of the organization helps divert attention from their true meaning. Even at high levels of an organizational hierarchy, actions demanded by the top leader may become routinized when officials are entrapped by a sense of overriding loyalty to the leadership and obligation to carry out its programs. Such officials do make decisions, but these tend to be almost entirely operational, focusing on how to carry out a given action rather than on whether to carry it out. The decision to perform the assignment is automatic; no alternative definition of the situation is ever entertained. Obligation to the leader overrides all other considerations, including any moral scruples or value commitments that might otherwise play a role. Questions about the meaning and purpose of the action simply do not arise.

The total elimination of routine is an unrealistic goal, since the existence and flowering of bureaucracy is predicated upon routinization. It should be possible, however, even in military bureaucracies, to delimit the tasks that are carried out in routine fashion: to distinguish between those that do and do not require a regimented routine and confine routinized activity to a carefully demarcated sphere. Moreover, even this categorization of tasks can be subjected to periodic reviews, which would help maintain awareness of those domains that are governed by routine and in which, therefore, questions of meaning are probably not being raised and moral choices not being made. In decision-making units, the tendency to succumb to overriding obligations to the leader can be avoided by following some of Janis's (1972) recommendations, discussed above, for counteracting groupthink. These procedures represent systematic ways of introducing alternative perspectives and thus reduce the likelihood that a single definiton of the situation will automatically prevail.

At the societal level, it is possible to develop and reiterate norms against the routine treatment of acts of violence and cruelty and violations of human rights. Failure to challenge such acts and a tendency to react to them matter-of-factly or even approvingly contribute to their normalization and legitimization within the society. The cumulative effect of such incidents is to encourage people to view orders to perform similar acts as legitimate and to obey such orders routinely. For example, research on aggression suggests that observation of sanctioned violence has a desensitizing and disinhibiting effect (Bandura, 1973). And messages that violence is normal and legitimate abound in our society and throughout the world—in military policies and strategic thinking, in security operations, in gun lobby campaigns, and in media presentations, to give just a few illustrations (Kelman, 1973). Corrective efforts might take the form of systematically reminding the public, whenever acts of violence or violations of human rights manifest themselves, that such acts are not normal and socially acceptable. Such reminders, institutionalized through watchdog organizations and embedded in educational programs at all levels, can help build social norms and moral sensitivities that would activate opposing forces in situations with the potential for crimes of obedience.

The Target: Human Consequences. Opposing forces to crimes of obedience should arise, finally, to the extent that individuals are aware of the human consequences: of the effect of the action they are ordered to perform on the target of that action. Physical or psychological distance of the victim reduces actors' awareness of the human consequences of their actions, and thus, as we noted in chapter 6, opposing forces are less likely to be activated. Psychological distancing often occurs when the victims have been dehumanized—categorized as inferior or dangerous beings and identified by derogatory labels—so that they are excluded from the bonds of human empathy and protection of moral rules. In some bureaucratic contexts, as we suggested above, awareness of the human consequences of the action may be muted by neutralization rather than dehumanization of the victims. Actors—characteristically in organizations whose goals and procedures do not normally call for intended harm to anyone—may simply ignore the target or even lose awareness that there *is* a human target who is affected by the action. The resort to both dehumanization and neutralization of the victim is often facilitated, particularly among the higher echelons in a hierarchy, by commitment to a transcendent mission, which supersedes the usual moral standards and automatically justifies whatever human costs it may necessarily or inadvertently entail.

Dehumanization, neutralization, and the trap of the transcendent mission can be avoided by two kinds of strategies: increasing the salience of the victims as *victims* and increasing their salience as *fellow human beings.* In those settings in which the victims are neutralized—in effect, forgotten—their existence as victims should be systematically brought to actors' attention. We suggest that policy groups in such organizations make a point of considering consequences to potential victims, as a way of correcting for the tendency to focus exclusively on the transcendent goals of the organization. In fact, numerous works on corporate crime (for example, Stone, 1975) propose that organizations designate watchdogs—typically internal consumer advocates—and stress the importance of taking the views of such advocates into account. Often, "neutralized" victims can gain salience only by overtly complaining: by engaging in legal conflict or publicity. To an extent, then, neutralization can also be countered by our earlier suggestions regarding participation. For example, when citizens and groups who are potential victims participate more fully and equally—are more vocal in asserting their own value preferences and needs—they automatically make themselves more salient to the decision makers who might otherwise remain inattentive to their vulnerability.

In those situations in which victims are dehumanized, extensive social-psychological investigation under a variety of labels—such as prejudice, stereotyping, and ethnocentrism—suggests the potential usefulness of strategies that emphasize the actor's and victim's shared humanness (for example, Allport, 1954;

Tajfel, 1982). To summarize these findings briefly, to the extent that actor and victim (or members of that victim's category) have the opportunity for peaceful and noncompetitive contact, in a setting in which they can communicate as equals and engage in interdependent tasks, the individual's ability and inclination to dehumanize the victim will be reduced. In the relationship between enemies, who often engage in mutual victimization, the attempt to build a complex understanding of the other's needs and fears and a differentiated view of the other's intentions and ideology, through "realistic empathy" (White, 1984) or the sharing of perspectives (Kelman, 1987), may counter some of the categorical thinking entailed in dehumanization.

At the societal level, we recommend encouragement of structural arrangements, educational programs, media practices, and advocacy groups promoting social norms against dehumanization. One practice that particularly needs to be countered is the definition of certain categories of people—whether they be ethnic minorities, or drug users, or political protesters—"as fair game, whose victimization is socially sanctioned and approved" (Kelman, 1973, p. 54). The use of such categories not only targets the groups included in them as potential victims of crimes of obedience, but legitimizes the concept that certain groups of people are less than human and expendable. One corrective effort is to individualize victims wherever possible; as long as they remain anonymous members of stereotyped categories, it is easier to dehumanize them. Moreover, attempts to exclude any group from the human community need to be challenged, particularly when they come from high authorities who are in a position to legitimize the establishment of a pariah category and subsequent actions directed against it. It is also necessary to be critically alert to dehumanizing messages conveyed by ideologies that glorify and romanticize violence—whether in a military or a revolutionary context—or that discount the concrete human consequences of political actions in the name of an abstract transcendent mission. It is such ideologies that provide the atmosphere and justification for crimes of obedience.

A deeply moving demonstration of the power of social norms against dehumanization was provided by the small Protestant village of Le Chambon in southern France in the years 1940 to 1944, during the period of the Vichy government and the Nazi occupation (Hallie, 1979). Under the leadership of their pastor, the villagers organized themselves into a place of refuge for victims of persecution, most of whom were Jews—and not even French Jews, but refugees from Germany and Eastern Europe. At great cost and in the face of enormous dangers, the people of Le Chambon established houses of refuge for children, sheltered refugees in their own homes, provided them with identity and ration cards, took care of their needs, and helped them escape when the necessity or opportunity arose. Through their efforts, thousands of children and adults were saved from arrest, deportation, and certain death. Many factors combined to launch and sustain this project of organized resistance to government authority: the history of the Protestants in France; the Chambonnais' sense of obligation to a higher, religious, authority; the character of André Trocmé, the pastor, and the villagers' relationship to him; the solidarity of the community. But the motive force behind the resistance, according to Philip Hallie, was the concern for individual human beings shared by the community's leaders and members—a concern marked by an attitude of caring, a responsiveness to others' pain, and a sense of duty to help human beings in need. The Chambonnais refused to go along with attempts to dehumanize the victims. When André Trocmé was informed by a high official about the need to deport the Jews, he replied: "We do not know what a Jew is. We know only men" (Hallie, 1979, p. 103). This response contrasts tellingly with Lieutenant Calley's statement, cited earlier: "I did not sit down and think in terms of men, women, and children. They were all classified the same . . . just as enemy soldiers" (Hammer, 1971, p. 257).

We began this book with the story of a village in which a crime of obedience was committed during the Vietnam War. It is appropriate that we end the book with the recollection of another village, at another time and place, whose occupants individually and collectively resisted destructive authorities and refused complicity in an officially sanctioned crime. Despite the continuing prevalence of crimes of obedience and the widespread readiness to submit to authority without question, we draw some optimism from the knowledge that the world of modern bureaucracies provides the setting not only for My Lais but also for Le Chambons. Our optimism is reinforced by the democratization of disobedience that has proceeded in tandem with the growth of bureaucracy. Perhaps societies and organizations will increasingly learn that fostering value orientation among their members, although it entails short-term costs, can contribute to their long-term stability. Thus authorities that acknowledge the right to say no may be making a wise choice, if only because the conditions of bureaucratic life make no the wise answer at least some of the time. With the democratization of disobedience, we dare to hope that more and more individuals will avail themselves of that right to say no—that indeed they will develop the feeling of obligation and the courage to do so. The choice to say no, as the preceding discussion reminds us, ultimately rests on our saying yes to some of the distinct qualities that make us human: a sense of personal agency, an awareness of the consequences of our actions, and a caring attitude toward our fellow human beings.

Appendixes
References
Index

Appendix A
Information about and Interest
in the Calley Trial:
Findings from the 1971 Survey

As indicated in chapter 7, the questionnaire began with innocuous questions about where the respondents obtained "news of the world today," in order to lead them gradually into an interview that included potentially sensitive questions. Respondents were then asked how closely they had followed news of the recent trial and conviction of Lieutenant Calley. If they said "very closely" or "fairly closely," they were asked the full set of questions in the survey. If they said "not too closely" or "hardly at all," their knowledge was probed with a further question: "Did you read or hear anything about the trial of Lieutenant Calley, or is this something you missed?"

What respondents told us about following the trial is summarized below in two constructed variables: whether respondents had heard of the trial or not, and, if so, how closely they followed it. Respondents are counted as not having heard of the trial only when they gave negative or "don't know" answers to both the original question about following the trial and the follow-up probe. These respondents were given a restricted version of the interview (see chapter 7). Not surprisingly, respondents who had not heard of the trial tended to answer "don't know" to many other items. Since our strategy was to focus only on definite responses to questions, excluding "don't know" answers, these respondents have played a minimal role in this book.

Who Knew about Lieutenant Calley?

Most respondents in the spring of 1971 had heard of Lieutenant Calley, in keeping with the intense media attention to his trial. Nineteen percent of the entire sample ($N = 990$) said they had followed the trial "very closely" and 49 percent said "fairly closely." Even the 23 percent who said "not too closely" and the 9 percent who said "hardly at all" had generally heard something about the trial. On the follow-up probe, 71 percent of the latter two groups of respondents acknowledged having "heard something." Thus in the entire sample only ninety-nine people, exactly 10 percent, steadfastly maintained that they had not heard about Calley's trial and conviction. Ninety percent is quite a high rate of public recognition of *any* public figure, let alone a previously obscure army lieutenant.

In that period of intense public awareness of the trial, those who had not heard of Calley were significantly more likely to be uneducated, old, poor, black, and residing in rural areas. Respondents who were not asked the subsequent trial items therefore tend to fit a familiar profile; the same demographic groups are often overrepresented among other surveys' nonresponses or "don't know" responses (see, for example, Francis and Busch, 1975). To illustrate this familiar cluster of predictors, we show in the upper left panel of table A-1 the relationship of respondents' *educational attainment* to their claim of having heard of the trial. Those respondents with less than a high school degree were substantially more likely to deny knowledge of the trial than were those who had either obtained a high school degree or attended college.

As the upper right panel of the table indicates, information about the Calley trial—or a respondent's claim thereto—also had one unusual demographic correlate. Respondents with some *military experience* claimed to have heard of Calley at a higher rate than respondents without such experience. This pattern, although not characteristic of surveys in general, is not surprising here, given the subject matter.

Overall, the extent of public information about the Calley trial was remarkable. True, some categories of respondents (such as the less educated or rural residents) seemed to have heard of the trial less often; but most members of all demographic groups claimed at least to have heard of it.

Following the Trial: Extent of Public Interest

Among those who had heard of the Calley trial, the majority indicated that they had followed the trial "fairly closely." We next probed the extent to which variations in following the trial were related to demographic and attitudinal items. The lower half of table A-1 illustrates the patterns that emerged by using the same two predictor variables: educational level and military experience. This subtable *excludes* the ninety-nine respondents who had not heard of the trial. (When those who had not heard of it are included in analyses of "followed trial" among the "not closely" respondents, results reported here become more powerful and additional predictors become significant.)

In general, the degree to which respondents claimed to have followed the trial was predicted by the same demographic variables as hearing of the trial in the first place. Less educated and black respondents followed the trial significantly less closely; the lower left panel presents results for educational groups to illustrate this pattern. (If the ninety-nine excluded respondents are added to the analysis as part of the "not closely" group, we find that older, poorer, and rural respondents also prove to have followed the trial significantly less closely.) The lower right panel indicates that military experience predicted a respondent's level of interest in the trial as well as whether or not the person had simply heard of it. Those with some military experience claimed to have followed the Calley trial more closely.

Two new variables, not tabulated, also predicted respondents' having followed the trial: *sex* and *region of residence*. Females reported themselves less likely to have followed the trial closely. Some 82 percent of the males who had heard of the case claimed to have followed the trial "very closely" or "fairly closely," as compared to 69 percent of females. It might be possible to explain this finding as simply a result of military experience, since females were less likely to have served in the military. (In this sample only nine females

Table A-1 Predicting Information about and Interest in the Calley Trial: The Role of Education and Military Experience

Items	Education				Military Experience		
	Low (<12 years) (%)	Medium (12) (%)	High (13+) (%)	All Respondents (%)	No (%)	Yes (%)	All Respondents (%)
A. Heard of Calley trial?							
No	20	5	4	10	12	5	10
Yes	80	95	96	90	88	95	90
All respondents (%)	35	35	30	100 (977)	76	24	100 (967)
B. Followed trial							
Not closely	31	22	21	25	27	16	24
Fairly closely	47	61	55	54	54	55	55
Very closely	22	17	25	21	18	29	21
All respondents (%)	31	37	32	100 (879)	75	25	100 (870)

Note: To simplify the presentation, this table shows *percentages* for each category in the table's body and totals. The overall number of respondents (N) appears in parentheses below the 100% figure. Both the rows and the columns headed "All respondents" sum to 100% (with some rounding error), so that the N for any given row, column, or cell can be calculated as needed. Within each table, the *column* variable is presumed to be the independent variable, and percentages add to 100% down the columns (again with occasional rounding error). For information about statistical significance of the relationships presented here, see note to table 7.1.

had served in the armed forces.) However, male-female differences were significant even when we compared females with males who had not served in the military. Perhaps the explanation can be found in some difference in how the sexes are socialized about aggression. Even modern industrialized societies differentiate between the sexes such that males are given more encouragement, or license, to display aggression or to take an interest in it (see, for example, Maccoby and Jacklin, 1974). This may account for their greater interest in a military trial.

Since respondents from the South and Midwest tended to respond similarly to this as well as to other survey items, as did persons from the Northeast and Far West, we grouped regions into the two broad categories of Northeast/Far West versus South/Midwest for computational convenience. Respondents living in the Northeast or Far West were less likely to have followed the trial closely than those from the South or Midwest: Among northeastern and western respondents who had heard of the trial, 16 percent responded "very closely" in comparison to 28 percent of those living in the South or Midwest. Observed regional differences are consistent with the notion that there may be regional "cultures." In particular, the South seems to be characerized by promilitary sentiment in this and other surveys. The fact that the trial was held in the South may also have contributed to interest in it.

In general, each of these relatively unusual demographic predictors of trial interest—military experience, sex, and region of residence—seemingly touches on involvement with or sympathy for the military. Promilitary sympathies need not, in our view, represent a self-conscious ideology. Sympathy or empathy for military figures may have reflected respondents' social-structural positions, roles, or life experiences without necessarily entailing an abstract position on war per se or the war in Vietnam. However, these same variables generally predicted overt expressions of interest in, or "sympathy for," the Vietnam War in particular.

Opinions about the war, in turn, were related to having heard of and having followed the Calley trial. Specifically, hawks attended to the trial more closely. This tendency was observable across a set of items about Vietnam policy views and more global attitudes; it was usually of statistical significance. (This was true both in simple cross-tabulations and when we tabulated war opinion by trial interest while controlling for respondents' military experience, sex, or region of residence. Such controls were important since respondents who were hawks regarding the Vietnam War tended to have served in the military, to be male, and to live in the South or Midwest.)

Overall, the demographic and attitudinal predictors of American interest in the Calley trial formed two clusters. First, certain familiar demographic factors—age, social status, education, race, and urban residence—predicted having heard of the Calley trial and, less powerfully, having followed it. Second, we identified a package of predictors that were distinctively tied to military experience or sympathies, including military experience itself, sex, region of residence, and attitudes toward the Vietnam War. These two sets of predictors may represent two psychologically distinct wellsprings of opinion. The first cluster indexes higher position in the social structure and sophistication in public affairs. These variables may mainly affect how people *think* about the issues. The other cluster appears to be more motivational than cognitive; it may indicate experientially based *identification* with the defendant.

Appendix B
Differences between
the 1971 and 1976
Survey Populations

The follow-up survey occurred five years after the original and drew upon a single metropolitan sample instead of a national cross-section. Therefore the comparability of the two survey samples is an important issue. Two types of comparability—demographic and attitudinal—were to be evaluated, but how to do such an evaluation was not immediately obvious. Simple statistical tests for differences between the samples were not appropriate because there is no reasonable sense in which Boston in 1976 and the nation in 1971 can be considered two samples of the same universe. If they were, the problem would not exist in the first place. We chose instead to make informal comparisons among the 1971 national sample, the 1976 Boston sample, and the 1971 Northeast regional respondents. The last group was the best available subset of the national sample that might give a clue to how Boston would have responded in 1971. Still smaller chunks of data were available. The smallest such unit was the New England region's responses. This admittedly closer regional match contributed only sixty respondents to the 1971 study, however. So only by aggregating to the level of a larger unit could we find enough respondents to make a reasonable comparison.

The comparative strategy was to use the Northeast regional data to evaluate differences. For example, if the 1976 Boston sample differed from the 1971 national one on a critical attitude variable, such as responsibility orientation, we could ask whether Boston in 1976 resembled the Northeast as a whole in 1971. If it did, we could assume that something about the .region, rather than the timing of the survey, produced the difference; if it did not, we would be inclined to attribute the difference at least in part to a change in attitude between 1971 and 1976. This rough comparison is feasible only because the variable *region* did not interact with other predictors in 1971. Regions did differ, but in an analytically manageable way. They differed in *percent of respondents holding a view* (such as percent saying they would shoot) rather than in the *effect of one variable on another* (such as the impact of education on responsibility orientation). Only the latter effect would make regional differences threatening to the validity of our analyses. The statistical "inertness" of region makes the comparison of the 1971 Northeast and 1976 Boston area more conclusive than it would otherwise be. Where possible, we also drew on data supplied by Floyd J. Fowler, director of the Survey Research Program at the University of Massachusetts, Boston, to fill in gaps about what Boston itself was like in 1971.

Although a nation's demographic composition changes over time, a five-year span is a rather narrow period in which to expect major shifts. Therefore any 1971–76 differences in a variable such as education were likely to be due to the specific locale of the later survey rather than to changes over time in the American educational profile.

Attitudes are far more ephemeral. It is plausible to imagine the attitudes of a national sample changing sharply within five years. Political parties, for example, can be brought into and cast out of power in a shorter interval. When we turned to some attitudinal comparisons among the 1971 national, the 1971 Northeast, and the 1976 Boston samples, it was less clear whether time or place was the source of observed differences. Other national and regional studies had to be drawn on for relevant data such as distributions of political party affiliation.

Demographic Predictors

The demographic variables of interest here are the national sample's significant predictors of DR-AR orientation and "shoot-refuse" positions. Important demographics in the earlier study for which Boston data are available include education, religion, age, sex, and military experience. (Among the earlier study's predictor variables, region and metropolitan/rural residence were excluded from the present comparisons since they did not vary in the 1976 survey. Socioeconomic status was excluded because it was replaced in the 1976 study by the income question described in chapter 10.) Given the informality of the comparisons involved, we used the criterion that a group difference should be 10 percent or more before we considered it noteworthy. By that criterion, only the sample differences in education and religion are substantial. Table B-1 presents the distributions of these two variables for the two samples overall, with the 1971 Northeast regional subsample also included in an intermediate position.

In 1971 the Northeast was only slightly more educated than the nation as a whole. The Boston of 1976 was an exaggerated East. A substantially lower proportion of Boston respondents had less than a high school education, and there was an almost equivalent differential in Boston's favor in the percentage who had at least some college education. The entire educational spectrum had shifted upward in Boston. Boston is a white-collar and educational center, whenever education levels are assessed (Fowler, personal communication).

Another of Boston's predictable deviations, religion, appears in item B. Boston was far more Catholic than the nation, and substantially more so than the Northeast as a whole. It also included a higher proportion of respondents classified as Jewish, other, or none in religious preference. Such demographic differences could be assumed to be stable over time. For example, 1969–70 surveys of the Boston S.M.S.A. that employed probability samples indicated that Boston was 50 percent Catholic, 36 percent Protestant, and 14 percent other religions (Fowler, personal communication).

These sample differences in education and religion deserve attention when we examine the impact of demographic variables in 1976. As chapters 7 and 9 stressed, in 1971 these variables were important determinants of responsibility orientations and related attitudes about My Lai and the Calley trial.

Table B-1 Key Demographic Comparisons among Three Samples

Items	1971 National (%)	1971 Northeast (%)	1976 Boston (%)
A. Education			
Low (<12)	35	31	20
Medium (12)	35	38	39
High (13+)	30	31	41
Total	100	100	100
	(979)	(423)	(379)
B. Religion			
Catholic	27	39	50
Protestant	61	46	30
Jewish, Other, None	12	15	20
Total	100	100	100
	(976)	(421)	(388)

Attitudes

Comparisons among samples on relevant attitudes are more difficult, as we noted above. Time and place may be crucial in shaping attitudes. The issue of the Vietnam War seems to have been the most time-bound issue here. Early in the Boston interview we asked respondents for a retrospective self-identification regarding their attitude toward the war to replace the more detailed 1971 self-identification on the dove-hawk dimension. The Boston sample recalled being solidly dovish. Only 8 percent claimed they had been continuously in favor of the Vietnam War, in contrast to the 52 percent who asserted they had been continuously opposed. Some 38 percent reported shifting from a pro- to an antiwar position. Less than 3 percent responded "don't know." In contrast, our 1971 national figures showed 22 percent self-proclaimed hawks, 47 percent middle-of-the-road or "don't know," and 31 percent doves; and the Northeast was only slightly more dovish then than the nation as a whole. Boston's apparent dovishness—or change in the dovish direction between 1971 and 1976—need not have particular implications for responses to crimes of obedience, however. We have seen in earlier chapters that the nation as a whole was quite dovish in *policy* terms by 1971, and attitudes toward the war were only weakly linked to responsibility orientations.

Bostonians also differed from the earlier national sample in their political party identification and self-professed liberalism versus conservatism. Since neither of these variables was a significant predictor of trial views in 1971, we summarize these differences more briefly. Political party identification was virtually the same in the 1971 national and Northeastern regional samples. The 1976 Boston figures, in contrast, showed fewer Republicans (11 percent) and more independents (44 percent) versus the national sample's 26 percent Republican and 22 percent independent. Figures on party independence seem to represent a real change from 1971, probably reflecting the impact of Watergate. Self-proclaimed liberal or conservative tendencies, however, did not suggest a clear-cut pattern of change.

Boston respondents in 1976 differed from the nation (and the Northeast region) in 1971 by being more likely to identify as *either* conservative or liberal, avoiding the "don't know" and "middle-of-the-road" choices.

CALLEY TRIAL ATTITUDES

The fundamental question of baseline differences in response to the Calley trial remains. The distribution of answers to a question can govern how that question relates to—predicts or is predicted by—other items. Therefore we must ask: Did the surveys differ sharply in respondents' knowledge about the issues, in their inclinations to assert individual responsibility, in their claim that they would refuse to shoot, and the like? If Boston in 1976 resembled the nation in 1971 in average attitude judgments, it would be relatively simple to draw theoretical conclusions from a comparison of the two studies. Replication in 1976 of the pattern of relationships found in 1971 would clearly confirm the underlying orientations to authority and responsibility identified in chapters 8 and 9; failure to replicate would cast serious doubts on that theoretical formulation. On the other hand, if the two studies revealed differences in average attitude judgments, the theoretical implications might be more difficult to draw. Failure to replicate under these circumstances might be due to either baseline differences or the instability of the phenomenon. It can be argued, however, that replication of the pattern of relationships found in the earlier study under these circumstances would provide particularly persuasive confirmation of the underlying orientations. It would demonstrate the stability of the phenomenon *despite* baseline differences.

Table B-2 presents average responses about knowledge of the trial and responses to core attitude items: approval/disapproval of the Calley trial; DR-AR orientation; and what "most people" and respondents themselves would do in a My Lai–type situation.

A first key question was whether the comparison between Boston in 1976 and the nation in 1971 was really a comparison of those who had forgotten Calley and those who cared deeply about him. A five-year gap could certainly be expected to cause some diminution of intensity and information; chapter 7 suggested that such a diminution occurred even within months of the trial. Therefore it was important to determine how large the gulf in information and interest between surveys was likely to be. Item A shows averages for the nation, the Northeast, and Boston for the relevant query. The wording of this item actually differed between surveys, as described in the table. The original question asked *how closely the respondent had followed the Calley trial*. The replication, because of its placement in the questionnaire, was worded in terms of *remembering the My Lai incident*. The new wording may have inflated positive responses. One can remember the My Lai incident without having followed the trial, whereas it would have been virtually impossible to have followed the trial without remembering the incident.

With this caveat in mind, we can conclude from item A that My Lai had persisted in the public memory of Boston some five years after Calley's conviction. Our fear that interest in and remembrance of the issue might have faded appeared unfounded. Boston respondents instead appeared potentially *more* interested (if remembering is indicative of interest) than was true in the earlier survey. We are inclined to downplay the significance of this high level of claimed remembrance—and possible interest—for two reasons. First, it was easier to respond positively to the 1976 wording. Second, the higher education levels in Boston were likely to increase average remembrance, since more educated respondents followed the trial more closely in 1971 and claimed to remember My Lai better in 1976.

Table B-2 Comparisons among Three Samples on Trial Interest and Key Trial Attitudes[a]

Items	1971 National (%)	1971 Northeast (%)	1976 Boston (%)
A. Followed trial (Remembered My Lai)[b]			
Very closely (Very well)	19	16	34
Fairly closely (Fairly well)	49	53	50
Not closely (Not well)	32	30	17
Total	100	100	100
	(987)	(425)	(389)
B. Attitude toward Calley trial (Approve/Disapprove)			
Approve	37	43	63
C. Responsibility orientation (Deny/Assert)			
Deny	65	59	42
D. "Shoot-Refuse" responses			
Consistent Shooters	63	60	35
Deviant Refusers	15	18	26
Consistent Refusers	22	22	39

[a]In items A and D, column percentages add to 100% except for rounding error. In items B and C, responses to the omitted alternative can be obtained by subtracting the figure presented from 100%. Except where noted, wordings were essentially identical among surveys, with necessary changes in verb tenses.
[b]In the national study we asked if respondent followed the trial; in the Boston study, where five years had intervened and where the item came after a set of questions about Vietnam, we asked instead about remembrance of the My Lai incident. The query read: "One event in Vietnam that caused a great deal of public reaction was the trial of Lt. William Calley for his part in the My Lai incident. Would you say you remembered the My Lai incident very well" . . . and so on.

Overall, it appears that differences between the surveys cannot reasonably be attributed to Bostonians' ignorance or indifference.

The good memories of Bostonians, however, were associated with quite different views from those of the nation in 1971, as the other items in the table indicate. Furthermore, the 1971 Northeast regional sample is similar to the nation as a whole in respondents' tendencies to approve of the trial (item B), to take DR or AR positions (item C), and to respond to questions about whether "most people" and "you" would follow orders and shoot (item D). In both the nation and the Northeast, the majority of respondents in 1971 disapproved of the trial and, if they chose a reason involving responsibility, took the DR rather than AR stance. A majority responded *both* that "most people" would shoot and that they would personally do so (item D), making them Consistent Shooters by our definition in chapter 7. Bostonians, in contrast, generally recalled approving of the trial and held an assert-responsibility orientation (items B and C). Perhaps most striking was Bostonians' tendency to be Refusers, especially Consistent Refusers (item D); that is, they were likely to assert that both "most people" and they personally would refuse to shoot if ordered to do so in a situation like My Lai. (Examining these separate items revealed that Bostonians in 1976 were somewhat more likely to say "most people" would refuse to shoot in a My Lai–type setting and much more likely to say they personally would refuse, in comparison to the nation or the Northeast in 1971.) Overall, for Bostonians in 1976, the assertion of individual responsibility for actions appeared to be the baseline, the norm. In 1971 the denial of subordinates' responsibility was the baseline both for the nation as a whole and for the Northeast.

It is unclear why baseline responses should be so different, and it is always possible that these differences reflect something about Boston. For example, its residents' dovish views and high levels of education might have yielded these results had we surveyed Boston in 1971. But we think timing has much to do with the ascendancy of an AR response, particularly in view of the differences between Boston in 1976 and the Northeast in 1971. By 1976 the Calley trial itself was long over. Its outcome had not resulted in the crumbling of military morale or any of the many other dire outcomes that had once been suggested. Punishment for crimes of obedience in wartime had thereby been reinforced as the legal norm. And more indirectly, a president had been forced to resign over a scandal involving issues of obedience and command responsibility.

References

Abelson, R. P. (1982). Three modes of attitude-behavior consistency. In M. P. Zanna, E. T. Higgins, & C. P. Herman (Eds.), *Consistency in social behavior* (pp. 131–146). Hillsdale, N.J.: Erlbaum.

Adorno, T. W.; Frenkel-Brunswik, E.; Levinson, D. J.; & Sanford, R. N. (1950). *The authoritarian personality.* New York: Harper.

Ajzen, I., & Fishbein, M. (1977). Attitude-behavior relations: A theoretical analysis and review of empirical research. *Psychological Bulletin, 84,* 888–918.

Albright, W. F. (1949). The biblical period. In L. Finkelstein (Ed.), *The Jews: Their history, culture, and religion* (Vol. 1, pp. 3–69). Philadelphia: Jewish Publication Society.

Allport, G. W. (1954). *The nature of prejudice.* Cambridge, Mass.: Addison-Wesley.

Andenberg, M. R. (1973). *Cluster analysis for applications.* New York: Academic Press.

Arendt, H. (1964). *Eichmann in Jerusalem: A report on the banality of evil.* New York: Viking Press.

Argentine National Commission on the Disappeared. (1986). *Nunca más: The report of the Argentine National Commission of the Disappeared.* New York: Farrar, Straus & Giroux. (Original report published 1984)

Asch, S. E. (1951). Effects of group pressure upon the modification and distortion of judgments. In H. Guetzkow (Ed.), *Groups, leadership, and men* (pp. 177–190). Pittsburgh: Carnegie Press.

———. (1956). Studies of independence and conformity: A minority of one against a unanimous majority. *Psychological Monographs, 70* (9, Whole No. 416).

Bakan, D. (1966). *The duality of human existence.* Chicago: Rand McNally.

Bandura, A. (1973). Social learning theory of aggression. In J. F. Knutson (Ed.), *Control of aggression: Implications from basic research.* Chicago: Aldine-Atherton.

———. (1977). Self-efficacy: Toward a unifying theory of behavioral change. *Psychological Review, 84,* 191–215.

Baumrind, D. (1964). Some thoughts on ethics of research: After reading Milgram's "Behavioral study of obedience." *American Psychologist, 19,* 421–423.

Beauchamp, T. L.; Faden, R. R.; Wallace, R. J., Jr.; & Walters, L. (Eds.). (1982). *Ethical issues in social science research.* Baltimore: Johns Hopkins University Press.

Bedau, H. A. (1974). Genocide in Vietnam. In V. Held, S. Morgenbesser, & T. Nagel (Eds.), *Philosophy, morality, and international affairs* (pp. 5–46). New York: Oxford University Press.

Berman, H. J. (1983). *Law and revolution.* Cambridge, Mass.: Harvard University Press.

Bernstein, C., & Woodward, B. (1974). *All the president's men.* New York: Simon & Schuster.

Bernstein, R. (1987, May 17). Lawyer for Barbie tries to indict all of France. *The New York Times,* p. E3.

Bettelheim, B. (1943). Individual and mass behavior in extreme situations. *Journal of Abnormal and Social Psychology, 38,* 417–452.

Bigongiari, D. (1953). *The political ideas of St. Thomas Aquinas.* New York: Hafner.

Blau, P. M. (1964). *Exchange and power in social life.* New York: Wiley.

———. (1968). The hierarchy of authority in organizations. *American Journal of Sociology, 73,* 453–467.

Bloom, A. H., III. (1974). *Social principledness and social humanism.* Unpublished Ph.D. dissertation, Harvard University, Cambridge, Mass.

———. (1977). Two dimensions of moral reasoning: Social principledness and social humanism in cross-cultural perspective. *Journal of Social Psychology, 101,* 29–44.

Blum-West, S., & Carter, T. J. (1983). Bringing white collar crime back in: An examination of crimes and torts. *Social Problems, 30,* 545–554.

Boffey, P. M. (1987, January 28). Engineer who opposed launching Challenger sues Thiokol for $1 billion. *The New York Times,* p. A16.

Bosch, W. J. (1970). *Judgment on Nuremberg: American attitudes toward the major German war-crime trials.* Chapel Hill: University of North Carolina Press.

Botz, G. (1987). Österreich und die NS-Vergangenheit: Verdrängung, Pflichterfüllung, Geschichtsklitterung. In D. Diner (Ed.), *Ist der Nationalsozialismus Geschichte?* (pp. 141–152). Frankfurt a. M.: Fischer.

Brandon, S. G. F. (1968). *The fall of Jerusalem.* London: S.P.C.K.

Brickman, P.; Ryan, K.; & Wortman, C. (1975). Causal chains: Attribution of responsibility as a function of immediate and prior causes. *Journal of Personality and Social Psychology, 32,* 1060–1067.

Brooke, C. (1971). *Medieval church and society.* London: Sidgwick & Jackson.

Brophy, J. E., & Good, T. (1974). *Teacher-student relationships: Causes and consequences.* New York: Holt, Rinehart & Winston.

Brophy, J. E.; Rashid, H.; Rohrkemper, M.; & Goldberger, M. (1983). Relationships between teachers' presentations of classroom tasks and students' engagement in those tasks. *Journal of Educational Psychology, 75,* 544–552.

Browning, F., & Forman, D. (Eds.). (1972). *The wasted nations: Report of the International Commission of Enquiry into United States Crimes in Indochina, June 20–25, 1971.* New York: Harper & Row.

Buck, L. P., & Zophy, J. W. (Eds.). (1972). *The social history of the Reformation.* Columbus: Ohio State University Press.

Burger, J. M. (1981). Motivational biases in the attribution of responsibility for an accident: A meta-analysis of the defensive attribution hypothesis. *Psychological Bulletin, 90,* 496–512.

Campbell, A.; Gurin, G.; & Miller, W. E. (1954). *The voter decides.* Evanston, Ill.: Row, Peterson.

Carlyle, R. W., & Carlyle, A. J. (1936). *A history of medieval political theory in the West* (Vol. 6). London: Blackwood & Sons.

Chang, J. (1987, September 11). What Bork did in Watergate was obstruction. [Letter to the editor]. *The New York Times,* p. A30.

Chanowitz, B., & Langer, E. (1980). Knowing more (or less) than you can show: Understanding control through the mindlessness/mindfulness distinction. In M. E. P. Seligman & J. Garber (Eds.), *Human helplessness* (pp. 97–130). New York: Academic Press.

Christian, S. (1987, May 9). Argentina urgently seeking way to ease army tension over trials. *The New York Times,* p. 2.

Christie, R., & Jahoda, M. (Eds.). (1954). *Studies in the scope and method of the authoritarian personality.* Glencoe, Ill.: Free Press.

Church, G. J. (1987, July 13). Ollie's turn. *Time,* pp. 22–26.

Claburn, E. (1968). *Deuteronomy and collective behavior.* Unpublished Ph.D. dissertation, Princeton University, Princeton, N.J.

Clinard, M. B. (1983). *Corporate ethics and crime: The role of middle management.* Beverly Hills, Calif.: Sage.

Cohen, M.; Nagel, T.; & Scanlon, T. (Eds.). (1974). *War and moral responsiblity.* Princeton, N.J.: Princeton University Press.

Cole, R. E. (1979). *Work, morality, and participation: A comparative study of American and Japanese industry.* Berkeley: University of California Press.

Coleman, J. S. (1980). Authority systems. *Public Opinion Quarterly, 44,* 143–163.

Collins, B. E. (1974). Four components of the Rotter internal-external scale: Belief in a difficult world, a just world, a predictable world, and a politically responsive world. *Journal of Personality and Social Psychology, 29,* 381–391.

Committee on the Judiciary, House of Representatives. (1980). *Corporate crime* (Committee Print No. 10). Washington, D.C.: U.S. Government Printing Office.

Converse, P. (1964). The nature of belief systems in mass publics. In D. Apter (Ed.), *Ideology and discontent* (pp. 206–261). New York: Free Press.

———. (1970). Attitudes and non-attitudes: Continuation of a dialogue. In E. R. Tufte (Ed.), *The quantitative analysis of social problems* (pp. 168–189). Reading, Mass.: Addison-Wesley.

Cooley, W. W., & Lohnes, P. R. (1971). *Multivariate data analysis.* New York: Wiley.

Cowan, C.; Thompson, W.; & Ellsworth, P. (1984). The effects of death qualification on a juror's predisposition to convict and on the quality of deliberation. *Law and Human Behavior, 8,* 53–70.

Craig, G. A. (1986, October 9). The Waldheim file. *The New York Review of Books,* pp. 3–6.

Crawford, T. J. (1972). In defense of obedience research: An extension of the Kelman ethic. In A. G. Miller (Ed.), *The social psychology of psychological research* (pp. 179–186). New York: Free Press.

Critchlow, B. (1985). The blame in the bottle: Attributions about drunken behavior. *Personality and Social Psychology Bulletin, 11,* 258–274.

Darley, J. M.; Klosson, E. C.; & Zanna, M. P. (1978). Intentions and their contexts in the moral judgments of children and adults. *Child Development, 49,* 66–74.

Darley, J. M., & Zanna, M. P. (1982). Making moral judgments. *American Scientist, 70,* 515–521.

Davies, J. G. (1965). *The early Christian Church.* New York: Holt, Rinehart & Winston.

deCharms, R. (1968). *Personal causation.* New York: Academic Press.

DeJong, W. (1979). An examination of self-perception mediation of the foot-in-the-door effect. *Journal of Personality and Social Psychology, 37,* 2221–2239.

Department of the Army. (1956). *The law of land warfare* (Field Manual, No. 27–10). Washington, D.C.: U.S. Government Printing Office.

Deutscher, I. (1973). *What we say/What we do.* Glenview, Ill.: Scott, Foresman.

Dickinson, W. B., Jr. (Ed.). (1973). *Watergate: Chronology of a crisis* (2 vols.). Washington, D.C.: Congressional Quarterly.

Diener, E. (1979). Deindividuation, self-awareness, and disinhibition. *Journal of Personality and Social Psychology, 37,* 1160–1171.

DiMona, J. (1972). *Great court-martial cases*. New York: Grosset & Dunlap.

Dinstein, Y. (1965). *The defense of obedience to superior orders in international law*. Leyden, Netherlands: A. W. Sijthoff.

Disch, E. (1987, August-September). For the people of Argentina, it's not yet "punto final." *Resist Newsletter*, No. 198, pp. 4–7.

Dixon, W. J. (Ed.). (1983). *BMDP statistical software* (1985 reprint). Berkeley: University of California Press.

Douvan, E., & Walker, A. M. (1956). The sense of effectiveness in public affairs. *Psychological Monographs, 70* (22, Whole No. 429).

Dowie, M. (1977, September-October). Pinto madness. *Mother Jones*, pp. 18–24, 28–32.

Doyle, J. (1977). *Not above the law: The battles of Watergate prosecutors Cox and Jaworski*. New York: William Morrow.

Drane, J. (1982). *Early Christians*. San Francisco: Harper & Row.

Draper, T. (1987, October 8). The rise of the American junta. *The New York Review of Books*, pp. 47–58.

———. (1987, October 22). The fall of an American junta. *The New York Review of Books*, pp. 45–57.

Drossman, E., & Knappman, E. W. (Eds.). (1974). *Watergate and the White House: July-December, 1973* (Vol. 2). New York: Facts on File.

Duncan, O. D. (1961). A socioeconomic index for all occupations. In A. J. Reiss et al. (Eds.), *Occupation and social status* (pp. 109–138). New York: Free Press of Glencoe.

Durkheim, E. (1947). *The division of labor in society*. New York: Free Press.

Easton, D. (1965). *A systems analysis of political life*. New York: Wiley.

Eisenstein, E. L. (1974). The advent of printing and the Protestant revolt: A new approach to the disruption of Western Christendom. In R. M. Kingdon (Ed.), *Transition and revolution* (pp. 235–270). Minneapolis: Burgess.

Eisenstein, P. A. (1987, July 3). Chrysler chairman tries to make amends—and boost image. *Christian Science Monitor*, p. 11.

Elms, A. C., & Milgram, S. (1966). Personality characteristics associated with obedience and defiance toward authoritative command. *Journal of Experimental Research in Personality, 1*, 282–289.

Elon, A. (1986, July 21). Letter from Argentina. *The New Yorker*, pp. 74–86.

Ermann, M. D. (1985). Accounting for corporate crime. *Contemporary Sociology, 14*, 158–161.

Ervin, S. J., Jr. (1980). *The whole truth: The Watergate conspiracy*. New York: Random House.

Escalona, S. (1968). *The roots of individuality: Normal patterns of development in infants*. Chicago: Aldine.

Falk, R. A. (Ed.). (1968). *The Vietnam War and international law*. Princeton, N.J.: Princeton University Press.

Falk, R. A.; Kolko, G.; & Lifton, R. J. (Eds.). (1971). *Crimes of war*. New York : Vintage Books.

Ferguson, L. W. (1942). The isolation and measurement of nationalism. *Journal of Social Psychology, 16*, 215–228.

Ferguson, T., & Rule, B. G. (1982). Influence of inferential set, outcome intent, and outcome severity on children's moral judgments. *Developmental Psychology, 18*, 843–851.

Fincham, F. D. (1985). Outcome valence and situational constraints in the responsibility attributions of children and adults. *Social Cognition, 3,* 218–233.

Fincham, F. D., & Jaspars, J. M. (1979). Attribution of responsibility to the self and other in children and adults. *Journal of Personality and Social Psychology, 37,* 1589–1602.

———. (1980). Attribution of responsibility: From man the scientist to man as lawyer. In L. Berkowitz (Ed.), *Advances in experimental social psychology* (Vol. 13, pp. 81–138). New York: Academic Press.

———. (1983). A subjective probability approach to responsibility attribution. *British Journal of Social Psychology, 22,* 145–162.

Fincham, F. D., & Shultz, T. R. (1981). Intervening causation and the mitigation of responsibility for harm. *British Journal of Social Psychology, 20,* 113–120.

Fishbein, M., & Ajzen, I. (1973). Attribution of responsibility: A theoretical note. *Journal of Experimental Social Psychology, 9,* 148–153.

FitzGerald, F. (1972). *Fire in the lake: The Vietnamese and the Americans in Vietnam.* Boston: Atlantic–Little, Brown.

———. (1987, May 10). Reagan's band of true believers. *The New York Times Magazine,* pp. 36–39, 42–43, 84.

Fox, A. (1974). *Beyond contract: Work, power, and trust relations.* London: Faber & Faber.

Francis, J. D., & Busch, L. (1975). What we know about "I don't knows." *Public Opinion Quarterly, 39,* 207–218.

Frank, J. D. (1944). Experimental studies of personal pressure and resistance: II. Methods of overcoming resistance. *Journal of General Psychology, 30,* 43–56.

Franklin, J. H. (1967). Constitutionalism in the sixteenth century: The Protestant monarchomachs. In D. Spitz (Ed.), *Political theory and social change* (pp. 117–132). New York: Atherton.

Freedman, J. L., & Fraser, S. C. (1966). Compliance without pressure: The foot-in-the-door technique. *Journal of Personality and Social Psychology, 4,* 195–202.

Freire, P. (1971). *Pedagogy of the oppressed* (M. B. Ramos, trans.). New York: Herder & Herder.

———. (1973). *Education for critical consciousness.* New York: Seabury.

French, J. R. P., Jr., & Raven, B. H. (1959). The bases of social power. In D. Cartwright (Ed.), *Studies in social power* (pp. 150–167). Ann Arbor, Mich.: Institute for Social Research.

French, P. (Ed.). (1972). *Individual and collective responsibility: The massacre at My Lai.* Cambridge, Mass.: Schenkman.

Freud, A. (1946). *The ego and the mechanisms of defense.* New York: International Universities Press.

From Mt. Moriah: The sacrifice of Isaac and contemporary man. (1975). *Shdemot,* No. 4, 6–22.

Fromm, E. (1941). *Escape from freedom.* New York: Rinehart.

Fuller, L. L. (1969). *The morality of law* (rev. ed.). New Haven, Conn.: Yale University Press.

Gager, J. G. (1975). *Kingdom and community: The social world of early Christianity.* Englewood Cliffs, N.J.: Prentice-Hall.

Gal, R. (1985). Commitment and obedience in the military: An Israeli case study. *Armed Forces & Society, 11,* 553–564.

Gamson, W. A. (1968). *Power and discontent.* Homewood, Ill.: Dorsey.

Gamson, W. A.; Fireman, B.; & Rytina, S. (1982). *Encounters with unjust authority.*

Homewood, Ill.: Dorsey.

Gierke, O. (1958). *Political theories of the Middle Age.* Boston: Beacon Press.

Gillers, S. (1987, September 11). His legal ethics. [Letter to the editor]. *The New York Times,* p. A30.

Gilligan, C. (1982). *In a different voice.* Cambridge, Mass.: Harvard University Press.

Glazer, M. P., & Glazer, P. M. (1986, August 13). The whistle-blower's plight. *The New York Times,* p. A23.

Gold, A. R.; Christie, R.; & Friedman, L. N. (1976). *Fists and flowers: A social psychological interpretation of student dissent.* New York: Academic Press.

Goldstein, J.; Marshall, B.; & Schwartz, J. (Eds.). (1976). *The My Lai massacre and its cover-up: Beyond the reach of law?* (The Peers report with a supplement and introductory essay on the limits of law). New York: Free Press.

Gonzalez, F. (1987, July 19). Argentina's "invisible generation." *The Boston Globe Magazine,* pp. 18–40.

Gordis, R. (1949). The Bible as a cultural monument. In L. Finkelstein (Ed.), *The Jews: Their history, culture, and religion* (Vol. 2, pp. 457–496). Philadelphia: Jewish Publication Society.

Grant, M. (1968). *The climax of Rome.* London: Weidenfeld & Nicholson.

Grant, R. M. (1977). *Early Christianity and society.* San Francisco: Harper & Row.

Gray, J. G. (1959). *The warriors: Reflections on men in battle.* New York: Harper & Row.

Greenberg, M. (1978). Rabbinic reflections on defying illegal orders: Amasa, Abner, and Joab. In M. M. Kellner (Ed.), *Contemporary Jewish ethics* (pp. 211–220). New York: Sanhedrin Press.

Greenspan, M. (1959). *The modern law of land warfare.* Berkeley: University of California Press.

Greenstein, F. I. (1969). *Personality and politics: Problems of evidence, inference, and conceptualization.* Chicago: Markham.

Gurin, P.; Gurin, G.; & Morrison, B. M. (1978). Personal and ideological aspects of internal and external control. *Social Psychology, 41,* 275–296.

Hacohen, G. (1987, Summer). The officer's right to dissent: A military perspective. *Jerusalem Quarterly,* No. 43, 122–134.

Hallie, P. P. (1979). *Lest innocent blood be shed.* New York: Harper & Row.

Hamilton, V. L. (1975). *The crime of obedience: Jury simulation of a military trial.* Unpublished Ph.D. dissertation, Harvard University, Cambridge, Mass.

————. (1976). Individual differences in ascriptions of responsibility, guilt, and appropriate punishment. In G. Bermant, N. Vidmar, & C. Nemeth (Eds.), *Psychology and the law: Research frontiers* (pp. 239–264). New York: Lexington Books.

————. (1978a). Obedience and responsibility: A jury simulation. *Journal of Personality and Social Psychology, 36,* 126–146.

————. (1978b). Who is responsible? Toward a *social* psychology of responsibility attribution. *Social Psychology, 41,* 316–328.

————. (1980). Intuitive psychologist or intuitive lawyer? Alternative models of the attribution process. *Journal of Personality and Social Psychology, 39,* 767–772.

————. (1986). Chains of command: Responsibility attribution in hierarchies. *Journal of Applied Social Psychology, 16,* 118–138.

Hamilton, V. L.; Blumenfeld, P. C.; & Kushler, R. H. (1988). A question of standards: Attributions of blame and credit for classroom acts. *Journal of Personality and Social Psychology, 54,* 34–48.

Hamilton, V. L., & Rotkin, L. (1979). The capital punishment debate: Public perceptions of crime and punishment. *Journal of Applied Social Psychology, 9,* 350–376.

Hamilton, V. L., & Rytina, S. (1980). Social consensus on norms of justice: Should the punishment fit the crime? *American Journal of Sociology, 85,* 1117–1144.

Hamilton, V. L., & Sanders, J. (1981). Effects of roles and deeds on responsibility judgments: The normative structure of wrongdoing. *Social Psychology Quarterly, 44,* 237–254.

Hamilton, V. L., & Sanders, J. (with Y. Hosoi, Z. Ishimura, N. Matsubara, H. Nishimura, N. Tomita, & K. Tokoro). (1983). Universals in judging wrongdoing: Japanese and Americans compared. *American Sociological Review, 48,* 199–211.

Hammer, R. (1970). *One morning in the war.* New York: Coward-McCann.

———. (1971). *The court-martial of Lt. Calley.* New York: Coward, McCann, & Geoghegan.

Harmon, H. H. (1976). *Modern factor analysis* (3rd rev. ed.). Chicago: University of Chicago Press.

Harris, B. (1977). Developmental differences in the attribution of responsibility. *Developmental Psychology, 13,* 257–265.

Harris, M. (1974). *Cows, pigs, wars, and witches.* New York: Random House.

Hart, H. L. A. (1968). *Punishment and responsibility.* New York: Oxford University Press.

Hart, H. L. A., & Honoré, A. M. (1959). *Causation in the law.* Oxford, England: Clarendon Press.

Harvey, J. H.; Ickes, W. J.; & Kidd, R. F. (Eds.). (1976). *New directions in attribution research* (Vol. 1). Hillsdale, N.J.: Erlbaum.

———. (Eds.). (1978). *New directions in attribution research* (Vol. 2). Hillsdale, N.J.: Erlbaum.

Harvey, M. D., & Rule, B. G. (1978). Moral evaluations and judgments of responsibility. *Personality and Social Psychology Bulletin, 4,* 583–588.

Healey, R. (1987, July 15). Looking to Reagan, not North, for answers. *The Boston Globe,* p. 15.

Heider, F. (1958). *The psychology of interpersonal relations.* New York: Wiley.

Hemphill, L. (1985). Curriculum responses to the threat of nuclear war. In B. Zars, B. Wilson, & A. Phillips (Eds.), *Education and the threat of nuclear war* (pp. 90–95). Cambridge, Mass.: Harvard Educational Review.

Herrman, S. (1973). *A history of Israel in Old Testament times.* Philadelphia: Fortress Press.

Hersh, S. (1970). *My Lai 4: A report on the massacre and its aftermath.* New York: Vintage Books.

———. (1972). *Cover-up.* New York: Random House.

Hesselbart, S., & Schuman, H. (1976). Racial attitudes, educational level, and a personality measure. *Public Opinion Quarterly, 40,* 108–114.

Hill, R. J. (1981). Attitudes and behavior. In M. Rosenberg & R. H. Turner (Eds.), *Social psychology: Sociological perspectives* (pp. 347–410). New York: Basic Books.

Hirschman, A. O. (1970). *Exit, voice, and loyalty.* Cambridge, Mass.: Harvard University Press.

Hofeller, M. A. (1966). *The processes of legitimacy: A social psychological theory.* Unpublished Ph.D. dissertation, University of Michigan, Ann Arbor, Mich.

Hofling, C. K.; Brotzman, E.; Dalrymple, S.; Graves, N.; & Pierce, C. M. (1966). An experimental study of nurse-physician relationships. *Journal of Nervous and Mental*

Disease, 143, 171–180.

Hollander, E. P. (1958). Conformity, status, and idiosyncrasy credit. *Psychological Review, 65*, 117–127.

Holusha, J. (1987, July 2). Chrysler acts in false mileage case. *The New York Times*, pp. D1, D9.

Homans, G. (1976). Commentary. In L. Berkowitz & E. Walster (Eds.), *Advances in experimental social psychology* (Vol. 9, pp. 231–244). New York: Academic Press.

Iran-contra affair: A defiant tale of evasive actions. (1987, July 12). *The New York Times*, p. E1.

Iran-contra hearings/Excerpts from Poindexter's testimony. (1987, July 16). *The Boston Globe*, p. 13.

The Iran-contra hearings at a glance. (1987, August 4). *The New York Times*, p. A6.

Jackman, M. (1973). Education and prejudice or education and response set? *American Sociological Review, 38*, 327–339.

Janis, I. L. (1972). *Victims of groupthink: A psychological study of foreign-policy decisions and fiascoes*. Boston: Houghton Mifflin.

Jaworski, L. (1976). *The right and the power: The prosecution of Watergate*. New York: Reader's Digest Press.

Jones, E. E., & Davis, K. E. (1965). From acts to dispositions: The attribution process in person perception. In L. Berkowitz (Ed.), *Advances in experimental social psychology* (Vol. 2, pp. 219–266). New York: Academic Press.

Jones, E. E.; Kanouse, D. E.; Kelley, H. H.; Nisbett, R. E.; Valins, S.; & Weiner, B. (Eds.). (1972). *Attribution: Perceiving the causes of behavior*. Morristown, N.J.: General Learning Press.

Jones, E. E., & Nisbett, R. E. (1971). *The actor and the observer: Divergent perceptions of the causes of behavior*. Morristown, N.J.: General Learning Press.

Jurow, G. (1971). New data on the effect of a death qualified jury on the guilt determination process. *Harvard Law Review, 84*, 567–611.

Kadish, M. R., & Kadish, S. H. (1973). *Discretion to disobey: A study of lawful departures from legal rules*. Stanford, Calif.: Stanford University Press.

Kantorowicz, E. H. (1957). *The king's two bodies*. Princeton, N.J.: Princeton University Press.

Karniol, R. (1978). Children's use of intention cues in evaluating behavior. *Psychological Bulletin, 85*, 76–85.

Keasey, C. B. (1978). Children's developing awareness and usage of intentionality and motives. In C. B. Keasey (Ed.), *Nebraska Symposium on Motivation, 1977* (pp. 219–260). Lincoln: University of Nebraska Press.

Keegan, J. (1976). *The face of battle*. New York: Viking Press.

Kelley, H. H. (1967). Attribution theory in social psychology. In D. Levine (Ed.), *Nebraska Symposium on Motivation, 1967* (pp. 192–238). Lincoln: University of Nebraska Press.

Kelman, H. C. (1958). Compliance, identification, and internalization: Three processes of attitude change. *Journal of Conflict Resolution, 2*, 51–60.

———. (1961). Processes of opinion change. *Public Opinion Quarterly, 25*, 57–78.

———. (1963). The role of the group in the induction of therapeutic change. *International Journal of Group Psychotherapy, 13*, 399–432.

———. (1968). *A time to speak: On human values and social research*. San Francisco: Jossey-Bass.

———. (1969). Patterns of personal involvement in the national system: A social-psychological analysis of political legitimacy. In J. N. Rosenau (Ed.), *International politics and foreign policy* (2nd ed., pp. 276–288). New York: Free Press.

———. (1972). The rights of the subject in social research: An analysis in terms of relative power and legitimacy. *American Psychologist, 27,* 989–1016.

———. (1973). Violence without moral restraint: Reflections on the dehumanization of victims and victimizers. *Journal of Social Issues, 29*(4), 25–61.

———. (1974a). Attitudes are alive and well and gainfully employed in the sphere of action. *American Psychologist, 29,* 310–324.

———. (1974b). Social influence and linkages between the individual and the social system: Further thoughts on the processes of compliance, identification, and internalization. In J. T. Tedeschi (Ed.), *Perspectives on social power* (pp. 125–171). Chicago: Aldine.

———. (1976). Some reflections on authority, corruption, and punishment: The social-psychological context of Watergate. *Psychiatry, 39,* 303–317.

———. (1978). Attitude and behavior: A social-psychological problem. In M. Yinger & S. J. Cutler (Eds.), *Major social issues: A multidisciplinary view* (pp. 412–420). New York: Free Press.

———. (1980). The role of action in attitude change. In H. E. Howe, Jr., & M. M. Page (Eds.), *Nebraska Symposium on Motivation, 1979: Attitudes, values, and beliefs* (pp. 117–194). Lincoln: University of Nebraska Press.

———. (1987). The political psychology of the Israeli-Palestinian conflict: How can we overcome the barriers to a negotiated solution? *Political Psychology, 8,* 347–363.

Kelman, H. C., & Barclay, J. (1963). The F-scale as a measure of breadth of perspective. *Journal of Abnormal and Social Psychology, 67,* 608–615.

Kelman, H. C., & Hamilton, V. L. (1974). Availability for violence: A study of U.S. public reactions to the trial of Lt. Calley. In J. D. Ben-Dak (Ed.), *The future of collective violence: Societal and international perspectives* (pp. 125–142). Lund, Sweden: Studentlitteratur.

Kelman, H. C., & Lawrence, L. H. [Hamilton, V. L.]. (1972a). American response to the trial of Lt. William Calley. *Psychology Today, 6*(1), 41–45, 78–81.

———. (1972b). Assignment of responsibility in the case of Lt. Calley: Preliminary report on a national survey. *Journal of Social Issues, 28*(1), 177–212.

Kelman, H. C.; Miller, F. D.; Hamilton, V. L.; & Winkler, J. D. (1977). [Political orientation and attachment scales: Detroit and Windsor samples]. Unpublished data.

Kerckhoff, A. (1973). *Socialization and social class.* Englewood Cliffs, N.J.: Prentice-Hall.

Key sections of conspiracy indictment in Iran-contra affair. (1988, March 17). *The New York Times,* p. D26.

Kilham, W., & Mann, L. (1974). Level of destructive obedience as a function of transmitter and executant roles in the Milgram obedience paradigm. *Journal of Personality and Social Psychology, 29,* 696–702.

King, M. L., Jr. (1969). Letter from Birmingham City Jail. In H. A. Bedau (Ed.), *Civil disobedience: Theory and practice* (pp. 72–89). New York: Pegasus.

Kinghorn, S. (1984). *Corporate harm: A structural analysis of the criminogenic elements of the corporation.* Unpublished Ph.D. dissertation, University of Michigan, Ann Arbor, Mich.

Kirschenbaum, A. (1974). A cog in the wheel: The defence of "obedience to superior orders" in Jewish law. *The Israel Yearbook on Human Rights, 4,* 168–193.

Kirscht, J. P., & Dillehay, R. C. (1967). *Dimensions of authoritarianism: A review of research and theory.* Lexington: University of Kentucky Press.

Kluckhohn, C. (1952). Values and value-orientation in the theory of action: An exploration in definition and classification. In T. Parsons & E. A. Shils (Eds.), *Toward a general theory of action* (pp. 388–433). Cambridge, Mass.: Harvard University Press.

Knappman, E. W. (Ed.). (1973). *Watergate and the White House: June 1972–July 1973* (Vol. 1). New York: Facts on File.

Kohlberg, L. (1969). Stage and development: The cognitive-developmental approach to socialization. In D. A. Goslin (Ed.), *Handbook of socialization theory and research* (pp. 347–480). Chicago: Rand McNally.

———. (1984). *The psychology of moral development: The nature and validity of moral stages.* San Francisco: Harper & Row.

Kohn, M. L. (1977). *Class and conformity: A study of values, with a reassessment* (2nd ed.). Chicago: University of Chicago Press.

Kohn, M. L., & Schooler, C. (1983). *Work and personality: An inquiry into the impact of social stratification.* Norwood, N.J.: Ablex.

Koven, R. (1987, May 13). Barbie says he acted under orders in war. *The Boston Globe*, pp. 1, 12.

Kren, G. M., & Rappoport, L. (1980). *The Holocaust and the crisis of human behavior.* New York: Holmes & Meier.

Kurland, P. B. (1978). *Watergate and the Constitution.* Chicago: University of Chicago Press.

La Boétie, E. de (1975). *The politics of obedience: The discourse of voluntary servitude* (H. Kurz, trans.; with an introduction by M. N. Rothbard). New York: Free Life Editions. (Original work published in 1574.)

Lang, G. E., & Lang, K. (1983). *The battle for public opinion: The president, the press, and the polls during Watergate.* New York: Columbia University Press.

Lang, K. (1968). Military. In D. L. Sills (Ed.), *International encyclopedia of the social sciences* (Vol. 10, pp. 305–312). New York: Macmillan & Free Press.

Langer, E. J. (1988). *Minding matters: The consequences of mindlessness/mindfulness.* Unpublished manuscript, Harvard University.

Langer, E. J.; Blank, A.; & Chanowitz, B. (1978). The mindlessness of ostensibly thoughtful action. *Journal of Personality and Social Psychology, 36,* 635–642.

Langer, E., & Piper, A. (1987). The prevention of mindlessness. *Journal of Personality and Social Psychology, 53,* 280–287.

Laski, H. J. (1919). *Authority in the modern state.* New Haven, Conn.: Yale University Press.

Latané, B. (1981). The psychology of social impact. *American Psychologist, 36,* 343–356.

Latané, B., & Darley, J. M. (1970). *The unresponsive bystander: Why doesn't he help?* New York: Appleton-Century-Crofts.

Lawrence, L. H. [Hamilton, V. L..], & Kelman, H. C. (1973). Reactions to the Calley trial: Class and political authority. *Worldview, 16*(6), 34–40.

Lerner, M. J. (1970). The desire for justice and reactions to victims. In J. Macaulay & L. Berkowitz (Eds.), *Altruism and helping behavior* (pp. 205–229). New York: Academic Press.

———. (1971). Observer's evaluation of a victim: Justice, guilt, and veridical perception. *Journal of Personality and Social Psychology, 20,* 127–135.

———. (1980). *The belief in a just world: A fundamental delusion.* New York: Plenum.

Levinson, S. (1973). Responsibility for crimes of war. *Philosophy and Public Affairs, 2,* 244–273.

Lewin, K. (1947). Group decision and social change. In T. M. Newcomb & E. L. Hartley (Eds.), *Readings in social psychology.* New York: Holt.

Lewis, A. (1987, August 23). Bork and Watergate. *The New York Times,* p. E23.

Lewis, E. (1954). *Medieval political ideas* (Vol. 1). New York: Alfred A. Knopf.

Lickona, T. (Ed.). (1976). *Moral development and behavior.* New York: Holt, Rinehart & Winston.

Lifton, R. J. (1956). "Thought reform" of Western civilians in Chinese Communist prisons. *Psychiatry, 19,* 173–195.

———. (1971). Existential evil. In N. Sanford, C. Comstock, & Associates, *Sanctions for evil: Sources of social destructiveness.* San Francisco: Jossey-Bass.

———. (1973). *Home from the war—Vietnam veterans: Neither victims nor executioners.* New York: Simon & Schuster.

———. (1986). *The Nazi doctors: Medical killing and the psychology of genocide.* New York: Basic Books.

Lipset, S. M. (1960). *Political man: The social bases of politics.* New York: Doubleday.

Liska, A. E. (Ed.). (1975). *The consistency controversy.* New York: Wiley.

Maccoby, E., & Jacklin, C. N. (1974). *The psychology of sex differences.* Stanford, Calif.: Stanford University Press.

Magnuson, E. (1987, June 22). Shredded policies, arrogant attitudes. *Time,* pp. 21–22.

Magruder, J. S. (1974, May 19). Means: Watergate reflections. *The New York Times Magazine,* pp. 31, 103–112.

Mankiewicz, F. (1975). *U.S. v. Richard M. Nixon: The final crisis.* New York: Quadrangle.

Mann, L. (1973). Attitudes toward My Lai and obedience to orders: An Australian survey. *Australian Journal of Psychology, 25*(1), 11–21.

Mantell, D. M., & Panzarella, R. (1976). Obedience and responsibility. *British Journal of Social and Clinical Psychology, 15,* 239–245.

Manual for courts martial, United States (rev. ed.). (1969). Washington, D.C.: U.S. Government Printing Office.

Markham, J. M. (1987, May 17). Austrians seem to cut support for Waldheim. *The New York Times,* pp. 1, 20.

Markus, R. A. (1974). *Christianity in the Roman world.* London: Thames & Hudson.

McClosky, H. (1958). Conservatism and personality. *American Political Science Review, 52,* 27–45.

McGraw, K. M. (1985). Subjective probabilities and moral judgments. *Journal of Experimental Social Psychology, 21,* 501–518.

McIlwain, C. H. (1947). *Constitutionalism ancient and modern* (rev. ed.). Ithaca, N.Y.: Cornell University Press.

Mendenhall, G. E. (1955). *Law and covenant in Israel and the ancient Near East.* Pittsburgh: Biblical Colloquium.

Milbrath, L. (1968, November-December). The nature of political beliefs and the relationship of the individual to the government. *American Behavioral Scientist, 12,* 28–36.

Milgram, S. (1963). Behavioral study of obedience. *Journal of Abnormal and Social Psychology, 67,* 371–378.

———. (1964a). Group pressure and action against a person. *Journal of Abnormal and Social Psychology, 69,* 137–143.

————. (1964b). Issues in the study of obedience: A reply to Baumrind. *American Psychologist, 19*, 848–852.

————. (1965). Liberating effects of group pressure. *Journal of Personality and Social Psychology, 1*, 127–134.

————. (1974). *Obedience to authority: An experimental view.* New York: Harper & Row.

Miller, A. G. (1986). *The obedience experiments: A case study of controversy in social science.* New York: Praeger.

Mills, C. W. (1940). Situated actions and vocabularies of motive. *American Sociological Review, 5*, 904–913.

Mixon, D. (1971). Behaviour analysis treating subjects as actors, rather than organisms. *Journal for the Theory of Social Behaviour, 1*, 19–31.

Moeller, B. (1972). *Imperial cities and the Reformation.* Philadelphia: Fortress Press.

Moore, B. (1978). *Inequality: The social bases of obedience and revolt.* White Plains, N.Y.: M. E. Sharpe.

————. (1984). *Privacy.* Armonk, N.Y.: M. E. Sharpe.

Morgan, T. (1987, August 2). Voices from the Barbie trial. *The New York Times Magazine*, pp. 20–27, 36, 44, 58–59.

Mueller, J. H.; Schussler, K. F.; & Costner, H. L. (1978). *Statistical reasoning in sociology.* Boston: Houghton Mifflin.

Murray, E. J. (1956). A content-analysis method for studying psychotherapy. *Psychological Monographs, 70* (13, Whole No. 420).

Myrdal, G. (1944). *An American dilemma: The Negro problem and modern democracy.* New York: Harper.

NASA falls from grace. (1986, March 10). *U.S. News and World Report*, pp. 20–22.

New York Times Staff. (1973a). *The Watergate hearings: Break-in and cover-up* (Proceedings of the Senate Select Committee on Presidential Campaign Activities). New York: Viking.

New York Times Staff. (1973b). *The White House transcripts* (Submission of recorded presidential conversations to the Committee on the Judiciary of the House of Representatives by President Richard Nixon). New York: Viking.

Nisbett, R., & Ross, L. (1980). *Human inference: Strategies and shortcomings of social judgment.* Englewood Cliffs, N.J.: Prentice-Hall.

Noble, K. B. (1987, July 26). Law vs. principle: Out of Watergate comes new view of Bork. *The New York Times*, p. 23.

Noth, M. (1958). *The history of Israel.* London: Adam and Charles Black.

Oates, W. J. (Ed.). (1948). *Basic writings of St. Augustine* (Vols. 1–2). New York: Random House.

Orne, M. T., & Holland, C. H. (1968). On the ecological validity of laboratory deceptions. *International Journal of Psychiatry, 6*, 282–293.

Paige, J. (1975). *Agrarian revolution: Social movements and export agriculture in the underdeveloped world.* New York: Free Press.

Painton, F. (1987, July 13). A verdict on the butcher. *Time*, p. 40.

Panel's case: Bullets and the rule of law. (1987, July 15). *The New York Times*, p. A13.

Parsons, T. (1947). Introduction. In M. Weber, *The theory of social and economic organization* (pp. 3–86). New York: Oxford University Press.

Peabody, R. L. (1968). Authority. In D. Sills (Ed.), *International encyclopedia of the social sciences* (Vol. 1, pp. 473–477). New York: Macmillan & Free Press.

Penner, L.; Hawkins, H. L.; Dertke, M. C.; Spector, P.; & Stone, A. (1973). Obedience as a function of experimenter competence. *Memory and Cognition, 1*, 241–245.

Pennock, J. R., & Chapman, J. W. (Eds.). (1970). *Political and legal obligation* (Nomos XII). New York: Atherton Press.

Perrucci, R.; Anderson, R. L.; Schendel, D. E.; & Trachtman, L. E. (1980). Whistle-blowing: Professionals' resistance to organizational authority. *Social Problems, 28*, 149–164.

Perry, S. (1985). Interview of draft counselor trainers. *The Reporter for Conscience' Sake, 42*(8), 3–6.

Peters, C., & Branch, T. (1972). *Blowing the whistle: Dissent in the public interest*. New York: Praeger.

Piaget, J. (1965). *The moral judgment of the child* (M. Gabain, trans.). New York: Free Press. (Original work published 1932)

Popkin, S. L. (1979). *The rational peasant: The political economy of rural society in Vietnam*. Berkeley: University of California Press.

Prentice-Dunn, S., & Rogers, R. W. (1980). Effects of deindividuating situational cues and aggressive models on subjective deindividuation and aggression. *Journal of Personality and Social Psychology, 39*, 104–113.

Rank, S. G., & Jacobson, C. K. (1977). Hospital nurses' compliance with medication overdose orders: A failure to replicate. *Journal of Health and Social Behavior, 18*, 188–193.

Rasinski, K.; Tyler, T. R.; & Fridkin, K. (1985). Exploring the function of legitimacy: Mediating effects of personal and institutional legitimacy on leadership endorsement and system support. *Journal of Personality and Social Psychology, 49*, 386–394.

Raven, B. H. (1965). Social influence and power. In I. D. Steiner & M. Fishbein (Eds.). *Current studies in social psychology* (pp. 371–382). New York: Holt, Rinehart & Winston.

———. (1983). Interpersonal influence and social power. In B. H. Raven & J. Z. Rubin, *Social psychology* (pp. 399–444). New York: Wiley.

Raven, B. H., & French, J. R. P., Jr. (1958). Legitimate power, coercive power, and observability in social influence. *Sociometry, 21*, 83–97.

Remy, R. C. (1977). Promoting citizen competence. *Mershon Center Quarterly Report, 2*(2), 1–7.

Remy, R. C., & Turner, M. J. (1979). Basic citizenship competencies: Guidelines for educators, policymakers, and citizens. *Mershon Center Quarterly Report, 5*(1), 1–8.

Report of the Presidential Commission on the Space Shuttle Challenger Accident. (1986). Washington, D.C.: The Commission.

Rest, J. R. (1983). Morality. In P. Mussen (Ed.), *Handbook of child psychology* (Vol. 3, pp. 556–629). New York: Wiley.

Rights advocates bitter over Argentine amnesty. (1987, June 27–28). *International Herald Tribune*, p. 3.

Rokeach, M. (1973). *The nature of human values*. New York: Free Press.

———. (1980). Some unresolved issues in theories of beliefs, attitudes, and values. In H. E. Howe, Jr., & M. M. Page (Eds.), *Nebraska Symposium on Motivation, 1979: Attitudes, values, and beliefs* (pp. 261–304). Lincoln: University of Nebraska Press.

Rosenberg, M. J.; Verba, S.; & Converse, P. E. (1970). *Vietnam and the silent majority*. New York: Harper & Row.

Rosenthal, R. (1966). *Experimenter effects in behavioral research*. New York: Appleton-Century-Crofts.

Ross, L. (1977). The intuitive psychologist and his shortcomings. In L. Berkowitz (Ed.), *Advances in experimental social psychology* (Vol. 10, pp. 173–220). New York: Academic Press.

Rotter, J. B. (1966). Generalized expectancies for internal versus external control of reinforcement. *Psychological Monographs, 80* (1, Whole No. 609).

Samelson, F. (1986). Authoritarianism from Berlin to Berkeley: On social psychology and history. *Journal of Social Issues, 42*(1), 191–208.

Sanford, N.; Comstock, C.; & Associates. (1971). *Sanctions for evil: Sources of social destructiveness.* San Francisco: Jossey-Bass.

Sanger, D. E. (1987, January 28). A year later, two engineers cope with Challenger horror. *The New York Times*, pp. A1, D27.

Schank, R. C., & Abelson, R. P. (1977). *Scripts, plans, goals, and understanding.* Hillsdale, N.J.: Erlbaum.

Schein, E. H.; Schneier, I.; & Barker, C. H. (1961). *Coercive persuasion: A social-psychological analysis of "brainwashing" of American civilian prisoners by the Chinese Communists.* New York: W. W. Norton.

Schell, J. (1968). *The military half.* New York: Vintage Books.

Schirmer, D. B. (1971, April 24). My Lai was not the first time. *New Republic*, pp. 18–21.

Schmemann, S. (1988, February 9). Inquiry for Austria declares Waldheim knew of war crimes. *The New York Times*, pp. A1, A8.

Schuman, H., & Johnson, M. P. (1976). Attitudes and behavior. In A. Inkeles (Ed.), *Annual review of sociology* (pp. 161–207). Palo Alto, Calif.: Annual Reviews.

Schuman, H., & Presser, S. (1981). *Questions and answers in attitude surveys.* Orlando, Fla.: Academic Press.

Scott, M. B., & Lyman, S. (1968). Accounts. *American Sociological Review, 33*, 46–62.

Sedlak, A. (1979). Developmental differences in understanding plans and evaluating actors. *Child Development, 50*, 536–560.

Semin, G. R., & Manstead, A. S. R. (1983). *The accountability of conduct.* London: Academic Press.

Shannon, W. V. (1987, July 15). Finding a niche for a gung-ho personality. *The Boston Globe*, p. 15.

———. (1987, August 5). Reagan wins, but suspicion of cover-up lingers. *The Boston Globe*, p. 15.

Shaver, K. G. (1970). Defensive attribution: Effects of severity and relevance on the responsibility assigned for an accident. *Journal of Personality and Social Psychology, 14*, 101–113.

———. (1975). *An introductin to attribution processes.* Cambridge, Mass.: Winthrop.

———. (1985). *The attribution of blame.* New York: Springer.

Shaver, K. G., & Drown, D. (1986). On causality, responsibility, and self-blame: A theoretical note. *Journal of Personality and Social Psychology, 50*, 697–702.

Shaw, M. E., & Iwawaki, S. (1972). Attribution of responsibility of Japanese and Americans as a function of age. *Journal of Cross-Cultural Psychology, 3*, 71–81.

Shaw, M. E., & Reitan, H. T. (1969). Attribution of responsibility as a basis for sanctioning behavior. *British Journal of Social and Clinical Psychology, 8*, 217–226.

Shaw, M. E., & Sulzer, J. L. (1964). An empirical test of Heider's levels in attribution of responsibility. *Journal of Abnormal and Social Psychology, 69*, 39–46.

Sheehan, N. (1971, March 28). Should we have war crime trials? *The New York Times Book Review*, pp. 1–3, 30–34.

Shenon, P. (1988, March 17). North, Poindexter and 2 others indicted on Iran-contra fraud and theft charges. *The New York Times*, pp. A1, D27.

Shils, E. A., & Janowitz, M. (1948). Cohesion and disintegration in the Wehrmacht in World War II. *Public Opinion Quarterly, 12*, 280–315.

Shultz, T. R., & Schliefer, M. (1983). Towards a refinement of attribution concepts. In J. Jaspars, F. D. Fincham, & M. Hewstone (Eds.), *Attribution theory and research* (pp. 37–62). London: Academic Press.

Shultz, T. R.; Wright, K.; & Schliefer, M. (1986). Assignment of moral responsibility and punishment. *Child Development, 57*, 177–184.

Smith, M. (1971). *Palestinian parties and politics that shaped the Old Testament*. New York: Columbia University Press.

Snow, R., & Goodman, L. (1985). A decisionmaking approach to nuclear education. In B. Zars, B. Wilson, & A. Phillips (Eds.), *Education and the threat of nuclear war* (pp. 105–113). Cambridge, Mass.: Harvard Educational Review.

Southern, R. W. (1970). *Western society and the church in the Middle Ages*. Harmondsworth, England: Penguin Books.

Stinchcombe, A. (1968). *Constructing social theories*. New York: Harcourt, Brace, World.

Stone, C. D. (1975). *Where the law ends: The social control of corporate behavior*. New York: Harper & Row.

Strayer, J. R. (1970). *On the medieval origins of the modern state*. Princeton, N.J.: Princeton University Press.

Strobel, L. P. (1980). *Reckless homicide*. South Bend, Ind.: And Books.

Suedfeld, P.; Hakstian, A. R.; Rank, D. S.; & Ballard, E. J. (1985). Ascription of responsibility as a personality variable. *Journal of Applied Social Psychology, 15*, 285–311.

Sykes, G. M. (1958). *The society of captives: A study of a maximum security prison*. Princeton, N.J.: Princeton University Press.

Tajfel, H. (Ed.). (1982). *Social identity and intergroup relations*. Cambridge, England: Cambridge University Press.

Tapp, J. (1987, September). *Legal socialization across age, culture, and context: Psychological considerations for children and adults in the criminal and legal justice systems*. Paper presented at the Conference on Education in Law and Internalization of Values, Newark, N.J.

Tawney, R. H. (1962). *Religion and the rise of capitalism*. Gloucester, Mass.: Peter Smith.

Taylor, T. (1970). *Nuremberg and Vietnam: An American tragedy*. Chicago: Quadrangle Books.

Thomas, A., & Chess, S. (1977). *Temperament and development*. New York: Brunner/Mazel.

Tolstoy, L. (1957). *War and peace*. Harmondsworth, England: Penguin Books.

The Trial of the major war criminals before the International Military Tribunal. (1947–49). (42 vols.). Nuremberg: International Military Tribunal.

Trials of war criminals before the Nuernberg military tribunals. (1949–53). (15 vols.). Washington, D.C.: U.S. Government Printing Office.

Tyler, T. R. (1984). The role of perceived injustice in defendants' evaluations of their courtroom experience. *Law and Society Review, 18*, 51–74.

———. (1987). *Why people follow the law: Procedural justice, legitimacy, and compliance*. Unpublished manuscript, Northwestern University.

Tyler, T. R., Rasinski, K. A., & Griffin, E. (1986). Alternative images of the citizen: Implications for public policy. *American Psychologist, 41*, 970–978.

Tyler, T. R., Rasinski, K. A., & McGraw, K. M. (1985). The influence of perceived injustice on the endorsement of political leaders. *Journal of Applied Social Psychology,* 15, 700–725.

Vaughan, D. (1983). *Controlling unlawful organizational behavior: Social structure and corporate misconduct.* Chicago: University of Chicago Press.

Vidich, A. J. (1977). Political legitimacy in bureaucratic society: An analysis of Watergate. In J. D. Douglas & J. M. Johnson (Eds.), *Official deviance: Readings in malfeasance, misfeasance, and other forms of corruption* (pp. 145–169). New York: Lippincott.

Vidmar, N., & Crinklaw, L. (1974). Assignment of responsibility for an accident: A methodological and conceptual critique. *Canadian Journal of Behavioral Science, 6,* 112–130.

Vidmar, N., & Ellsworth, P. (1974). Public opinion and the death penalty. *Stanford Law Review, 26,* 1245–1270.

von Lang, J., with Sibyll, C. (Eds.). (1983). *Eichmann interrogated: Transcripts from the archives of the Israeli police* (R. Manheim, trans.). New York: Farrar, Straus & Giroux.

Walster, E. (1966). Assignment of responsibility for an accident. *Journal of Personality and Social Psychology, 3,* 73–79.

Walzer, M. (1970). *Obligations: Essays on disobedience, war, and citizenship.* Cambridge, Mass.: Harvard University Press.

———. (1976). *The revolution of the saints.* New York: Atheneum.

———. (1977). *Just and unjust wars: A moral argument with historical illustrations.* New York: Basic Books.

Weber, M. (1947). *The theory of social and economic organization* (T. Parsons, Ed.; A. M. Henderson & T. Parsons, Trans.). New York: Oxford University Press.

Weisband, E., & Franck, T. M. (1975). *Resignation in protest: Political and ethical choices between loyalty to team and loyalty to conscience in American public life.* New York: Grossman.

Whistle blower to get award. (1987, January 28). *The New York Times,* p. A9.

White, R. K. (1984). *Fearful warriors: A psychological profile of U.S.-Soviet relations.* New York: Free Press.

White, R. W. (1959). Motivation reconsidered: The concept of competence. *Psychological Review, 66,* 297–333.

Wicker, A. W. (1969). Attitudes versus actions: The relationship of verbal and overt behavioral responses to attitude objects. *Journal of Social Issues, 25*(4), 41–78.

Wicker, T. (1987, July 11). War ain't peace yet. *The New York Times,* p. 31.

Wider Argentine immunity bill is sent to Alfonsín for signature. (1987, June 6). *The Boston Globe,* p. 3.

Wilks, M. (1963). *The problem of sovereignty in the later Middle Ages.* Cambridge, England: Cambridge University Press.

Willey, F. (1987, February 23). The dirty war's dirty laundry. *Newsweek,* p. 40.

Williams, B. (1985, April 14–15). "I will never forgive," says My Lai survivor. *Jordan Times* (Amman), p. 4.

Willis, R. H. (1965). Conformity, independence, and anti-conformity. *Human Relations, 18,* 773–788.

Wilson, B. (1985). Education for democratic participation: Intended and unintended lessons of schooling. In B. Zars, B. Wilson, & A. Phillips (Eds.), *Education and the threat of nuclear war* (pp. 77–89). Cambridge, Mass.: Harvard Educational Review.

Wolf, E. (1969). *Peasant wars of the twentieth century.* New York: Harper & Row.

Woodward, B., & Bernstein, C. (1976). *The final days.* New York: Simon & Schuster.

Yinger, J. M. (1961). *Religion in the struggle for power.* New York: Russell & Russell.

Yolton, W. L. (1986). Form 22 reformed, problems still persist. *The Reporter for Conscience' Sake, 43*(1), 1–2, 4.

Zimbardo, P. G. (1970). The human choice: Individuation, reason, and order versus deindividuation, impulse, and chaos. In W. J. Arnold & D. Levine (Eds.), *Nebraska Symposium on Motivation, 1969* (pp. 237–307). Lincoln: University of Nebraska Press.

Index

Abelson, R. P., 90

Abraham and Isaac story: obedience dilemma in, 59–60

Accidents, judging responsibility for, 199

Accountability: mechanisms of, for authorities, 124, 131; hierarchical differences in, 202–04. *See also* Law; Responsibility

Adorno, T. W., 262, 266, 278

Age. *See* Demographic factors: age

Aggression: and sanctioned massacres, 15; desensitization to, 335; socialization of, 344

Ajzen, I., 168, 199

Albright, W. F., 61

Alfonsín, Raúl, 35, 36

Alienated citizen (Walzer), 270. *See also* Citizen, role of

Allport, G. W., 336

Alternative perspectives on authority demands and definition of situation, 61–63, 138, 139–47, 155, 158–62, 322, 328–32. *See also* Higher authority, appeals to

American Civil Liberties Union, 327

Amnesty International, 327

Analysis, levels of: of social influence, 112–16. *See also* Social influence

Andenberg, M. R., 282

Arendt, Hannah, 14, 15, 18, 46, 318

Argentina, and "due obedience" law, 34–37

AR orientation. *See* Assert-responsibility (AR) orientation

Asch, Solomon E., 158

Aspirations, morality of, 203, 204

Assert-responsibility (AR) orientation: defined and described, 216, 225–26, 315; attitude toward My Lai–type and Calley actions, trial, 216–25 and tables 9.3–9.4, 231–34, 243–46, 248–51 and table 10.2, 258–59; attitude

toward Nuremberg, Yamashita trials, 223 (table 9.4), 224; attitude toward draft-board protest, 224–25; attitude toward crime/punishment, 246–48; attitudes toward Watergate, hypothetical obedience situations, 251–56 and tables 10.3–10.4, 259; and social status, 262–63, 319; and self-direction, 265–66; relation to political orientation, 275, 296, 316, 317, 318–20; and internality, 280; samples compared, 349–50 and table B-2. *See also* Demographic factors

Association responsibility, 198 (table 8.1), 199, 200, 203–04

Attachment. *See* Instrumental attachment; Sentimental attachment

Attitudes: toward Calley trial, 51, 75, 167, 168–69, 171–72, 181–83 and table 7.3, 211–18 and table 9.1, 222–25 and table 9.4, 231–34, 245–46, 296–99 and table 12.5, 348–50 and table B-2; toward crimes of obedience, 51–52, 251–56; toward My Lai or My Lai–type actions, 75, 172–81 and tables 7.1–7.2, 216–18 and table 9.2, 219–22, 231–34, 243, 245, 248–51 and table 10.2, 259, 297 and table 12.5, 302; distinguished from behavior, 168; toward Vietnam War, 171–72, 186–88 and table 7.4, 216, 218, 344, 347; toward Nuremberg, Yamashita trials, 182 (table 7.3), 183–85, 223 (table 9.4), 224; toward draft-board protest, 182 (table 7.3), 186, 223 (table 9.4), 224–25; of AR/DR-oriented groups, 216–26 and tables 9.3–9.4, 231–35, 243–56 and tables 10.1–10.4, 258–60, 262–63; toward COs, draft amnesty, 246, 297 (table 12.5), 298, 299, 302; toward crime/punishment, 246–48; toward Watergate, 251–55 and tables 10.3–10.4, 259. *See also* Demographic factors;

Bureaucratic authority. *See* Authority: bureaucratic
Burger, J. M., 199
Busch, L., 342
Butterfield, Alexander, 27

Calley, Lt. William L., Jr.: described, 2, 234; actions at My Lai, 3, 5, 6–9, 17, 49, 75, 163–64, 338
Calley trial: charges, 5–6, 7; testimony at, 7–8, 10–12, 47, 48; focus of, 50*n*; attitudes toward, 51, 75, 167, 168–69, 171–72, 181–83 and table 7.3, 211–18 and table 9.1, 222–25 and table 9.4, 231–34, 245–46, 296–99 and table 12.5, 348–50 and table B-2; outcry against, 167, 168–69, 171–72, 211, 212, 231, 232–34; surveys concerning, 168–72, 211–35, 236–60; reasoning behind verdicts, 208; awareness of, interest in, 341–44 and table A-1, 348, 349 (table B-2). *See also* My Lai massacre
Campbell, A., 266
Carter, Pfc. Herbert, 8
Carter, T. J., 311
Casey, William, 38, 39, 41
Catholicism: and development of divided authority, 65–69. *See also* Christianity; Demographic factors: religion
Causal judgments: defined, 195; and attribution theory, 195–99; as expressed in language, 200–01; of responsibility, 204–10, 248–51 and table 10.2, 252–56, 258–60, 319, 334
Central Committee for Conscientious Objectors, 327
Chains of command: and Watergate, 26; responsibility allocation in, 202–10, 248–51 and table 10.2, 252–56, 258–60, 319, 334; as factor in crimes of obedience, 308–15
Challenger disaster, 308, 311, 312–13
Chang, J., 37
Chanowitz, B., 90
Charismatic authority, 54, 126–28, 130–31
Chess, S., 107
Choice. *See* Preference
Christian, S., 36
Christianity: and norms legitimating disobedience, 58, 63–65; and development of divided authority, 65–70; and conscientious objection, 140–41. *See also* Demographic factors: religion
Christie, Richard, 241, 279
Chrysler Corporation, 45–46

Church, G. J., 40, 41
CIA, 39
Citizen, role of: social contract with authority, 55; encouraging adherence to, 93–94; identification as orientation to, 113; as seen in political orientations, 268–77; enhancing sense of efficacy in, 322–27, 334; redefining, 329–32. *See also* Role obligations; Socialization
City of God, The (St. Augustine), 66
Civil disobedience: prerequisite of, 56–57; as extralegal challenge, 137; as appeal to alternative, higher authority, 139–47; as obligation of citizenship, 330; as collective action, 332, 333. *See also* Disobedience; Value orientation
Civil rights movement, 145
Claburn, E., 57*n*
Class. *See* Social status/class
Clinard, M. B., 208
Coercion. *See* Power: coercive
Cognitive processes: as affected by demographic factors, 172, 228–29
Cole, R. E., 325*n*
Coleman, J. S., 54*nn*, 90, 91, 128
Collective action: and challenging authority, 57, 160–62; as empowerment of individuals and redefinition of authority situation, 327, 332, 333
Collins, B. E., 241, 280, 288
Command responsibility: as role obligation, 184–85; distinguishing from subordinates', 204–09
Commission responsibility, 198 (table 8.1), 199, 200
Commitment, activation of, 91, 157
Company C ("Charlie"), at My Lai, 1–9
Compliance: as process of social influence, 104, 109–16, 129, 269 (table 11.1), 271–72. *See also* Rule orientation
Comstock, C., 180
Conformity: pressures for, 158, 162; groupthink, 329, 335
Conscience: as justification for disobedience, 75–76; and civil disobedience, 139–40; and conscientious objection, 141–42. *See also* Disobedience: principled; Moral restraints
Conscientious objection, 140–43; attitudes toward, 246, 297 (table 12.5), 298, 299
Consensus: as pressure for conformity, 158
Consequences of obedience: actors' distancing from, 162–66, 309, 310–15; focus on, in judging responsibility, 193, 206–10, 231–32,

Markham, J. M., 33, 34
Markus, R. A., 57*n*
Martinez, Eugenio, 25
Massacres, sanctioned, 12–20. *See also* Crimes of obedience
Massera, Adm. Emilio, 35
McClosky, H., 279, 291, 294, 295 and *n*, 303
McCord, James, Jr., 25
McDonald, Allan, 313 and *n*
McGraw, K. M., 123, 196*n*
McIlwain, C. H. 57*n*
Meadlo, Pfc. Paul, 6, 7, 8
Medina, Capt. Ernest, 2, 3, 7, 10
Mendenhall, G. E., 58
Mens rea, 200, 231
Milbrath, L. 281, 285 (table 12.1*n*)
Milgram, Stanley, 23, 57, 136, 168, 239; and obedience experiments, 148–66, 174, 207, 233, 264*n*, 266–67, 309, 310
Military. *See* Authority: military; Demographic factors: military experience; Law: military
Miller, Arthur, 150*n*, 239*n*
Miller, Frederick D., 281, 285
Mills, C. W., 206
Mitchell, John, 26
Mixon, D., 164, 310
Moeller, B., 57*n*
Moore, B., 57*n*, 333
Moral development: models of, 197, 198 (table 8.1); effect on obedience, 267; levels of, in political orientations, 269 (table 11.1), 273
Morality: of duty, 173–74, 203; of aspirations, 203, 204; principles of, in political orientations, 269 (table 11.1), 272–73; of obedience, 272. *See also* Moral development; Moral restraints
Moral judgment, independent. *See* Assert-responsibility (AR) orientation; Value orientation
Moral restraints: forces outweighing, 14–20, 29–31, 162–66; cited by survey respondents, 177–78, 180–81, 185–86, 192. *See also* Conscience; Moral development
Morgan, T., 32
Morton Thiokol: and *Challenger* disaster, 312–13
Mother Jones, and exposé of Ford Pintos, 311
Motivational processes: as affected by demographic factors, 172
Motives, vocabulary of, 206, 275, 276
Motives for obedience: focus on, in judging responsibility, 206–10, 274–75
Mueller, J. H., 171

Murphy, Justice Frank: and Yamashita's conviction, 74
Murray, E. J., 78
My Lai massacre: events recounted, 1–9; investigation of, 1, 2, 10; cover-up of, 1, 9–10; charges, trials stemming from, 5, 6, 7, 8–9, 10–12, 50*n*; as sanctioned massacre, 13, 15, 17; attitudes toward, 75, 172–81 and tables 7.1–7.2, 216–18 and table 9.2, 219–22, 231–34, 243, 245, 248–51 and table 10.2, 259, 297 and table 12.5, 302; and dehumanization, 163–64, 180. *See also* Calley trial
Myrdal, G., 146*n*

NASA: and *Challenger* disaster, 308, 311, 312–13
National Commission on the Disappeared (Argentina), 35
Nationalism: bases of, 116–18, and instrumental/sentimental attachments, 118–22 and table 5.2
National Security Council (NSC), 39
Nazism, 12, 13, 18, 46, 318; dispositional explanations of, 14, 15; and Barbie trial, 31–33; and Waldheim, 33–34; and routinization, 165; resistance to, 337–38
Neutralization: of victim, 313, 336
Ninety-five Theses (Luther), 68
Nisbett, R., 209
Nixon, Richard: involvement in Calley case, 12*n*, 75; and Watergate, 25–31, 65–66, 203, 251, 252
Nkrumah, Kwame, 127 and *n*
Noble, K. B., 37, 38
Norms, social: for obedience, 57, 59, 167, 173–74, 176–78, 191, 192; for disobedience, 57–58, 59, 70, 176–77, 192; governing authorities' actions, 123–24; and moral congruence, 176. *See also* Role obligations; Socialization; Values
North, Lt. Col. Oliver, 38, 39, 40–42, 46, 51
Noth, M., 57*n*
Nuremberg trials, 30, 35, 41–42, 50*n*, 71–74, 76, 207, 208; attitudes toward, 182 (table 7.3), 183–84, 223 (table 9.4), 224

Obedience: as duty, in military law, 5–6, 10–11; unquestioning, 17, 59, 125, 137–38, 315; Bork's, in Watergate affair, 28, 37–38; defining, 48–51; norms for, 57, 59, 167, 173–74, 176–78, 191, 192; limits upon, in Bible, 59–61; Aquinas's strictures on, 67–68; to legitimate demands, preferences affecting,